NatureScape alberta

Creating and caring for wildlife habitat at home

by Myrna Pearman and Ted Pike

Foreword by Robert Bateman

Illustrated by Gary Ross

Red Deer River Naturalists
Red Deer, Alberta

Federation of Alberta Naturalists
Edmonton, Alberta

THE PUBLISHERS

Red Deer River Naturalists
Box 785
Red Deer, Alberta
T4N 5H2

Federation of Alberta Naturalists
Box 1472
Edmonton, Alberta
T5J 2N5

Canadian Cataloguing in Publication Data

Pearman, Myrna, 1956-
NatureScape Alberta

Co-published by: Federation of Alberta Naturalists.
Includes bibliographical references and index.
ISBN 0-9685765-0-8

1. Wildlife habitat improvement--Alberta. 2. Gardening to attract wildlife--Alberta. 3. Wildlife attracting--Alberta. I. Pike, Ted, 1954-II. Ross, Gary, 1961- III. Red Deer River Naturalists. IV. Federation of Alberta Naturalists. V. Title.
QH77.C3P42 2000 639.9'2'097123 C00-910403-8

Editor: R. Edrea Daniel

Graphic Design and Layout: Judy Cook, Broken Arrow Solutions

Illustrations: Gary Ross

Garden Graphic Design: Cynthia Pohl

Front Cover Illustration: Gary Ross

Back Cover Photographs: Wood frog ~ Tom Webb; all other photographs ~ Myrna Pearman

Printing: Bolder Graphics (Edm) Inc., Edmonton, Alberta

Printed in Canada

Table of Contents

TABLES

APPENDIXES

Acknowledgments

We would like to acknowledge Geoff Holroyd, Loney Dickson and Sarah Baker of Environment Canada, and Jim Robertson of the Kerry Wood Nature Centre, for their role in promoting the idea of a backyard biodiversity program. In its first incarnation, *NatureScape Alberta* was part of a national *Backyard Wildlife Habitat Manual* produced through the support of Environment Canada's Green Plan initiative. The manual, whose production was overseen by Ellis Bird Farm Ltd., was developed with contributions from Bill Merilees (British Columbia); Bob Kreba, Myrna Pearman, Tom Reaume and Karyn Scalise (Prairie Provinces); Kim Gavine (Ontario); Corinne Tastyre (Quebec); and Dan McAskill (Atlantic Provinces). Our thanks to all these contributors, with a special thanks to Bob Kreba and Karyn Scalise, because their work formed the foundation from which this book was written.

Our sincere thanks also to Rod Silver, Sylvia Pincott and the others involved with Naturescape B.C. for their pioneering vision, for permitting us to use the name "naturescape," for their freely shared advice and for their ongoing support and inspiration.

The volunteer support of Red Deer River Naturalists (RDRN) members, coupled with the logistical support of the Federation of Alberta Naturalists (FAN), has been instrumental in getting this book published. We would like to say a very special thank-you to RDRN's NatureScape Committee Chair, Bill Heinsen, for his singular devotion to this project and for his amazing ability to work with budgets and spread sheets. FAN's support of NatureScape Alberta has been critical to its production, and FAN's Executive Director, Glen Semenchuk, is to be commended for his ability to calm us down as required, and for his business savvy and ongoing encouragement.

We owe a special debt of gratitude to the experts who so willingly and patiently reviewed and re-reviewed material. We have acknowledged our many technical reviewers in each chapter but would like to say a special thanks to those who truly extended themselves to help us out: Elisabeth Beaubien, James Bowick, Gordon Heaps, Derek Johnson, Heinjo and Jan Lahring, Clancy Patton, Carolyn Rallison, Ruth Staal and Tom Webb (from Turner Valley). To our overall technical reviewers—Ron Bjorge, Dorothy Dickson, J. Cam and Joy Finlay, and Sylvia Pincott—thanks for meeting our impossible deadlines! To Gary Ross, our incredibly talented artist; to Cynthia Pohl, who worked so diligently and creatively on the garden plans; and to Howard Troughton, who drafted and redrafted the Backyard Watch form—our sincere thanks!

Every photograph in this book was donated, a tribute to the talent and generosity of the photographers. We would like to say a special thank-you to photographers John Acorn, Russ Amy, Gordon Court, Betty Fisher, Sylvia Glass, Jan Heaps, Christiana Johnson, Derek Johnson, Gordon Johnson, Doug Leighton, Wayne Lynch, Carrol Perkins, Ruth Stewart and Tom Webb (from Edmonton) for sharing their talents with us. Thanks also to Sean Abbott, Elisabeth Beaubien, William Bergen, Kevin Berner, Mary Coughlin, Terry Didychuk, Vera Halliday (deceased), Cy Hampson (deceased), James R. Hill, III, Marijke Jalink, Gavin Kernaghan, Heinjo Lahring, Bob Lane, Robin Leech, Jean and Glenn McCullough, Mike McNaughton, the Medicine River Wildlife Rehabilitation Centre staff, Greg Ohm, Clancy Patton, Godo Stoyke and Bob Young for their excellent photos. Kudos, as well, to the Provincial Museum of Alberta for donating the use of Edgar T. Jones' fine images.

To the many patient gardeners, especially Margaret Brown, Donna Dawson, Lorraine Nagel, Clancy Patton and Carolyn Rallison, who let Myrna wander through and photograph their yards and gardens, our thanks. Trevor Wiens donated his time and expertise to produce the excellent Natural Regions map, for which we are grateful. Thanks also to Dave Ealey, who answered some difficult editing questions.

Many thanks to the Ellis Bird Farm (EBF) for allowing us to reproduce some of Gary Ross's illustrations from previous publications, and to the EBF Board of Directors, for understanding the commitment that Myrna had to make to this project.

We would like to thank our families and friends for standing by us through this long and sometimes difficult process. Myrna would like to say a special thanks to Marie, Shelley, Janelle and Jolynne for always being there, and Ted would like to thank his wife, Betty, and sons, Jon and Nathan.

This book would not have happened without the devoted leadership and meticulous editorship of Edrea Daniel. Thank you, Edrea, not only for your hundreds of volunteer hours, but also for putting up with us for so many months and for never wavering in your belief that this book would eventually, someday, become a reality. And we owe the beauty of these pages to the magical touch of Judy Cook (Broken Arrow Solutions).

Last, but certainly not least, we would like to thank all the agencies, organizations and businesses that provided us with financial assistance. Their support has made NatureScape Alberta possible.

Community Lottery
Board Region #78
Society

Foreword

NatureScaping is an idea whose time has come. In fact, it may just be in the nick of time. Since the Neolithic, we have been forcing nature into a mould for human convenience, and since the 1950s, the force has multiplied manyfold due to dazzling technology and unbridled growth. In his song *After the Gold Rush*, Neil Young says, "Look at Mother Nature on the run / In the nineteen seventies."

At the dawn of the twenty-first century, the run has become a stampede, and the human imprint is everywhere. We have settled into almost every habitat and, with our settlement, have razed, altered and evicted, believing these spaces to be empty of anything worthwhile. But there is no such thing as "empty" in the natural world. Every inch of this Earth supports a complex citizenry living in a dynamic and ordered community.

The concept of NatureScaping gives us the chance to redevelop an active, living community that will benefit not only nature, but ourselves. As Wes Jackson says in his important little book *Becoming Native to This Place*:

> It is possible to love a small acreage in Kansas as much as John Muir loved the entire Sierra Nevada. This is fortunate, for the wilderness of the Sierra will disappear unless little pieces of nonwilderness become intensely loved by lots of people.

If we come to cherish those places where wilderness has long since disappeared, perhaps we will also be moved to protect what is left of our wild places.

One of my pet "hobby horses" is to advocate that everyone should get to know his or her neighbours of other species. This basic, traditional knowledge should be passed on from parent to child, from teacher to student. Sadly, such teachings are rare. Now, through *NatureScape Alberta*, you can learn the names and habits of some of those neighbours. By applying the principles outlined in this book, you can encourage new neighbours to come.

It will be like a block party. It will be better than a party. In an increasingly alienated world, NatureScaping will get people away from the TV and computer monitor, and out there with reality. NatureScaping will bring together families, human neighbours and communities.

The great environmentalist, David Brower, said, "What this planet needs is CPR; not cardio-pulmonary resuscitation, but Conservation, Preservation and Restoration." Imagine the effect if backyards, front yards, school yards and city parks were all developed as NatureScapes!

~ Robert Bateman

But ask now the beasts, and they shall teach thee; and the fowls of the air and they shall tell thee. Or speak to the earth, and it shall teach thee: and the fishes of the sea shall declare unto thee.

~ BOOK OF JOB

Chapter 1
Why NatureScape?

MYRNA PEARMAN

Mother and son looking at cosmos flower

In lamenting the demise of the passenger pigeon, Aldo Leopold, perhaps North America's greatest conservation icon, wrote, "Men still live who, in their youth, remember pigeons. Trees still live who, in their youth, were shaken by a living wind. But a decade hence, only the oldest oaks will remember, and at long last only the hills will know."

It has been more than half a century since Leopold wrote these words in his famous *A Sand County Almanac*. Sadly, thousands of other species have now followed the way of the passenger pigeon. As our society becomes increasingly urbanized, and as technology lures us deeper and deeper into a "virtual reality," our understanding of the primal link between humans and the natural environment is becoming increasingly tenuous. Children grow to adulthood not knowing where milk and eggs come from, or how the forests help create the oxygen they breathe.

NatureScaping gives us insight into that vital link.

EXTINCTION OF EXPERIENCE

Perhaps never having seen a weasel or a warbler, this generation of Albertans has fewer opportunities to experience nature than any other generation in history, and the extinction of species such as the passenger pigeon is the ultimate finality. We, our children and grandchildren will never know the phenomenon of pigeons in flocks the size of cities. We will never experience the power of the wild buffalo thundering across the open prairie. "Extinction of experience" describes this reduced opportunity.

If we are not diligent, generations to come will not have the opportunity to enjoy a wild blossom, or watch butterflies flit from one flower to another, except in a conservatory. To prevent extinction of experience is perhaps one of the best reasons to NatureScape your piece of the Earth.

HABITAT LOSS

There are some who claim that the habitat provided on an acreage or in an urban yard is insignificant, especially on a global or national scale. But as more and more of the earth becomes fragmented, paved, drained and clear-cut, the conservation of these small parcels becomes increasingly important.

Habitat loss is often incremental—a new neighbourhood, shopping mall or highway here; a seismic line, forestry road or clear-cut there. NatureScaping can help offset these losses. NatureScaped yards, especially those that are linked together, and perhaps joined to a ravine, greenspace or park, provide significant wildlife habitat.

By NatureScaping your yard, you are—in a small, but meaningful way—contributing to the well-being of the planet.

When we build a shopping mall, we lose wildlife habitat

WHAT IS AN ECOSYSTEM?

Here is a basic definition: An ecosystem is the totality of a community and all the abiotic (nonliving) components and functions in a given area.

Ecosystems can vary in space, time and complexity. A puddle formed from snowmelt, or a window box, are examples of small, ephemeral and quite simple ecosystems; Alberta's lakes, boreal forest and grasslands are examples of larger, ancient and more complex ecosystems.

BIODIVERSITY

Biodiversity is the diversity, or variety, of all living things; if we are going to sustain life on this planet, we need high biodiversity. Biodiversity occurs at three different levels, encompassing all life as we know it—from the level of the DNA in cells to that of the Earth's global ecosystem.

Genetic diversity refers to the gene variation of individuals that make up a species. This diversity is the reason why we all look different from one another, except those of us who are identical twins, triplets, etc. A species can go extinct if there is not enough genetic diversity within its individuals.

Species diversity is the number of different species within an ecosystem. We often know about or can recognize some of the more obvious members of an ecosystem—like spruce trees, black bears and great gray owls in the boreal forest. But what about the northern starflowers, hoary elfin butterflies and black-throated green warblers that also live there? When we protect or enhance species diversity we are looking after all the members, from the obvious to the obscure, of an ecosystem.

The parkland ecosystem with aspen trees, grassland and slough

Ecosystem diversity refers to the number and variety of different ecosystems in an area. If you live in or around Lethbridge, some of the dominant ecosystems in your area include the cottonwood forests along the Oldman River valley, the short grass prairie, alkali sloughs and marshes. If you live near Big Valley, aspen groves, fescue grassland and potholes or sloughs are some of the easily recognizable ecosystems. The greater the diversity of ecosystems, the higher the number of species that can be supported.

Biodiversity is lost when a patch of native habitat is destroyed to make way for a monocrop, an industrial park or housing development. It is also lost when a lawn is put in where native grasses once grew, when a pasture is overgrazed, a riverside bank is trampled or a forest cleared. To put biodiversity in perspective, just think about the number of creatures you might see in the middle of a large mall parking lot, the ultimate of ecological deserts!

Through NatureScaping, you are creating and enhancing biodiversity.

LESS WELL-KNOWN DWELLERS OF THE BOREAL FOREST

Hoary elfin butterfly

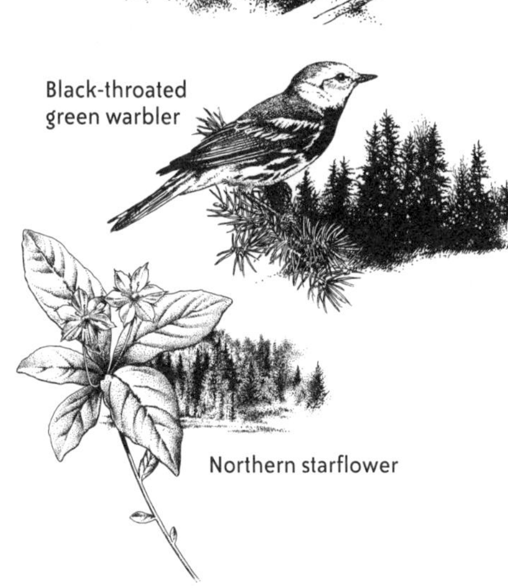

Black-throated green warbler

Northern starflower

NATURESCAPING VALUES AND US

NatureScaping is about increasing biodiversity and conserving species and ecosystems. It is also about being nurturing to both ourselves and those humans and nonhumans with whom we share our homeplace. It is about becoming directly involved with primal, natural processes right within our living spaces, and becoming good stewards of nature.

NatureScaping is about melding the hobby and tradition of gardening with the biological principles of habitat development. It is about complementing centuries of horticultural knowledge with millennia of life wisdom. It is about learning and appreciating, marvelling and studying. It is about creating beauty.

NatureScaping is about inviting living creatures into our world for the sheer enjoyment of watching them, observing their antics and studying their behaviour. It is about pausing to consider and examine, instead of rushing for the spray can or trap.

NatureScaping is about satisfying a basic human need to care, to be helpful and to make a difference. It is acknowledging that we are one link in an infinitely complex and very finely tuned natural system. It is about respect.

WHAT THIS BOOK WILL DO FOR YOU

We hope that this book will help you see your yard and garden through different eyes. Presenting information from the perspective of wildlife, we lead you through the elements of habitat development and tell you why many of the creatures you may have always loved to hate are actually your friends!! We provide you with ideas on how to attract insects (yes, bugs!), amphibians (yes, frogs!), reptiles (yes, snakes!), birds and mammals. We show you how to make a plan for your property. We list the plantings—from trees to annuals and perennials—that will attract the widest variety of wildlife. We give you details on how to attract wildlife with water, from a simple birdbath to a water garden. Tips on how to deal with sick and injured wildlife are provided, and ideas on how to coexist with wildlife are outlined. We write about how to NatureScape a school yard, and how to get involved in a variety of educational and interesting projects and programs. We encourage you to become an "official" NatureScaper by applying to have your yard certified (see side bar).

Finally, we hope to hear from you! There are still many unknowns out there, especially when it comes to the smaller creatures, such as insects and spiders. Please share your observations with us! Tell us all about the discoveries you make, and the triumphs and challenges you face as you work to transform your yard into a haven for you and your wild friends. Feel free to fill out and send us the Backyard Watch form enclosed at the back of this book (Appendix 6). Our website (www.naturescape.ab.ca) will link you to other NatureScape-related sites and will provide updates and summaries of the NatureScape Alberta program.

We invite you to become an OFFICIAL NATURESCAPE ALBERTA PARTICIPANT

If you provide wildlife habitat in your yard or garden, or have NatureScaped your school yard, we invite you to apply to have the area "certified." All you have to do is complete the Certification Application form on page 189 (Appendix 7). The form is also available on our website (www.naturescape.ab.ca). Take a few minutes to tell us what you have done to provide habitat; then mail or fax the form to NatureScape Alberta.

For your efforts, we will provide you with a small, attractive sign suitable for hanging on a gate or fence, or attaching to a small stake in your yard or garden. Not only will this sign provide you with recognition for your efforts, but it will also show others that NatureScaping is a worthwhile and beneficial endeavour.

It is our hope that NatureScape Alberta will be the key that opens the door to a world of mystery, beauty, study and entertainment—right in your own backyard!

ACKNOWLEDGMENTS

Kevin Timoney (Ecologist, Treeline Ecological Research, Sherwood Park, Alberta)

SIGNIFICANT REFERENCES

Leopold, A. 1966 (first published in 1949). *A Sand County almanac*. Ballantine Books, New York, by arrangement with Oxford University Press, New York.

www.naturescape.ab.ca

Barn swallows

Chapter 2
Create the Habitat and They Will Come

Wild creatures respond quickly to the provision of their basic requirements: **space** within which they can find **food**, **water** and **shelter**. Like humans, they can survive and thrive if these basic needs are met.

PROVIDING THE NECESSITIES OF LIFE

Space

Many landowners think of their property in terms of square footage and property lines. But wild creatures don't exist in two-dimensional space. Theirs is a three-dimensional world, and their habitat requirements have less to do with surface boundaries than spatial arrangement. A chipping sparrow, for example, sings from a treetop, builds its nest in low bushes and feeds on the ground. A garter snake will spend the summer skulking about through the grass and leaf litter, then find a deep burrow in which to pass the winter.

When you consider that habitat can extend from the rooting depth of tall trees to hundreds of metres up into the sky, and that it encompasses the space in and around every plant, water body and nesting site, you can begin to appreciate just how much habitat potential there is even in a typical city-sized lot. Imagine the volumes of wildlife living space that could be created if significant numbers of people took the initiative to NatureScape!

Different animal species need different amounts of space. A city yard or small acreage may constitute the entire home range for some creatures, whereas for others, it provides only a portion of their spatial requirements. Tree swallows, for example, defend a very small territory around a nest site, so more than one pair could take up residence in a small yard. Several pairs could nest in a typical neighbourhood. On the other hand, a pair of flickers, which need approximately 16 ha (40 ac.)[1] for a home range, may end up nesting in one yard, then frequenting others in the neighbourhood to forage for food.

Given this wide variation in habitat requirements, it will be helpful for you to assess your yard in a larger context. For those animals whose ranges are larger than a single yard, the likelihood of attracting them to an area increases if their requirements are met at a neighbourhood or community level. The chance of attracting these species especially increases if a yard is connected to a larger habitat area by a corridor or "greenway."

Obviously, the larger and more diverse a yard is, the more species of wildlife it can accommodate. Although it is true that rural properties or acreages are more likely to provide habitat for a greater diversity of wild creatures than city yards, even urban areas can provide important oases for a surprising diversity of species. As

[1] Most measurements have been provided to us in Imperial or U.S. units. In making conversions to metric equivalents, we have rounded off the figures (e.g., 1 m = 3 ft.; 2 m = 6 ½ ft.), except where exact measurements are required (e.g., nestbox hole diameters).

individuals, neighbours and communities begin to work together with developers, urban planners and landscape planners to conserve and enhance habitat, our urban and suburban landscapes could become linked together into a mosaic of connected, diverse and vibrant ecoscapes.

Plants are the foundation of a typical food chain: a polyphemus moth caterpillar munches saskatoon leaves; the caterpillar is eaten by a Baltimore oriole; and the oriole is eaten by a merlin

Food

Food in a yard or garden can be supplied through plantings, by the animals attracted to these plantings (e.g., insects or other similar, small creatures) and by supplemental feeding stations. Plants are important because they are at the bottom of the food chain—they are the foundation upon which all wildlife depends. They supply food directly by way of sap, nectar, blossoms, fruit, seeds or other plant parts. The myriad animal species that depend directly on plants for their survival continue to fuel the food chain because they are eaten by predatory creatures. These animals, in turn, may be eaten by other predators (see sidebar).

Each animal species has its own unique food requirements. These requirements may change from season to season and during the course of an animal's life.

Plant communities also change from season to season and over time. This transformation over time is called plant succession. In an urban or acreage yard, as in any habitat, succession translates into a changing community of wildlife species. A young spruce tree, for example, provides only limited food for wildlife. As the tree matures, it increases in size and begins to produce cones, so will attract species that want to dine on its seeds or on the insects the tree harbours. Even as the tree ages, dies and falls to the ground, it continues to supply food and habitat for a wide variety of animal species.

ALL CREATURES NEED WATER: American goldfinches will use a birdbath to both drink and bathe.

There is information in several of the following chapters on how to provide food for wildlife species.

Water

Water is a life-sustaining requirement for all creatures and is needed, in some form (a few animals actually eat snow), all year round. For certain animals, water is the medium through which they pass one or more life cycles; for others, it is needed for drinking, cleaning food, cooling down or bathing. We discuss the provision of water in detail in Chapters 5 and 14.

Shelter

For wild creatures, shelter means many things—protection from the elements, safe resting spots, places for roosting, hiding areas from predators, and secure spaces to safely raise young. Shelter is most critical to wildlife during cold or inclement weather and during the nesting season.

ALL CREATURES SEEK SHELTER

Different wildlife species have different shelter requirements. The little brown bats that dart about your yard at dusk might be perfectly content to hang out during the day behind the door of your garden shed, whereas the pair of breeding tree swallows will prefer the nestbox you've set up at the back of your yard. The tangle of rose bushes along the far fence may be a dream home for a pair of yellow warblers, but a least weasel will select the old brush pile (after you've finally convinced your significant other that the pile is indeed a habitat feature) as its favourite haunt. If you let the grass grow tall in the corner of your garden, a pair of juncos might construct a small nest among the thatch. That same patch of grass, if beside a small pond, could provide the ideal hiding spot for a frog. An overwintering mourning cloak butterfly might shelter beneath those

LAWN AND GARDEN PESTICIDES—THE HEALTH RISKS

Chemical pesticides (which, for the purpose of this book, include herbicides, fungicides and insecticides) are toxic substances designed to kill plant, fungus and insect "pests." There is growing concern about the dangers to human and animal health associated with pesticide use, including use in homes and gardens, as well as on school and public playgrounds. The range of known or potential health effects of exposure to some pesticides includes cancer, immune system suppression, chromosomal abnormalities, reproductive abnormalities, developmental problems, neurobehavioural deficits and alterations in endocrine function. Children are both relatively more often exposed, and more sensitive, to pesticides compared to other age groups. The impact of pesticide use on non-target backyard wildlife is unknown.

The Canadian Environmental Law Association and the Ontario College of Family Physicians (Environmental Health Committee) have co-authored a study that addresses the health effects of pesticides, and their regulation in Canada. For a copy of the study or more information, contact the Canadian Environmental Law Association (see Appendix 5).

few old logs you've never bothered to move, whereas your resident hairy woodpecker is likely to spend a winter night safely tucked away in a cavity in one of the old aspens on the far side of the garden.

Not surprisingly, wild creatures are experts when it comes to finding shelter or a home. The secret is to provide them with enough habitat so that they can find that special nook, cranny, patch of grass, branch or hole. Trees and treed areas, especially those with a dense shrub undercover, provide the most important sources of shelter for the widest variety of wildlife. Although most creatures prefer to find or construct their own nesting sites, some will accept human-made abodes such as bird, bat or toad houses, and bee blocks.

We discuss how you can provide shelter for your backyard neighbours in a number of chapters.

DESIGNING YOUR NATURESCAPE WILDLIFE HABITAT

When you choose to shift from traditional gardening to wildlife gardening, you will likely find that your focus will be less on pure aesthetics and more on biodiversity. Your carefully manicured lawn will appear less appealing as you come to realize that it is really an expensive, high-maintenance, water-hungry and toxic ecological desert, almost as devoid of life as a mall parking lot or concrete sidewalk. (For a chemical-free lawn, see below.)

The Basics

The greater the variety of habitat components you provide, the greater the variety of wildlife you will attract. You will want to incorporate a wide mix of plant species, emphasizing plants native to Alberta, and consider vertical, as well as horizontal, diversity. It is a good idea to mix conifers with deciduous trees, plant understories of shrubs, and design your perennial and annual gardens so that they are layered. You should consider trees and shrubs that will supply year-round benefits, and plan your garden so that the blooming season extends as long as possible. To a matrix of well-positioned plantings, you can add water features and such structural attractants as nestboxes, log piles and brush piles. All of these principles and ideas are discussed in more detail in later chapters.

A NatureScaped yard is vibrant and alive

NatureScaping seeks to emulate the curves, clusters, clumpings and vibrant diversity found in nature, not the careful symmetry and straight lines of traditional planning standards. Features like overgrown tangles of underbrush, snags, rock piles, brush piles, patches of tall grass and wet areas become valued for both their inherent beauty and their contribution to biodiversity.

NINE STEPS TO A CHEMICAL-FREE LAWN

1. **Mowing.** Allow your grass to grow to 10 cm (4 in.), then cut it back to about 7.5 cm (3 in.). Following this procedure will protect grass blades from the sun and allow grass roots to penetrate more deeply into the soil, making the plants more resistant to drought and pests. Stronger turf will prevent weeds from growing.
2. **Watering.** Grass needs about 2.5 cm (1 in.) of water every seven to ten days. Water in the morning to avoid burning your grass. Watering at night and not letting the lawn dry out between waterings encourages disease.
3. **Hardy plants.** Plant grass species that are hardy and resistant to drought. Apply a thin layer of screened compost or manure in the early spring or late fall, then overseed with hardy grass seed.
4. **Grass-cycling.** Leave grass clippings on the lawn, thereby cycling nutrients back into the soil, protecting grass blades from the sun and controlling weeds.
5. **Soil testing.** If you have a problem lawn, have the soil tested to determine its chemical composition and pH level. This kind of testing can help you diagnose the problem and give you the basis for proper treatment measures.
6. **Organic fertilizer.** Grass clippings, compost and manure can provide everything your lawn needs. Chemical fertilization is not necessary with a well-structured soil full of earthworms and other beneficial soil life.
7. **Aeration.** Aerate your grass once a year to help oxygen get down to the roots. Aeration encourages root system development and, therefore, creates a thicker lawn that is more resistant to drought and weed invasion.
8. **Shop around.** If you use a lawn care company, ask for a program using organics only. State clearly that you want NO pesticides.
9. **Reduce your lawn area.** Do you really need that vast expanse of lawn? NatureScape instead! One way to begin is to replace your turf with ground covers. Steeply sloped or shaded areas, or parts of your yard with poor soil, are good places to start this changeover.

Adapted from Thunder Bay 2002. 1998. *Ten steps to a chemical-free yard*. In: *Enjoy a Chemical-free Yard*. Thunder Bay 2002, Thunder Bay. (Booklet)

Although a NatureScaped yard will require less water and no, or minimal, chemical inputs, we're not implying that NatureScaping means ignoring your whole yard and leaving it entirely to the vagaries of nature. Although it is true that NatureScaped yards might appear less ordered than their well-manicured counterparts, they, too, must be carefully designed and lovingly maintained. What you consider lovingly maintained, however, might be interpreted by your neighbours as being a ghastly mess and a threat to neighbourhood property values. Gently try to educate these neighbours.

It is also important to remember that, no matter how enthusiastic your efforts, wildlife habitat is not created overnight. Developing a NatureScaped habitat is an ongoing process that is best undertaken in small, manageable chunks. Some aspects of wildlife gardening will yield immediate results, whereas others may take up to 30 or 40 years. For example, it may take only a few days to attract birds to a birdbath, bird feeder or a nestbox, but it may take decades for some trees to mature to the point where they will be large enough for woodpeckers to excavate a nesting cavity.

You should also give some thought to what creatures you want to attract. If birds are a priority, consideration should be given to appropriate selection and placement of plantings, bird feeders, nesting structures and a birdbath or watering area. Routes for birds should also be provided around feeding stations and through your yard. If emphasis is to be placed on creating habitat for amphibians and reptiles, a water garden encircled with appropriate habitat should be considered. If it is butterflies you are interested in, then suitable plantings and sunning spots in areas sheltered from the wind need to be included in your garden plan.

COMMON BACKYARD WILDLIFE

Red squirrel

It is important to be realistic about what animals you can attract. For starters, no matter where you live or how much you landscape, you will attract only those species that naturally occur in your region. In a typical urban landscape, adaptable and gregarious species (waxwings, house sparrows, ants, red squirrels) are more likely to visit your yard than those that are less tolerant of disturbance (hermit thrushes, Cooper's hawks), are large in size (moose) or are at the top of the food chain (cougars). Similarly, animals with specialized feeding or nesting/breeding requirements (sharp-tailed grouse), or those with nesting habits that put them at risk in an urban area (ground-nesting sparrows), are less likely to flourish. Yards located near or adjacent to native habitat will be more likely to attract less common species, and properties located in older neighbourhoods will attract more wildlife than those in newly developed areas.

A yard should be designed to minimize unnecessary wildlife mortality. However, natural predation by native predators (e.g., weasels, hawks, owls or snakes) will be inevitable and should be viewed as part of the natural process. Ideas on how to deal with non-native species such as house sparrows and European starlings, as well as with domestic predators (e.g., cats) are outlined in Chapters 17 and 18.

You may also have to deal with the touchy problem of being "too successful." You may be thrilled to have deer wandering in and out of your yard, but they quickly wear out their welcome when you discover their insatiable appetite for fresh garden vegetables, backyard shrubs and the sunflower seeds in your bird feeder. You may appreciate how valuable skunks are in the big scheme of things, but you are probably not going to be very happy if they take up residence under the garden shed. We discuss the issue of co-existing with wildlife in Chapter 18.

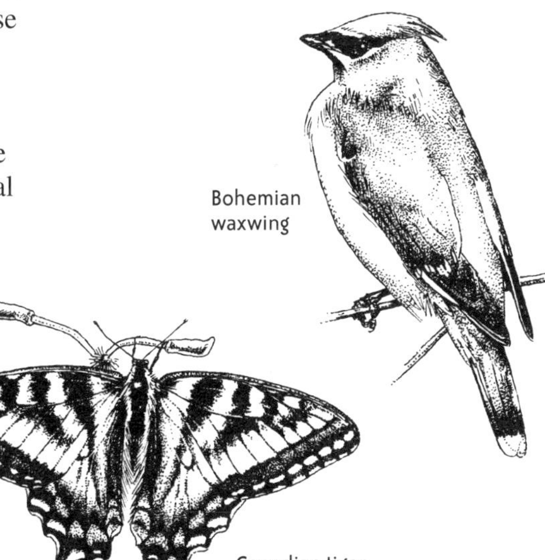

Bohemian waxwing

Canadian tiger swallowtail butterfly

In thinking through a long-term yard development plan, you should give consideration to the time and financial commitment that your NatureScaping project will entail. How much will it cost to plant trees, move trees, install a water garden, put up a purple martin house, or provide supplemental food on a year-round basis? How much maintenance will a butterfly garden require, and how much time will be needed to regularly clean a birdbath and hummingbird feeder?

ALBERTA ONE CALL/CALL BEFORE YOU DIG

Be sure that you have clearly identified all underground utilities, especially power lines and natural gas lines, before you begin your NatureScaping project. Check with **Alberta One Call** at **1-800-242-3447** for procedures.

You will also need to consider the possible effects on the neighbourhood. How will your yard look in 5, 10 or 15 years? What if your neighbours hate the serenading chorus of frogs each night, or complain about the bird droppings on their newly painted fence? Will the trees you plant interfere with overhead power lines, or will invasive root systems interfere with your (or your neighbour's) water lines or septic system? To reduce potential conflict, be sure to contemplate possible future effects of your NatureScaping activities, and check out local regulations regarding property use, weeds, unsightly premises and zoning, before you start your project.

PLANNING THE WORK AND WORKING THE PLAN

Inventory Base Map

Before you get out your shovel or rush off to the nearest hardware store, we recommend you do two things: First, take a deep breath and take a slow, deliberate walk around your property. Look carefully at all the built features, terrain, landscape and vegetation. Then, do a simple, scale outline of the property or area you wish to NatureScape, on graph paper, and map the features listed below. The process does not have to be complex or difficult—using graph paper makes the task easy.

SOIL TESTING

If you want to know more about your soil, have it tested. You can get detailed information about soil type, nutrient levels and pH in a soil test. Call Alberta Agriculture, Food and Rural Development, a private soil-testing laboratory, or your local greenhouse/nursery to find out who does soil tests in your area, what a soil test costs and how to collect samples.

(This inventory base map, which records what currently exists on your property, is what you will be working from. Photocopy several copies of it because you'll need it during the entire planning process.)

Ideally, four different elements should be mapped: **above-ground built features** (e.g., house, garage, deck, sheds, sidewalks, fences, overhead lines, garden area, lawn area); **surface features** (e.g., drainage pattern, hills, slopes, wet areas/wetlands); **underground built structures** (e.g., utility lines, septic tank, septic field); and **existing wildlife features** (e.g., bird feeders, brush piles, wild spaces, flower beds, trees, shrubs). Soil types (you may want to test your soil) may also be important. Note on your diagram if there is wildlife habitat next to or near your land, or even an adjacent wildlife corridor.

You may want to put arrows on your diagram to show the prevailing wind directions for summer and winter, since these winds will modify the wildlife use of the property. The creation of wind buffers and cover are important in most naturalized gardens.

You should also prepare sketches of the various shade types (heavy shade, light shade, full sunlight) on the property generated by existing vegetation, buildings and other structures at various times of the day. The degree of shade is important when it comes to selecting your plant species.

How to draw a profile map of your property

If your yard is steeply sloped, you may want to prepare a profile map, also to scale.

Illustrated on the following page are two examples of inventory base maps—one of an urban property (which will be the base of the bubble diagram and site plans in this chapter, and the butterfly gardens in Chapter 9), and another of an acreage property. These maps are adaptations of actual Alberta lots.

Inventory base map of an urban property

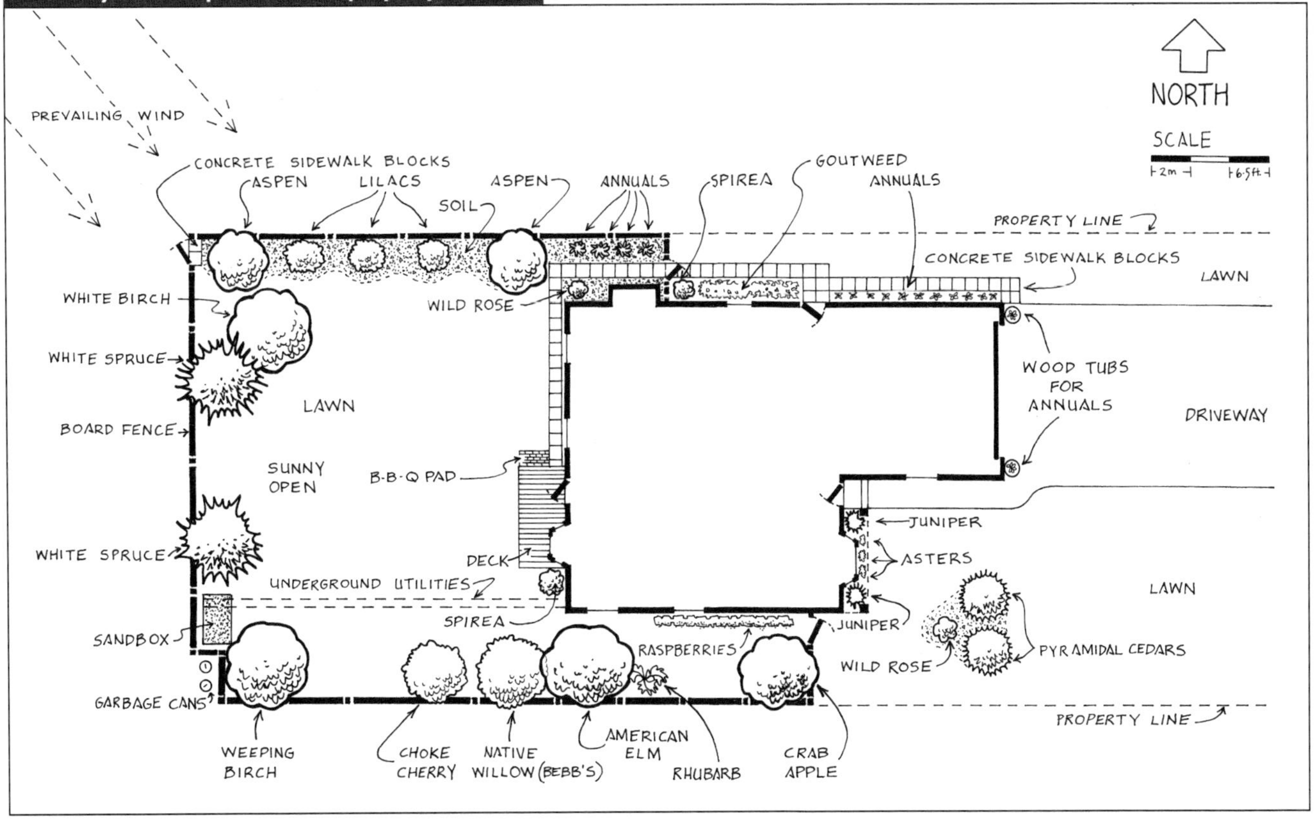

Inventory base map of an acreage property

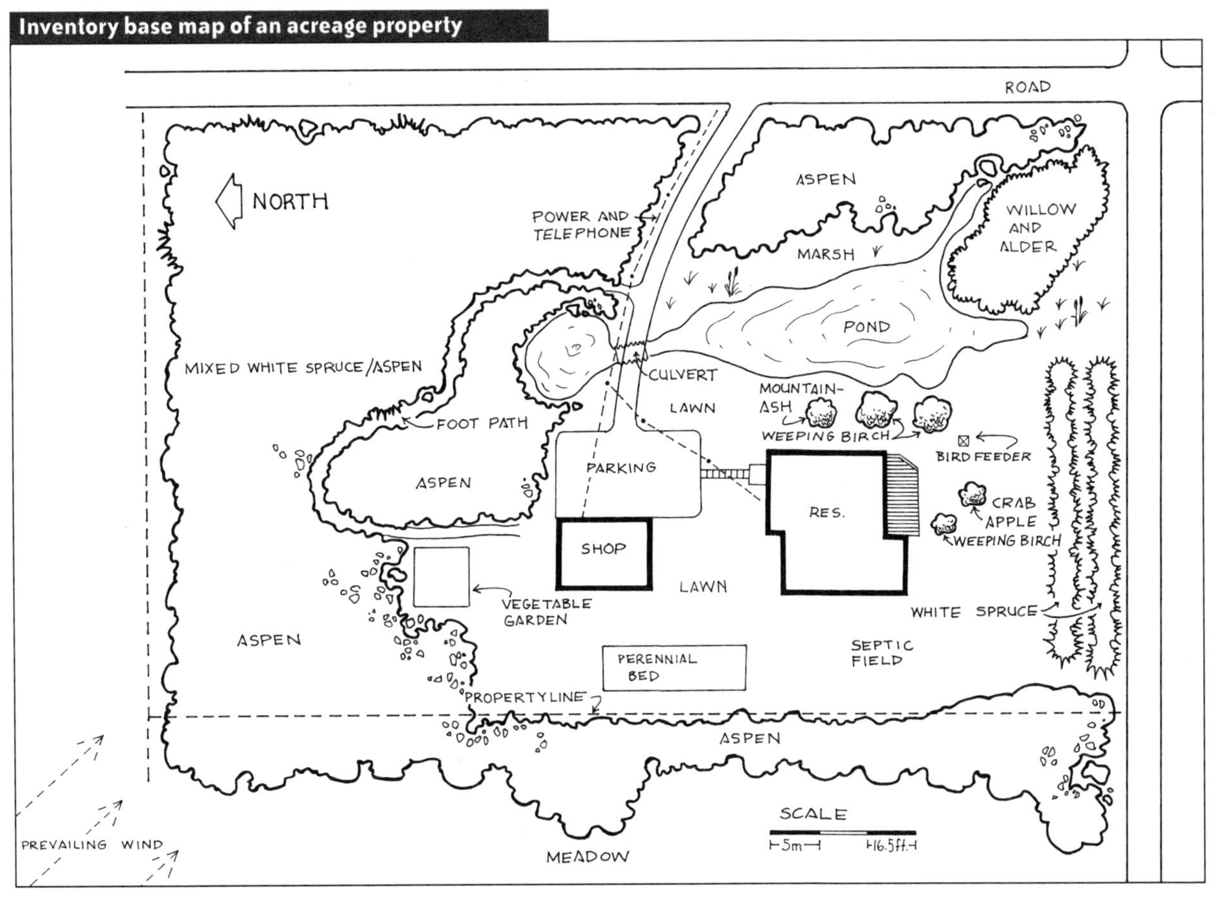

Bubble Diagram

The next step in the design process is to draw one or more simple bubble diagrams based on your inventory map. One method is to draw directly on the map; another is to use tracing paper or overhead transparency sheets so that you can work with several layers of features.

On a bubble diagram, identify potential uses for different parts of your yard. Sketch in the areas specifically for your use (e.g., vegetable garden, viewing benches, storage shed, play areas), as well as the areas that you might want to develop for wildlife (e.g., a wild corner, brush pile, water garden, rock garden, butterfly garden, hummingbird garden, wooded or shrubby area). Be sure to take into account such factors as present yard use, existing topographical features (e.g., slopes, well-drained or poorly drained areas), existing wildlife habitat in your yard and adjacent areas, shade and prevailing winds.

If possible, keep most human activity concentrated in one section of your yard and away from the most sensitive wildlife areas. Also consider how domestic pets can be kept away from wildlife. Be sure to set trees back at least 10 m (33 ft.) from water wells, water lines, drainage pipes and septic systems, and don't forget to leave adequate travel corridors for heavy equipment to access wells, septic tank systems, and underground pipes or wires.

If you are planning a windbreak, make sure it won't cause future problems with snow accumulation on driveways and sidewalks. Windbreaks cause an accumulation of snow for a distance of ten times their height downwind and several times their height upwind.

Below is a bubble diagram for NatureScaping a typical Alberta urban lot.

Bubble diagram for NatureScaped property (based on urban property shown on page 9)

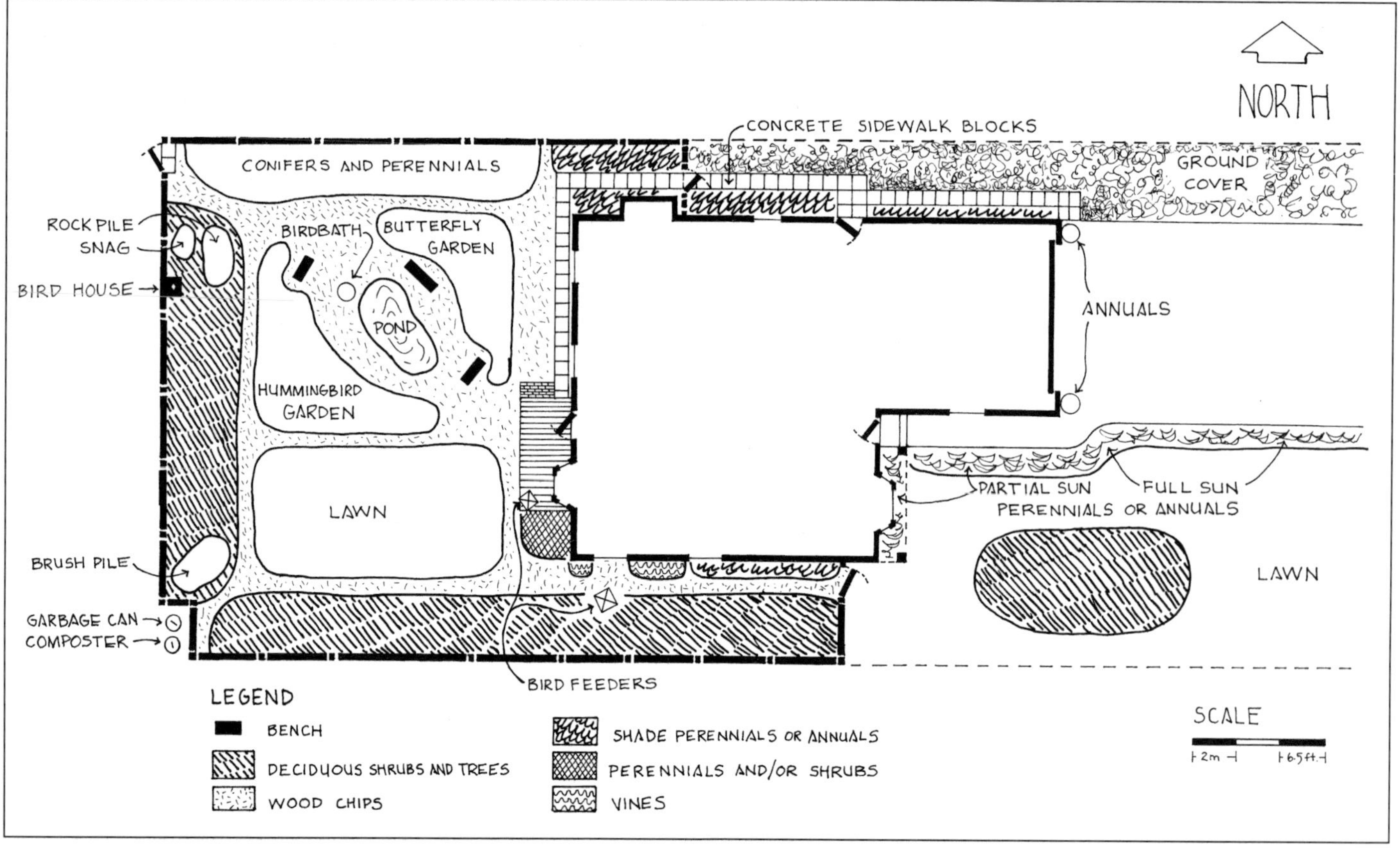

NORTH
CONCRETE SIDEWALK BLOCKS
CONIFERS AND PERENNIALS
GROUND COVER
ROCK PILE
SNAG
BIRD HOUSE
BIRDBATH
BUTTERFLY GARDEN
POND
ANNUALS
HUMMINGBIRD GARDEN
LAWN
PARTIAL SUN
FULL SUN
PERENNIALS OR ANNUALS
LAWN
BRUSH PILE
GARBAGE CAN
COMPOSTER
BIRD FEEDERS
LEGEND
BENCH
DECIDUOUS SHRUBS AND TREES
WOOD CHIPS
SHADE PERENNIALS OR ANNUALS
PERENNIALS AND/OR SHRUBS
VINES
SCALE
2 m
6.5 ft.

MYRNA PEARMAN

Naturalized yard in southern Alberta

Site Plan

Once you have decided on the basic plan, you are ready to develop a specific landscape or site plan. Many people will enjoy making their own site plan, but if you don't want to tackle the process on your own, one option is to get professional assistance from a landscape designer or horticulturist. Alternatively, if you count among your friends a landscape designer or someone with considerable talent when it comes to gardening, now is the time to take them out to dinner or otherwise cajole them into giving you some free advice.

At this point, you make decisions as to which plants to choose, and the locations and dimensions of all the other features, such as water gardens and nestboxes, that you want to include. Make sure you consider the height and foliage spread of mature trees and shrubs in your planning.

Also think about how trees and shrubs can contribute to energy conservation. If you plant coniferous trees on the north and west sides of your house, not only will you provide critical shelter for overwintering birds, but you will also reduce your home heating costs by sheltering your house from harsh winter winds. Deciduous trees planted on the south side provide food and nesting habitat for wildlife while at the same time providing shade from the hot summer sun. During the fall and winter, when they have no leaves, these trees allow your house to enjoy maximum solar gain.

Your last step is to arrange the structural components. Place nestboxes and feeders at appropriate heights and locations, install bumble bee boxes well away from where children play, and carefully plan where to build rock piles, brush piles, and so on.

Following are potential site plans for three separate natural regions (grassland, parkland, boreal forest) and two natural regions combined (foothills and Rocky Mountain). The site plans are based on the bubble diagram on page 10.

Site plans for a NatureScaped property in different natural regions ~ GRASSLAND
(based on urban property shown on page 10)

GRASSLAND (e.g., Lethbridge, Medicine Hat)

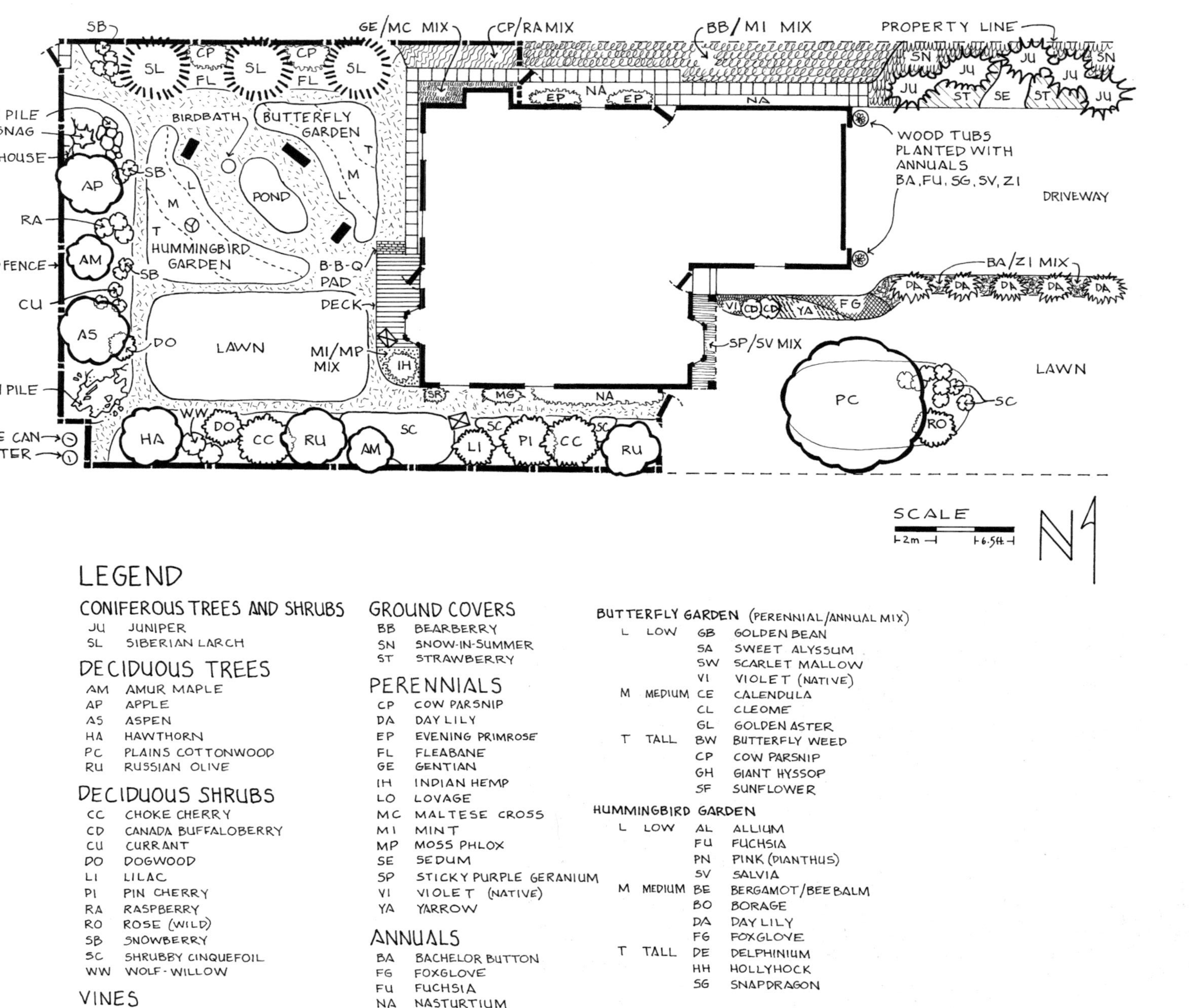

Site plans for a NatureScaped property in different natural regions ~ PARKLAND

(based on urban property shown on page 10)

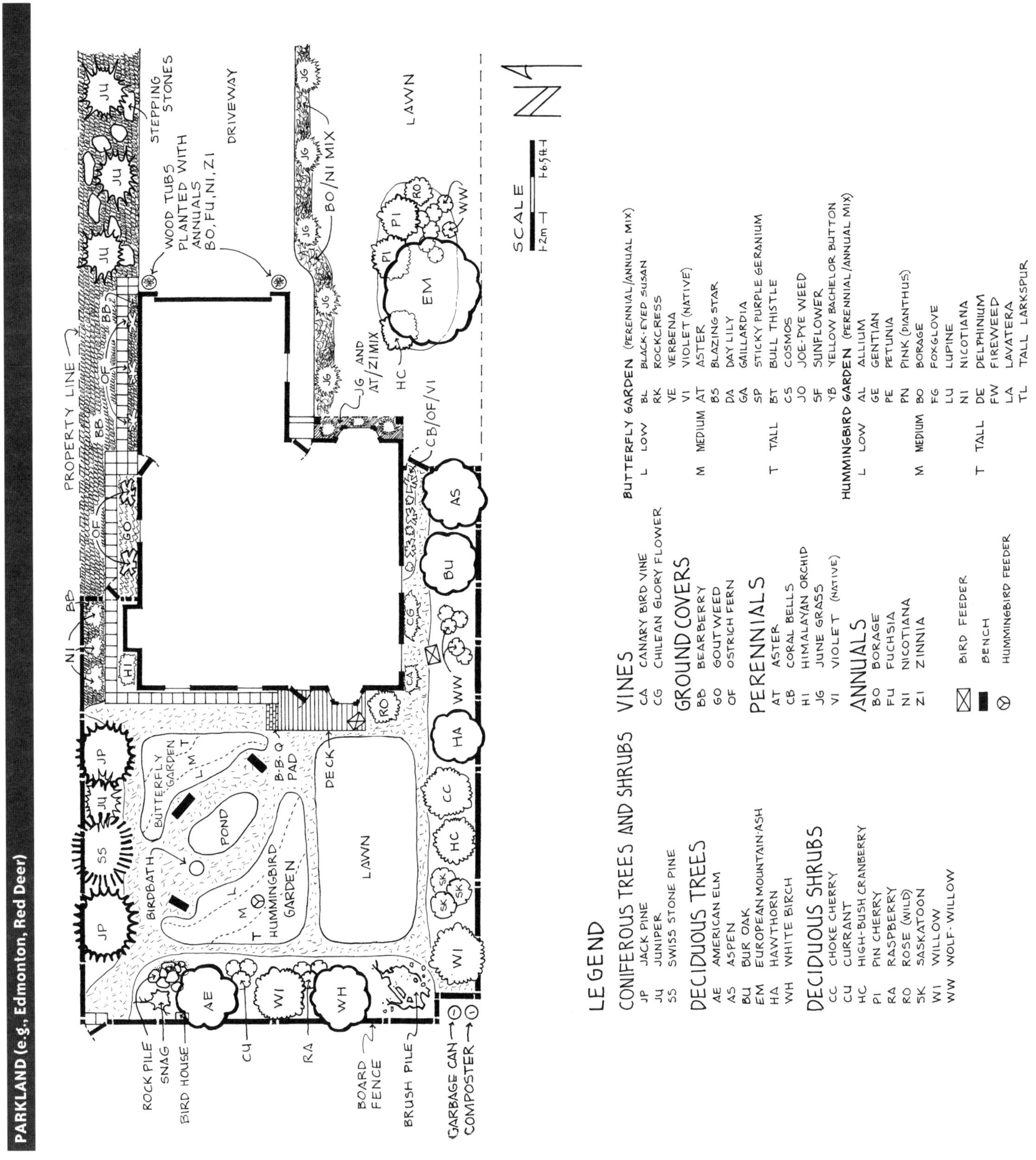

SCALE 2m 6.5ft

LEGEND

CONIFEROUS TREES AND SHRUBS
- JP JACK PINE
- JU JUNIPER
- SS SWISS STONE PINE

DECIDUOUS TREES
- AE AMERICAN ELM
- AS ASPEN
- BU BUR OAK
- EM EUROPEAN MOUNTAIN-ASH
- HA HAWTHORN
- WH WHITE BIRCH

DECIDUOUS SHRUBS
- CC CHOKE CHERRY
- CU CURRANT
- HC HIGH-BUSH CRANBERRY
- PI PIN CHERRY
- RA RASPBERRY
- RO ROSE (WILD)
- SK SASKATOON
- WI WILLOW
- WW WOLF-WILLOW

VINES
- CA CANARY BIRD VINE
- CG CHILEAN GLORY FLOWER

GROUND COVERS
- BB BEARBERRY
- GO GOUTWEED
- OF OSTRICH FERN

PERENNIALS
- AT ASTER
- CB CORAL BELLS
- HI HIMALAYAN ORCHID
- JG JUNE GRASS
- VI VIOLET (NATIVE)

ANNUALS
- BO BORAGE
- FU FUCHSIA
- NI NICOTIANA
- ZI ZINNIA

- ☒ BIRD FEEDER
- ■ BENCH
- ⊗ HUMMINGBIRD FEEDER

BUTTERFLY GARDEN (PERENNIAL/ANNUAL MIX)

L	LOW	BL	BLACK-EYED SUSAN
		RK	ROCKCRESS
		VE	VERBENA
		VI	VIOLET (NATIVE)
M	MEDIUM	AT	ASTER
		BS	BLAZING STAR
		DA	DAY LILY
		GA	GAILLARDIA
		SP	STICKY PURPLE GERANIUM
T	TALL	BT	BULL THISTLE
		CS	COSMOS
		JO	JOE-PYE WEED
		SF	SUNFLOWER
		YB	YELLOW BACHELOR BUTTON

HUMMINGBIRD GARDEN (PERENNIAL/ANNUAL MIX)

L	LOW	AL	ALLIUM
		GE	GENTIAN
		PE	PETUNIA
		PN	PINK (DIANTHUS)
M	MEDIUM	BO	BORAGE
		FG	FOXGLOVE
		LU	LUPINE
		NI	NICOTIANA
T	TALL	DE	DELPHINIUM
		FW	FIREWEED
		LA	LAVATERA
		TL	TALL LARKSPUR

Site plans for a NatureScaped property in different natural regions ~ BOREAL FOREST

(based on urban property shown on page 10)

BOREAL FOREST (e.g., Athabasca, Ft. McMurray)

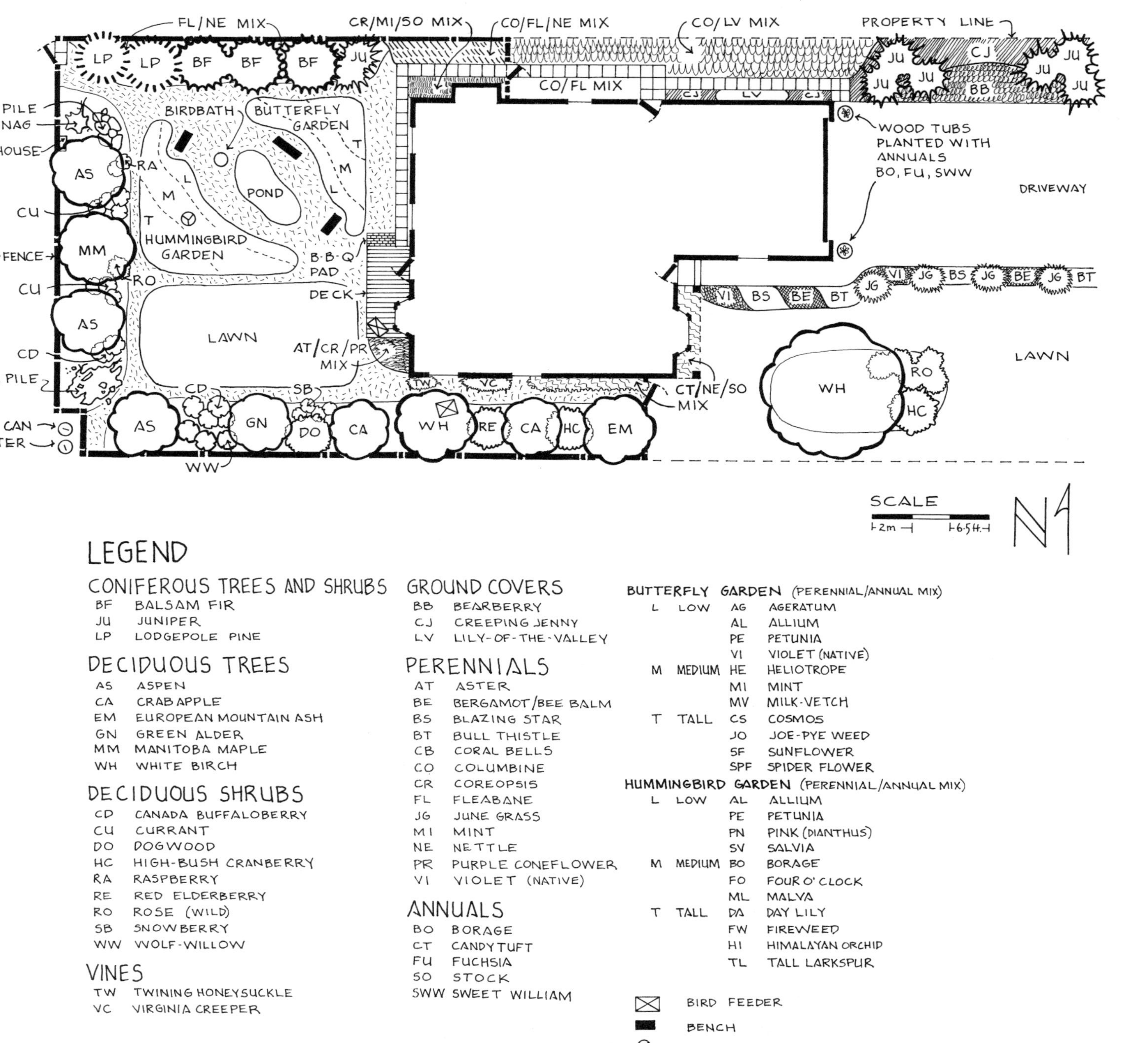

Site plans for a NatureScaped property in different natural regions ~ FOOTHILLS/ROCKY MOUNTAIN
(based on urban property shown on page 10)

FOOTHILLS/ROCKY MOUNTAIN (e.g., Edson, Banff)

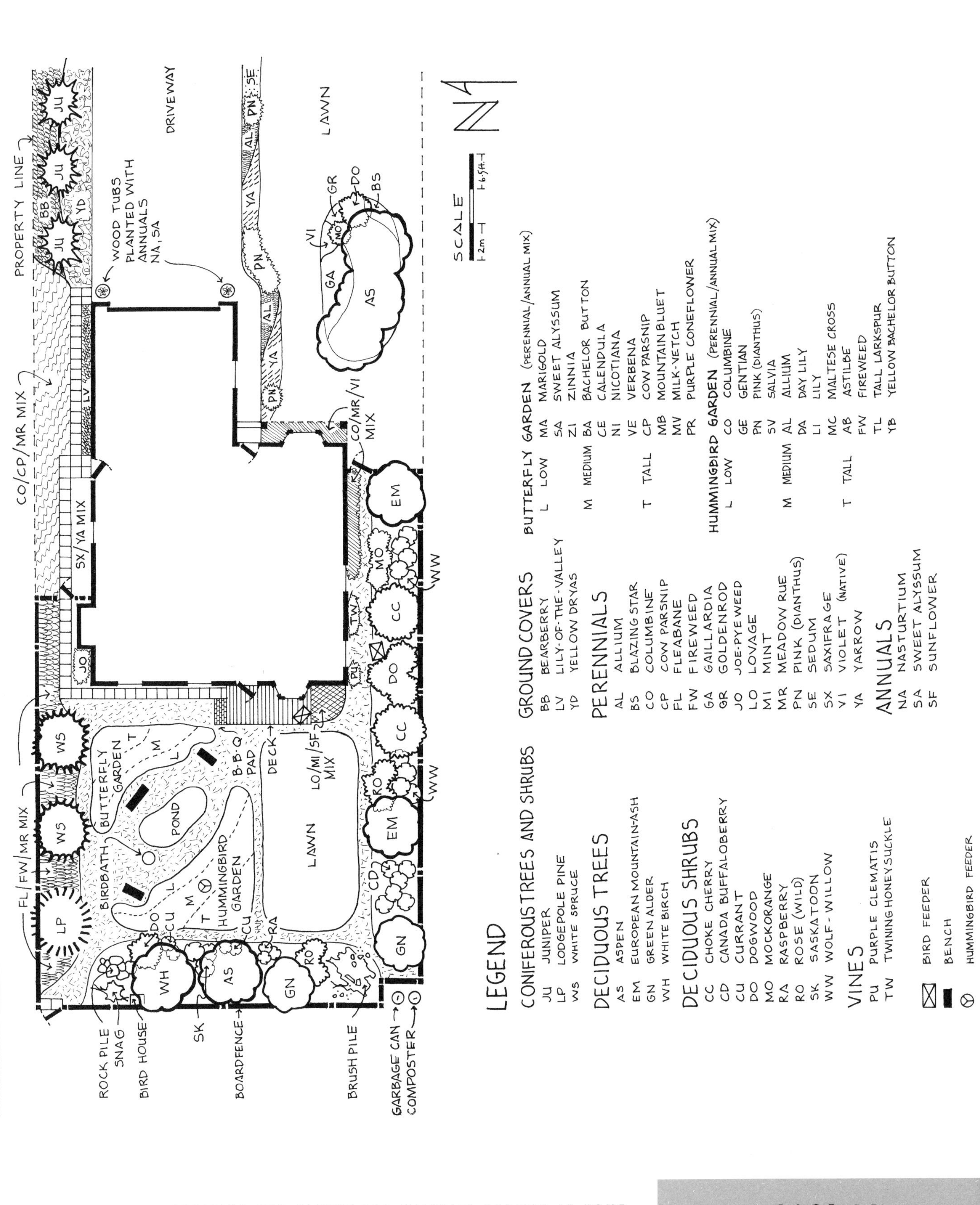

FL/FW/MR MIX
CO/CP/MR MIX
PROPERTY LINE
JU BB JU JU YD
LP WS WS
JO
SX/YA MIX
LV
ROCK PILE
SNAG
BIRD HOUSE
WH
DO
CU
BIRDBATH
BUTTERFLY GARDEN
T M L
POND
L M T
HUMMINGBIRD GARDEN
SK
AS
BOARDFENCE
CU
RA
B-B-Q PAD
DECK
WOOD TUBS PLANTED WITH ANNUALS NA, SA
DRIVEWAY
GN
RO
LAWN
LO/MI/SF MIX
BRUSH PILE
GARBAGE CAN
COMPOSTER
GN
CD
EM
RO
WW
CC
DO
CC
MO
WW
EM
PU
TW
CO/MR/VI MIX
PN YA AL PN YA AL PN SE
AS GA VI MO GR DO BS
LAWN
SCALE
2m
6.5ft.
N

LEGEND

CONIFEROUS TREES AND SHRUBS
- JU JUNIPER
- LP LODGEPOLE PINE
- WS WHITE SPRUCE

DECIDUOUS TREES
- AS ASPEN
- EM EUROPEAN MOUNTAIN-ASH
- GN GREEN ALDER
- WH WHITE BIRCH

DECIDUOUS SHRUBS
- CC CHOKE CHERRY
- CD CANADA BUFFALOBERRY
- CU CURRANT
- DO DOGWOOD
- MO MOCKORANGE
- RA RASPBERRY
- RO ROSE (WILD)
- SK SASKATOON
- WW WOLF-WILLOW

VINES
- PU PURPLE CLEMATIS
- TW TWINING HONEYSUCKLE

- ⊠ BIRD FEEDER
- ▬ BENCH
- ⊗ HUMMINGBIRD FEEDER

GROUND COVERS
- BB BEARBERRY
- LV LILY-OF-THE-VALLEY
- YD YELLOW DRYAS

PERENNIALS
- AL ALLIUM
- BS BLAZING STAR
- CO COLUMBINE
- CP COW PARSNIP
- FL FLEABANE
- FW FIREWEED
- GA GAILLARDIA
- GR GOLDENROD
- JO JOE-PYE WEED
- LO LOVAGE
- MI MINT
- MR MEADOW RUE
- PN PINK (DIANTHUS)
- SE SEDUM
- SX SAXIFRAGE
- VI VIOLET (NATIVE)
- YA YARROW

ANNUALS
- NA NASTURTIUM
- SA SWEET ALYSSUM
- SF SUNFLOWER

BUTTERFLY GARDEN (PERENNIAL/ANNUAL MIX)

L LOW	MA	MARIGOLD
	SA	SWEET ALYSSUM
	ZI	ZINNIA
M MEDIUM	BA	BACHELOR BUTTON
	CE	CALENDULA
	NI	NICOTIANA
	VE	VERBENA
T TALL	CP	COW PARSNIP
	MB	MOUNTAIN BLUET
	MV	MILK-VETCH
	PR	PURPLE CONEFLOWER

HUMMINGBIRD GARDEN (PERENNIAL/ANNUAL MIX)

L LOW	CO	COLUMBINE
	GE	GENTIAN
	PN	PINK (DIANTHUS)
	SV	SALVIA
M MEDIUM	AL	ALLIUM
	DA	DAY LILY
	LI	LILY
	MC	MALTESE CROSS
T TALL	AB	ASTILBE
	FW	FIREWEED
	TL	TALL LARKSPUR
	YB	YELLOW BACHELOR BUTTON

RECORDING YOUR EXPERIENCE

Chronicle the ongoing transformation of your yard as you NatureScape it. Take photos, write poems! You may even want to keep a scrapbook of notes, words of advice, interesting experiences and observations. Share what you see and your experiences with NatureScape Alberta by filling in the Backyard Watch form at the back of the book (Appendix 6) or contacting us on the web at www.naturescape.ab.ca . You may also want to have your yard certified as "official" NatureScaped habitat. See the sidebar in Chapter 1 (page 3) for details. You will be amazed at how quickly your yard transforms—and how rewarding the result will be after all your work!

ACKNOWLEDGMENTS

Cynthia Pohl (Landscape designer/gardener, Delburne, Alberta)
Jackie Powell (Arborist and landscape gardener, Lacombe, Alberta)

A special thanks to Jackie Powell for doing the natural region garden designs.

SIGNIFICANT REFERENCES

Canadian Environmental Law Association and Ontario College of Family Physicians Environmental Health Committee. 2000. *Environmental standard setting and children's health*. In press.

Canadian Wildlife Federation (Mycio-mommers, L., S. Fisher and S. Uriarte). 1996. *Backyard habitat for Canada's wildlife*. Canadian Wildlife Federation, Ottawa.

Dennis, J. V. 1985. *The wildlife gardener*. Alfred A. Knopf, New York.

Ernst, R. S. 1993. *The naturalist's garden: How to garden with plants that attract birds, butterflies, and other wildlife*. The Globe Pequot Press, Old Saybrook, Connecticut.

Henderson, C.L. 1987. *Landscaping for wildlife*. Nongame Wildlife Program - Section of Wildlife, Minnesota Department of Natural Resources. Minnesota's Bookstore, St. Paul, Minnesota.

Kavanagh, J. 1991. *Nature Alberta: An illustrated guide to common plants and animals*. Lone Pine Publishing, Edmonton.

Leedy, D.L., and L.W. Adams. 1984. *A guide to urban wildlife management*. National Institute for Urban Wildlife, Columbia, Maryland.

Merilees, B. 1989. *Attracting backyard wildlife*. Whitecap Books, Vancouver.

Municipal Districts of Rocky View, Pincher Creek and Foothills, Alberta Agriculture, Food and Rural Development, Agriculture & Agri-Food Canada—Prairie Farm Rehabilitation Administration, "Cows and Fish Project" and Alberta Environmentally Sustainable Agriculture Program. n.d. *Caring for Alberta's landscapes: Tips and references for owners of small farms and acreages*. N.p. (Booklet)

Ontario Ministry of Natural Resources. 1990. *Landscaping for wildlife*. Queen's Printer, Ontario. (Booklet)

Rubin, C. 1989. *How to get your lawn and garden off drugs*. Friends of the Earth, Ottawa.

Scalise, K. 1996. *Wildlife gardening in Saskatchewan*. Saskatchewan Environment and Resource Management, Regina.

Schneck, M. 1993. *Your backyard wildlife garden*. Rodale Press, Emmans, Pennsylvania.

Thunder Bay 2000. 1998. *Enjoy a chemical-free yard*. Thunder Bay 2000, Thunder Bay. (Booklet)

Tufts, C. 1988. *The backyard naturalist*. National Wildlife Federation, Washington, D.C.

Vick, R. 1987. *Gardening on the prairies*. Greystone Books, Vancouver.

NatureScaped garden in Calgary, Alberta

Chapter 3

Variety is the Spice of Life: Creating Habitat with Plants

Plants are the underpinnings of an ecosystem; they are the base upon which all else depends. The biodiversity, beauty and vibrancy of your NatureScape project will depend, to a large extent, on what plants you choose and how you arrange these plants in your yard. By following the guidelines outlined in this chapter, you will have the opportunity to meld traditional gardening practices with the principles of habitat development.

BIODIVERSITY AND PLANTS

Here are some ecological factors and principles to consider that will help you increase wildlife habitat in your yard.

The Layered Look

Different wildlife species inhabit different "levels" of habitat: some live underground, others spend their time scurrying about at ground level, some inhabit low bushy cover, and others spend their time high in the treetops. Some will use more than one level, depending on what they are doing. By providing many levels of habitat, the needs of a variety of species can be met.

Planting in layers

When planning for the "layered look," make sure you arrange your plantings so that the lowest level is near your house or viewing site and the tallest plants are farthest away. Of course, you will have to take into consideration the mature height and spread of all trees and shrubs, making sure that your plantings will not interfere with your view, underground services, overhead wires, neighbouring walkways and so on.

EDGE

The creation of edge, although beneficial in a small NatureScape, may actually reduce biodiversity in forests and other ecosystems.

The Edge Effect

The place where two different types of habitat meet and blend is called an edge. It is in this area that most wildlife activity takes place. By maximizing the amount of edge in your yard, you can encourage a larger number of wildlife species to enter your yard.

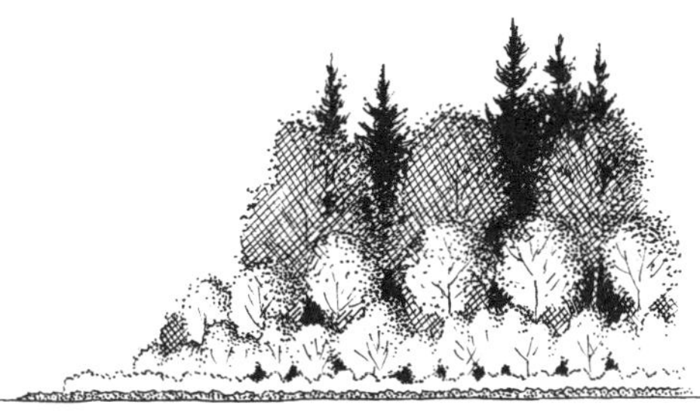

Maximizing edge

One way to create edge is to graduate the heights of vegetation. If you have large trees, add an edge by planting a border of increasingly smaller shrubs. Ground covers can also be used to provide an edge between lawns and adjacent shrubs. Other ways to increase edge are to alternate clumps of plantings with open space and to curve your plantings, rather than having them in straight lines. Unpruned or irregularly pruned trees, shrubs and hedges also tend to provide more edge than those that are carefully manicured.

Planting in Groups

Group plantings, rather than individual plants, are more likely to attract wildlife. Not only will a clump of plants be more visible to a passing animal, but planting in clumps provides creatures with a concentrated food source. When a butterfly finds a blossom, or a bird, a seedhead, to its liking, it will linger longer if there is lots to eat.

Planting in groups

Thoughtful planting in several yards can create a wildlife corridor (above, for birds)

Wildlife Corridors

Corridors or "greenways" are also important for wildlife. These corridors can be provided on a "micro" level in a yard by providing safe travel routes to and from a water garden, birdbath or bird-feeding station. Travel corridors can also be provided on a larger scale by using trees and shrubs to link larger habitat areas. Animals tend to prefer travelling along safe, protected and familiar routes, so these links allow free movement by a variety of species.

If you have natural habitat or a wooded area adjacent to your property, be sure to maximize this habitat feature by planting trees and shrubs adjacent to it. If you live between two habitat areas, plant rows of shrubs and trees to form a wildlife corridor.

Planting for Year-Round Use

When NatureScaping, try to choose plants so that food will be provided year-round. One way to do this is to make sure the different plant species you select produce their flowers, fruit and seeds at different times through the season, and be sure to plant some early-blooming species. By including at least some fruit-bearing trees and shrubs that hold their fruits and seeds into the winter, you will ensure that winter residents will have food.

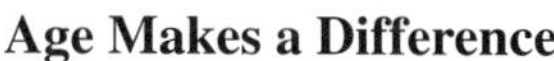

Mature poplar with *(l. to r.)* warbling vireo, hairy woodpeckers and black-capped chickadee

Age Makes a Difference

As trees mature, their value to wildlife changes. A small poplar seedling, for example, has limited wildlife value when it is first planted. However, by the time it reaches the ripe old age of 30, it will be a virtual wildlife "condo" and "cafeteria." To maximize the value of a wooded area over the long-term, you may want to plant additional trees every few years so that more than one age class is represented. And, even in death, trees remain an important habitat component. See page 26 for information on the ecology of snags and how to include them in your NatureScaped yard.

The Advantages of Native Plants

Where and when possible, use native plants. These indigenous plant species have evolved over time in a particular ecosystem, and so may rely less on water, energy and chemicals than introduced plants. Native plants are well suited to local soils, climate and light levels, and are often less stressed by local insects than are cultivated species or varieties (unless that species or variety has been bred especially to resist a particular insect).

Try to use native material from within the natural region where it will be planted (see map of Alberta's natural regions on the following page). By planting native species, you help to ensure the genetic health and biodiversity of your area.

GUIDELINES FOR THE COLLECTION OF NATIVE PLANTS

Where to Collect

- Avoid protected lands such as national, provincial and municipal parks and protected natural areas. It is illegal to collect from many of these areas.
- Obtain necessary permits to collect on forestry reserves.
- Obtain permission from the landowner or lease holder to collect on private or leased land.
- Avoid busy highways and roads. Roadside collecting is dangerous and may encourage indiscriminate collecting by others.
- Avoid rare or fragile habitats such as sand dunes or wetlands.
- Where possible, collect from areas destined to be developed or destroyed in the near future. Obtain permission from the landowner or lease holder.

Know Your Species

- Know the flora of the area before you collect. Do not collect rare or endangered species (see Alberta Natural Heritage Information Centre [ANHIC] tracking and watch lists; to contact the ANHIC, see Appendix 5).
- Identify the plants before collecting seeds or cuttings.
- Collect common species or those with a large population.
- Avoid collecting single specimens or from small populations with fewer than 50 plants.

Collect Seeds or Cuttings, Not Plants

- Collect only seeds or cuttings, not entire plants.
- Flag or label plants with a marker while in bloom, or be able to identify plants in seed.
- Collect undamaged, ripe seeds (firm, plump and dry).
- Leave 50 percent of the seed in place to allow natural propagation, and to provide food and habitat for insects, birds and small mammals.
- Do not intensively collect the same area year after year.
- In areas that may be subjected to further collecting by the general public or where grazing reduces natural regeneration, collecting should be minimal (no more than 10 percent of the plants).

Adapted from D. Bush, ed. 1998. *Guidelines for the collection & use of native plants.* Alberta Native Plant Council, Edmonton, Alberta. (From the ANPC website)

Alberta's Natural Regions

Grassland Natural Region. This region occupies the southern part of the province, east of the Rocky Mountains. It is characterized by flat or gently rolling topography with mixedgrass or fescue grasslands, and deep river valleys dominated by deciduous forests. Much of the natural vegetation of this natural region has been replaced by agricultural crops; the extensive areas of native rangeland that remain are managed mainly for livestock grazing.

Parkland Natural Region. With the exception of the Peace River parkland area, the parkland natural region is a transitional zone between the grasslands of the plains and the coniferous forests of the boreal forest and Rocky Mountains. The southern parkland is dominated by deciduous forests (especially aspen and balsam poplar) and fescue grasslands. The Peace River parkland is dominated by mixedwood forests (with both coniferous and deciduous trees) and grasslands lacking the rough fescue (*Festuca scabrella*) of the southern region. The parkland is the most densely populated natural region in Alberta, so the landscape has been greatly altered.

Boreal Forest Natural Region. The boreal forest is the largest natural region in Alberta. It consists of broad, lowland plains and isolated hill systems, and is dominated by coniferous and mixedwood forests. It includes extensive wetlands in low-lying areas and peatland complexes.

Foothills Natural Region. The foothills natural region is a transitional zone between the Rocky Mountains and both the boreal forest and parkland natural regions, with some northern outlying hill masses (outliers). It is dominated by mixed and coniferous (e.g., lodgepole pine, black spruce) forests.

Rocky Mountain Natural Region. This region is defined by the Rocky Mountains, with vegetation zones (including coniferous forests, grasslands and heath tundra) changing according to altitude. Most of Alberta's rivers have their headwaters in this region.

Canadian Shield Natural Region. This small region in the northeastern corner of the province is characterized by exposed bedrock, pine forests and peatlands. Because of its small size and remote location, this natural region is not discussed in this book.

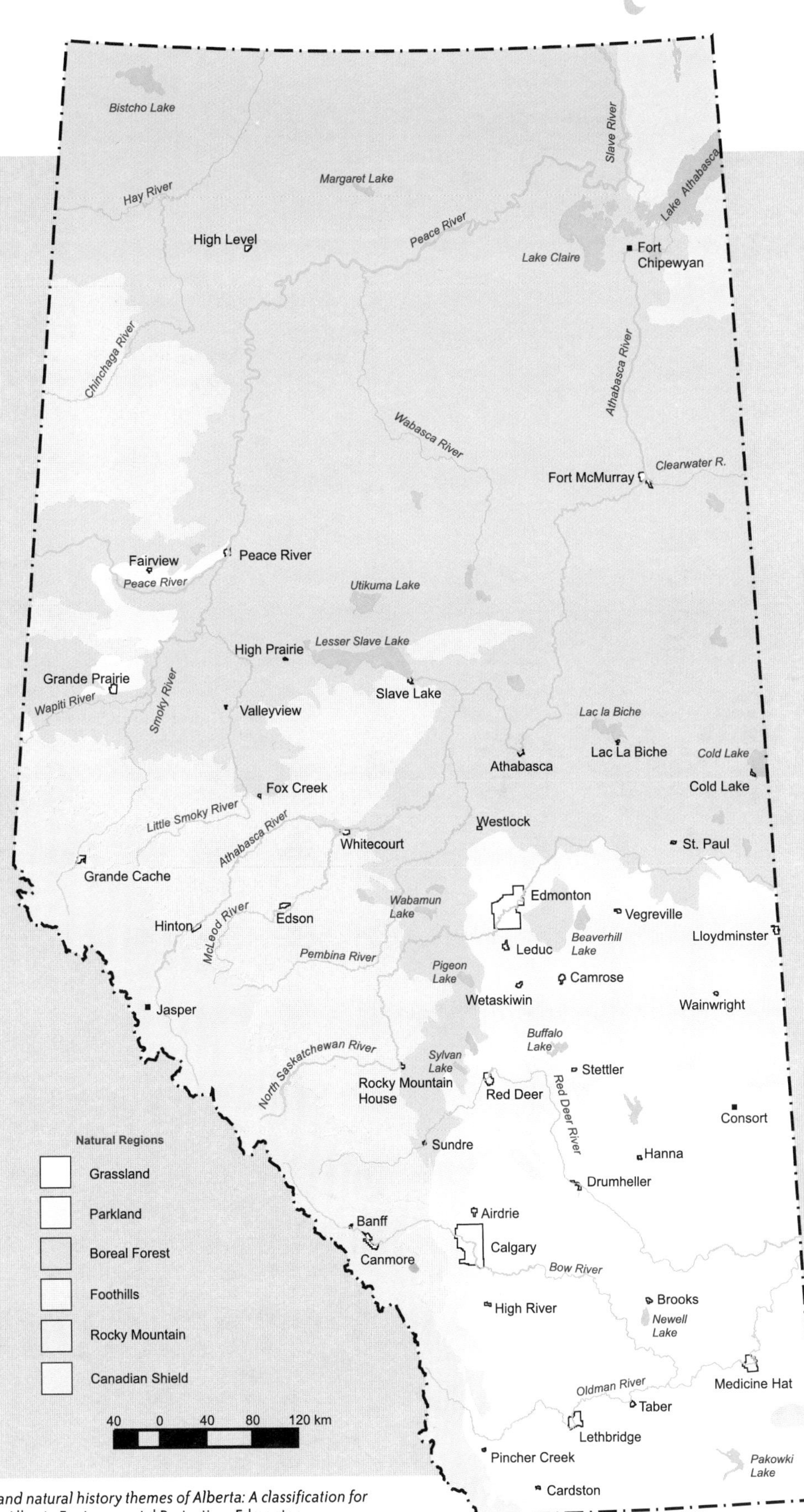

Text adapted from P.L. Achuff. 1994. *Natural regions, subregions and natural history themes of Alberta: A classification for protected areas management*. 2d ed. Prepared for Parks Services, Alberta Environmental Protection, Edmonton.

Natural region boundaries supplied by Alberta Environment.

When aquiring native seeds or plants, check with your local nursery first. Your request will indicate to the nursery that there is interest in native species. If the nursery can't help you, then try a native plant or seed supplier. See Appendix 5 for a list of these suppliers.

If you are purchasing native plants from a nursery, make sure that the plants are nursery-propagated. Many wild species of cactus, fern, orchid and lily are dug from the wild and have become threatened by the trade in wild plants. Please do not purchase wild-collected plants.

You may wish to collect your own seeds or cuttings of native plants from the wild. If you do, it is extremely important to follow the Alberta Native Plant Council (ANPC) guidelines for this kind of collection (see page 18). Rare or threatened plants should not be collected from the wild.

WHAT TO CONSIDER WHEN CHOOSING YOUR PLANTS

When you are deciding what plants to use in your NatureScaped yard, you will need to consider broad factors such as natural region and hardiness zone, and very specific features such as soil, drainage/moisture and sunlight.

Natural Region

Alberta's climate is classified as continental, with cold winters and short, relatively cool summers. Within the province, there are wide variations of average temperature, and there are also differences in average precipitation, vegetation types, soils and landforms. Some areas of southern Alberta are prone to chinook winds. A classification system has been set up of "natural regions" that share similar characteristics. These broad areas have been further subdivided into subregions.

The map, on the previous page, shows all of Alberta's natural regions. Understanding the broad bioregional context of where you live will give you a greater appreciation of the general landscape features and vegetation types you might expect to find in your area. The tables in Appendix 1 provide information on wildlife-attracting plants that will grow well in your natural region.

Hardiness Zone

Hardiness is the ability of a plant to thrive in a particular climate. It is determined by the adaptability of the plant to local soils, humidity, precipitation, length of growing season, as well as summer and winter temperature extremes. Several different hardiness zone systems and maps have been developed, of which, the USDA (United States Department of Agriculture) system is one of the most popular.

Hardiness zones and hardiness zone maps can be useful guideposts, but they do not take into account local climatic variables, drainage patterns, soil conditions, aspect and other microsite characteristics. Plants that are not listed for a particular area (e.g., a northern zone) can often do well in such a location, provided they are grown in the correct microclimate and given a little "tender loving care."

For these reasons, it is always wise to take note of what plants grow well in your area and to check with local nurseries and greenhouses for advice about what plantings are best suited to your particular location or site. The ultimate test, of course, is to try growing a particular plant yourself! But even if you want to experiment with marginally hardy species, make sure that the foundation plants—those that form the permanent framework of your yard—are locally hardy and suited to your particular site conditions.

Microclimates

Although natural regions and hardiness zones share general characteristics, a wide variety of climatic differences can be found within each of these areas. If these unique conditions are in relatively small areas, they are called microclimates.

There are, for example, strong microclimatic differences in the city of Calgary. Folks up in the northwest part of the city have a harder time growing things than gardeners living at lower elevations in the Elbow River valley in the southwest. The northwest has little natural vegetation cover and, because of its high elevation, is exposed to harsh northwest winds. Many gardens in the Elbow River valley are sheltered by the valley, and tree cover offers additional protection from the wind.

Within the confines of a single yard, several very small microclimates will exist. The south side of your house, for instance, will be much warmer and sunnier than the north side. Fences, tall trees and other large structures will intercept wind, alter rainfall patterns and will affect how much sun is able to reach the area around them. The aspect and slope of your yard will also exert a microclimatic influence. Through experience, you will be able to find out what plants grow best in different areas of your yard. Your local nursery may also be able to give you some advice.

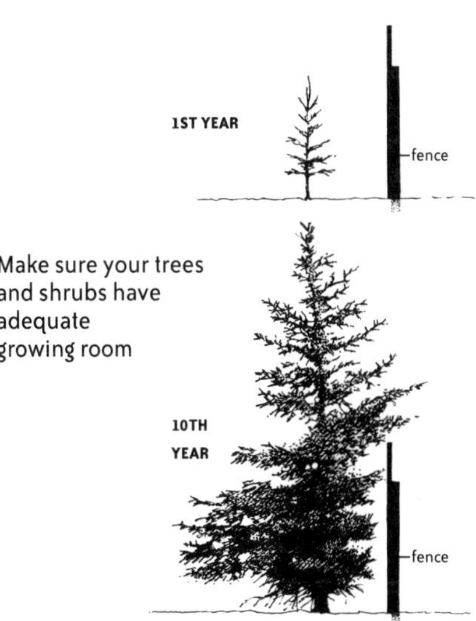

Make sure your trees and shrubs have adequate growing room

Space Requirements

When compiling the list of trees and shrubs you want to plant, take into account their mature height and spread (see Appendix 1). Small trees and shrubs that are spaced properly may look a little forlorn when they are first planted, but they will fill in eventually. It is important to remember that there is a wide variation in height and spread values, depending on the species or variety planted, the specific site conditions (e.g., soil type, climate, sun availability, moisture, competition from other species, exposure), and what you are able to provide your plants (e.g., water, mulch, fertilizer, winter protection).

Soil

Soil composition will greatly influence which plants will grow in your yard and how well they will do. The soil type will also determine how much work your NatureScaping projects might take!

You may have to improve your soil's structure, water-holding capacity and/or chemical balance.

SOIL AND NATURESCAPING

Soil is arguably the most complex and neglected component of the biosphere. Built from inorganic molecules, and living and dead organisms, including plants, animals, fungi and bacteria, soil is literally the foundation of all terrestrial life.

The best soils contain high numbers of living things. Almost all these creatures are small and poorly understood. They include moulds, bacteria, myriapods (mostly centipedes), microscopic spiders, mites, beetles, fly larvae and springtails. In Alberta, ants and worms are probably the most obvious living components of soils.

Healthy soil is essential for successful NatureScaping. A good garden centre will help you build your soil, if that is necessary, but perhaps the best advice for most of our urban soils is to add organic material by way of compost or mulch.

Water and Drainage

The ideal soil condition for the growth of most garden plants is "well-drained." However, some plants love soggy soils and others thrive under very dry conditions, so know the conditions in your yard and pick your plants carefully. From a NatureScaping point of view, it makes sense to use plants you would find in your natural surroundings rather than spend time, money and energy trying to make your yard into a foreign landscape.

If you don't like yard work, try xeriscaping—the practice of landscaping with plants to minimize the use of water. Xeriscaping make sense from a water conservation perspective, and xeriscaped gardens require very little maintenance, but you will need to start with a well-drained soil.

To create a xeriscaped garden, use plants that require little water, can hold water well and/or have dormant periods (deciduous trees, for instance). Look for plants that have grey or silver leaves, which reflect sunlight, like wolf-willow; succulent leaves, which hold water, such as stonecrop/sedum; and hairy leaves, which prevent or

reduce evapotranspiration (loss of water from the plant), like yellow dryas. When shopping for xeriscaping plants, be sure to ask your local nursery or native seed/ plant supplier for advice on what plants will work best for your particular region and site.

Sunlight and Shading

Different species of plants have different shade/sun preferences. Sun-loving plants, such as pin cherry, aspen and white birch, tend to be early successional species—they are found soon after a fire or other disturbance. These species usually grow quickly but don't live very long.

Shade-loving, or what botanists call shade-tolerant, plants (like white spruce) tend to be slow-growing and long-lived, so they eventually out-compete the faster-growing but shorter-lived sun-lovers. These plants grow in shady conditions, such as a forest understory, until they become well established, at which time they can better cope with the increased light.

To achieve maximum diversity, try mixing trees and shrubs with different degrees of shade tolerance together. You will create various layers of vegetation all the way from the canopy down to the ground, expanding the number of potential niches that plants and animals can utilize, thus increasing the number and variety of species that can be supported.

WHAT IS A NICHE?

A niche, in ecology, refers to both the habitat in which a species is found and the role of the species in its habitat. So, the niche of an organism consists of both where it lives and what it does. In a wetland, for example, wood frog tadpoles and adults occupy different niches, the tadpoles being aquatic and the adults a combination of terrestrial and aquatic.

Native, Introduced or Cultivar?

There are some gardeners who feel that wildlife gardens must contain only native material, and we advocate the use of native species wherever possible (see page 18 for the benefits).

Although it is preferable to use as much native material as possible, the selection and availability of native plants is still limited in Alberta. (We urge you to support native seed and plant growers, and encourage nurseries to carry more native material.) Furthermore, there are many cultivars and introduced plants that are readily sought out by wildlife. Some cultivars also have traits that potentially make them more desirable to a gardener than native varieties (longer blooming period, for example).

Sometimes, however, cultivars are not as attractive to wildlife as the original wild varieties. Violets (*Viola* spp.) are a striking example of this principle—butterflies are attracted only to native species. Also, certain species of plants—native, introduced or cultivar—may be attractive to wildlife in some parts of the continent, but not in others. Use the Appendixes of this book to decide what plants to grow, and let us know about other species and varieties attractive to wildlife here using the Backyard Watch form (Appendix 6).

It is important to remember that cultivars exhibit specific characteristics in the first generation but can be vastly different in succeeding ones. You cannot collect and replant the seeds of cultivars and expect the resulting plants to be the same as the parents. However, open-pollinated (pollinated by insects, the wind or other natural methods), native flowers will retain their characteristics generation after generation.

The degree to which you choose to use native material will likely depend on your gardening goals. If you want to be involved in the very important role of preserving the native gene pool, you may want to grow only native species. If you want to maximize the wildlife use of your plantings, then you may decide to choose the

NATIVE AND INTRODUCED PLANTS, AND CULTIVARS

A **native** plant is one that is indigenous to an area. Commonly, native plants in Alberta are defined as species that occurred in the province before the time of Euro-American settlement.

An **introduced** plant, or **exotic,** is a plant that is indigenous to a region, country or continent different from the one where it is presently located, sometimes an area with different growing conditions. In other words, it is a plant that is not in its native environment.

A **cultivar** is a clone of (1) a plant species, (2) a plant hybrid, or (3) a plant produced by mutation.

A clone is genetically identical to its parent; in plants it is created by tissue culture or vegetative propagation. A flower such as *Lilium orientalis* can come in a variety of colours, but the cultivar *Lilium orientalis* 'Star Bright' will be one specific colour, just like the parent.

A plant hybrid is a plant created by the cross-pollination of two plants of the same species with different characteristics. Plants grown from the seeds of a hybrid will not necessarily produce plants the same as the parent plant.

A mutation or "sport" is an individual that has characteristics that are different from the normal limits of variation in a species.

plants—native or introduced, or cultivars—that are the most attractive to the widest variety of wild creatures. If you are a more traditional gardener who wants to maximize the showiness of your garden, you may end up with mostly cultivars and exotics. You may also choose cultivars and exotics over native varieties if you want plants that have been bred to grow well in your particular area or site.

Invasiveness and Problem Plants

If your property happens to border a woodland, wetland or other natural area, avoid selecting species for your yard known to be invasive. Birds, wind and shoes, for instance, can carry seeds into a natural area, and suckers and rhizomes can also invade. Control or remove noxious weeds and eradicate restricted weeds (see definitions in side bar). A good website to look up information about invasive plants is http://infoweb.magi.com/~ehaber/ipcan.html .

Disease

Check out a plant's susceptibility to various insects or diseases before you plant it. Talk to plant experts at your local nursery or garden centre, or native seed/plant supplier, for information on plants for your area. If you have, or want to grow, elms (especially American elm [*Ulmus americana*]), great vigilance is required because of Dutch elm disease (see side bar).

Wildlife Features

When deciding what trees, shrubs and other plants to purchase, take into account all their wildlife-attracting qualities, particularly their ability to supply food and shelter. If you live in a neighbourhood dominated by mature conifers, increase the biodiversity of the area by planting more deciduous trees, and vice versa.

Plants for Food

Plants are the most important source of food in a NatureScaped yard. Many insects, birds and herbivorous (plant-eating) mammals eat plant parts, including their buds, blossoms, nectar, pollen, fruit, leaves, bark, sap and seeds—all this, without a single trip to the supermarket! Some creatures don't eat plants but feast instead upon the insects and other animals that dine on plants.

Plants for Shelter

The most effective way to provide shelter is to provide the habitat in which creatures can find their own hiding and resting spots. To maximize the shelter provided by your plantings, plant trees and shrubs in groups. Include hedges or shrubs with tight branching structure, and plant a mix of coniferous and deciduous trees and shrubs. If you let your trees and shrubs grow without pruning them very much, allow the understory beneath your trees to develop, retain as many dead and dying trees as possible, and—where feasible—leave deadfall on the ground, you will be amazed at the diversity of wild creatures that will find homes!

Blue jay sheltering in white spruce

PLANTS FOR NATURESCAPING

The placement of trees is of critical importance because these plants form the foundation of your NatureScaped yard and are the main features around which all other components must fit. In most cases, trees are also your most expensive and longest-term investment.

RHIZOME

Some plants have a rhizome or underground stem. The rhizome is usually horizontal and contains food reserve material. It can produce shoots above ground and roots below.

RESTRICTED AND NOXIOUS WEEDS

Restricted weeds are plants that possess characteristics of rapid spread and superior competition, and have to be eradicated from a property. These plants are usually found in small numbers in Alberta and are designated "restricted" to prevent their establishment.

Noxious weeds have the ability to spread rapidly, and have to be controlled to prevent further establishment, and spread.

For more information, contact your local Alberta Agriculture (Alberta Agriculture, Food and Rural Development) or Alberta Environment office.

DUTCH ELM DISEASE

Dutch elm disease (DED) was introduced into North America from Europe in 1930 and has destroyed millions of American elm trees since that time. Other elms, such as Siberian or Japanese elm, can also be affected. At present, Alberta has the largest DED-free American elm stands in the world.

The disease is caused by a fungus that clogs the elm tree's water conducting system, causing its leaves to wilt and the tree to die, usually within one or two seasons. The fungus is spread from one elm tree to another primarily by the European elm bark beetle and the native elm bark beetle. These beetles breed under the bark of dead or dying elm tree wood. When a new generation of beetles emerges from a diseased tree, the insects carry the fungal spores with them to healthy trees.

Because elm bark beetles breed in dead and dying elm tree wood, pruning is necessary to eliminate breeding sites in the elms. This preventative pruning must be done between September 30 and April 1, when the elm bark beetles are inactive. Wood removed during pruning should be burned or buried immediately. Elm tree stumps must be removed or the stump ground to 10 cm (4 in.) below the soil surface.

For information, call your local office of Alberta Agriculture, Food and Rural Development, and to report the suspected presence of DED or signs of beetle activity call the Provincial DED Hotline: First call the Rite Line 310-0000 (toll free), then 362-1300.

CONIFEROUS TREE SILHOUETTES

Balsam fir
Abies balsamea

American larch/Tamarack
Larix laricina

Siberian larch
Larix sibirica

Norway spruce
Picea abies

White spruce
Picea glauca

Colorado spruce
Picea pungens

Bristlecone pine
Pinus aristata

Jack pine
Pinus banksiana

Swiss stone pine
Pinus cembra

Lodgepole pine
Pinus contorta var. *latifolia*

Scots pine
Pinus sylvestris

Coniferous Trees

Coniferous trees are cone-bearing trees that retain their needles throughout the year (with the exception of the larches, which drop their needles each fall). Conifers are very important to wildlife because their dense foliage provides nesting cover during the summer, and thermal protection from the cold and wind during winter. Conifers are also important as food trees because they attract insects, which are eaten by a wide variety of birds, and because they produce cones, the seeds of which are consumed by both birds and mammals.

Because of these exceptional wildlife-attracting qualities, conifers should be the first plants to consider in a wildlife garden. An exception would be in neighbourhoods where conifers are already the dominant tree cover. Choose conifers that suit the size of your yard.

Coniferous trees that can work well in a NatureScaped yard in Alberta include *fir (*Abies* spp.),[1] *larch (*Larix* spp.), *spruce (*Picea* spp.) and *pine (*Pinus* spp.). For information on wildlife-attracting coniferous trees, see Appendix 1.

SOME CONIFEROUS TREES FOR NATURESCAPING IN ALBERTA

MYRNA PEARMAN

Siberian larch
Larix sibirica

MYRNA PEARMAN

White spruce
Picea glauca

MYRNA PEARMAN

Jack pine
Pinus banksiana

Deciduous Trees

Deciduous trees provide more food than their coniferous counterparts: they attract insects, produce a wide variety of fruit, and are often browsed on by mammals. The nectar of some deciduous species is also used by wildlife, and the buds of some—especially poplars—provide an important winter food source for a variety of bird species. Sap will run on the outside of a tree at wound sites, at places where branches have broken off and at sapsucker wells. This sap is sought out by several species, from moths and butterflies, to hummingbirds and red squirrels (see side bar on the following page).

During the summer, the foliage of deciduous trees provides safe nesting cover for many bird species. Although deciduous trees offer little thermal protection during the winter, they do continue to offer important protective cover from predators. Again, choose a tree that is appropriate in its mature height and spread for the size of your yard.

Some of the common deciduous trees useful for wildlife are maple *(*Acer* spp.), *birch (*Betula* spp.), *hawthorn (*Crataegus* spp.), ash (*Fraxinus* spp.), apple and crab apple (*Malus* spp.), *poplar (*Populus* spp.), mayday tree (*Prunus padus* var. *commutata*), *willow (*Salix* spp.) and *mountain-ash (*Sorbus* spp., especially European mountain-ash [*S. aucuparia*] and American mountain-ash [*S. americana*]). See Appendix 1 for detailed information on deciduous trees. Check with your local greenhouse or nursery for the best local varieties.

[1] If a plant has an asterisk, it is native to Alberta, or species native to Alberta are available.

SOME DECIDUOUS TREES FOR NATURESCAPING IN ALBERTA

MYRNA PEARMAN
Manitoba maple
Acer negundo

MYRNA PEARMAN
European white birch
Betula pendula (cultivar unknown)

MYRNA PEARMAN
Hawthorn
(Round-leaved hawthorn)[2]
Crataegus spp. (*C. rotundifolia*)

MYRNA PEARMAN
Russian olive
Elaeagnus angustifolia

MYRNA PEARMAN
Green ash
Fraxinus pennsylvanica var. *subintegerrima*

MYRNA PEARMAN
Crab apple
Malus sp.

DEREK JOHNSON
Balsam poplar
Populus balsamifera

MYRNA PEARMAN
Plains cottonwood
Populus deltoides

ELISABETH BEAUBIEN
Aspen
Populus tremuloides

MYRNA PEARMAN
Mayday tree
Prunus padus var. *commutata*

JAN HEAPS
Ussurian pear
Pyrus ussuriensis

MYRNA PEARMAN
Bur oak
Quercus macrocarpa

MYRNA PEARMAN
Willow (Laurel leaf willow)
Salix spp. (*S. pentandra*)

MYRNA PEARMAN
Mountain-ash
Sorbus sp.

MYRNA PEARMAN
American elm
Ulmus americana

Snags and Logs As Habitat

A dead or dying tree that is still standing is called a snag. If you are lucky enough to have a snag or two in your backyard—enjoy! Some NatureScapers actually "plant" them in their yards. If you are worried about a snag falling over, top it at about 3 m (10 ft.). If it becomes unstable, brace it with a post or fasten it to a live tree. You can

[2] Where we have identified a particular species/cultivar of a plant that has many species/cultivars, the information has been put in parentheses.

Sapsucker wells provide food for many creatures

SPEAKING OF SAPSUCKERS...

Sapsuckers are often blamed for destroying backyard trees, especially pines and birches. Although sapsucker activity may hasten the demise of some trees, the importance of this bird in the forest ecosystem cannot be understated.

Although they are best known for their habit of eating sap, sapsuckers also feed on fruit, insects (particularly ants), tent caterpillars, spiders and small flying insects. To obtain sap, sapsuckers excavate small holes called "sap wells," by pecking out a few small wells in a horizontal row. If the sap isn't sweet enough, they move to another branch or tree. If the sap "vein" is sweet, they excavate vertical rows of wells. These wells are tended (enlarged) each day to prevent them from drying up. Pairs of sapsuckers maintain many active wells, called "sap well orchards," during the nesting season.

Sapsuckers wells are usually more extensive on diseased or stressed trees than healthy ones because these trees produce sweeter sap than healthy ones. A tree is not usually killed directly by the sapsuckers, but its wounds may attract harmful insects and provide access for disease or rot-causing fungi. Squirrels and chipmunks will also gnaw at sap wells, sometimes causing extensive damage.

Fascinating activity develops around active sapsucker wells. If you ever have the opportunity to sit and watch some wells on a tree, take it. On a warm spring or summer day, the wells are like Grand Central Station with hummingbirds, butterflies, wasps, bees, ants, flies and other insects all vying for an opportunity to get at the sap. At night, moths move in to eat. Interestingly, sap wells are one of the main food sources for hummingbirds in the early part of the season, before many flowers are in bloom; hummingbirds also visit wells in the summer. Nuthatches, warblers, chickadees and kinglets also check out well sites in search of insects to eat.

If the sapsuckers are riddling your single favourite birch, you will likely want to take steps to discourage them (see Chapter 18). If, however, you have lots of trees in your yard and they have singled out one or two—leave the birds be. It will take many years for the tree to die! In the meantime, the sapsucker and its wells will have contributed greatly to the interest, health and biodiversity of your yard!

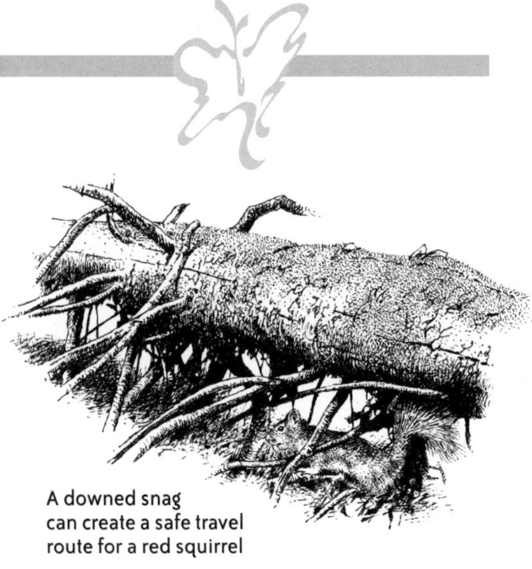
A downed snag can create a safe travel route for a red squirrel

plant vines such as scarlet trumpet honeysuckle or scarlet runner bean around the base of your snag. These plants will add beauty to your backyard and will be irresistible to neighbourhood hummingbirds. During the winter, a snag provides a great location for hanging suet or seed feeders.

Dead trees or logs on the ground offer habitat to many creatures; allowing a dead tree to fall (safely), or bringing one into your yard, will increase the habitat you offer to wildlife. If it is not possible to let a tree fall or to leave it where it falls, cut it up into long pieces and pile the pieces in a sheltered corner of your yard. Leave the pieces to deteriorate undisturbed. Not only will this log pile provide a cool, moist habitat for salamanders, frogs and invertebrates, it might also attract overwintering mourning cloak or Milbert's tortoise shell butterflies. If you drill holes into some of the logs and branches, you can also attract interesting insects, such as leaf-cutter bees (see Chapter 11 for details).

Shrubs

Shrubs are important for many reasons. They reach maturity relatively quickly, and many species produce wildlife-attracting fruits—some of which persist into the winter. A variety of shrubs should be planted to ensure a year-round supply of fruit.

Shrubs also provide wildlife with cover, and when planted as an understory, will increase the number of microhabitats in a garden. If planted between treed and grassy areas, they increase the amount of edge. In a NatureScaped yard, shrubs are most useful if planted in groups and not as lonely sentinels.

In areas where you want to increase the number of native species, suckering shrubs are good choices because they spread quickly. Suckering shrubs (such as common lilac) are not desirable in small yards or where the shrubs need to be contained. Thorny shrubs (e.g., thorny buffaloberry), which provide excellent protective cover for many wildlife species, should not be used in yards where small children play. Note that some shrubs can grow into small trees as they mature (e.g., choke cherry, pin cherry and saskatoon).

THE IMPORTANCE OF DEAD AND DYING TREES (SNAGS) AS HABITAT

Once the fascinating ecology of dying trees is understood, these stately, old relics take on a new and interesting beauty.

These trees provide a growth substrate for fungi, mosses and lichens, and in the crannies under the bark or within the wood, a host of insects and other invertebrates find both food and shelter. Snags are especially important to forest-dwelling birds because they provide many habitat components, including food (many birds eat invertebrates), nesting sites, roosting sites, perching sites, foraging perches and territorial markers. A woodpecker may take advantage of a snag's resonance to tap out Morse code-like mating tunes. Mammals, especially squirrels and bats, use snag cavities for roosting or to raise young.

When trees first start to decay, primary cavity-nesters (such as woodpeckers or nuthatches) may choose them as a place to excavate a nesting or roosting hole. Some species, such as sapsuckers, typically choose aspen trees that have been afflicted with a heart-rot fungus. This common fungus (*Phellinus tremulae*) can be easily identified by the large, brownish spore bodies that protrude along the outside of the tree trunk (see photo on page 38). *Phellinus tremulae* rots only the inside core of the tree, leaving the outer sapwood shell intact. A woodpecker has only to excavate through the thin, hard exterior before it reaches the easy-to-clean, powdery core. Then, voilà, a pair has an easily-excavated house with secure outer walls! Snags that rot in this manner are called case-hardened snags.

Case-hardened snags rot from the inside out, but soft snags decay in the opposite direction—from the surface towards the centre. Birch trees rot in this manner. Chickadees and nuthatches, both lacking powerful beaks, often choose these soft, punky snags in which to excavate their cavities.

Whether a cavity is excavated in a case-hardened or soft snag, the excavation is eventually likely to become home to a secondary cavity-nester. Secondary cavity-nesters lack the carpentry abilities of the primary excavators but still need roofs over their heads. This nesting requirement makes them reliant on woodpeckers to provide their housing for them. Secondary cavity-nesters, whether birds, squirrels or bats, will use these cavities for a variety of purposes—for nesting, resting, hibernating, roosting or even storing food.

As a snag continues to age, the outside bark begins to peel away and slough off. Chickadees will poke in and under the loose bark and woodpeckers will drill into the dead wood, both searching for insect morsels. Brown creepers might tuck their tiny nests under a piece of loose bark, and bats may find a spot to wedge themselves into for their daytime slumber. Other, non-cavity nesting birds may also take advantage of snags: an exposed dead limb may provide a flycatcher a vantage point to hawk for insects, and a songbird a perch from which it can sing for a mate.

Eventually, the snag collapses to the ground. Although no longer valuable as a source of cavities to birds, it remains important for other reasons. A ruffed grouse might choose it as a drumming log, or it may become a den for a snowshoe hare. If the tree or its branches are large, the trunk may stay far enough off the ground to provide a snow-free highway for squirrels and other small mammals. Mosses and lichens can usually be seen growing on decomposing logs, which teem with beetles and a host of other invertebrates.

In the final stages of its decay, a snag returns to enrich the soil from which it grew.

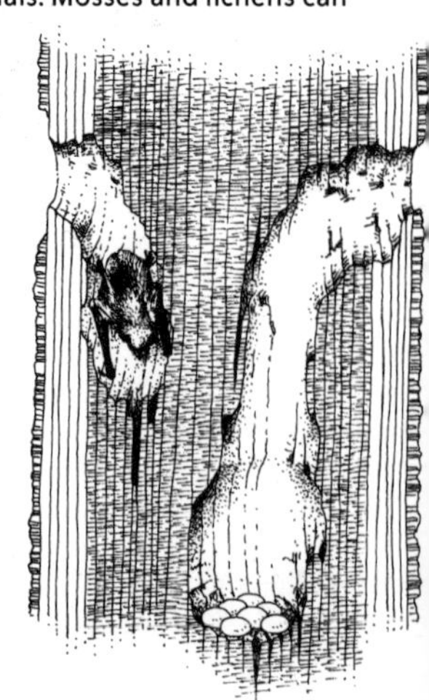
Snags provide wildlife with places to roost (little brown bat) and nest (northern flicker)

Some common deciduous shrubs useful for wildlife are *saskatoon (*Amelanchier alnifolia*), butterfly bush (*Buddleja davidii*), *dogwood (*Cornus* spp.), cotoneaster (*Cotoneaster* spp.), *wolf-willow (*Elaeagnus commutata*), *honeysuckle (*Lonicera* spp.), *shrubby cinquefoil (*Potentilla fruticosa*), *pin cherry (*Prunus pensylvanica*), *choke cherry (*Prunus virginiana*), *currant and gooseberry (*Ribes* spp.), *rose (*Rosa* spp.), *raspberry (*Rubus* spp.), *willow (*Salix* spp.), *Canada buffaloberry (*Shepherdia canadensis*), *snowberry and buckbrush (*Symphoricarpos* spp.), lilac (*Syringa* spp.) and *high-bush cranberry (*Viburnum trilobum*).

See Appendix 1 for information on these and other deciduous shrubs that attract wildlife.

*Common juniper (*Juniperus communis*) and *creeping juniper (*Juniperus horizontalis*) are native coniferous shrubs (with many cultivars) that are very popular and useful for NatureScaping. Non-native junipers (e.g., *Juniperus sabina*) and their cultivars are also grown. Other common coniferous shrubs include mugo pine (*Pinus mugo*) and cedar (*Thuja* spp.). Information on coniferous shrubs can be found in Appendix 1.

SOME DECIDUOUS SHRUBS FOR NATURESCAPING IN ALBERTA

SYLVIA GLASS
Saskatoon *Amelanchier alnifolia*

MYRNA PEARMAN
Red-oiser dogwood *Cornus stolonifera/C. sericea*

MYRNA PEARMAN
Beaked hazelnut *Corylus cornuta*

MYRNA PEARMAN
Cotoneaster *Cotoneaster sp.*

MYRNA PEARMAN
Wolf-willow *Elaeagnus commutata*

MYRNA PEARMAN
Bracted honeysuckle *Lonicera involucrata*

MYRNA PEARMAN
Tatarian honeysuckle *Lonicera tatarica*

MYRNA PEARMAN
Ninebark *Physocarpus opulifolius*

MYRNA PEARMAN
Shrubby cinquefoil *Potentilla fruticosa*

MYRNA PEARMAN
Nanking cherry *Prunus tomentosa*

MYRNA PEARMAN
Choke cherry *Prunus virginiana*

MYRNA PEARMAN
Currant (Red currant) *Ribes spp. (R. rubrum)*

SHRUBS AND TREES THAT BEAR FRUIT

It is important to pay attention to the type of fruit a plant produces, fruiting periods and how persistent the fruit is into the winter. When choosing a fruit-bearing shrub or tree at a nursery or garden centre, or from a native plant/seed seller, inquire about fruit production as well as local suitability. Varieties that produce abundant fruit will be much more useful to wildlife than their non- or less productive counterparts. Common types of fruit are listed and illustrated below, and are mentioned in various tables in Appendix 1.

Achene: a dry, single-seeded fruit that stays closed when mature (e.g., yellow dryas)

Berry: a small, juicy fruit with embedded seeds (e.g., blueberry, currant)

Capsule: a dry fruit, usually containing many seeds (e.g., lilac)

Drupe: a fleshy fruit with one or more seeds, each encased in a hard layer (e.g., dogwood)

Druplet: a small drupe, usually growing in a group to form a larger fruit (e.g., raspberry)

Nut: a hard fruit that does not split open (e.g., hazelnut)

Nutlet (winged): a small version of a nut, held in a catkin before being released (e.g., alder, birch)

Pome: a fruit with a seed-containing core surrounded by fleshy fruit (e.g., crab apple, saskatoon)

Samara: a dry, winged fruit, usually with one seed (e.g., ash, elm, maple)

SOME COMMON FRUITS OF DECIDUOUS SHRUBS AND TREES (not to scale)

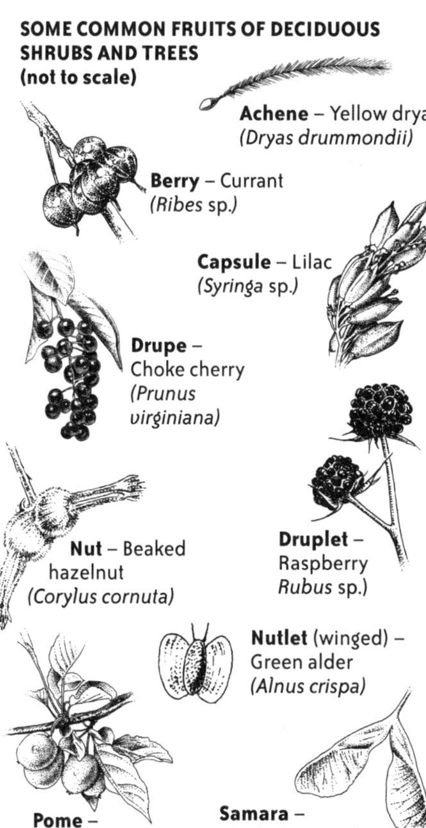

SOME DECIDUOUS SHRUBS FOR NATURESCAPING IN ALBERTA . . . CONTINUED

Rose (Common wild rose) ***Rosa* spp.** *(R. woodsii)*

Raspberry ***Rubus* sp.**

Willow (Drummond's willow) ***Salix* spp.** *(S. drummondiana)*

Red elderberry ***Sambucus racemosa***

Canada buffaloberry ***Shepherdia canadensis***

Spirea (Birch-leaf spirea) ***Spiraea* spp.** *(S.* 'Rosabella'*)*

Common snowberry ***Symphoricarpos albus***

Lilac (Common lilac) ***Syringa* spp. and cultivars** *(S. vulgaris)*

High-bush cranberry ***Viburnum opulus* ssp. *trilobum*/*V. trilobum***

SOME CONIFEROUS SHRUBS FOR NATURESCAPING IN ALBERTA

Juniper (Rocky Mountain juniper)[2] ***Juniperus* spp.** *(J. scopulorum)*

Mugo pine ***Pinus mugo***

Cedar (Eastern white cedar) ***Thuja* spp.** *(T. occidentalis)*

Vines and Ground Covers

Vines provide vertical diversity in a NatureScaped yard, and many species will add colour to your garden from spring through fall. Many are attractive to hummingbirds and various insects, including butterflies. Ground covers can provide a pleasing, low-maintenance alternative to lawn, while at the same time providing cover for wildlife or an understory to a NatureScaped area.

Some perennial vines useful to wildlife are *clematis (*Clematis* spp.), hops (*Humulus lupulus*), perennial sweet pea (*Lathyrus latifolius*) and *creamy peavine (*Lathyrus ochroleucus*). NatureScaping vines that are annuals in Alberta include Chilean glory flower (*Eccremocarpus scaber*), morning glory (*Ipomoea* spp.), sweet pea (*Lathyrus odoratus*), scarlet runner bean (*Phaseolus coccineus*) and canary bird vine (*Tropaeolum peregrinum*). American bittersweet (*Celastrus scandens*), *twining honeysuckle (*Lonicera dioica*), scarlet trumpet honeysuckle (*Lonicera* x *brownii* 'Dropmore Scarlet') and Virginia creeper (*Parthenocissus quinquefolia)* are examples of vine-like shrubs that are very attractive to wildlife. See Appendix 1 for information on wildlife-attracting vines.

Perennial ground covers include goutweed (*Aegopodium podograria*), snow-in-summer (*Cerastium tomentosum*), lily-of-the-valley (*Convallaria majalis*), bishop's hat (*Epimedium* spp.), *strawberry (*Fragaria* spp.), yellow archangel (*Lamiastrum galeobdolon*), lamium (*Lamium maculatum*), creeping Jenny (*Lysimachia nummularia*), *ostrich fern (*Matteuccia struthiopteris*), pulmonaria (*Pulmonaria* spp.) and thyme (including woolly thyme, *Thymus pseudolanuginosus*, and creeping thyme, *Thymus serpyllum*). *Bearberry/kinnikinnick (*Arctostaphylos uva-ursi*), *yellow dryas (*Dryas drummondii*) and low-growing junipers such as *creeping juniper (*Juniperus horizontalis*) are woody ground covers (shrubs) that are attractive to wildlife. Check Appendix 1 for information about ground covers.

SOME VINES FOR NATURESCAPING IN ALBERTA

SYLVIA GLASS — Western clematis *Clematis ligusticifolia*

MYRNA PEARMAN — Yellow clematis *Clematis tangutica*

MYRNA PEARMAN — Chilean glory flower *Eccremocarpus scaber*

MYRNA PEARMAN — Hops *Humulus lupulus*

MYRNA PEARMAN — Morning glory (Common morning glory) *Ipomoea purpurea*

DEREK JOHNSON — Creamy peavine *Lathyrus ochroleucus*

MYRNA PEARMAN — Scarlet trumpet honeysuckle *Lonicera x brownii* 'Dropmore Scarlet'

MYRNA PEARMAN — Twining honeysuckle *Lonicera dioica/L. glaucescens*

MYRNA PEARMAN — Scarlet runner bean *Phaseolus coccineus*

MYRNA PEARMAN — Canary bird vine *Tropaeolum peregrinum*

SOME GROUND COVERS FOR NATURESCAPING IN ALBERTA

MYRNA PEARMAN — Goutweed *Aegopodium podograria*

DEREK JOHNSON — Bearberry/Kinnikinnick *Arctostaphylos uva-ursi*

MYRNA PEARMAN — Snow-in-summer *Cerastium tomentosum*

MYRNA PEARMAN — Lily-of-the-valley *Convallaria majalis*

SYLVIA GLASS — Yellow dryas *Dryas drummondii*

MYRNA PEARMAN — Strawberry *Fragaria sp.*

MYRNA PEARMAN — Creeping juniper *Juniperus horizontalis* (*J. horizontalis* 'Calgary Carpet')

MYRNA PEARMAN — Lamium *Lamium maculatum*

MYRNA PEARMAN — Pulmonaria *Pulmonaria sp.*

JAN HEAPS — Thyme (Woolly thyme and creeping thyme [in bloom]) *Thymus* spp. (*T. pseudolanuginosus* and *T. serpyllum*)

Perennials, Annuals and Biennials

Perennials are plants that have a life cycle lasting more than two years. Annuals grow into mature plants that produce flowers and seeds in a single growing season, then die. Some annuals self-seed, so may appear to be perennials. Biennials have a two-year life cycle. They produce leaves in the first year that overwinter; then they flower and produce seeds the second year before dying. Some biennials are treated as annuals in Alberta, so we have listed these plants in Appendix 1 with the annuals. Other biennials are included with the perennials. We have noted in the tables if a plant is biennial.

Annuals, which require yearly planting (either as seeds or bedding out plants), very often have a longer blooming period than perennials but tend not to be showy until late June. As a result, they cannot provide the essential early spring nectar needed by some wildlife species. The blooming season of most annuals can be lengthened by dead-heading (removing old blossoms).

Perennials are more expensive initially than annuals and generally have a shorter period of bloom. However, many bloom early, so they can be planted to add colour to your garden and attract wild creatures before your annuals have reached their peak.

Perennials can generally be grown from seed or propagated by dividing the plants themselves, and have the advantage of not requiring yearly planting. However, perennial beds sometimes become weedy and overcrowded.

To maximize attractiveness and lengthen blooming periods, plant a mixture of both annuals and perennials in your NatureScaped garden. Information on wildlife-attracting perennials, biennials and annuals can be found in Appendix 1. Chapter 4 lists perennials and annuals that will attract hummingbirds.

SOME PERENNIALS FOR NATURESCAPING IN ALBERTA

Yarrow (Common yarrow) *Achillea spp. (A. millefolium)*

Giant hyssop *Agastache foeniculum*

Allium (Wild chives) *Allium spp. (A. schoenoprasum)*

Angelica *Angelica gigas*

Spreading dogbane *Apocynum androsaemifolium*

Indian-hemp *Apocynum sibiricum/A. cannabinum var. hypericifolium*

Columbine *Aquilegia sp.*

Swamp milkweed *Asclepias incarnata*

Showy milkweed *Asclepias speciosa*

Aster *Aster sp.*

Milk-vetch (Ground plum) *Astragalus spp. (A. crassicarpus)*

Harebell *Campanula rotundifolia*

Yellow bachelor button *Centaurea macrocephala*

Bull thistle *Cirsium vulgare*

Coreopsis *Coreopsis spp. (Coreopsis 'Flying Saucers')*

SOME PERENNIALS FOR NATURESCAPING IN ALBERTA . . . CONTINUED

MYRNA PEARMAN — Delphinium *Delphinium* spp. (*D. elatum*)

SYLVIA GLASS — Tall larkspur *Delphinium glaucum*

JAN HEAPS — Pink (Maiden pink) *Dianthus* spp. (*D. deltoides*)

MYRNA PEARMAN — Purple coneflower *Echinacea purpurea*

MYRNA PEARMAN — Globe-thistle *Echinops ritro*

MYRNA PEARMAN — Fireweed *Epilobium angustifolium*

MYRNA PEARMAN — Fleabane *Erigeron* sp.

SYLVIA GLASS — Yellow umbrella plant *Eriogonum flavum*

DEREK JOHNSON — Spotted Joe-pye weed *Eupatorium purpureum* var. *maculatum*/*E. maculatum*

JAN HEAPS — Gaillardia *Gaillardia* spp. (*Gaillardia x grandiflora* 'Goblin')

MYRNA PEARMAN — Gentian (Blue gentian) *Gentiana* spp. (*G. dahuria*)

CHRISTIANA JOHNSON — Sticky purple geranium *Geranium viscosissimum*

DEREK JOHNSON — Gumweed *Grindelia squarrosa*

DEREK JOHNSON — Spiny ironplant *Haplopappus spinulosus*

MYRNA PEARMAN — Day lily *Hemerocallis* sp.

MARIJKE JALINK — Cow parsnip *Heracleum lanatum*

MYRNA PEARMAN — Sweet rocket *Hesperis matronalis*

MYRNA PEARMAN — Golden aster *Heterotheca villosa*

MYRNA PEARMAN — Coral bells *Heuchera* spp. (*H. sanguinea*)

MYRNA PEARMAN — Hosta *Hosta* sp.

SYLVIA GLASS — Colorado rubberweed *Hymenoxys richardsonii*

MYRNA PEARMAN — Daisy (Shasta daisy) *Leucanthemopsis* spp. (*Leucanthemopsis x superbum*)

MYRNA PEARMAN — Lovage *Levisticum officinale*

MYRNA PEARMAN — Blazing star (Dotted blazing star) *Liatris* spp. (*L. punctata*)

MYRNA PEARMAN — Lily *Lilium* sp.

MYRNA PEARMAN — Dwarf yellow flax *Linum flavum* 'Compactum'

DEREK JOHNSON — Yellow puccoon *Lithospermum ruderale*

JAN HEAPS — Lupine *Lupinus* spp. (*L. polyphyllus*)

MYRNA PEARMAN — Maltese cross *Lychnis chalcedonica*

DEREK JOHNSON — Canescent aster *Machaeranthera canescens*

SOME PERENNIALS FOR NATURESCAPING IN ALBERTA . . . CONTINUED

MYRNA PEARMAN 
Malva
Malva spp.
(M. sylvestris mauritiana)

SYLVIA GLASS 
Mint (Wild mint)
Mentha spp. *(M. arvensis)*

MYRNA PEARMAN 
Bergamot/Bee balm
Monarda spp. *(M. didyma)*

SYLVIA GLASS 
Evening primrose
(Yellow evening primrose)
Oenothera spp. *(O. biennis)*

JAN HEAPS 
Prickly pear cactus
(Brittle prickly pear cactus)
Opuntia spp. *(O. fragilis)*

MYRNA PEARMAN 
Oregano
Origanum vulgare

MARIJKE JALINK 
Loco-weed
Oxytropis sp.

CHRISTIANA JOHNSON 
Penstemon
(Smooth blue beard-tongue)
Penstemon spp. *(P. nitidus)*

CHRISTIANA JOHNSON 
Purple prairie clover
Petalostemon purpureum/
Dalea purpurea

JAN HEAPS 
Arrow-leaved coltsfoot
Petasites sagittatus

SYLVIA GLASS 
Hood's phlox
Phlox hoodii

MYRNA PEARMAN 
Summer phlox
Phlox paniculata

MYRNA PEARMAN 
Obedient plant
Physostegia virginiana

MYRNA PEARMAN 
Prairie cone-flower
Ratibida columnifera

MYRNA PEARMAN 
Black-eyed Susan
Rudbeckia hirta

DEREK JOHNSON 
Saxifrage (Purple saxifrage)
Saxifraga spp. *(S. oppositifolia)*

MYRNA PEARMAN 
Pincushion flower
(Fischer's scabious)
Scabiosa spp. *(S. fischeri)*

MYRNA PEARMAN 
Stonecrop/Sedum
Sedum spp./*Hylotelephium* spp.
(*Hylotelephium* 'Autumn Joy')

TED PIKE 
Moss campion
Silene acaulis

MYRNA PEARMAN 
Goldenrod
Solidago sp.

SYLVIA GLASS 
Scarlet mallow
Sphaeralcea coccinea

CLANCY PATTON 
Meadow rue (Columbine meadow rue)
Thalictrum spp. *(T. aquilegifolium)*

SYLVIA GLASS 
Golden bean
Thermopsis rhombifolia

DEREK JOHNSON 
Clover (Red clover)
Trifolium spp. *(T. pratense)*

MYRNA PEARMAN 
Nettle (Stinging nettle)
Urtica spp. *(U. dioica)*

JAN HEAPS 
Speedwell (Spike speedwell)
Veronica spp. *(V. spicata)*

CHRISTIANA JOHNSON 
Violet
Viola sp.

SOME ANNUALS FOR NATURESCAPING IN ALBERTA

MYRNA PEARMAN 
Ageratum
Ageratum houstonianum

MYRNA PEARMAN 
Hollyhock
Alcea rosea

MYRNA PEARMAN 
Snapdragon
Antirrhinum* x *hybrida

MYRNA PEARMAN 
Borage
Borago officinalis

MYRNA PEARMAN 
Calendula
Calendula officinalis

JAN HEAPS 
Bachelor button
Centaurea cyanus

MYRNA PEARMAN 
Spider flower
Cleome hasslerana/ C. hassleriana

MYRNA PEARMAN 
Cleome
Cleome serrulata

MYRNA PEARMAN 
Cosmos
***Cosmos* spp. (*C. bipinnatus*)**

MYRNA PEARMAN 
Foxglove
Digitalis purpurea

MYRNA PEARMAN 
Fuchsia
Fuchsia* spp./*Fuchsia* x *hybrida
(*F. triphylla* 'Gartenmeister Bonstedt')

MYRNA PEARMAN 
Sunflower
***Helianthus* spp. (*H. annuus*)**

MYRNA PEARMAN 
Heliotrope
Heliotropium arborescens

MYRNA PEARMAN 
Candytuft
Iberis umbellata

MYRNA PEARMAN 
Himalayan orchid
Impatiens glandulifera/I. royleii

MYRNA PEARMAN 
Sweet pea
Lathyrus odoratus

MYRNA PEARMAN 
Lavatera
(Annual rose mallow/Tree mallow)
***Lavatera* spp. (*L. trimestris*)**

MYRNA PEARMAN 
Sweet alyssum
Lobularia maritima

MYRNA PEARMAN 
Forget-me-not
Myosotis sylvatica

MYRNA PEARMAN 
Nicotiana
***Nicotiana* spp. (*N. alata*)**

MYRNA PEARMAN 
Opium poppy
Papaver somniferum

MYRNA PEARMAN 
Petunia
Petunia* x *hybrida

DEREK JOHNSON 
Polygonum (Bistort)
***Polygonum* spp. (*P. bistortoides*)**

MYRNA PEARMAN 
Salvia (Mealy-cup sage)
***Salvia* spp. (*S. farinacea*)**

MYRNA PEARMAN 
Marigold
Tagetes* spp./*Tagetes* x *hybrida

MYRNA PEARMAN 
Nasturtium
Tropaeolum majus

MYRNA PEARMAN 
Verbena (Common verbena)
***Verbena* spp. (*Verbena* x *hybrida*)**

MYRNA PEARMAN 
Zinnia
Zinnia elegans

Herbs

There are several herbs that attract wildlife, especially bees and butterflies. Herbs have been included with perennials and annuals in Appendix 1.

Grasses

Grasses can be grown in large or small yards. In large yards or on acreages, uncut grasses provide habitat for many ground-nesting birds, such as mallard, blue-winged teal and vesper sparrow. Grasses and grass-like plants, such as sedges and rushes, at the edge of water gardens also provide shelter for amphibians. Many butterflies like to use grass stems as perches.

Grasses also provide forage for herbivores like deer, rabbits, hares, mice and voles. During the winter, grasses provide food for overwintering microtine rodents (those that remain active under the snow), which in turn provide food for predators such as hawks, owls and coyotes. Grasses whose seeds remain above the snow provide an important source of food for overwintering birds.

Some native grasses that can be planted for wildlife include northern wheat grass (*Agropyron dasystachyum*), western wheat grass (*Agropyron smithii*), plains reed grass (*Calamagrostis montanensis*), Hooker's oat grass (*Helictotrichon hookeri*), sweet grass (*Hierochloe odorata*), June grass (*Koeleria macrantha*), early bluegrass (*Poa cusickii*), needle and thread grass (*Stipa comata*), western porcupine grass (*Stipa curtiseta/Stipa spartea*) and green needle grass (*Stipa viridula*). Ornamental grasses may also be useful in a NatureScaped garden.

Grasses that have rhizomes (e.g., plains reed grass [*C. montanensis*]) are invasive, so you may want to keep them contained.

A FEW GRASSES FOR NATURESCAPING IN ALBERTA

DEREK JOHNSON

Northern wheat grass
Agropyron dasystachyum

DEREK JOHNSON

Plains reed grass
Calamagrostis montanensis

DEREK JOHNSON

June grass
Koeleria macrantha

DEREK JOHNSON

Green needle grass
Stipa viridula

DEREK JOHNSON

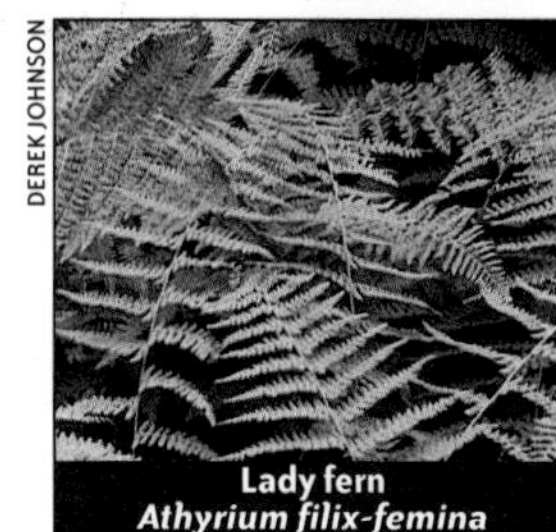

Lady fern
Athyrium filix-femina

DEREK JOHNSON

Ostrich fern
Matteuccia struthiopteris

Ferns

Ferns belong to a group of plants that reproduce with spores instead of seeds. These plants are quite easy to identify because they have large leaves that are usually divided into several "leaflets"; as buds, the leaves are generally curled, forming what are called "fiddleheads." The stems are often covered with scales, and the spore bodies (called sporangia) are found in small clusters (the sori) on the underside or at the margins of the leaves.

Native species include lady fern (*Athyrium filix-femina*), found in wet forests and thickets, and along stream banks; fragile fern (*Cystopteris fragilis*), which grows in moist rock crevices and among boulders; oak fern (*Gymnocarpium dryopteris*), which grows in moist woods and on rocky hillsides; and ostrich fern (*Matteuccia struthiopteris*), found in moist forests and along stream banks. Depending on where you live and the conditions available—many ferns like damp, shady locations—one or more of these species may establish themselves in your yard.

Many other fern species are available at local garden centres and nurseries. Check with your nursery to make sure the species you want are hardy for your area.

THE SMALL AND OBSCURE
(Horsetails, Club-Mosses, Lichens, Mosses and Liverworts)

A healthy yard and garden will become home to many plants that will colonize on their own, like some of the ferns mentioned above. Of the less-well-known plant families that you may see, some will be vascular plants like the plants we have already discussed. (These plants have internal tubes called xylem and phloem for conducting water and food.) Horsetails and club-mosses are vascular plants. Others will be non-vascular plants (plants without conducting tissue), including lichens, mosses and liverworts. All these plants inhabit a Lilliputian world that is fascinating but easily overlooked. They are often misunderstood, so many people treat them as if they were weeds or unwelcome invaders. However, in a NatureScaped yard these plants add interest and help create the microclimates that allow wildlife species to thrive.

Horsetails

These interesting plants are easy to identify because they have clusters of leaves that are fused in a whorl around the stem; only the leaf tips are free. Like ferns, they reproduce by spores instead of seeds. The stems and branches are rough to the touch because they are coated with silicon dioxide. This feature was appreciated by early pioneers, who sometimes used these plants to clean their dishes—hence the common name "scouring rush." The most common horsetail species in Alberta, common horsetail *(Equisetum arvense)*, is abundant in moist woods, wet areas and along road edges. Wood horsetail *(Equisetum sylvaticum)* grows in the moist woods of the boreal forest, foothills and mountains, and swamp horsetail *(Equisetum fluviatile)* is found in marshes and wet ditches. These common plants are very likely to show up in a NatureScaped yard.

DEREK JOHNSON

Common horsetail
Equisetum arvense

DEREK JOHNSON

Swamp horsetail
Equisetum fluviatile

Club-Mosses

Club-mosses are rather strange-looking plants; several species look like miniature pine or spruce trees. Some of the more common species include stiff club-moss (*Lycopodium annotinum*), running club-moss *(Lycopodium clavatum)*, ground pine (*Lycopodium obscurum*) and ground-cedar (*Lycopodium complanatum*). Depending on where you live and the nature of your yard, club-mosses could appear.

DEREK JOHNSON

Stiff club-moss
Lycopodium annotinum

DEREK JOHNSON

Ground-cedar
Lycopodium complanatum

Lichens

Lichens are actually two organisms, a fungus and an alga, joined together. The fungus provides the "skeleton" of the plant and the alga provides the "organs." If your yard is well established, look around. You will likely find lichens everywhere. They come in four basic forms: crustose (encrusted on rocks, trees or even unused lawn furniture); foliose (leafy forms on tree trunks or in shady places on the ground); squamulose (usually upright stems and a leaf-like base, often on soil or rotting wood); and fruticose (stringy hairs hanging from tree branches). Perhaps the most familiar to most people are the various fruticose forms called "old man's beard," which are often seen hanging from spruce trees, not old men.

Lichens propagate either by windborne fragments or by producing tiny spores (called ascospores). Lichens are quite sensitive to air pollution, so scientists use them to monitor air quality in industrial areas.

Wild creatures will feed on some of the fruticose lichens, especially the reindeer lichens (*Cladina* spp.), but most are not eaten.

Although there are about 650 species of lichens in Alberta, some of the more common ones are quite easy to identify.

Crustose

Crusted orange lichen	*Caloplaca cerina*
No common name	*Caloplaca holocarpa*
No common name	*Candelariella vitellina*
Green map lichen	*Rhizocarpon geographicum*

Foliose

No common name	*Cetraria ericetorum*
Icelandmoss	*Cetraria islandica*
Powdered sunshine	*Cetraria pinastri/Vulpicida pinastri*
Monk's hood lichen	*Hypogymnia physodes*
Waxpaper lichen	*Parmelia sulcata*
Freckle pelt/Studded leather lichen	*Peltigera aphthosa*
Dog pelt/Dog lichen	*Peltigera canina*
Hooded rosette	*Physcia adscendens*
Gray-eyed rosette	*Physcia aipolia*
Elegant orange lichen	*Xanthoria elegans*
Powdered orange lichen	*Xanthoria fallax*
Pincushion orange	*Xanthoria polycarpa*

Squamulose

Stump cladonia, ribbed cladonia, brown-foot cladonia and various pixie cups	*Cladonia* spp.

Fruticose

Horsehair lichen	*Bryoria* spp.
Green reindeer lichen	*Cladina mitis*
Spruce moss	*Evernia mesomorpha*
Old man's beard	*Usnea* spp.

SOME LICHENS YOU MAY FIND IN A NATURALIZED ALBERTA GARDEN

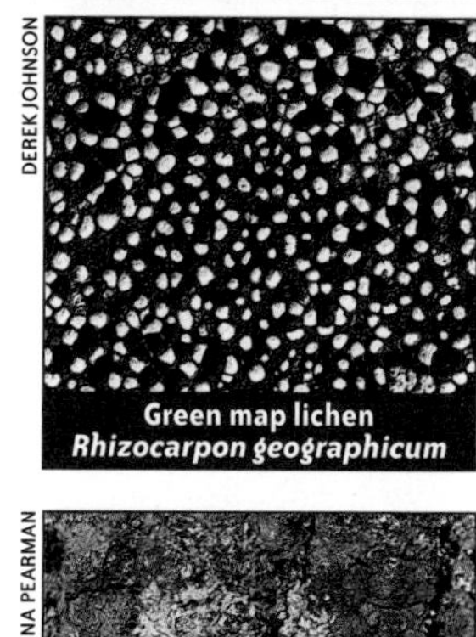
DEREK JOHNSON

Green map lichen
Rhizocarpon geographicum

DEREK JOHNSON

Waxpaper lichen
Parmelia sulcata

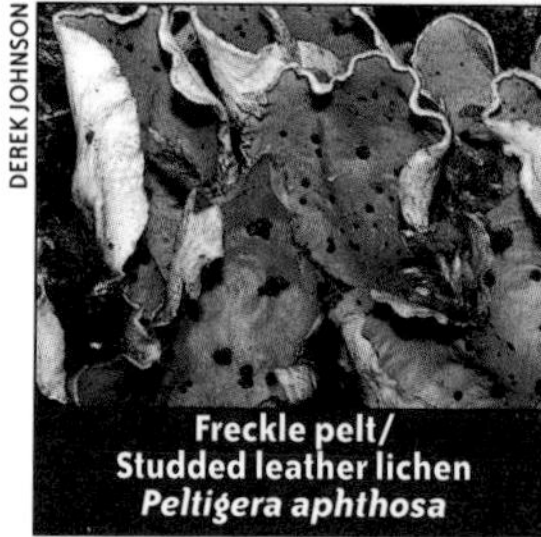
DEREK JOHNSON

Freckle pelt/ Studded leather lichen
Peltigera aphthosa

MYRNA PEARMAN

Gray-eyed rosette
Physcia aipolia
Powdered orange lichen
Xanthoria fallax

DEREK JOHNSON

Cladonia (Red pixie cup)
Cladonia* spp. *(C. borealis)

DEREK JOHNSON

Old man's beard
(Scruffy old man's beard)
Usnea* spp. *(U. scabrata)

Mosses

Mosses, like ferns and club-mosses, don't have seeds—they use sporophytes and spores to reproduce. Mosses tend to be found wherever there is moisture. They rarely grow as individuals; rather, they form extensive colonies on moist wood, rocks or soil. If you snoop around in some of the cool, shady corners of your yard, you will find moss.

Some common Alberta mosses include

Golden ragged moss	*Brachythecium salebrosum*
Silvery bryum	*Bryum argenteum*
Purple horn-toothed moss	*Ceratodon purpureus*
Cord moss	*Funaria hygrometrica*
Stair-step moss	*Hylocomium splendens*
Woodsy leafy moss	*Plagiomnium cuspidatum*
Big red stem	*Pleurozium schreberi*
Juniper hair-cap	*Polytrichum juniperinum*
Knight's plume	*Ptilium crista-castrensis*
Stocking moss	*Pylaisiella polyantha*
Hairy screw moss	*Tortula ruralis*

MOSS CAPSULES

When mosses reproduce they develop a sporophyte, the tip of which enlarges into a spore-bearing capsule. These capsules are fascinating to study, as each species has its own distinctive capsule and way of releasing the spores.

Three common Alberta mosses with capsules

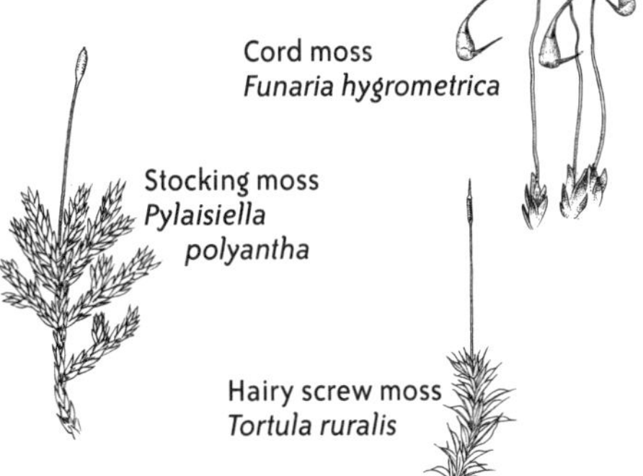

SOME COMMON MOSSES OF A NATURESCAPED YARD

MYRNA PEARMAN

Purple horn-toothed moss
Ceratodon purpureus

DEREK JOHNSON

Juniper hair-cap
Polytrichum juniperinum

MYRNA PEARMAN

Knight's plume
Ptilium crista-castrensis

MYRNA PEARMAN

Stocking moss
Pylaisiella polyantha

Liverworts

Liverworts are similar to mosses in many ways but differ in appearance and in the way their sporophytes develop. Of the liverworts found in Alberta, there are two that are easily recognizable: green-tongue liverwort (*Marchantia polymorpha*), which occurs on wet soil and in roadside ditches, on rock walls and stream banks in all but the grassland natural region, and snake liverwort (*Conocephalum conicum*), found on moist, inorganic soils.

MYRNA PEARMAN

Green-tongue liverwort
Marchantia polymorpha

FUNGI

Fungi are, structurally, very simple organisms that are no longer considered to be plants. They now have their own kingdom (Fungi). The two groups of fungi of most interest to NatureScapers are the Ascomycetes, such as morels and cup fungi, and the Basidiomycetes, such as rusts, shelf fungi, puffballs and mushrooms.

Unlike typical plants, fungi don't have chlorophyll, and very few show any green colour (green is usually associated with chlorophyll). They have no true roots, leaves, stems, buds, flowers or seeds. Some are woody and live for years; others, particularly mushrooms, appear mysteriously and last only for a few days. Some fragile grassland mushrooms last for only a few hours, shriveling and dying soon after the sun finds them.

HOW A MUSHROOM GROWS

If a mushroom spore lands in a spot where conditions are right, it begins to germinate and forms a complex web of filament-like fungal cells called hyphae. Different species can't be told apart at this stage, as the hyphae (which form a structure called a mycelium) all look like cottony white or yellow growths. This network of cells may live for months or years underground, or in wood, feeding on decaying matter.

When enough nutrients have been absorbed and moisture conditions are appropriate (light and temperature often being critical to this process), the mature mycelium forms tiny, bud-like growths. These buds can expand rapidly, often overnight, bursting from the ground and resulting in a crop of mushrooms. A mushroom can release thousands of microscopic, single-celled spores that will produce others of its kind.

Because fungi have no chlorophyll, they cannot produce the energy needed for growth from sunlight as most green plants do. Instead, they consume organic material from plants (living or dead), animal waste or soil.

Mushrooms

It is not known exactly how many kinds of mushrooms grow in Alberta. Across the prairie provinces, there are at least 500-1,000 species, growing in all habitats ranging from grassland to forest, and in all the varied microhabitats found in these plant communities. In an urban or rural yard, one might see 50-100 different species of mushrooms over a period of many years, depending on the area and habitat. The more natural and varied the yard, the more species of mushrooms and other fungi will be seen. They are usually found in four main habitats: associated with lawns or grassy areas; on trees, stumps or roots; in rich soils, as in gardens, flower beds and hedges; or in organic landscape material, such as bark mulch.

Consider any wild mushroom or other fungus poisonous unless proven otherwise. If you want to learn to identify these curious organisms, do so only with a highly qualified resource person. Please watch small children closely if you have mushrooms or other fungi growing in your yard. Protect your dog or cat from poisonous varieties.

SOME COMMON ALBERTA FUNGI

SEAN ABOTT — Meadow mushroom *Agaricus sp.*

SEAN ABOTT — Honey mushroom *Armillaria ostoyae*

GAVIN KERNAGHAN — Shaggy mane *Coprinus comatus*

MIKE MCNAUGHTON — Cort *Cortinarius sp.*

SEAN ABOTT — Oyster mushroom *Pleurotus ostreatus*

MIKE MCNAUGHTON — Coral fungus *Clavicorona sp.*

MYRNA PEARMAN — True tinder conk *Fomes fomentarius*

MIKE MCNAUGHTON — Earthstar *Geastrum sp.*

MIKE MCNAUGHTON — Comb tooth *Hericium sp.*

MYRNA PEARMAN — Puffball *Lycoperdon sp.*

MYRNA PEARMAN — False tinder conk *Phellinus tremulae*

Some common, native gilled mushrooms include

Meadow mushroom/Field mushroom	*Agaricus* spp.
Honey mushroom	*Armillaria ostoyae*
Inky cap	*Coprinus atramentarius*

Shaggy mane	*Coprinus comatus*
Cort	*Cortinarius* spp.
Poison pie	*Hebeloma crustuliniforme*
Shaggy parasol	*Macrolepiota rhacodes*
Fairy ring mushroom	*Marasmius oreades*
Oyster mushroom	*Pleurotus ostreatus*
Suburban psathyrella	*Psathyrella candolleana*
Russula	*Russula* spp.

Some native non-gilled fungi you might see include

Coral fungus	*Clavicorona* spp.; *Ramaria* spp.
Bird's nest fungus	*Cyathus* spp.
True tinder conk/Horse's hoof fungus	*Fomes fomentarius*
Earthstar	*Geastrum* spp.
Comb tooth	*Hericium* spp.
Puffball	*Lycoperdon* spp.
Dog stinkhorn	*Mutinus caninus*
False tinder conk	*Phellinus tremulae*
Birch conk/Birch polypore	*Piptoporus betulinus*

COMPOSTING

Composting, which involves the break down of organic waste into humus, is an efficient and sensible way to ensure a ready supply of garden fertilizer and mulch. The practice of composting also reduces organic waste buildup in local landfills.

To compost, you can either purchase a commercial composter or make your own. A container is not essential, but it will keep your compost pile tidy and will exclude animals. A composter should be at least 1 m^3 (1.3 cu. yd.) in size to maximize the efficiency of decomposition, and it should be located in an accessible area, protected from cold winds, and in partial shade. A cover keeps the pile neat and prevents rain from getting in. The area should also have adequate drainage.

If you build a composter yourself, be sure that there is adequate air circulation—space the boards of the composter or drill holes around each side. Some people build their composter on a raised floor with air holes to let air into the bottom layer.

With the exception of meat, animal feces, weeds, diseased plants and the kitchen sink, almost anything can be added to the compost. Just make sure what you add comes from a plant!

You will need to alternate "green" and "brown" layers. "Green" is usually easy—it can come from any plant material in your yard. "Brown" can come from such items as dead, dry plants in the spring, topsoil, sawdust, shredded brown paper, dried coffee filters, coffee grounds, old tea bags, and so on.

Make sure you keep the compost moist, especially during dry periods. Turning the material every so often and adding a few handfuls of a high nitrogen fertilizer (e.g., blood meal) will speed up the decomposition process. The compost is ready to use once the material has turned dark brown or black.

Composting can also be done by following the above process using a garbage bag as the composter. Place your organic wastes into the bag, add a small amount of topsoil or coffee grounds, then place the bag in a sunny location.

VERMICOMPOSTING

Worm composting is a simple way for apartment dwellers and householders to turn organic household waste into compost. it is especially useful for those who don't have space for a backyard composter.

For information on this type of composting, read Alberta Environment's pamphlet *Taking Action Through Vermicomposting to Reduce Kitchen Waste*, or call the Alberta Recycle Info Line at 1-800-463-6326. You can also read *Worms Eat My Garbage* or *Squirmy Wormy Composters* (see **Significant References** at the end of this chapter).

Note: Moss (1983) is the source of most scientific names used for native plants in this chapter. See **Significant References** below.

ACKNOWLEDGMENTS

Donna Balzer (Horticulturist/garden consultant, Calgary, Alberta)

Elisabeth Beaubien (Research Associate, Devonian Botanic Garden, c/o University of Alberta, Edmonton, Alberta)

Jim Bowick (Owner, The Conservancy and Old Strathcona Garden Shoppe, Edmonton, Alberta)

Donna Dawson (Gardener, and Webmaster, IcanGarden.com Website, Edmonton, Alberta)

Gordon Heaps (Horticulturist, and Operations Supervisor, Muttart Conservatory, Edmonton, Alberta)

Derek Johnson (Botanist, Canadian Forest Service, Edmonton, Alberta)

Ed Karpuk (Resource Inventory Specialist, Parkland Region, Alberta Environment, Red Deer, Alberta)
Gavin Kernaghan (Researcher, Department of Renewable Resources, University of Alberta, Edmonton, Alberta)
Robert Kreba (Interpretive Specialist, Royal Saskatchewan Museum, Regina, Saskatchewan)
Cathy Kurio (Gardener, and member of Calgary Horticultural Society and Calgary Rock and Alpine Garden Society)
Jean and Glenn McCullough (Gardeners, Calgary, Alberta)
Ken Mallett (Forest Pathologist, Canadian Forest Service, Edmonton, Alberta)
Paul Martin (Horticulturist, Lacombe Research Station, Agriculture and Agri-Food Canada, Lacombe, Alberta)
Clarence (Clancy) Patton (Gardener, and member of Calgary Horticultural Society, Calgary, Alberta)
Jackie Powell (Arborist, and landscape gardener, Lacombe, Alberta)
Carolyn Rallison (Owner, Last West Gardens, Bluffton, Alberta)
Joan Redelback (Manager, Brooks Garden Centre, Brooks, Alberta)
Karyn Scalise (Wildlife Ecologist, Fish and Wildlife Branch, Saskatchewan Environment and Resource Management, Regina, Saskatchewan)
Ruth Staal (Manager, Golden Acre Garden Sentre South, Calgary, Alberta)
Barbara Walters (Gardener, Clive, Alberta)
Terry Warke (Instructor, Landscape Gardener Apprenticeship Program, Olds College, Olds, Alberta)
Trevor Wiens (Computer consultant, Edmonton, Alberta)

5 BASICS
NATURESCAPING WITH PLANTS

1. Plant wildlife-attracting trees, shrubs and flowers.
2. Use native plants whenever possible.
3. Plant in groups and create lots of "edge."
4. Plant your yard so food is available for wildlife all year round.
5. Minimize your lawn space, and avoid using lawn or garden chemicals.

SIGNIFICANT REFERENCES

General

Agricultural Industry Fieldmen, Alberta Environmental Protection, Ducks Unlimited Canada and TELUS. n.d. *Weed identification in Alberta*. N.p. (Booklet)

Alberta Agriculture, Food and Rural Development. n.d. *Dutch elm disease*. Alberta Agriculture, Food and Rural Development. (Pamphlet)

Alberta Environmental Protection and Action on Waste. n.d. *Taking action through backyard composting to reduce household waste*. N.p. (Pamphlet)

————. n.d. *Taking action through vermicomposting to reduce kitchen waste*. N.p. (Pamphlet)

Apelhof, M. 1997. *Worms eat my garbage*. 2d ed. Flower Press, Kalamazoo, Michigan.

Bush, D., ed. 1998. *Guidelines for the collection & use of native plants*. Alberta Native Plant Council, Edmonton.

Dzikowski, P., and R.T. Heywood. n.d. *Agroclimatic atlas of Alberta*. Agdex 071-1. Conservation and Development Branch, Alberta Agriculture, Edmonton.

Gerling, H.S., M.G. Willoughby, A. Schoepf, K.E. Tannas and C.A. Tannas. 1996. *A guide to using native plants on disturbed lands*. Alberta Agriculture, Food and Rural Development, Edmonton, and Alberta Environmental Protection, Edmonton.

Gould, J. 1999. *Plant species of special consideration*. Alberta Natural Heritage Information Centre, Alberta Environmental Protection, Edmonton.

Kalman, B., and J. Schaub. 1992. *Squirmy wormy composters*. Crabtree Publishing Company, Niagara-on-the-Lake.

McAskill, D. n.d. *The Prince Edward Island forest wildlife manual*. Prince Edward Island Department of Agriculture, Fisheries and Forestry, Charlottetown.

Stenberg, K., and W.W. Shaw, eds. n.d. *Wildlife conservation and new residential developments*. Proceedings of a National Symposium on Urban Wildlife, 20-22 January, 1986. Tucson, Arizona. University of Arizona, Tucson, Arizona.

Tuer, C. 1989. *Good planets are hard to find: Prescriptions for everyday environmental action*. Biddel Publishing, Calgary.

White, D.J., E. Haber and C. Keddy. 1993. *Invasive plants of natural habitats in Canada: An integrated review of wetland and upland species and legislation governing their control*. Report prepared for the Canadian Wildlife Service, Environment Canada, in cooperation with the Canadian Museum of Nature, and with support from the North American Wetlands Conservation Council (Canada), Ottawa.

Natural Regions

Achuff, P.L. 1994. *Natural regions, subregions and natural history themes for Alberta: A classification for protected areas management*. 2d ed. Prepared for Parks Services, Alberta Environmental Protection, Edmonton.

Plant Description, Identification and Classification

Ansley, J., K.G. Beck, C. Bell, et al. *Weeds of the West*. 1996. 5th ed. Western Society of Weed Science, Newark, California.

Brown, L. 1997. *Wildflowers and winter weeds*. W.W. Norton & Co., New York and London.

Currah, R., A. Smreciu and M. Van Dyk. 1983. *Prairie Wildflowers*. Friends of the Devonian Botanic Garden, Edmonton.

Farrar, J.L. 1995. *Trees in Canada*. Fitzhenry & Whiteside Ltd., Markham, Ontario, and Canadian Forest Service, Natural Resources Canada in cooperation with Canada Communication Group - Publishing, Supply and Services Canada, Ottawa.

Gadd, B. 1995. *Handbook of the Canadian Rockies*. 2d. ed. Corax Press, Jasper.

Inkpen, W., and R. Van Eyk. n.d. *Guide to the common native trees and shrubs of Alberta*. Pesticide Management Branch, Environmental Regulatory Services, Alberta Environmental Protection.

Johnson, D., L. Kershaw, A. MacKinnon and J. Pojar (with contributions from T. Goward and D. Vitt). 1995. *Plants of the western boreal forest and aspen parkland*. Lone Pine Publishing, Edmonton.

Kershaw, L., A. MacKinnon and J. Pojar. 1998. *Plants of the Rocky Mountains*. Lone Pine Publishing, Edmonton.

Moss, E.H. 1983. *Flora of Alberta*. 2d ed., revised by J.G. Packer. University of Toronto Press, Toronto.

Royer, F., and R. Dickinson. 1996. *Wildflowers of Edmonton and central Alberta*. University of Alberta Press, Edmonton.

———. 1996. *Wildflowers of Calgary*. University of Alberta Press, Edmonton.

———. 1999. *Weeds of Canada and the northern United States*. Lone Pine Publishing, Edmonton, and the University of Alberta Press, Edmonton.

Scotter, G.W., and H. Flygare. 1986. *Wildflowers of the Canadian Rockies*. Hurtig Publishers (McClelland & Stewart), Toronto.

Strickler, D. 1986. *Prairie wildflowers*. The Flower Press, Columbia Falls, Montana.

Vance, F.R., J.R. Jowsey, J.S. McLean and F.A. Switzer. 1999. *Wildflowers across the prairies*. Greystone Books, Vancouver.

Vitt, D., J. Marsh and R. Bovey. 1994. *Mosses, lichens and ferns of northwest North America*. Lone Pine Publishing, Edmonton.

Wilkinson, K. 1990. *Trees and shrubs of Alberta*. A Habitat Field Guide. Lone Pine Publishing, Edmonton.

———. 1999. *Wildflowers of Alberta: A guide to common wildflowers and other herbaceous plants*. The University of Alberta Press, Edmonton, and Lone Pine Publishing, Edmonton.

Gardening

Barkley, S. 1999. *Alberta yards & gardens: What to grow*. Alberta Agriculture, Food and Rural Development, Edmonton.

Bishop, W. n.d. *Trees & shrubs for the prairies*. Landscape Alberta Nursery Trades Association, Edmonton.

Duncan, B., ed. 1999. *The 1999 prairie garden: Featuring perennials*. The Prairie Garden Committee, Winnipeg Horticultural Society, Winnipeg.

Ernst, R. S. 1993. *The naturalist's garden: How to garden with plants that attract birds, butterflies, and other wildlife*. The Globe Pequot Press, Old Saybrook, Connecticut.

Hole, L. 1995. *Lois Hole's perennial favorites*. Lone Pine Publishing, Edmonton.

Hole, L. (with J. Fallis). 1994. *Lois Hole's bedding plant favorites*. Lone Pine Publishing, Edmonton.

Knowles, H. 1995. *Woody ornamentals for the prairies*. Rev. ed. University of Alberta, Faculty of Extension, Edmonton.

Leatherbarrow, L., and L. Reynolds. 2000. *101 best plants for the prairies.* Fifth House, Calgary.

Sands, D. 1992. *Herbs for northern gardeners*. Lone Pine Publishing, Edmonton.

Toop, E.W. 1993. *Annuals for the prairies*. University of Alberta, Faculty of Extension, Edmonton, and University of Saskatchewan, Extension Division, Saskatoon, and Lone Pine Publishing, Edmonton.

Toop, E.W., and S. Williams. 1991. *Perennials for the prairies*. University of Alberta, Faculty of Extension, Edmonton.

Vladicka, B. 1994. *Alberta horticultural guide*. Alberta Agriculture, Food and Rural Development, Edmonton.

Williams, S. 1997. *Creating the prairie xeriscape*. University Extension Press, University of Saskatchewan, Saskatoon.

Fungi

Bossenmaier, E.F. 1997. *Mushrooms of the boreal forest*. University Extension Press, University of Saskatchewan, Saskatoon.

Katsaros, P. 1996. *Familiar mushrooms*. National Audubon Society Pocket Guide. Chanticleer Press, New York.

Miller, O. 1978. *Mushrooms of North America*. E.P. Dutton, New York.

Schalkwijk-Barendsen, H.M.E. 1991. *Mushrooms of western Canada*. Lone Pine Publishing, Edmonton.

MYRNA PEARMAN

Chapter 4

Creating a Hummingbird Garden

TOM WEBB

Rufous hummingbird feeding young

Hummingbirds are fascinating creatures that can be attracted to many Alberta yards and gardens. The ruby-throated hummingbird is the most common and can be found from north central Alberta south, mostly in the southern boreal and parkland regions. Alberta's other nesting hummingbirds, the calliope and rufous, are western species that are found in the province's central and southern Rocky Mountain and foothills regions; the black-chinned hummingbird also occasionally wanders into this area.

HUMMINGBIRD FACTS

Hummingbirds are truly extraordinary birds. Two of their amazing abilities are flying backwards, and feeding while hovering. Darting about on wings that beat from 40 to 80 times per second, hummingbirds fly at speeds of 40 km-48 km (25-30 mi.) per hour, with bursts of up to 80 km (50 mi.) per hour. Because of their speed, hummingbirds can visit up to 1500 flowers in a single day!

The hummingbird nesting season begins with elaborate courtship displays by the male. Aggressive "sky dances" may also be performed—male with male and female with female—which consist of diving toward the ground in a wide arc.

Once mating has taken place, the male offers no assistance with building the nest or rearing the young. The female builds a very tiny nest, usually about 38 mm (1.5 in.) in diameter, using plant down, spiderwebs and bits of lichen. Some species build a new nest atop the one they used the previous year.

After nest building, the female lays two white eggs. She starts to incubate immediately after laying the first egg, and lays a second egg two or three days later. Incubation lasts, depending on the species, from 12 to 15 days. After the young hatch, they remain in the nest for 18 to 23 days.

Typical hummingbird flower
(*Fuchsia* x hybrida 'Swingtime')

Hummingbirds have an extremely high metabolism and, therefore, need to feed frequently. Their main food sources are tiny insects, which they catch on the wing or find in flower heads, and nectar, which they acquire from plants or sugar-water feeders. During the night or during periods of stress, such as cold weather, hummingbirds are able to conserve energy by slowing their metabolism (heartbeat and breathing rate) and entering a state of torpor.

As noted above, hummingbirds have the remarkable ability to withdraw nectar from flowers while hovering on the wing. As they move about from plant to plant, extracting nectar, they also perform the important service of pollination. Hummingbird tongues are well adapted for removing the nectar. While hovering in front of a flower, the bird pushes its beak into the blossom, then extends the top of its tongue, which is forked, into the "pot" of nectar. The split portion of the tongue is folded into a tube, which holds the liquid until the tongue is pulled back into the mouth, whereupon the nectar is swallowed.

Flowers that hummingbirds favour are tubular-, cup- or trumpet-shaped, have no fragrance, are brightly coloured (usually red, but also orange-red, orange, blue, purple/

WILLIAM BERGEN

Ruby-throated hummingbird
Archilochus colubris

violet or pink) and are physically arranged in such a way that the birds can hover near them. Plants that are used by hummingbirds typically have protruding stamens (pollen-bearing male organs) and stigmas (tips of female organs where the pollen lands) so that pollen can be easily transported from the male to the female plants. They usually produce multiple flowers in open inflorescences (clusters), and the flowers are positioned on the outside of the plant.

Not all of the plants that attract hummingbirds to a garden produce nectar. A hummingbird might be drawn simply by the colour of a plant, or by the plant having lots of tiny insects for the hummer to feed on.

PLANNING A HUMMINGBIRD GARDEN

To create a hummingbird garden, follow the design steps outlined in Chapter 2: create an inventory base map, bubble diagram(s) and a final site plan for the area you want to NatureScape for these delightful birds.

DOUG LEIGHTON

Black-chinned hummingbird
Archilocus alexandri

A successful hummingbird garden consists of hummingbird-attracting plants that are highly visible and placed so that they are easily accessible to the birds. It is best to put your tall plants and vines at the back of a garden area, with progressively smaller species to the front. Plants should be chosen and arranged so that there is a continual bloom throughout the summer—the best way is to mix annuals and perennials, and include flowers that have a long blooming season. Flowers with short blooming periods can be planted so that they are in full bloom during the nesting season, when the demand for nectar is the highest.

One way to provide blooms early in the season is to use container plants such as fuchsias, nasturtiums and petunias. Container plants are also useful in areas with limited space. Another way to ensure hummers have early spring food is to encourage sapsuckers (see Chapter 3).

WILLIAM BERGEN

Calliope hummingbird
Stellula calliope

Unlike a butterfly garden, which should be in full sun, hummingbird gardens need areas of dense shade, partial shade and full sun. To provide these conditions, a combination of trees, shrubs, vines, perennials and annuals can be used.

Trees are important because they provide shade, and nesting and roosting sites. They also provide a source of nesting materials. Shrubs should be planted in small clusters so the birds can easily manoeuvre around them. Open spaces are important to hummingbirds, so avoid cluttering a yard with too many trees and shrubs.

A hummingbird feeder will supplement natural nectar sources and will bring the birds within close viewing range. Chapter 14 contains details on supplemental feeding stations for hummingbirds.

BETTY FISHER

Rufous hummingbird
Selasphorus rufus

HUMMINGBIRD PLANTS

The following plants are very attractive to hummingbirds. For more information on these plants, see Appendix 1. Photographs of some of these plants are in Chapter 3.

Deciduous Trees
Hawthorn (*Crataegus* spp.)
Apples and crab apples (*Malus* spp.)

Shrubs
Caragana (*Caragana arborescens*)
Tatarian honeysuckle (*Lonicera tatarica*)
Flowering currant (*Ribes* spp.)
Lilac (*Syringa* spp.)

Vines
Chilean glory flower (*Eccremocarpus scaber*, annual in Alberta)
Morning glory (*Ipomoea purpurea* and *Ipomoea tricolor*, annuals)
Creamy peavine (*Lathyrus ochroleucus*, perennial)
Scarlet trumpet honeysuckle (*Lonicera* x *brownii* 'Dropmore Scarlet,' shrub)

Twining honeysuckle (*Lonicera dioica*, shrub)
Scarlet runner bean (*Phaseolus coccineus*, annual)
Canary bird vine (*Tropaeolum peregrinum*, annual)

Flowers (Perennials)
Giant hyssop (*Agastache foeniculum*)
Hollyhock (*Alcea rosea*)
Allium/Ornamental onions, garlic, chives (*Allium* spp.)
Spreading dogbane (*Apocynum androsaemifolium*)
Columbine (*Aquilegia* spp.)
Yellow bachelor button (*Centaurea macrocephala*)
Delphinium (*Delphinium* spp.)
Tall larkspur (*Delphinium glaucum*)
Pink/Dianthus (*Dianthus* spp.)
Fireweed (*Epilobium angustifolium*)
Gentian (*Gentiana* spp.)
Day lily (*Hemerocallis* spp.)
Coral bells (*Heuchera* spp.)
Hosta (*Hosta* spp.)
Lily (*Lilium* spp.)
Lupine (*Lupinus* spp.)
Maltese cross (*Lychnis chalcedonica*)
Malva (*Malva* spp.)
Bergamot/Bee balm (*Monarda* spp.)
Penstemon (*Penstemon* spp.)
Salvia (*Salvia* spp.)
Speedwell (*Veronica* spp.)

Flowers (Annuals)
Snapdragon (*Antirrhinum* spp.)
Borage (*Borago officinalis*)
Spider flower (*Cleome hasslerana*)
Cleome/Pink bee plant (*Cleome serrulata*)
Pink/Dianthus (*Dianthus* spp.)
Foxglove (*Digitalis purpurea*)
Fuchsia (*Fuchsia* spp.)
Himalayan orchid (*Impatiens glandulifera/I. royelii*)
Lavatera (*Lavatera* spp.)
Malva (*Malva* spp.)
Four o'clock (*Mirabilis jalapa*)
Nicotiana (*Nicotiana* spp.)
Petunia (*Petunia* x hybrida)
Salvia (*Salvia* spp., especially scarlet sage [*Salvia splendens*])
Nasturtium (*Tropaeolum majus*)

HUMMINGBIRD GARDEN AT THE ELLIS BIRD FARM, LACOMBE, ALBERTA

MYRNA PEARMAN

LEGEND
Plants with an asterisk are not hummingbird plants.

Coniferous Trees and Shrubs

Mugo pine	MP*

Vines

Canary bird vine	CA
Scarlet runner bean	SR
Hummingbird feeder	HF

Perennials

Bergamot/Bee balm	BE
Columbine	CO
Coral bells	CB
Day lily	DA
Pink/Dianthus	PN
Summer phlox	SP*

Annuals

Calendula	CE*
Cosmos	CO*
Foxglove	FG
Nasturtium	NA
Nicotiana	NI
Petunia	PE
Salvia	SV
Snapdragon	SG
Sunflower (bird-planted)	SF*

HUMMINGBIRDS AND WATER

Hummingbirds will use shallow birdbaths. (See Chapter 14 for how to set up a birdbath.) They also like to bathe by flying through the spray generated from a garden hose, lawn sprinkler, water mister or water garden waterfall. Water gardens are discussed in Chapter 5.

NOTE: The source of hummingbird scientific names used in this chapter is the American Ornithologists' Union (1998). The source of native plant scientific names is Moss (1983). See **Significant References** below.

5 BASICS
NATURESCAPING FOR HUMMINGBIRDS

1. Plant flowers in your garden that will attract hummingbirds; red tubular ones are best.
2. Provide early spring nectar sources by putting out plant containers with fuchsias, nasturtiums and petunias.
3. Provide both shaded and sunny spots in your garden.
4. Put up a hummingbird feeder.
5. If you don't have a water garden with a waterfall, set up a birdbath or water mister.

ACKNOWLEDGMENTS

Judy Clayton (Site Manager, Ellis Bird Farm, Lacombe, Alberta)
Clifton Lee Gass (Associate Professor, Department of Zoology, University of British Columbia, Vancouver, B.C.)
Gordon Heaps (Horticulturist, and Operations Supervisor, Muttart Conservatory, Edmonton, Alberta)
Andrew Hurly (Associate Professor, Department of Biological Sciences, University of Lethbridge, Lethbridge, Alberta)
Bob Sargent (President, Hummer/Bird Study Group Inc., Clay, Alabama)

SIGNIFICANT REFERENCES

Hummingbird Gardens

Butler, E. 1991. *Attracting birds*. Lone Pine Publishing, Edmonton.

Dennis, J., and M. Tekulsky. 1991. *How to attract hummingbirds & butterflies*. Ortho Books, Chevron Chemical Company, San Ramon, California.

Editors of Sunset Books and Sunset Magazine. 1990. *An illustrated guide to attracting birds*. Sunset Publishing Corporation, Menlo Park, California.

Henderson, C. 1987. *Landscaping for wildlife*. Nongame Wildlife Program - Section of Wildlife, Minnesota Department of Natural Resources. Minnesota's Bookstore, St. Paul, Minnesota.

Newfield, N., and B. Nielsen. 1996. *Hummingbird gardens*. Chapters Publishing Ltd., Shelburne, Vermont.

Schneck, M. 1993. *Creating a hummingbird garden*. Fireside, New York.

Stokes, D., and L. Stokes. 1989. *The hummingbird book: The complete guide to attracting, identifying, and enjoying hummingbirds*. Little, Brown and Company, Boston, New York, Toronto and Boston.

Hummingbirds

American Ornithologists' Union. 1998. *Check-list of North American birds*. 7th ed. American Ornithologists' Union, Washington, D.C.

Fisher, C., and J. Acorn. 1998. *Birds of Alberta*. Lone Pine Publishing, Edmonton.

McGillivray, W.B., and G.P. Semenchuk. 1998. *The Federation of Alberta Naturalists field guide to Alberta birds*. Federation of Alberta Naturalists, Edmonton.

Semenchuk, G.P., ed. 1992. *The atlas of breeding birds of Alberta*. Federation of Alberta Naturalists, Edmonton.

Plant Classification

Moss, E.H. 1983. *Flora of Alberta*. 2d ed., revised by J.G. Packer. University of Toronto Press, Toronto.

Water garden in southern Alberta

Chapter 5

The Wet and Wonderful: How to Create a Water Garden

Water is an often overlooked and underestimated wildlife attractant. Within the confines of a typical urban backyard, water is usually provided through birdbaths, water gardens and boggy areas. In this chapter we discuss how to create a backyard water garden.

BUILDING A BACKYARD WATER GARDEN

Backyard water gardens can range from a simple container, to a pond or "bog." If you are planning to install a water body deeper than 60 cm (24 in.), be warned that it may pose a hazard to small children and pets. Some municipalities consider deeper ponds or water gardens to be swimming pools and have strict guidelines related to fencing and keeping the area locked when there is no supervision. These crucial considerations may influence how, and where, you place your water garden.

From a wildlife point of view, the ecosystem created by a backyard water garden has two, inextricably linked components: the water itself and the habitat that surrounds the water. We'll start with the surroundings first.

The Habitat Surrounding Your Water Garden

A water garden placed in the middle of a vast expanse of well-manicured turf will be of little value to wildlife; most wild animals feel secure only when they are within flying, running or jumping distance (usually 3 m [10 ft.]) of protective vegetation. Birds look for safe approaches to a water source, and their well-used routes will thread to and fro through surrounding trees and overhanging branches. Berry-producing trees and shrubs, as well as a snag or two, near your water garden will provide many wildlife species with both food and shelter.

If you place vegetation adjacent to your water garden, make sure the pond isn't excessively shaded. However, tall grasses and ferns, thick tangles of shrubs and relatively dense plantings of tall annuals or perennials around a pond edge will offer shelter to amphibians, which appreciate some shade. You may be pleasantly surprised to find that non-vascular plants, especially mosses, and sometimes lichens and liverworts, will naturally establish themselves around your water garden (see Chapter 3).

Do not locate your water garden where tree roots can puncture the pond's liner, or where runoff from your lawn will drain into the water, especially if you apply fertilizers or pesticides (which we strongly discourage; see Chapter 2).

If feasible, avoid removing the leaf litter and deadfall debris that accumulate around a pond throughout the year. This extra layer of habitat will increase the population of ground-dwelling insects, which not only add biodiversity to your yard, but also attract creatures such as salamanders, frogs, toads and insect-eating birds. Thick leaf litter can also provide sufficient cover for an overwintering wood frog or mourning cloak butterfly.

In addition to the plantings around your water garden, you can also increase its habitat value by adding structural attractants such as rock piles, old boards, wooden slabs with

AMPHIBIANS AND WATER GARDENS

Although a small water garden may not support breeding populations of amphibians, adults will happily spend their summers in and around your pond if you provide adequate food and habitat for them. You can encourage these fascinating creatures to take up residence in your neighbourhood by transplanting a few native frog, toad or salamander eggs or tadpoles into your pond (try to avoid species at risk, for example, northern leopard frogs and Canadian toads). Don't move the adults; it is too stressful for them. Frog eggs occur in jelly-like clumps, toad eggs in rope-like strands and salamander eggs in compact clusters or singly. All are attached to the submerged parts of aquatic plants. Never put an exotic or pet store-raised amphibian in your pond.

AMPHIBIAN EGGS

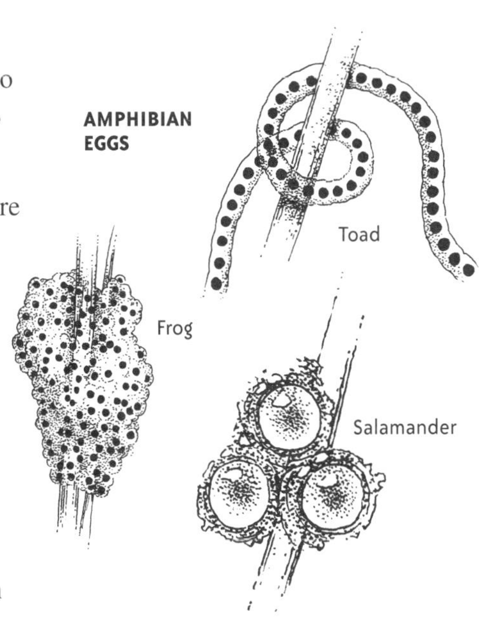

the bark still attached, large logs (>25 cm [10 in.] diameter) of trees that decompose quickly (e.g., poplar), brush piles or amphibian houses. These attract many creatures, from millipedes and overwintering butterflies, to frogs and salamanders.

Depending on the location of your pond and habitat, garter snakes might be attracted to both the water and to sunning areas around it. A few strategically placed large boulders, rock piles or stone walls near a pond are favoured sunning spots for these delightful critters (see Chapter 8).

If your pool is fairly large, you can place nestboxes nearby in hopes of attracting a pair of tree swallows. Depending on where you live and the habitat within and around your yard, a nestbox placed in trees or shrubbery near a water garden could attract a house wren (especially if you live south of Peace River).

Large mammals, such as deer, moose and elk—again depending on where you live—may also stop in to pay a visit (and test your liner's strength!).

WHAT IS PHOTOSYNTHESIS?

Photosynthesis is the process whereby chlorophyll-bearing plants manufacture carbohydrates, proteins and other materials. Through this process, carbon dioxide, water and light (in the presence of enzyme systems associated with chlorophyll) result in the production of glucose and oxygen.

The Water in a Water Garden

The ecosystem created in a water garden is much more complex and interesting than you might suspect from just casual observation. It is an intricate web of interactions between water, minerals, gases, animals and plants—all fuelled by sunshine. Through photosynthesis, submerged plants release oxygen and absorb carbon dioxide. The oxygen is consumed by aquatic invertebrates and fish, which in turn release carbon dioxide. Waste products and detritus are broken down by bacteria and other decomposers; the resulting nutrients are in turn used by primary producers (plants) and a variety of levels of consumers (invertebrates, fish). A balance between all these elements happens when each part of the food web is present and active. The illustration here shows part of a basic food web of a typical healthy water garden and a few of the more common creatures that you will find there.

It is important to remember that the workings of a natural ecosystem might come into conflict with your desire to grow beautiful lilies or raise expensive koi. Native aquatic predators, such as diving beetles, dragonfly larvae and backswimmers are

SIMPLE POND FOOD WEB WITH TYPICAL POND CREATURES

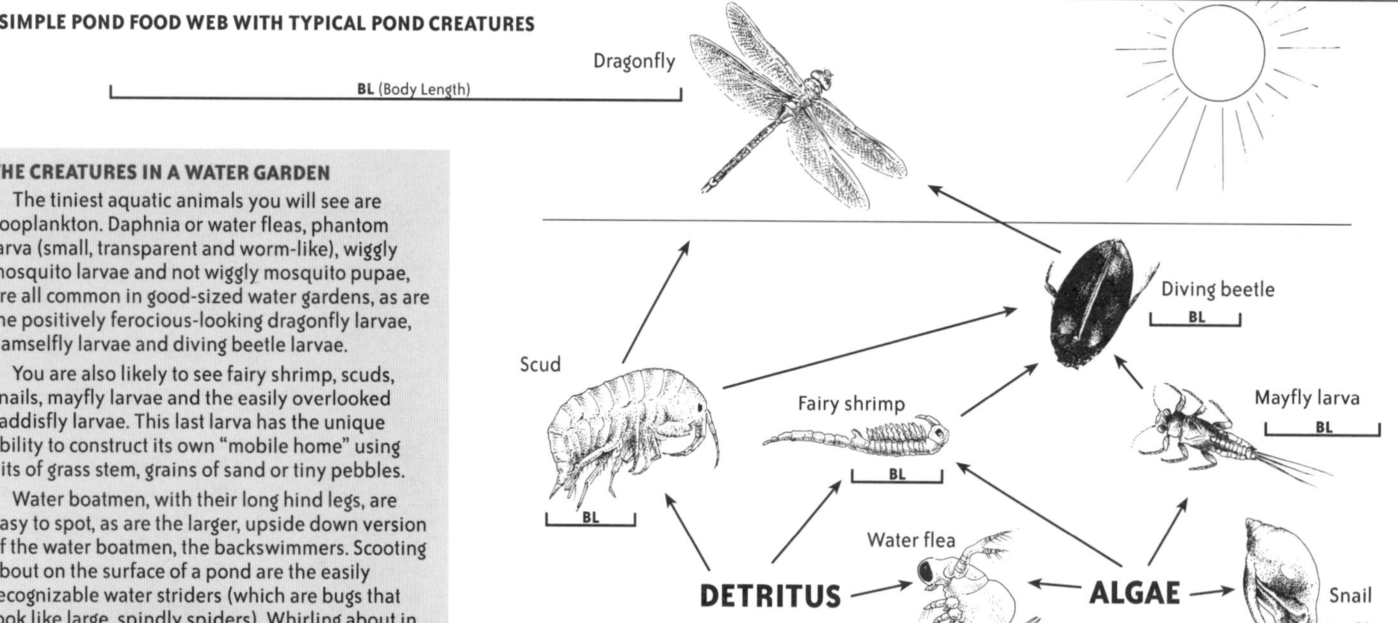

NOTE: The body lengths of the animals shown here will vary depending on age and species.

THE CREATURES IN A WATER GARDEN

The tiniest aquatic animals you will see are zooplankton. Daphnia or water fleas, phantom larva (small, transparent and worm-like), wiggly mosquito larvae and not wiggly mosquito pupae, are all common in good-sized water gardens, as are the positively ferocious-looking dragonfly larvae, damselfly larvae and diving beetle larvae.

You are also likely to see fairy shrimp, scuds, snails, mayfly larvae and the easily overlooked caddisfly larvae. This last larva has the unique ability to construct its own "mobile home" using bits of grass stem, grains of sand or tiny pebbles.

Water boatmen, with their long hind legs, are easy to spot, as are the larger, upside down version of the water boatmen, the backswimmers. Scooting about on the surface of a pond are the easily recognizable water striders (which are bugs that look like large, spindly spiders). Whirling about in small groups on the water surface are the pond dervishes—whirligig beetles.

efficient and ruthless in their attacks on ornamental fish fry. Insects may also attack and devour the leaves of prized water lilies. The action you take when these "problems" arise will depend on how "natural" you want to keep your garden or how "ornamental" you wish it to look.

WATER GARDENS: PONDS

Although there are several types of water gardens, the best for wildlife are earth (or clay) ponds, or water gardens lined with either flexible liners or preformed liners. Raised ponds and formal, brick-edged water gardens are less likely to attract wildlife. Concrete ponds, which are subject to cracking in the Alberta climate and require technical expertise to build, are not generally recommended.

Earth Ponds

If conditions are just right in your yard, (i.e., there is a good clay subsoil, proper contouring and adequate water input), you might be able to construct one of these ponds. Earth ponds most closely resemble natural wetlands, and as long as they are carefully placed and constructed to respect natural drainage patterns, can work well in a large backyard. You will need to do soil tests first to determine the feasibility of installing this type of pond, and you will likely need the services of a bobcat or other earth-moving equipment.

Flexible Liner Ponds

Flexible liner ponds are relatively easy to install, and the liners mould to virtually any shaped hole or watercourse. This latter characteristic makes it possible to incorporate curves and other features that allow a water garden to look more natural. Also, the edges of flexible liners are easy to hide, which is important if the pool is to resemble a natural pond. Flexible liners may decay and crack if they are exposed to sunlight, so it is very important to keep a pond full and, by so doing, protect the liner from ultraviolet (UV) exposure.

INSTALLING A FLEXIBLE LINER

Dig the Hole

Start digging a hole where you want your pond to be, making sure you won't dig into any underground utilities (call Alberta One Call; see page 8). Use a level on a two-by-four and stakes to make sure your pond is level. Then dig out the pond shape, making sure the sides slope inward at about a 20° angle to prevent them from collapsing. Some water gardeners suggest leaving a 20 cm-30 cm (8-12 in.) rim above ground level and sloping away from the pond, to prevent runoff from entering the water. If you want shelves, then dig down to the first shelf, making sure it is level before proceeding to the next. Shelves should be 20 cm-60 cm (8-24 in.) wide. Dig until the deepest section has been dug, digging and levelling all shelves as you go. In cases where the soil is loose, you may need a more gradual slope and wider shelves.

Install the Liner

Check the sides, shelves and bottom of your hole for sharp objects such as tree roots and rocks. Cover the pond floor and shelves with a protective underlay or about 5 cm (2 in.) of sand (some people suggest dampening the sand). Fold the liner and place it in the centre of the hole. Then unfold the liner and smooth it out in the hole, making folds and tucks, as necessary, to compensate for corners and angles. The liner should overlap the hole by about 30 cm (12 in.). Use rocks or bricks to hold the edges down. Try to install your liner on a warm day—it will be more flexible and easier to work with. Lay the liner out on warm grass, in full sun, just before you are ready to lay it in.

Add Water

Begin filling the pond with water. As the pond fills and the liner stretches, adjust or remove the weights holding the edges down. Carefully work out any wrinkles in the liner and do the final folds and pleats on the corners. Stop filling the pond when the water reaches about 5 cm (2 in.) below the edging.

Finish the Edge

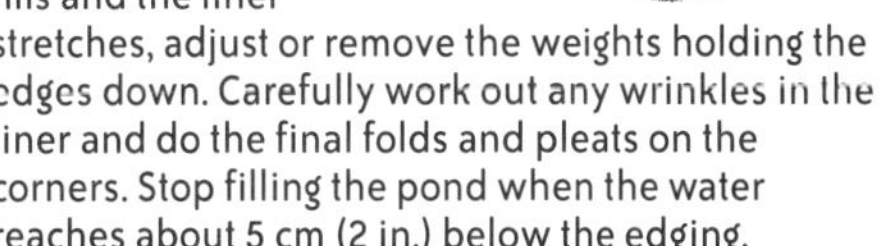

Trim any excess liner (you will want an overlap of about 30 cm [12 in] to hold the top of the liner), hide the liner with a suitable pond edge (see page 56), and fill your pond to the top.

Pond made with a flexible liner

MYRNA PEARMAN

FLEXIBLE POND LINERS

Flexible liners are usually made of polyvinylchloride (PVC), butyl rubber (isobutylene with isoprene) or EPDM rubber (containing ethylene propylene diene monomer). Butyl or EPDM rubber liners are initially more expensive but outlast those made from PVC, making them more economical in the long-run. The estimated lifespan of PVC liners is 10 to 12 years. Butyl/EPDM rubber liners will last 20 years or more. Rubber liners have the added bonus of being slightly rougher on the surface, allowing microorganisms to adhere better.

Polyethylene, once popular, has fallen out of favour because it is so sensitive to ultraviolet (UV) light and difficult to repair if it becomes brittle.

Given the challenges of the Alberta climate, the ideal thickness for a flexible liner is 45 mil (1 mil = 1/1000 in.). EPDM is available in thicknesses up to 60 mil. A new "super liner" is also available. This liner provides the same flexibility and weight as a 20-mil PVC liner (which many people use) but has the durability of the 45-mil EPDM.

Remember, never use a swimming pool liner for a water garden—most contain harmful biocides.

PROTECTING A FLEXIBLE LINER FROM PUNCTURES

Although flexible liners of 20-mil thickness or more are quite tough, they can still be punctured by a sharp object and need an underlay for protection. Commercial underlays can be used, although felt, old carpet, fibreglass insulation or 5 cm (2 in.) of sand will also work well. Wet newspaper and cardboard deteriorate quickly, so are not recommended.

If a butyl or EPDM liner gets punctured, it can be patched by heat-welding or with butyl mastic tape. PVC liners can be repaired with PVC adhesive. This adhesive bonds by chemical reaction, so you can do repairs underwater if necessary.

If deer, moose or elk are likely to visit, you will need additional protection for your liner where these animals walk. In these areas, cover your liner with about 10 cm (4 in.) of fill (use sand, small rocks and loam), or use an overlay of geotextile (a polyester product) and wire mesh, covered with fill.

HOW TO CALCULATE THE SIZE OF A FLEXIBLE LINER FOR A POND

Add the maximum width of the pond to twice the depth, then add on an overlap of 0.5 m (about 2 ft.); this calculation will give you the width of liner required. Then add the maximum length to twice the depth, and add on an overlap of 0.5 m (about 2 ft.) to get the length of liner.

These calculations include shelves and will work as long as the walls are vertical or slope towards the centre. If special edging is required, add extra lining to compensate. If the pond is circular, assume that its length and width are the same; if the pond has an irregular shape, you will have to adjust your calculations to fit accordingly.

If a pond is 2 m (6 ½ ft.) wide, 3 m (10 ft.) long and 0.5 m (2 ft.) deep, the calculation is as follows:

Width: 2 m + (0.5 m + 0.5 m) + 0.5 m = 3.5 m
6 ½ ft. + (2 ft. + 2 ft.) + 2 ft. = 12 ½ ft.

Length: 3 m + (0.5 m + 0.5 m) + 0.5 m = 4.5 m
10 ft. + (2 ft. + 2 ft.) + 2 ft. = 16 ft.

Measurement conversions are approximate.

Preformed Liner Ponds

Preformed, or rigid, liners allow for the "instant" water garden, complete with preformed shelves for placing plants. These liners come in a variety of shapes, survive our winters well and are easy to clean. However, ponds made with this type of liner can be more difficult to naturalize than those with a flexible liner, and their steep, slippery sides make it more difficult for wildlife to access the water. They are also quite expensive, considering the volume of water they hold. See below for instructions on how to install a preformed liner.

WATER GARDENS: BOGS

"Bogs" are small, low-lying wet areas that support the growth of moisture-loving plants. Although NatureScaped bogs will never resemble the true, natural bogs of central and northern Alberta, they are still diverse and interesting ecosystems. Human-made bogs can be created either as an integral part of a water garden or as an independent feature.

Cutaway view of a "bog" garden

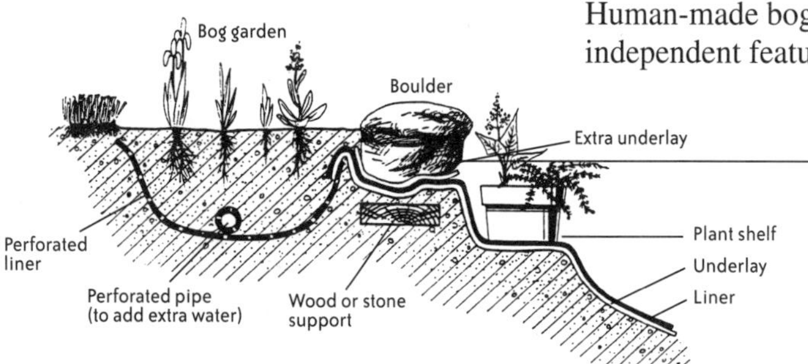

Because boggy areas need to be kept wet, but not saturated, they need to be designed so that slow drainage occurs. If you have a naturally occurring low area, plant the appropriate plants (see later) and keep the area suitably moist by watering it regularly.

If you would like to create a bog, dig out a small depression at least 1.2 m (4 ft.) in diameter in a suitable spot. Line the area with polyethylene sheeting or other liner material into which some holes have been punched to ensure slow drainage. Put down a layer of pea gravel and fill the hole with a mix of equal parts loam and peat moss. Water your bog regularly. Check the pH each spring—if it is higher than 6.5, add some peat moss. To prevent drying out over winter, make sure the area is well watered before freeze-up.

HOW TO CHECK THE pH OF YOUR POND

To test the pH of your pond soil or water, use a pH kit. These kits can be purchased at garden centres, nurseries and water gardening shops. To determine the pH, simply mix some soil or water with the kit solution and check the colour of the liquid against the chart provided.

INSTALLING A PREFORMED LINER

Dig the Hole

Be certain there are no underground utilities where you are going to dig (call Alberta One Call; see page 8). Place the preformed liner over the proposed hole and "sketch" its shape on the ground (use powdered chalk, wood ash, pebbles or the like, if you're working on a lawn). Dig the first few centimetres (couple of inches) slightly larger than the actual outline. Using stakes and a level on a two-by-four, make sure your pond is level. Dig the hole, including shelves, until the deepest section has been dug. Always check the level of each shelf as you go, and dig out a slightly larger area than that of the liner (adding an extra 8 cm [3 in.] is recommended). You will backfill this extra space later.

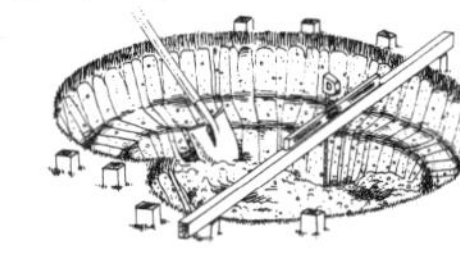

Install the Liner

Remove any sharp objects, such as roots or rocks, from the hole you have dug. Place loose, sifted sand at the bottom of the hole and compact the sand firmly (some water gardeners suggest using damp sand). Put the preformed pond shell in the hole and adjust the shell until it is perfectly level. The top rim of the shell can be slightly above ground level to prevent surface runoff from entering the pond water.

Add Water

Begin to fill the liner with water, stopping when the pond is firmly in place. Backfill behind the liner using loose soil or sand. Then continue to fill the liner with water and add backfill around the liner, making sure that the shelves and sides of the pond are well supported. Stop filling when the water is about 5 cm (2 in.) from the top.

Finish the Edge

Finish the edges (see page 56) and fill the pond to the top.

Pond made with a preformed liner

MYRNA PEARMAN

To create boggy areas around your water garden, dig small, shallow depressions around the rim—cavities just deep enough that a sufficient quantity of soil can be placed in them for bog plants to become established. The liner under these areas can be an extension of the main liner, or a separate sheet of liner material. Puncture the liner and fill the depression with soil, as described previously. Boggy areas should be separated from a the main water garden by a berm or ring of stones, which will ensure the soil is kept moist but not washed out into the main pond.

WATER GARDENS: CONTAINERS

Container water gardens are an inexpensive alternative to conventional water gardens. Some containers (Lerio® tubs) can even be buried. Although not as wildlife-friendly as an in-ground pond, container water gardens—which can be made from just about any watertight container—add variety and biodiversity to a yard, especially if they are located near a few trees or shrubs.

Container water garden

You can use your imagination in constructing a container garden (kitty litter trays and old bathtubs work well), or you can purchase a commercial one at a garden centre. Some commercial products come equipped with a built-in circulation and filter system.

PLANNING YOUR WATER GARDEN

A water garden is a fairly complex project, so take the time to plan it carefully. Once it's in, it's not that easy to move or modify! Be sure that you are physically capable, have budgeted enough time and have the necessary skills to complete the job. If not, be prepared to hire skilled labour.

The first step is to check out as many water gardens as you can, and visit water gardening stores, nurseries/garden centres that specialize in water gardening. You may want to visit the demonstration water garden at the Ellis Bird Farm, near Lacombe, to get an idea of the various features that can be incorporated into a backyard pond. Create a vision of what you want, then develop a budget (including additional labour costs if you need help) based on the type of pond you hope to install. Make some adjustments, if necessary, until both the vision and budget are in sync.

The next step is to follow the design procedure outlined in Chapter 2 (preparing an inventory base map, bubble diagram and site plan). Here are some tips:

- Pay particular attention to natural water patterns, as well as underground services (e.g., gas, telephone, electrical and sewage lines, septic systems).
- Make sure the type of pond you envisage and its size are suitable for your yard. Some yards can accommodate only a container water garden; a large backyard could have room for a large water garden with a boggy area. One way to get an idea of size is to outline the proposed area with your garden hose.
- A wildlife pond has to be large enough to balance itself and attain the equilibrium of a self-sustaining ecosystem. Small ponds tend to lose water quickly due to evaporation, and heat up a lot during the day, especially if they are not properly shaded. A wildlife pond should be no less than 4.5 m^2 (50 sq. ft.), and its average depth should be at least 45 cm-60 cm (18-24 in.). Ideally, it should have one deep area of about 90 cm-150 cm (35-60 in.).
- The amount of sunlight and shade is an important consideration in the placement of your water garden. Check the shade quality of potential sites in the morning, afternoon and evening. The ideal site for any water garden will receive some sun and some shade (either full or dappled) over the course of a day. If you want to grow lilies, your pond will need to receive at least six hours of full sun per day.
- Viewing perspective is also very important. Do you want the pond for the exclusive use of wildlife, and therefore hidden from view, or do you want to be able to see it

MYRNA PEARMAN

Container water garden with waterfall

from a kitchen or living room window, balcony, lawn chair or off the back deck? If your pond will be viewed from mainly one location, design it with that viewpoint in mind, staggering the height of your plantings, with low ones near the front, and shrubs and large trees in the background.
- To maximize the aesthetic quality of your pond, try to locate it so that reflections can be seen on the water surface during at least part of the day. Lay a couple of large mirrors down on the ground to get an idea of the reflective qualities of different sites.

Build your pond anytime after spring thaw and before fall freeze-up. Installing a pond during a period of warm, dry weather is preferable to struggling with an installation in the rain. If it starts to rain before you've been able to finish, be sure to cover the open hole with a sturdy tarp.

WATER GARDEN PLANTS

Plants are the foundation of a successful water garden, and wherever possible, representative species for different water depths should be included. The number and variety of water plants you can use will depend on the size of your pond and on the different water depths you provide.

Although there are many species and varieties of water plants available, try to choose locally hardy plants that are appropriate to the type of water garden that you want to create. Although a water garden filled with native species will be most like a natural pond, cultivars and exotics can contribute both to the attractiveness and health of a water garden.

Some nurseries have a wide selection of both native and non-native species; you may have to contact native plant/seed suppliers or collect from the wild to get native species. If you collect from the wild, do so with restraint, and follow the collection guidelines in Chapter 3. Never harvest rare or endangered plants (contact the Alberta Natural Heritage Information Centre [ANHIC] for lists [see Appendix 5]).

Cross-section of pond showing different types of vegetation

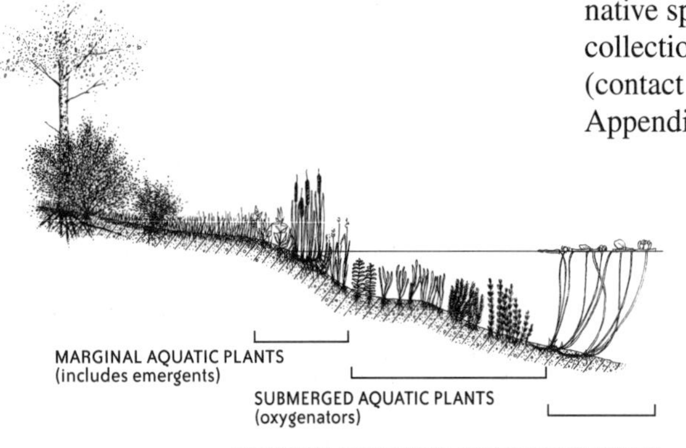

All types of aquatic vegetation provide wildlife with habitat. **Marginals** provide hiding spots for amphibians and shelter for insects. **Submergents/oxygenators** provide aquatic wildlife with shelter, food and shade, and help keep a water garden oxygenated. **Deep-water aquatics**, rooted plants such as water lilies, provide shade for underwater creatures and resting spots for frogs as well as dragonflies, butterflies and other insects. Unrooted **floating-leaved plants** provide shade and a good food source for fish (especially koi).

Marginals

Marginals (including emergents) are the plants that grow along the water's edge. They grow either in saturated soil or in the shallows (in water up to about 0.6 m [2 ft.]), and usually, most of their foliage is above water level. These plants provide good habitat for wildlife, especially insects, and their roots help to stabilize the shoreline. Native marginal perennials sustain freezing conditions well, as long as their roots are permitted to penetrate the mud and develop overwintering tubers or rhizomes.

To plant marginals, put them into pots and submerge the pots at the edge of the water garden, or plant the root stocks directly into the wet soil at the pond margin. Some native species may naturally establish themselves.

HANDLING AQUATIC PLANTS

If you want to make placement and removal of your plants a little easier, grow them in containers. Plant all water plants in heavy clay loam mixed with a bit of sand. Make sure the soil is herbicide- and pesticide-free, and avoid mixes that float (e.g., perlite, vermiculite, Peat-lite®). Top-dress a container with washed sand or washed pea gravel (1 cm-1.25 cm [3/8 - 1/2 in.]), being sure not to put any sand or gravel on the crown of the plant.

WATER GARDEN PLANTS—MARGINALS

MYRNA PEARMAN
Sweet flag/Ratroot
Acorus calamus

MYRNA PEARMAN
Water hawthorne 
Aponogeton distachyos

MYRNA PEARMAN
Water arum/Wild calla 
Calla palustris

MYRNA PEARMAN
Floating marsh-marigold 
Caltha natans

MYRNA PEARMAN
Yellow marsh-marigold 
Caltha palustris

HEINJO LAHRING
Canna
***Canna* spp.**
(*Canna* 'African Sunset')

MYRNA PEARMAN
Sedge (Water sedge)
***Carex* spp. (*C. aquatilis*)**

MYRNA PEARMAN
Brass buttons 
Cotula coronopifolia

MYRNA PEARMAN
Umbrella plant 
***Cyperus* sp.**

MYRNA PEARMAN
Creeping spike-rush 
Eleocharis palustris

MYRNA PEARMAN
Common mare's tail 
Hippuris vulgaris

BETTY FISHER
Siberian iris
Iris sibirica

MYRNA PEARMAN
Knotted rush
Juncus nodosus

MYRNA PEARMAN
Parrot feather 
Myriophyllum aquaticum

MYRNA PEARMAN
Coltsfoot 
***Petasites* sp.**

MYRNA PEARMAN
Water smartweed 
Polygonum amphibium

MYRNA PEARMAN
Pickerel weed 
Pontedaria cordata
Common water plantain
(left and flower stalk)
Alisma plantago-aquatica

SYLVIA GLASS
Yellow water crowfoot
Ranunculus gmelinii

JAN HEAPS
Western dock
Rumex occidentalis

MYRNA PEARMAN
Arrowhead (Common arrowhead)
***Sagittaria* spp. (*S. latifolia*)**

MYRNA PEARMAN
Common cattail 
Typha latifolia

MYRNA PEARMAN
Wild rice 
Zizania aquatica

Perennial marginal plants that overwinter in Alberta include *sweet flag/ratroot (*Acorus calamus*)[1], *common water plantain (*Alisma plantago-aquatica*), *marsh reed grass (*Calamagrostis canadensis*), *water arum/wild calla (*Calla palustris*), *floating marsh-marigold (*Caltha natans*), *yellow marsh-marigold (*Caltha palustris*), *sedges (*Carex* spp.), *creeping spike-rush (*Eleocharis palustris*), *horsetail/scouring-rush (*Equisetum* spp.), *common mare's tail (*Hippuris vulgaris*), Japanese iris (*Iris kaempferi*), Siberian iris (*Iris sibirica*), blue water iris/blue flag (*Iris versicolor*), *knotted rush (*Juncus nodosus*), aquatic mint/watermint (*Mentha aquatica*), *wild mint (*Mentha arvensis*), *coltsfoot (*Petasites* spp.), *common reed grass/giant reed grass (*Phragmites australis*), *water smartweed/swamp persicaria (*Polygonum amphibium*), pickerel weed (*Pontedaria cordata*), *white water crowfoot (*Ranunculus aquatilis*), *yellow water crowfoot (*Ranunculus gmelinii*), *western dock (*Rumex occidentalis/Rumex*

[1] In this chapter, all plants in plant lists are listed in alphabetical order by botanical or scientific name, and native species are preceded by an asterisk.

RARE SUBMERGENTS

Several pondweed species (*Potamogeton* spp.) are on the ANHIC "tracking" list (meaning they are rare or of some conservation concern) and should never be harvested from the wild.

fenestratus), *arrowhead (*Sagittaria* spp.), *arrow-grass (*Triglochin maritima*), pencil cattail (*Typha angustifolia*) and *common cattail (*Typha latifolia*).

Some perennial marginals that do not overwinter are water hawthorne (*Aponogeton distachyos*), canna (*Canna* spp.), brass buttons/golden buttons (*Cotula coronopifolia*), umbrella plant (*Cyperus* spp. including *C. alternifolius*), parrot feather (*Myriophyllum aquaticum*), water soldier (*Stratiotes aloides*) and hardy canna (*Thalia dealbata*).

Annual marginals include watercress (*Nasturtium officinale)* and wild rice (*Zizania aquatica*, including *Zizania palustris*). Botanists are currently discussing the taxonomy of wild rice and debating whether it is native to Alberta.

WATER GARDEN PLANTS – SUBMERGENTS

MYRNA PEARMAN

Hornwort/Coontail
Ceratophyllum demersum

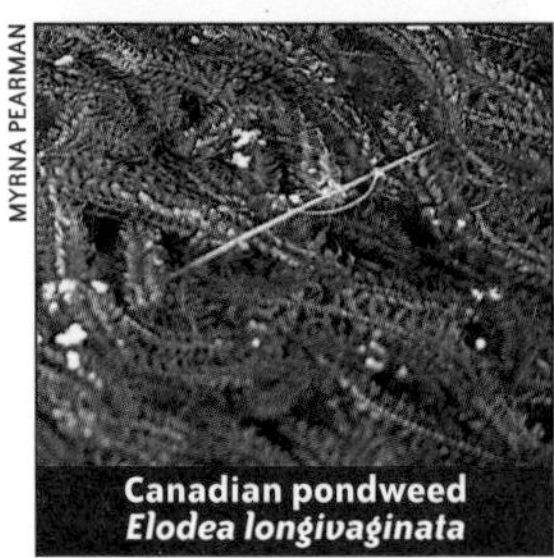
MYRNA PEARMAN

Canadian pondweed
Elodea longivaginata

MYRNA PEARMAN

Pondweed
(Zoster-like pondweed)
***Potamogeton* spp.**
(P. zosteriformis)

Submergents/Oxygenators

These plants are so called because they release oxygen into the water from their completely submerged foliage. Some varieties will grow slightly above the water surface if conditions permit, but the physical appearance of the plant parts that protrude into the air (e.g., leaves and flowering stalks) is different from that of parts that are submerged.

Submergents absorb nutrients directly through the leaf surface, and their roots act primarily as anchors. They compete with algae for nutrients so are considered the key to good water clarity. However, some of these plants can be invasive, so it is important to control excessive growth. Eurasian water milfoil *(Myriophyllum spicatum* var. *spicatum*) has caused severe problems in areas where it has been introduced and is now banned from import into Canada. There is a native variety of this plant—spiked water milfoil (*Myriophyllum spicatum* var. *excalbescans*).

It is recommended that one bunch of oxygenating plants be added for every 0.1 m^2 (1 sq. ft.) of exposed surface area in water gardens up to 10 m^2 (100 sq. ft.) in size, and one bunch per 0.2 m^2-0.3 m^2 (2-3 sq. ft.) be added in ponds larger than 10 m^2 (100 sq. ft.).

To plant submergents, pot them in large pots and place them on the pond bottom, or pot them in shallow trays and place them on shelves or in shallow water. Another technique is to wrap a few plants together, place a weight around them and let them sink to the bottom of the pond.

Varieties that do well in Alberta include *hornwort/coontail (*Ceratophyllum demersum*), *Canadian pondweed (*Elodea longivaginata*), *common mare's tail (*Hippuris vulgaris*), *pondweeds (*Potamogeton* spp.) and *common bladderwort (*Utricularia vulgaris*). Common mare's tail is also grown as a marginal species.

Deep-Water Aquatics (Water Lilies) and Floating-leaved Plants

This group of plants contains both rooted (deep-water) varieties (e.g., water lilies) and unrooted (floating-leaved) varieties (e.g., duckweeds). Both types use surface leaves for the bulk of their photosynthetic activity; their leaves lie flat on the water surface to absorb as much sunlight as possible. The rooted types overwinter with the aid of rhizomes that are anchored in mud below the ice. Some unrooted types (specifically duckweeds) form winter buds and sink to the pond floor until spring. Nonhardy floaters, such as fairy moss (*Azolla caroliniana/Azolla filiculoides*) have to be replenished each year.

BATHING BIRDS

Birds, especially robins, chickadees and siskins, love to use water lily leaves for bathing. This bathing routine is quite comical to watch because the birds have to practice a bit to find the best place to stand. They don't want to fall into the water, but the leaf needs to be submerged enough for them to get a good dip.

To plant water lilies, set a planted pot onto the pond bottom or wrap the plant's roots and some loam in burlap, attach a weight if necessary (e.g., put a rock in the sack) and drop the bundle to the bottom of the pond. Be sure the crown of the plant sticks out of the bundle. To plant floating-leaved aquatics, simply place them onto the water surface.

Water lilies include small pond lily *(Nuphar microphyllum)*, *small yellow pond lily/ spatterdock *(Nuphar variegatum)*, *white water lily *(Nymphaea tetragona)* and fragrant water lily *(Nymphaea odorata)*, as well as hundreds of varieties of cultivars and exotics. Consult a water gardening book or a water gardening centre for a complete list of water lilies.

In Alberta, hardy water lilies need a minimum water temperature of 15°C (60°F) to grow; tropical water lilies 24°C (75°F). Some very hardy lilies (e.g., some *Nuphar* species) will grow in cooler water if light levels are adequate. Check with your local nursery or a water garden expert to see what lilies are best for your particular water garden.

Floating-leaved aquatics include fairy moss (*Azolla caroliniana/Azolla filiculoides*), *common duckweed (*Lemna minor*), *ivy-leaved duckweed (*Lemna trisulca*), American frogbit (*Limnobium spongia*), water lettuce (*Pistia stratiotes*), butterfly fern *(Salvinia auriculata)* and floating water fern (*Salvinia natans*). In Alberta, only the duckweeds will overwinter. The rest can be treated like annuals: scoop them off the water's surface in the fall and put them in the compost pile.

RARE WATER LILIES

White water lily (*Nymphaea tetragona*) is on the ANHIC "tracking" list, so should not be taken from the wild.

WATER GARDEN PLANTS—DEEP WATER (L) AND FLOATING-LEAVED AQUATICS (R)

MYRNA PEARMAN
Small yellow pond lily/ Spatterdock
Nuphar variegatum

MYRNA PEARMAN
Ivy-leaved duckweed
Lemna trisulca

MYRNA PEARMAN
Fairy moss
Azolla caroliniana

MYRNA PEARMAN
Common duckweed
Lemna minor

MYRNA PEARMAN
Water lily
***Nymphaea* spp.**
(*Nymphaea* 'Attraction')

MYRNA PEARMAN
American frogbit
Limnobium spongia

MYRNA PEARMAN
Water lettuce
Pistia stratiotes

Plants for "Bogs"

Recommended plants for boggy areas include *sweet flag/ratroot (*Acorus calamus*), *yellow marsh-marigold (*Caltha palustris*), *sedges (*Carex* spp.), brass buttons/ golden buttons (*Cotula coronopifolia*), *creeping spike-rush (*Eleocharis palustris*), wild rhubarb (*Gunnera* spp.), hosta (*Hosta* spp.), ensata iris (*Iris ensata*), Siberian iris (*Iris sibirica*), cardinal plant (*Lobelia cardinalis*), skunk cabbage (*Lysichiton americanum*), *wild mint (*Mentha arvensis*), watercress (*Nasturtium officinale*), *coltsfoot (*Petasites* spp.), *creeping buttercup (*Ranunculus cymbalaria*), lizard's tail (*Saururus cernuus*), *arrow-grass (*Triglochin maritima*) and *cattails (*Typha* spp.), many of which are shown on page 53. Not all of these plants may be hardy in your area, so check for planting instructions when you purchase them.

INVASIVE WATER PLANTS

Some plants commonly recommended for water gardens in Alberta have been found to be invasive elsewhere and, for safety's sake, probably should not be planted here. These plants include flowering rush (*Butomus umbellatus*) and yellow iris/yellow flag (*Iris pseudacoris*), both marginals; European frogbit (*Hydrocharis morsus-ranae*), a submergent; and water hyacinth (*Eichhornia crassipes*), a floating-leaved plant. A website with information on invasive plants is http://infoweb.magi.com/ ~ehaber/ipcan.html .

MYRNA PEARMAN
Water hyacinth
Eichhornia crassipes

SETTING UP A STREAM OR WATERFALL

Streams and waterfalls are interesting to the eye and soothing to the ear, and can bring a water garden to life for their human admirers. Birds also love them because they are attracted to the sound and the motion of moving water. Many species of songbirds love to bathe in a stream of water, and hummingbirds will take aerial baths

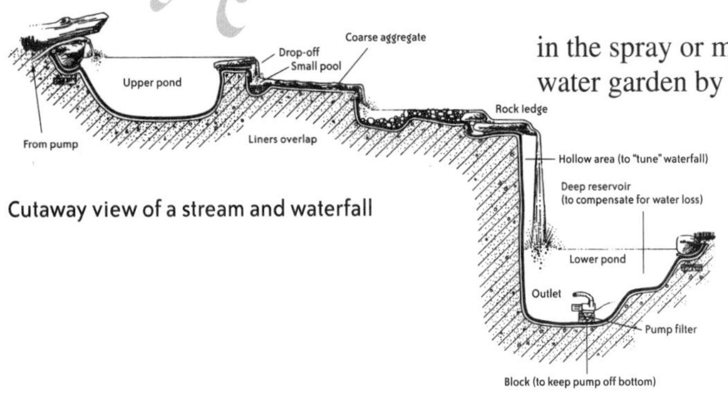

Cutaway view of a stream and waterfall

in the spray or mist of a waterfall. Moving water can also contribute to the health of a water garden by helping to aerate the water.

Building a watercourse or waterfall "from scratch" requires careful planning, some technical expertise and the installation of a pumping system (see side bar on page 57). To make this task easier, there are several styles of preformed waterfalls available commercially. Consult a water gardening book (see **Significant References** at the end of the chapter) or a water gardening expert for information and specific installation details.

WATERFALL AND STREAM FACTS

- Streams and waterfalls lose a lot of water through evaporation, capillary action along the edges, and general splashing, so water gardens with these features need to be topped up regularly.
- The longer the watercourse, the better the water will be filtered and cleaned.
- The more drop-offs to splash the water, the better the water will be aerated.
- You can use pockets of sand or loam among the stones or along the edge in protected locations for plantings.
- Angular stones above the waterline will be used by birds to clean their beaks; and birds will use flat stones just beneath the water level for bathing.
- Fish like to hang around the base of waterfalls and drop-offs so make sure these areas are deep enough for them.
- Use lots of large stones along the watercourse and in and around the pond itself. They act as a heat sink and will help keep the water warm through the night.

WATER GARDEN EDGES AND BEACHES

The purpose of an edge is to blend a water garden into its surroundings. In a wildlife pond, the idea is to keep the edges as natural as possible by using materials such as rocks, washed gravel, pebbles, sand, grass or wood. A "bog" can also edge a water garden. A few edges are illustrated here.

SOME WAYS TO EDGE A WATER GARDEN

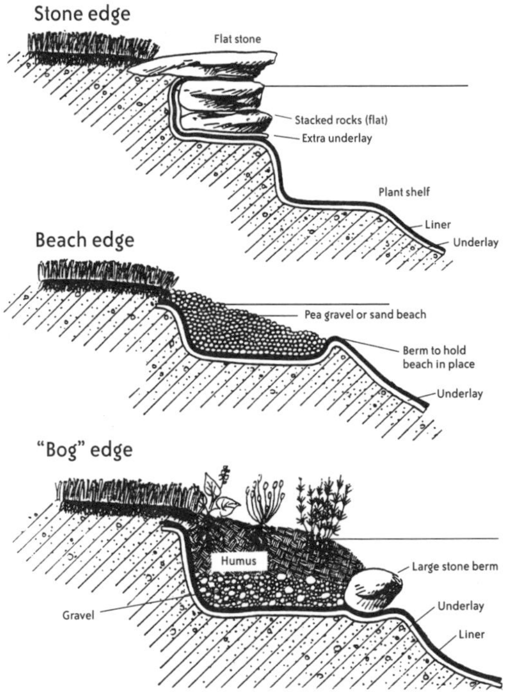

Stone edge

Beach edge

"Bog" edge

Beach edges are a great way to encourage wildlife use. Birds and mammals like these edges for drinking and bathing, and butterflies like to puddle in the moist, sandy areas adjacent to the water. (We describe the intricacies of puddling in Chapter 9.)

To create a beach, dig a shallow, gently sloped shelf on one side of a water garden. Run the liner up over the excavated area and extend it back and up to the soil surface, making sure the end is above the waterline. Then cover the liner with pea gravel or beach sand, or a combination of both. Sand is recommended if you want the area to be frequented by puddling butterflies. Because the liner runs beneath the sand, the area will remain permanently moist. A berm or a few strategically placed, large rocks will prevent the sand or gravel from drifting down into the main pond area. Rocks will also provide basking and drinking sites for wildlife such as birds and butterflies, and hopping stones for curious children.

If you don't have a beach edge or gently sloping side, make sure that you provide some way for pond creatures to easily enter and exit the pond. One example is a frog ramp—a rock or rough board that extends out of the water to a safe exit spot (see page 66 for illustration). The ramp can also serve as an insect lifeline.

MYRNA PEARMAN

Demonstration water garden at the Ellis Bird Farm, Lacombe, showing beach (foreground), stone edging with waterfall (left) and "bog" (far left).

FISH

Fish, like colourful goldfish and koi, add an interesting dimension to a water garden. Fish have big appetites, however, and will readily consume the aquatic invertebrates in your pond (just as enthusiastically as the invertebrates will devour fish fry). To maintain a true wildlife pond, consider stocking it with some sticklebacks or minnows, which can be netted from a nearby pond or lake.

Goldfish are fairly hardy and can handle temperatures from just above freezing to 29°C (85°F). Koi are less adaptable and need their water to be 10-29°C (50-85°F). Sticklebacks and minnows can generally handle a wide range of temperatures. Bring susceptible fish inside for the winter. The recommended density for fish is 2.5 cm (1 in.) of goldfish per 4.5 L (1 gal.) of pond water and 2.5 cm (1 in.) of koi per 23 L (5 gal.) of water.

If you plan to put fish into your water garden, and if the pond is located anywhere near a water channel, make sure the channel and the water garden never connect—even during periods of heavy rain. Never allow pond fish into a natural waterway!

MYRNA PEARMAN

Koi are a colourful addition to a water garden

BALANCING A WATER GARDEN

Once a balance between the plants and animals in a water garden is achieved, the pond will be able to maintain a healthy equilibrium. A balanced water garden will be teeming with life, and the water free of scum and quite clear (although suspended phytoplankton may make it appear slightly cloudy).

Here is the process for balancing a water garden. Remember, all new water gardens go through an initial algal bloom until excess nutrients are used up and algae-feeding populations build up. Plants and animals need time to adjust as they compete for nutrients and space.

To balance a pond:

- Fill the new pond with rainwater, if possible, and let the water stand for a few days. If chlorinated water has to be used, you can hasten chlorine removal by using an aquarium aerator attached to an air stone, or you can treat the water with a dechlorifier (follow the instructions on the label).
- Add appropriate plants in suitable locations.
- "Inoculate" the pond with invertebrates by adding about 23 L (5 gal.) of water collected from a nearby natural pond. Collect this water close to the shore (where the water is shallow), and be sure that it has an abundance of small creatures, including scavengers (snails, tadpoles). Take a dip net along if you want more creatures than can be scooped up with a pail.
- Be sure to monitor the temperature of your water garden before putting in fish, and stock it appropriately. If necessary, add a few water lilies to help shade the pond and keep the water cooler. Never overfeed your fish.
- Keep the pond well aerated using a fountain, stream, waterfall or filter. All of these require the use of a pump (see side bar). It is better to have a slightly oversized than undersized pump.
- Take precautions to avoid an overabundance of algae and other water quality problems (see next page).

PUMPS FOR PONDS AND WATERFALLS

There are two types of pumps: submersible (which run under water) and surface (which are put above ground). Most people buy submersible pumps, which are easy to install and have a wide range of output capacities.

If you are going to buy a pump, seek expert advice at your local nursery or garden centre. You will need to know what the pump is going to be used for; the volume of the pond (the flow rate per hour should not exceed the pond's volume); and for features like waterfalls, the height of the "head" (the greatest height of water that the pump will have to lift) and the output per hour that will be required. With this information, it will be possible to calculate the output capacity of the pump you should buy.

For a 1800-L (400 gal.) water garden, use at least a 900-L/h (200 gal./h) pump. The smallest waterfall will likely require a 300 gal./h (1350 L/h) pump, and a decent cascade will require a pump to deliver 500 gal./h (2250 L/h) or more. (We are using Imperial gallons here, but note that the capacity of many pumps is rated in U.S. gallons. One Imperial gallon is about 4.5 L and one U.S. gallon is about 3.75 L.)

In order to calculate the required litres or gallons per hour for a waterfall or stream, run a garden hose to the top end of the stream and turn it on to the desired volume of water. Use a pail to count how many gallons (litres) come out in one minute, then multiply by 60 to get gallons (litres) per hour.

HOW TO CALCULATE POND VOLUME

Calculate the volume of water in a water garden as follows:

Rectangular Pools

Length (ft.) x width (ft.) x depth (ft.) x 6.25 = Imperial gallon capacity

Length (ft.) x width (ft.) x depth (ft.) x 7.5 = U.S. gallon capacity

Length (m) x width (m) x depth (m) x 1000 = litre capacity

For example, a pond measuring 10 ft. x 6.5 ft. x 2 ft. = 130 cu. ft.; 130 x 6.25 = 812.5 Imperial gallons, or 130 x 7.5 = 975 U.S. gallons.

A similar pond measuring 3 m x 2 m x 0.6 m = 3.6 m^3; 3.6 x 1000 = 3600 litres.

Circular Pools

3.14 x radius^2 (ft.) x depth (ft.) x 6.25 = Imperial gallon capacity

3.14 x radius^2(ft.) x depth (ft.) x 7.5 = U.S. gallon capacity

3.14 x radius^2(m) x depth (m) x 1000 = litre capacity

For example, the volume of a pond measuring 10 ft. across with a depth of 2 ft would be

3.14 x 5^2 x 2 = 157 cu. ft; 157 x 6.25 = 981 Imperial gallons or 157 x 7.5 = 1177.5 U.S. gallons.

The volume of a similar pond measuring 3 m across with a depth of 0.6 m would be

3.14 x 1.5^2 x 0.6 = 4.24 m^2; 4.24 x 1000 = 4240 litres.

Irregularly Shaped Ponds

For these ponds, estimate the pond's dimensions, then do the appropriate calculations.

Note that 1 Imp. gal. = about 4.5 L; 1 U.S. gal. = about 3.75 L.

HOW TO MAINTAIN A WATER GARDEN

Water Levels

If rainfall hasn't been sufficient to keep the pond topped up, add water slowly with a hose. If the water loss is suspiciously high, check for leaks in your liner and repair them. When topping up with a hose, some water gardeners suggest you place the hose at the bottom of the pond to remove the cold, deoxygenated water found at the bottom and to stir up the bottom sediments. However, if you use this method and there is a lot of silt in the bottom sediments, it may take few days for the pond to clear again.

TO CONTROL ALGAE

- Do not overfeed your fish. If you have fish, use a pond filter.
- Do not fertilize plants until the water clears.
- Add more oxygenating plants.
- Add floating plants to block out the sunlight and help use up excess nutrients (30-50 percent of a pond surface should be covered with plant material).
- Aerate your water garden with a fountain or waterfall.
- Add an electrical aeration device with an air stone. This mechanism will bubble oxygen though the water.
- If you use fertilizer (e.g., manure) in your yard, check to make sure lawn or garden runoff is not entering your water garden.
- Introduce microorganisms by adding water from a healthy, clear, natural pond.
- Physically remove excess filamentous algae (e.g., by hand [twirl it around a stick or use a fan rake] or by using a pond vaccuum).
- Use a biological clarifier and/or install a pond filter; never use algicides to clear water.
- Stuff barley straw into a plastic net, gunnysack or pantyhose, and place the bundle under the water surface adjacent to moving water. Replenish as required (the bundle of material will shrink over time). If you overdo it with the barley straw, your water will turn brown.
- If necessary, drain the pond and refill it with fresh water.

Algae

Watch for imbalances in your water garden's ecosystem (e.g., algal blooms, stagnant water, excessively cloudy water). Correct these problems before they get out of hand (see side bar). Remember that a natural pond requires a certain amount of algae to feed other members of the food chain, so some algae will be active in a healthy pond all year round.

However, too much algae can be a problem partly because it clouds the water. Plants deprived of light because of algae are unable to properly carry out biochemical processes, such as photosynthesis, and die as a result. As they decompose, they release methane into the water, which causes the water condition to deteriorate further. Excessive algae also consumes oxygen vital for water-dwelling creatures.

Digging Out

Water gardens go through a kind of "natural succession" as they age. Vegetation will eventually grow in from the sides and bottom, displacing the open water. Earth ponds will need to be dug out every 10 or 20 years, and the plants in a preformed or flexible liner pond may have to be divided each year. You may need to remove accumulated debris from the bottom of your water garden every couple of years. If you do clean out your pond, be sure to leave a layer of organic matter on the pond floor so that bacteria, plankton and insect populations can reestablish themselves. Except when doing a complete clean-out, never remove more than two-thirds of the pond's water volume at one time.

Leaf Litter

If trees or shrubs overhang the pond and leaf litter is a problem, use a pond net (install the net in the fall and remove it in the spring).

Fertilizing Plants

Fertilize potted plants from time to time using slow-release fertilizer tablets or bonemeal. Repotting your plants into fresh, heavy clay loam each year will also stimulate lush growth. After repotting, be sure to top the plant pots with washed sand or pea gravel to avoid losing loam into the water.

OVERWINTERING YOUR WATER GARDEN

A typical Alberta winter can see a broad range of temperatures, from well above freezing to -40°C (-40°F), and ice on lakes or ponds can be 0.6 m-1.2 m (2-4 ft.) thick. Over countless thousands of years, our native flora and fauna have adapted to survive these conditions.

Here's what to do to overwinter your pond:

- Stop feeding your fish when the water temperature reaches approximately 5-10°C (40-50°F).
- Make sure the pond is full of water before freeze-up.
- Remove unneeded filters and pumps.

- Leave hardy marginal plants in place, and don't cut back the dead foliage on them. By leaving the dead leaves intact, you allow the root systems to "breathe"; also, a number of pond creatures are likely to overwinter on the dead blades.
- Protect your water lilies and less hardy plants. If your pond is less than 1.2 m (4 ft.) deep, you will either need to move all your water lilies and other, less hardy plants indoors (store them in water-filled tubs), or insulate the pond to prevent the mud from freezing. If your water garden is at least 1.2 m (4 ft.) deep, or has one or more areas this deep, move your plants from the shallower sections into the deeper sections. Attach ropes or handles to any pots so they can be easily retrieved in the spring.
- Leave some mud and organic debris in and around the pond for overwintering creatures.
- Remove or protect your fish. If you want to overwinter your fish, you will need to have a pond that won't freeze to the bottom (i.e., is deep enough or has a heater), and uses a bubbler or pump to help keep the water circulating. You will need to keep part of the water garden ice-free so that the fish have an adequate supply of oxygen, and waste gases can escape. Installing a stock tank de-icer with a timer is an easy way to keep your pond open.
  A cheaper method to protect your fish is to insulate the pond, leaving a small hole for gases to escape and light to enter; then use an aquarium heater (150-250 watts) on a timer (set it for a two-hour "on" cycle at least every four hours) to ensure that there is always an ice-free area on the pond surface, and an aquarium aerator to keep the water oxygenated. Don't over-aerate or the water might become "super-cooled" and freeze your fish.

HOW TO INSULATE A WATER GARDEN

To insulate a pond, place boards across it, then pile tightly packed straw bales on top of the boards (make sure the bales never touch the ice, and cover them with a tarp to keep them dry). Straw bales have an R40 insulation value. Fibreglass insulation can be used instead of straw bales but only where excess moisture will not build up in the fibreglass. In some areas, water gardeners use monocellular blue or pink styrofoam insulation sheets.

Note: Moss (1983) is the source of most scientific names used for native plant species (see **Significant References** below).

5 BASICS
CREATING A WATER GARDEN

1. If your water garden is an in-ground pool, make sure it is large enough to become a self-sustaining ecosystem; put in a container water garden if your yard is too small for an in-ground pool.
2. Choose a location for your water garden that will receive both sun (about six hours) and shade.
3. Inoculate your water garden with aquatic life from a nearby, healthy pond.
4. Plant a selection of aquatic plants in your water garden, and if you have an in-ground pool, plant wildlife-attracting vegetation on at least one side.
5. Make sure birds can drink/bathe safely along the edges of a water garden, and that frogs and other amphibians can easily enter and exit an in-ground pool.

ACKNOWLEDGMENTS

Elisabeth Beaubien (Research Associate, Devonian Botanic Garden, c/o University of Alberta, Edmonton, Alberta)
Barry Greig (Horticulturist, Devonian Botanic Garden, c/o University of Alberta, Edmonton, Alberta)
Curtis Jerrom (Owner, Common Sense Aquatics, Red Deer, Alberta)
Derek Johnson (Botanist, Canadian Forest Service, Edmonton, Alberta)
Heinjo and Jan Lahring (Owners, Bearberry Creek Water Gardens, Sundre, Alberta)
Grant Moir (Biologist, and Board Member, Red Deer River Naturalists, Red Deer, Alberta)
Jamie Pilkey (Owner, Backyard Dreams, Red Deer, Alberta)
Kim Schmitt (Biologist, Ducks Unlimited, Red Deer, Alberta)
Garry Wright (Owner, Aquatic Enterprises, Airdrie, Alberta)

Thanks also to Ellis Bird Farm Ltd., Lacombe, Alberta, for the use of Gary Ross's illustrations in *Water Gardening: A Prairie Guide*.

SIGNIFICANT REFERENCES

Clifford, H.F. 1991. *Aquatic invertebrates of Alberta*. The University of Alberta Press, Edmonton.

Gould, J. 1999. *Plant species of special consideration*. Alberta Natural Heritage Information Centre, Alberta Environmental Protection, Edmonton.

Harris P., and T. Warke. 1998. *The prairie water garden*. Red Deer College Press, Red Deer.

Heritage, B. 1994. *Ponds and water gardens*. Cassell Publishers Ltd., The Strand, London, England.

Hessayon, D.G. 1993. *The rock and water garden expert*. Transworld Publishers Ltd., London, England.

Lahring, H., and J. Lahring. 1995. *Water gardening: A prairie guide*. Ellis Bird Farm, Lacombe.

Matson, T. 1997. *Earth pond's sourcebook: The pond owner's manual & resource guide*. Countryman Press, Woodstock, Vermont.

Moss, E.H. 1983. *Flora of Alberta*. 2d ed, revised by J.G. Packer. University of Toronto Press, Toronto.

Nash, H. 1994. *The pond doctor*. Tetra Press, Blacksburg, Virginia.

Rees, Y. 1994. *Practical water gardening*. The Crowood Press Ltd., Marlborough, Wiltshire.

Robinson, P. 1997. *Complete guide to water gardening*. Reader's Digest Association (Canada) Ltd., Westmount, Quebec.

Slocum, P.D., and P. Robinson. 1996. *Water gardening: water lilies and lotuses*. Timber Press, Inc., Portland, Oregon.

Tomocik, J. 1996. *Water gardening*. Denver Botanic Gardens, Pantheon Books, Knopf Publishing Group, New York.

White, D.J., E. Haber and C. Keddy. 1993. *Invasive plants of natural habitats in Canada: An integrated review of wetland and upland species and legislation governing their control*. Report prepared for Canadian Wildlife Service, Environment Canada, in cooperation with the Canadian Museum of Nature, and with support from the North American Wetlands Conservation Council (Canada), Ottawa.

MYRNA PEARMAN

Sylvan Lake shoreline

Chapter 6
If You Live on a Lake or Waterway

Many people who live adjacent to a lake, creek, river or other permanent water body fully appreciate the beauty of these special areas and are diligent in ensuring that their activities do not spoil the natural environment. However, some waterside property owners see their land as an extension of their urban yardscape and set about "taming" the shoreline by replacing the natural vegetation, soil and rocks with lawns, sand beaches, riprap or gravel. Unfortunately, attempts to alter natural conditions are often destructive to the environment, expensive for the landowner and illegal.

HOW LANDOWNERS CAN PROTECT AND ENHANCE THEIR WATERFRONT PROPERTY

Because most waterside lots are small, some property owners may feel that the impact of their actions on the overall health of a water body is insignificant. However, the cumulative impact of small, incremental changes can be very significant over time. Adding to the complexity of the situation is the fact that there is often a lag time between when damage is caused to an aquatic ecosystem and when the results become obvious. By the time symptoms appear, it is usually very difficult (or expensive) to rectify the situation.

Living in harmony with the natural environment of any water body is preferable to trying to change it. Here are ways to maintain that harmony. Remember, to be a good steward of your shoreline, advise friends and visitors of what you are doing and why.

- Avoid removing tree cover or any other vegetation between a developed area and a water body. (To alter vegetation along a shoreline usually requires a permit). If you feel you must remove some vegetation from your property to have a better view, try selective delimbing first; you may be surprised at how a view can open up with this technique. A professional arborist could do your pruning for you. The extra cost is small compared with the value that trees provide to a lot. If you do need to remove some trees, be very selective and cut down as few as possible. Try to leave a buffer of vegetation at least 30 m (100 ft.) wide back from the bank or high water line.

- If the vegetation in front of your lot has been routinely removed, restore the shoreline by replanting species native to that water body. To determine what plants to use, find an undisturbed area of shoreline and see what is growing there. If your lot has similar growing conditions, you can collect some seeds or cuttings from these plants (see Chapter 3 for guidelines on collecting from the wild). Species such as willow, alder and dogwood are easy to grow from cuttings. An alternative is to buy plants or seeds from a local nursery or native plant source (see Appendix 5 for locations of native plant and seed suppliers). Along a shoreline, shrubs should be planted 45 cm (18 in.) or less apart and at least 25 cm (10 in.) from the water's edge.

- If nature didn't give you a beach, don't create one. It is illegal to dump sand and other materials on the shore of a water body without a permit. An

WHAT DO YOU OWN?

Waterfront property owners often assume they own the land right down to the water, which is not always the case. In Alberta, many shorelines, or portions of shorelines, have been designated as environmental reserves. These reserves are owned by the municipality and are to be left in their natural state to protect the shoreline and allow for public access. They cannot be altered without permission. Even if there is no reserve between your property and the water body, be advised that the shore and bed of a lake, river, stream or other permanent water body is usually considered to be public land. Check your land title and/or subdivision plan to see where your property boundary is located. Contact your local municipal government and the Public Lands Branch of Alberta Agriculture, Food and Rural Development to check out the regulations regarding use of public lands in your area.

SOME DEFINITIONS

The **bed** of a water body is the land upon which the water sits.

The **shore** (or shoreline) is the part of a water body below the bank but above the present water level. It is the part of the bed that is exposed when water levels are low.

The **bank** separates the shore and the bed of a water body from the "terrestrial" land; its location is not affected by occasional periods of drought or flooding.

Adapted from P. Valastin and W. Nelson. 1999. *Caring for shoreline properties*. Alberta Conservation Association, Edmonton, and Alberta Environmental Protection, St. Paul.

GOVERNMENT PERMITS

Anyone planning work that might affect the bed or shore of a water body, or an environmental reserve, will likely need a permit to proceed. Shoreline projects require approval from Alberta Environment or the Public Lands Branch of Alberta Agriculture, Food and Rural Development. These agencies have a "one window" approach so that applying for a permit from one means applying also to the other. Changes in an environmental reserve require a development permit from the municipality that owns the land.

artificial beach alters the natural characteristics of a water body, can negatively affect water quality and fish habitat, and often washes away anyway. As an alternative, build a "floating beach"—a floating dock or swimming platform that gives some of the same amenities as a beach but without any environmental damage.

- Should there be rocks in the shallows in front of your property, leave them be. Rocks help stabilize the shore, provide habitat for aquatic insects and fish, and have aesthetic value. If you must take some away for better swimming or to protect boat propellers, try to be selective and move them by hand.
- Occasionally, some control of aquatic plants may be necessary to open up the water in front of a lot, for example, to create a boat lane. Aquatic plants are considered to be fish habitat and are protected under the federal *Fisheries Act*. Also, except for very small-scale hand removal of aquatic vegetation, the elimination of aquatic plants from the provincially owned bed of a water body requires a government permit. Check with your Alberta Environment regional office (see Appendix 5) for the conditions under which a permit is granted to remove aquatic plants in a recreational cottage area. If you do take out aquatic plants, make sure the material is taken away from the shoreline so that, when the vegetation rots, it does not return nutrients to the water body.
- When creating a boat lane, try establishing a joint access channel with several neighbours, or get together with a neighbour to share a dock and boat access.
- When building a dock, consider floating, cantilever or post-supported docks. These structures minimize damage to the existing water body bottom and do not restrict the movement of fish and wildlife. You are allowed to put temporary structures into the water without a permit, but more permanent structures (e.g., docks, weirs, etc.) require a permit.
- Build your boathouse back from the shore and use a winch to take the boat out of the water.
- For properties with steeply sloped banks, the most effective protection against erosion is to leave the natural shoreline area undisturbed. Rather than building a retaining wall (which will likely require a permit) to control erosion at the shoreline, keep existing vegetation and/or add shrubs and small trees.
- Consider building stairs or a meandering path (maximum 2 m [6.5 ft.] wide) on slopes leading to the water. You can design the slope so that rainwater flows off the path, not straight down it into the water body. Try to keep the path or the area beneath any stairs fully vegetated (but cut, as necessary), rather than covered with dirt, sand or gravel. If the path is well used or steep, gravel can be used.
- Leave natural ice ridges in place (they slow meltwater runoff into a lake or waterway).
- Don't wash vehicles, dogs, clothes, hair or dishes in a lake, stream or other water body. Carry out these activities inside or as far back from the shore as possible, and do not dump water from another source into any water body.

Manicured waterfront yard

- Motor boats should be driven slowly in shallow water. Fast driving disturbs nutrient-rich bottom sediments and fertilizes the water above them. Motorized vehicles can also disturb fish and waterfowl.

- Never put garbage into a water body, and don't leave garbage on the ice in winter.

- Learn about your septic system and how to maintain it properly (for example, regular pumping, avoiding tank additives and minimizing the amount of water going into it). If necessary, repair or upgrade the system. If feasible, replace a septic field with a holding tank.

- Consider reducing the size of your lawn space. If you must have turf, try to restrict it to high traffic areas. A lawn should never run to the bank edge. Existing waterside lawns can be replanted or allowed to revegetate back to a natural buffer of grasses, shrubs or trees. Make sure there is some ground cover beneath any shrubs and trees.

- Avoid planting a garden on a slope leading toward a water body; bare soil is a nutrient source, and locating a garden on a sidehill will accelerate soil erosion and runoff.

- Avoid using lawn or garden pesticides (herbicides, fungicides, insecticides) or fertilizers; they can create problems for aquatic plants and animals (as well as terrestrial ones).

Unmanicured waterfront yard

- Try to reduce or stop your use of any products containing phosphorus. For example, choose laundry and dishwasher detergents that are low in or have no phosphorus, and cut down on dishwasher and washing machine use. Septic tank systems do not break down or dilute phosphorus—the chemical ends up in the ground around the cottage and, eventually, in the nearby water body.

- Rake and remove leaves from waterside lawn and unnaturalized garden areas, and compost grass clippings or vegetable wastes away from the bank. Never put these materials into the water. In wooded areas, don't rake up leaves or other forest floor debris; this material is needed to help trap and filter water.

- Most non-edible petroleum products contain toxins. Therefore, never dispose of any motor oil or other petroleum product on driveways or roads, or down drains. Instead, take it where it can be recycled.

- Refuel a boat and other machines/equipment carefully. Because fuel spills do occasionally happen, have kitty litter or some other absorbent substance on hand in order to soak up the fuel.

- Cattle and water bodies do not mix. Cattle contribute large quantities of nutrients through their manure, and their hooves break down banks, promoting erosion. Prevent cattle from getting direct access to lakes, creeks, rivers or other water bodies. Off-site watering stations (for example, nose-pumps or solar-powered pumps) are relatively easy to install and use.

- It makes good sense to keep heavy objects away from the bank of a water body. Such objects (like all-terrain vehicles [ATVs] or snowmobiles) can weaken the ground and cause it to break away and slip into the water. Locate walking and vehicular routes only where the land is very stable.

PROTECTING A SHORELINE

If you are interested in shoreline conservation, you may want to get in touch with either the Living by Water Project, through the Federation of Alberta Naturalists, or the Alberta Conservation Association (see Appendix 5 for contact information).

5 BASICS
IF YOU LIVE ON A LAKE OR WATERWAY

1. Leave a natural shoreline undisturbed.
2. If your shoreline is disturbed, revegetate it with native species.
3. Keep livestock and heavy objects away from the water edge.
4. Don't pollute the water with pesticides, fertilizers or runoff from septic fields.
5. Check with Alberta Environment before removing any aquatic plants, and before building a dock or boathouse.

ACKNOWLEDGMENTS

Sarah Kipp (Co-founder, Living by Water Project, Salmon Arm, B.C.)
Ian McFarlane (Biologist, Ducks Unlimited, Red Deer, Alberta)
R. Wayne Nelson (Fisheries Biologist, Natural Resources Service, Northeast Boreal Region, Alberta Environment, St. Paul, Alberta)
David Park (Regional Programs Manager, Alberta Conservation Association, Edmonton, Alberta)
Pat Valastin (Habitat Biologist, Alberta Conservation Association, Edmonton, Alberta)

SIGNIFICANT REFERENCES

Adams, B. 1998. *Caring for the green zone: Riparian areas and grazing management*. 2d ed. Alberta Riparian Habitat Management Project ("Cows and Fish Project"), Lethbridge. (Booklet)

Henderson, C.L., C.J. Dindorf and F.J. Rozumalski. n.d. *Lakescaping for wildlife and water quality*. Nongame Wildlife Program - Section of Wildlife, Minnesota Department of Natural Resources. Minnesota's Bookstore, St. Paul, Minnesota.

Living by Water Project. n.d. *Waterfront living: Simple tips—lasting benefits*. Living by Water Project. (Pamphlet)

Mitchell, P., and E. Prepas. 1990. *Atlas of Alberta lakes*. University of Alberta Press, Edmonton.

Valastin, P., and W. Nelson. 1999. *Caring for shoreline properties: Changing the way we look at owning lakefront property in Alberta*. Alberta Conservation Association, Edmonton, and Alberta Environmental Protection, St. Paul.

MYRNA PEARMAN

Chapter 7

Attracting Amphibians to Your Garden

Boreal toad

Welcome to the kiddie section! If you are genuinely interested in learning what to do to enhance amphibian populations in your garden, you are, indeed, among the very young at heart.

WHY ATTRACT AMPHIBIANS TO YOUR YARD

We can think of a number of reasons why you should try to provide habitat for amphibians in your NatureScaped yard.

First, we are finding that amphibian populations all over the world are declining at alarming rates. Some of the most interesting species, like the stomach brooding frogs of Australia and the golden toad of Costa Rica, are now believed to be extinct. In Alberta, the northern leopard frog, Canadian toad and Great Plains toad have been placed on the province's list of "at risk" species. Suspected causes of this general decline include global warming, increased ultraviolet (UV) radiation due to ozone depletion, parasites and agricultural chemicals.

Second, amphibians eat a large number of traditional garden "pests," like slugs, grasshoppers and caterpillars. A good population of frogs, salamanders and toads will help keep the populations of these "problem" creatures in check.

Third, children love to look for amphibians, which are usually easy to feed when captured. For example, kids find watching a fat toad down a large moth or cricket fascinating. After the fun (not for the insect that was eaten!), be sure to return the satisfied toad to the garden. Although most of our amphibians are harmless, a thorough washing of hands after handling is recommended, especially with toads and salamanders.

Last, there is something wonderfully soothing about listening to a group of hopeful gentleman frogs or toads in the spring as they describe their worthiness to the ladies and warn away their rivals.

GETTING TO KNOW AMPHIBIANS

Almost all amphibians require water for some part of their life cycle. All Alberta amphibians tend to spend their adult lives on land near water; they engage in water play during mating season; and the females lay their eggs in water. The young, known as tadpoles or pollywogs, live in water until their arms and legs are well enough developed that life on land is possible. In metamorphosing (changing form) from tadpole to adult, the tail and gills are usually resorbed. However, the two salamander species keep their tails. It takes a full spring and summer season for the eggs of most of the amphibians you will meet to hatch into tadpoles, then grow and transform into adult frogs, toads or salamanders. During this period of growth, young amphibians are very vulnerable.

ALBERTA'S AMPHIBIANS

Salamanders

- Long-toed salamander (*Ambystoma macrodactylum*)
- Tiger salamander (*Ambystoma tigrinum*)

Toads

- Plains spadefoot toad (*Scaphiopus bombifrons*)
- Boreal toad/Western toad (*Bufo boreas*)
- Great Plains toad (*Bufo cognatus*)
- Canadian toad (*Bufo hemiophrys*)

Frogs

- Boreal chorus frog/Striped chorus frog (*Pseudacris maculata*)
- Northern leopard frog (*Rana pipiens*)
- Spotted frog (*Rana pretiosa*)
- Wood frog (*Rana sylvatica*)

WILDLIFE PETS

We don't recommend keeping wild adult amphibians as pets. If you capture a frog, toad or salamander, keep it only a few hours, then return it to its natural habitat.

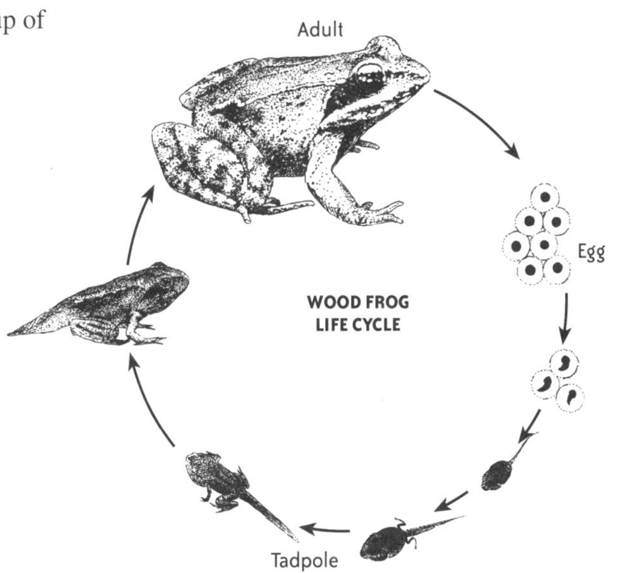

Amphibians are "cold-blooded"—they get their body heat from the environment and so have a fluctuating body temperature. When days are hot, adult amphibians will try to find cool, shaded areas to wait out the heat (e.g., the edge of a water garden). Large pieces of old bark, loose planks or the shelters described later on will also help make these creatures feel at home.

Cats and dogs will eat amphibians just like they do birds or other small animals. It is helpful to keep these pets away from that part of the yard in which you are trying to encourage amphibians.

Because amphibians have thin, permeable skins, they are particularly susceptible to lawn and garden pesticides (including fungicides and herbicides). Therefore, habitats without these chemicals are friendliest toward amphibians.

Wood frog tadpoles under water garden plants

Amphibians can be the victims of lawn mowers, especially in tall grass areas. The chance of inadvertently mincing a frog or toad will be reduced if you mow your lawn midafternoon, or on hot, sunny days when our hoppy friends are hiding in the shelters you have provided for them. As far as amphibians go, cool days and evenings are the most dangerous times to mow your lawn.

PLANTS FOR AMPHIBIANS

Because amphibians are carnivores, they really don't care a great deal about the types of plants you grow. However, they do attach their eggs to submerged aquatic vegetation. They also prefer shade (bright sun dries their skin and kills them quickly) and, therefore, need plants that will provide them with this life-preserving amenity. Tadpoles and mating adults tend to stay under or near marginal or floating vegetation in ponds, and adult frogs will sit on land near the edges of ponds and streams if the edges are shaded and vegetation overhangs the water.

Frog ramp

Therefore, to attract amphibians, you will need a large water garden, pond, boggy area or very slow-moving stream with floating and marginal vegetation. Shade some of the water body and leave at least a metre or two of uncut vegetation around part of it—making sure that this vegetation does not get too dense, or the amphibians won't be able to move around.

Your water garden, pond, bog or stream should have a gently sloping edge or a frog ramp so adult amphibians can easily get in and out of the water.

SHELTER FOR AMPHIBIANS

To successfully encourage amphibians, you have to consider their needs throughout the year.

Amphibians spend the winter hidden and quiescent. Technically, they do not hibernate but, rather, become dormant and torpid due to the low temperature. Each species hides in its own way and has its own special requirements.

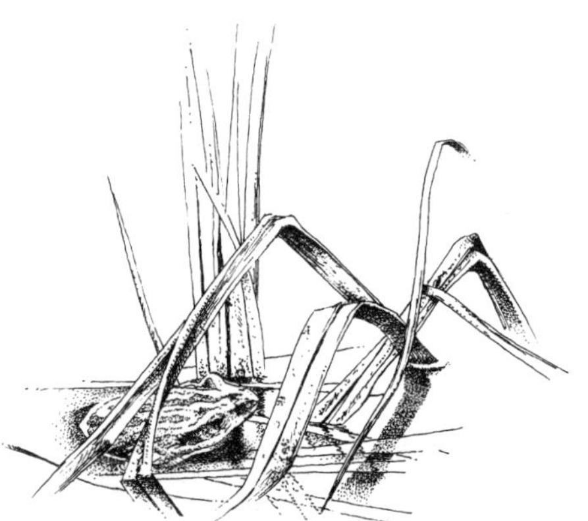

Boreal chorus frog sheltering under overhanging pond vegetation

Providing a water garden or pond can be critical for successful overwintering of some amphibians, but here we run into a problem. Not that much is known about how amphibians prepare themselves for the cold, nor do we have a great deal of information about how some of them spend the winter. Therefore, NatureScapers can provide important observations that may prove critical in assisting some amphibian species to survive (use the Backyard Watch form provided in Appendix 6).

We do know that some frogs actually freeze "solid" during the winter, although they can only freeze in this way for a few days and so need to be buffered from prolonged freezing. Wood frogs, for example, find a sheltered spot above ground under leaf litter or a fallen log. They may even burrow into logs if the wood is sufficiently decayed. As the cold sets in, a series of chemical reactions begins in their bodies that results in the production of a sugar-based antifreeze in critical tissues and organs. Fluids in other parts of their body actually freeze.

We suggest that one of the best ways to encourage such species to spend the winter is to set aside, near your pond or water garden, an area with a thick layer of leaf litter and a few, well-rotted logs. It is probably a good idea to fence off this area to ensure that the litter is not trampled during the winter. Amphibians will spend winter in this type of habitat only if there is normally a deep and constant snowpack.

Other species of frogs, like the northern leopard frog, spend the winter in sluggish contemplation of froggy things, at the bottom of ponds where the water doesn't freeze to the bottom. These frogs become dormant and absorb just enough oxygen through their skins to maintain life. If your pond has a liner, and reaches below the frost line (usually 1.5 m-2 m [5-6 1/2 ft.]), a thick layer of mud on the bottom will help these frogs overwinter.

Salamanders and toads tend to retreat into underground sanctuaries in winter. Often, such sanctuaries are mammal burrows, but if the soil is soft enough, the animals themselves can burrow deep enough to ensure survival.

Overwintering shelter for a salamander or toad

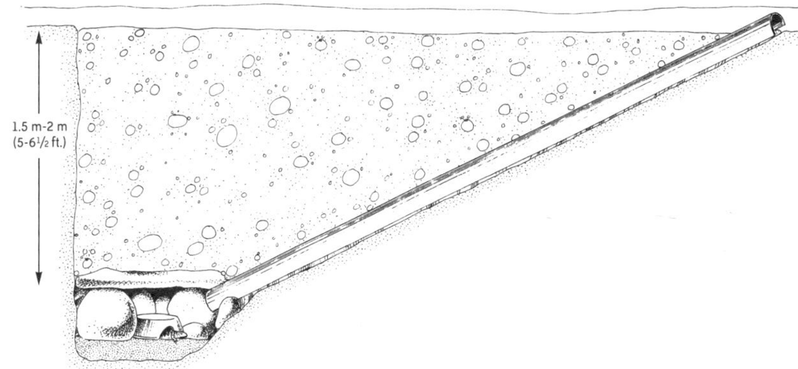

An overwintering shelter can be built for these amphibians with a burrowing nature, as follows. First, dig a large hole deep enough to reach below the frost line. Then put in a layer of sand and place a few large boulders on top of the sand, or put in a shallow, upturned plastic tub (e.g., a margarine container) on top of the sand before you place the boulders. The purpose of the boulders and plastic container is to provide open space underground.

To make an entranceway, lay PVC tubing or a concrete pipe (10 cm [4 in.] in diameter) at an angle of descent that mimics a rodent burrow. One end should be at ground level and the other in the cavity created by the rocks or plastic tub. If you use PVC tubing, cut it lengthwise so that the tunnel has a dirt floor.

Place a large, flat rock on top of the rock bed, then fill in the rock pile with soil. The flat rock will ensure that dirt will not fill in the space created for the overwintering amphibian.

Summer shelter for amphibians is easier to provide. Loose leaves, uncut vegetation beside a water garden plus floating and marginal plants will keep most amphibians happy through the spring and summer, but you can also provide shelter in other ways.

Tiger salamander sheltering under a wedge of bark

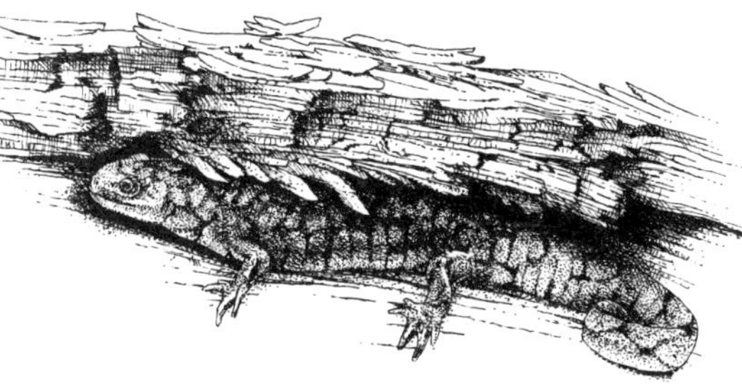

For a salamander, try putting out a 60 cm (2 ft.) board with a strip underneath one long side. Salamanders like to squeeze into the tight part of the resulting wedge area, as illustrated here with some bark. The board should be buried (with a space underneath it) so that its top is flush with the ground. This type of shelter is most likely to attract a salamander if the soil is moist.

Clay pot shelter with toad

A shelter for a frog, salamander or toad can be as simple as a small, overturned clay pot with a small hole broken or cut out of the side to act as an entrance or exit. Make sure the pot is no more than about 7.5 cm (3 in.) deep; if it is deeper, the delicate skin of the sheltering amphibian will tend to dry out. Place this kind of shelter in a shady, protected area. You can cover it with leaf litter, making sure the entrance hole is clear. This type of shelter works best where there is moist soil.

A toad "hotel"

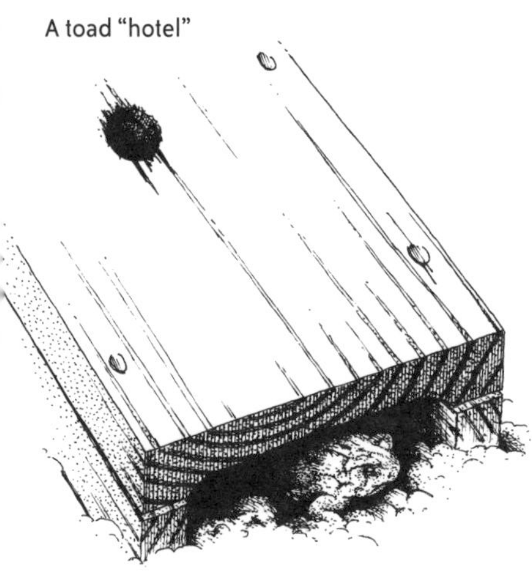

A toad "hotel" can be built from a 30-cm (1-ft.) piece of one-by-six nailed on top of two pieces of 2 cm (3/4 in.) wide one-by-six, one at each side (see illustration). You can build the toad hotel a bit higher by adding another piece of 2 cm (3/4 in.) one-by-six to each side. The entranceways can be sanded or routered, as in the illustration. Drill a hole 2 cm (3/4 in.) in diameter in the top, into which you should pour some water every few days. Flies will investigate the hole (much to the toad's delight), which means the toad can shelter and eat at the same time. Make a small depression in the ground by clearing away some leaf litter and soil, then place this shelter over the depression. Make sure the area is shaded.

TOAD LIGHT

A bright light over some lawn, ground cover or within vegetation attracts insects that eventually tire and land. (Put the light on a pole over short vegetation for best results). Toads will come to sit under the light on warm evenings and wait for "mana from heaven," so to speak.

AMPHIBIANS YOU ARE LIKELY TO SEE AND HEAR

Alberta supports ten species of amphibians. Some are rarely seen, others are more common, but even if you don't see them, you might hear them. There are really only a few that you have a good chance of attracting to your yard. Here they are.

WAYNE LYNCH

Tiger salamander
Ambystoma tigrinum

Tiger Salamander *(Ambystoma tigrinum)*

About 18 cm (7 in.) long as an adult and brightly coloured, the tiger salamander is most commonly seen south of Edmonton. It turns up in root cellars and near sump pumps, particularly in the fall, when the adults are searching for places to spend the winter. In spring and summer, tiger salamanders can be found underneath boards near water. The irregular black and yellow bands in young adults give way to a uniform green or gray in the elderly.

Salamander tadpoles hatch without legs, but these appendages quickly grow and are retained throughout the remaining larval stage. Gills are present at hatching and shrink when the time is near for the tadpole to leave the water. Because they have a large mouth at the front of the head, salamander pollywogs look rather otherworldly. (Frog and toad tadpoles have small mouths that are turned downward.)

Tiger salamander eggs are laid singly or in small clumps of perhaps a half dozen and are attached to rocks or vegetation (see page 47 in Chapter 5).

WAYNE LYNCH

Boreal toad
Bufo boreas

Boreal Toad/Western Toad *(Bufo boreas)*

Toads, in general, are less tied to water than salamanders or frogs, but close to water is the best place to look for them. The boreal toad is the typical toad of the mountains and foothills, but it is also found in the western half of the boreal forest region.

Adult boreal toads have a prominent light stripe along their largely greenish or brownish backs. They also have many raised bumps (tubercles) all over their backs; some people call these bumps "warts." (By the way, handling toads will not give *you* warts!) Smaller than tiger salamanders, adult boreal toads measure about 6 cm-12 cm (2 1/2-5 in.) in length. Their call is a quiet, repeated peeping.

To the untrained eye, toad tadpoles look much like frog tadpoles. Unfortunately, the differences may take a magnifying glass to see. The most obvious difference is the position of the spiracle or breathing tube. In frogs, the spiracle tends to be on the middle of the belly; in toads look for it on the animal's side.

Boreal toad eggs are laid in long strings in the spring (see page 47, Chapter 5). These strings are wrapped around vegetation in still water and hatch in only a few days. A single mother toad may lay 16,000 eggs each year!

Canadian Toad *(Bufo hemiophrys)*
The Canadian toad is green or brown like the boreal toad, but is smaller than its cousin (3.5 cm-7.5 cm [1 1/2-3 in.), lacks the prominent line down the back and has smaller tubercles. Its voice is a short, soft trill. Watch for the Canadian toad in the parkland and boreal forest areas of eastern Alberta; one of the best places to observe it in the wild is Elk Island National Park.

Canadian toad tadpoles are much like the tadpoles of the western toad, and the eggs of this species are also laid in long, tangled strings (see page 47, Chapter 5).

Boreal Chorus Frog/Striped Chorus Frog *(Pseudacris maculata)*
This singer is Alberta's smallest (adults are less than 4 cm [1 1/2 in.] long), most common and most commonly heard frog; it is found throughout the province. If you have a pond near your house and boreal chorus frogs live there, you will be sure to hear the males calling on warm, spring evenings. It is easy to spot the males as they begin calling because they inflate their throats like tiny balloons. Their voice is similar to the sound made by running your fingernail down the teeth of a comb.

The adult boreal chorus frog can be gray, brown or green, and has a series of light and dark stripes on its back, running from head to hips. Sometimes these stripes intermingle. At the back end of this frog, the stripes break into a series of irregular spots.

Adults tend to stay in or very near water, and occasionally you will see them hopping around on land.

The tadpoles of this species have silvery or coppery bellies, and tend to be quite small as our tadpoles go. The eggs are laid in blobs attached to submerged vegetation (see page 47 in Chapter 5).

If you have a water garden or pond with tall grass and marginal vegetation around the edge, the boreal chorus frog is the amphibian species you are most likely to see.

Wood Frog *(Rana sylvatica)*
The wood frog is larger than the boreal chorus frog but smaller than the northern leopard frog, which, because of its rarity, you are unlikely to see. The adult wood frog's usual size is 2.5 cm-6 cm (1-2 1/2 in.), and it tends to be brownish. As well, the wood frog has two obvious light stripes running down its back, and a dark mask about the eyes. Its call sounds like a duck quacking. Wood frogs are common throughout the province except in grasslands. Watch for the adults during daylight hours.

ALBERTA'S AMPHIBIAN MONITORING PROGRAM

The Alberta Amphibian Monitoring Program is helping us get a better understanding of the numbers, trends and distribution of amphibian populations in Alberta. Thus far, the program has been quite successful, with hundreds of records being submitted by volunteers. All 10 of Alberta's amphibian species have been recorded. Although a broad area of the province has been sampled, there are many areas that still need to be surveyed. See Appendix 5 for how to contact the Alberta Amphibian Monitoring Program.

WAYNE LYNCH

Canadian toad
Bufo hemiophrys

WAYNE LYNCH

Boreal chorus frog
Pseudacris maculata

WAYNE LYNCH

Wood frog
Rana sylvatica

Wood frog tadpoles get to be about 5 cm (2 in.) long, and are brown above and cream below, with a pinkish tint. Their eyes are located on the top of the body so that they seem to be looking up all the time.

The eggs of this species are laid in clumps attached to plants (see page 47 in Chapter 5). The clumps may contain 2000 to 3000 eggs. You are most likely to find them in clear, permanent and temporary ponds that are well shaded and have thick mats of aquatic vegetation growing on the pond bottom.

5 BASICS
NATURESCAPING FOR AMPHIBIANS

1. Provide a water source—water garden, pond, boggy area or slow-moving stream.
2. Make sure the water edge is shaded.
3. Leave some uncut vegetation (not too dense) and fallen leaves around a water body edge.
4. Provide a frog ramp or gently sloping edge so amphibians can get in and out of the water of a pond or water garden.
5. Put out amphibian shelters, such as well-rotted logs, a clay pot or a "toad hotel."

ACKNOWLEDGMENTS

Larry Powell (Research Associate, Department of Biological Sciences, University of Calgary, Calgary, Alberta)
Anthony P. Russell (Professor, Department of Biological Sciences, University of Calgary, Calgary, Alberta)

SIGNIFICANT REFERENCES

Alberta Environmental Protection. 1996. *The status of Alberta wildlife*. Wildlife Management Division, Natural Resources Service, Alberta Environmental Protection, Edmonton.

Behler, J.L., and F.W. King. 1979. *The Audubon Society field guide to North American reptiles and amphibians*. Alfred A. Knopf, New York.

Russell, A.P., and A.M. Bauer. 1993. *The amphibians and reptiles of Alberta*. University of Calgary Press, Calgary, and University of Alberta Press, Edmonton.

Stebbins, R.C. 1985. *Western reptiles and amphibians*. Houghton Mifflin Company, New York.

MYRNA PEARMAN

Plains garter snake

Chapter 8
NatureScaping for Reptiles

Reptiles are perhaps the most misunderstood of the animals you could attract to your yard. They are also the hardest group to convince gardeners to encourage and support. If you haven't already considered NatureScaping for reptiles, this chapter can help you incorporate habitats and structures that will allow these much-maligned creatures to feel at home.

WHY ATTRACT REPTILES TO YOUR GARDEN

We think there are some powerful arguments for you to help out reptiles. Unfortunately, the case that can be made for assisting these animals is often overshadowed by an unreasoning fear of them that is hard to displace. But here are our arguments.

First, in Alberta, wildlife habitat is disappearing; one result of this activity is that reptile populations are experiencing varying degrees of stress. Reptiles are an integral part of our native fauna, and without them, the natural order of life is just not as natural and will not function as well. You may not care if you ever see a red-sided garter snake, but can you guarantee your great grandchildren will feel the same way? We owe them the opportunity, at the very least.

Second, reptiles are not like what most people think: They are not slimy; they do not try to "get" you; they won't hide in your toilet; and they don't carry disease. All but one of the province's reptiles is harmless, and if you really don't want to attract prairie rattlers to your yard, we understand.

Third, children are often fascinated by reptiles—witness the rise in interest in dinosaurs and the popularity of zoo-type reptile houses. Supporting a child's interest in reptiles will go a long way toward ensuring any fear of these animals is not passed on or created.

Last, if reptiles are comfortable in your yard, it is less likely that they will venture into your house in search of appropriate winter habitat.

ALBERTA'S REPTILES

Turtles

Painted turtle (*Chrysemys picta*)

Lizards

Short-horned lizard (*Phrynosoma hernandesi*)

Snakes

Western hog-nosed snake (*Heterodon nasicus*)
Bull snake (*Pituophis catenifer*)
Wandering garter snake (*Thamnophis elegans*)
Plains garter snake (*Thamnophis radix*)
Red-sided garter snake (*Thamnophis sirtalis*)
Prairie rattlesnake (*Crotalus viridis*)

LEARNING ABOUT REPTILES

Reptiles are not tied to water the way that amphibians are, but much of their food is found near water, so they are more frequently seen there than not. This lack of dependence on water for reproduction allows reptiles to travel farther than amphibians and patrol larger territories.

Young reptiles come into this world looking much like their parents, most from eggs laid under the soil, or from eggs carried in the mother's body until hatching occurs (garter snakes, for example). A few reptiles have live young that are the result of a placenta-type relationship we associate more with mammals.

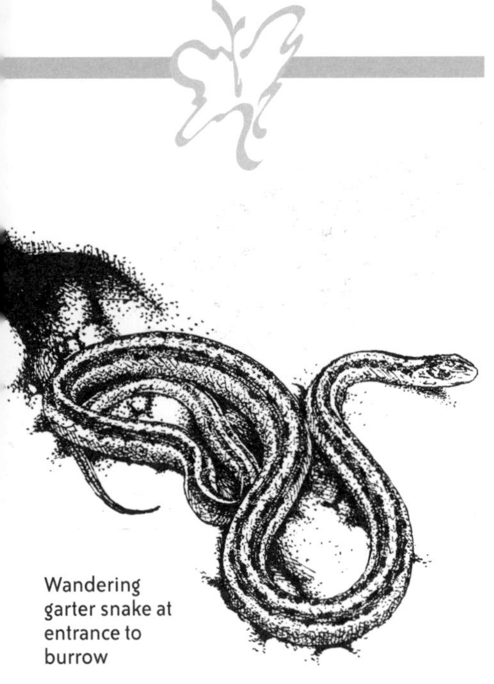
Wandering garter snake at entrance to burrow

Because most of Alberta's reptiles are at the northern boundaries of their natural range, they tend not to gather enough food and energy to reproduce every year. Thus, their populations are slow to recover from disasters, whether natural or man-made.

Like amphibians, reptiles are "cold-blooded." They cannot keep their body temperature stable without assistance from the environment. As a result, reptiles in climates like Alberta's tend to be sluggish in the early morning and late evening—the cooler parts of the day—and active during late morning and early afternoon. This dependence on environmental heat to get kick-started in the morning necessitates careful garden design if you want to make these creatures feel at home in your yard.

Reptiles can fall prey to cats and dogs, even though some of them (like the garter snakes) produce strongly scented chemicals to deter predators. Keeping your large, mammalian family members (including children) away from a NatureScaped area to which you want to attract reptiles will increase the chance that these animals will find your place to their liking.

Perhaps, for a reptile (as well as some humans), the most difficult part of living in Alberta is the winter. However, reptiles have developed some interesting mechanisms to cope with the white cold of this difficult season. You can read more about these strategies in the section on **Shelter for Reptiles**.

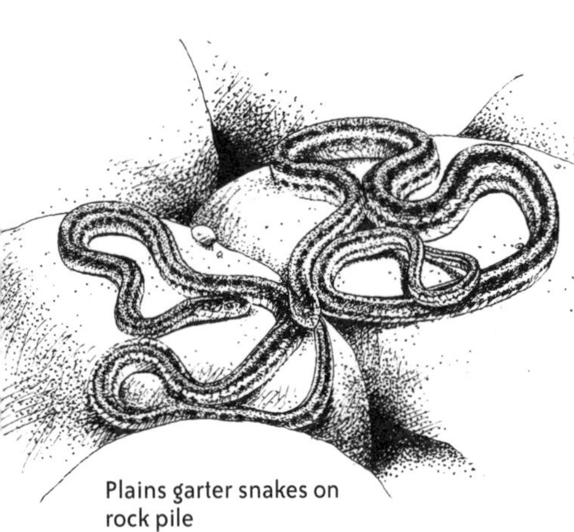
Plains garter snakes on rock pile

PLANTS FOR REPTILES

Like its amphibians, Alberta's native reptiles are primarily carnivores. An exception is the rarely seen painted turtle (common in parts of British Columbia), which eats aquatic vegetation. Because plants are of little housing or culinary interest to reptiles, they, like amphibians, really don't care a great deal about what you plant. They do, however, have some concerns about where you plant.

Let the grass grow where you want reptiles to feel comfortable feeding and searching for mates. Short grass exposes them to predators and lawn mowers. Lawn mowers are just as likely to mulch an unsuspecting reptile as to mince an unwary amphibian.

Reptiles rely on solar power and need to be able to access sunshine from a shelter. (You will often see reptiles sunning just outside their burrows on early summer mornings.) So make sure the opening of a shelter is not shaded from the morning sun. Keep the plants away.

SHELTER FOR REPTILES

There are two things you can build to provide extra shelter for reptiles and encourage them to come into your space. The first is a rock pile shelter. The second is a winter den or hibernaculum.

During the cooler parts of the day (night and early morning), when these animals are most vulnerable, they like to have protection, preferring to be underground, under something or between things.

A pile of large, loose rocks near a pond or water garden is an ideal motel for reptiles. Such a pile provides protection at night and while sunning in the morning, and quick shelter for getaways. If you choose colourful or unusually shaped rocks, the construction can become an interesting part of a rock garden.

REPTILE HIBERNACULA

One of the least understood aspects of reptile behaviour is where and how these creatures spend the winter. For the most part, we don't know where their overwintering dens (hibernacula) are, and because we don't know where they are, we can't protect them. The survival of Alberta's reptiles becomes less sure as a result.

If you know the location of a hibernaculum, or suspect the whereabouts of one, contact the Alberta Snake Hibernaculum Inventory (see Appendix 5).

All Alberta's reptiles, except the painted turtle, overwinter underground in burrows or deep crevices called hibernacula. In rural Alberta, places often will be named for these winter dens. There are a number of locally named "Snake Hills" renowned for the abundance of snakes in their vicinity. These places almost certainly mark locations of overwintering sites.

To survive the cold, overwintering snakes must get down to or below the frost line, about 1.5 m-2 m (5-6 1/2 ft.). If you want to make a hibernaculum, dig a wide, broad hole that reaches sufficiently deep; dump three or four layers of football-sized (or larger) boulders into the hole (make sure they are loosely packed); and for an entranceway, have a piece of PVC tubing leading into the rocks and up to the surface.

Garter snakes in human-made hibernaculum

The PVC tubing should be about 10 cm (4 in.) in diameter. If you cut the tubing lengthwise so that it forms a half-tube (see illustration), the tunnel will have an earth floor.

To keep soil from filling in the spaces between the rocks, use some old planks or a layer of plastic to cover the stones. Then fill up the hole with dirt and you may be lucky enough to encourage some of your local garter snakes to make this spot their winter home.

In Alberta, it seems that more than one species of snake will overwinter in the same hibernaculum. Expect only garter snakes in your yard though—the two other more common snakes in Alberta, bull snakes and rattlers, prefer riverside bluffs for their denning sites.

REPTILE PETS

If you capture a native reptile, keep it for a few hours only; then return it to its natural habitat.

Never release an exotic (non-native) or pet store-raised reptile into the wild. Take an unwanted pet to the SPCA, or ask the sales staff at a local pet store if they know someone who would like a new friend.

REPTILES YOU ARE LIKELY TO SEE

Alberta boasts only eight species of reptiles: one turtle, one lizard and six snakes (see side bar on page 71). Most of these species are very rarely seen. Some, like the short-horned lizard, have special habitat requirements that preclude attracting them to your yard unless you live right in the middle of their habitat. You are most likely to see reptiles on the prairies (grassland natural region), partly because it is warmer and partly because they are more visible there. Keep an eye out for the following species, which are the most common and widely distributed.

Wandering Garter Snake *(Thamnophis elegans)*

The wandering garter snake is up to a metre (three, and a bit, feet) in length, with one yellowish stripe on the back and light yellowish sides. Its upper side is also covered with dark spots. In Alberta, this lovely animal is commonly seen south of Red Deer.

WAYNE LYNCH

Wandering garter snake
Thamnophis elegans

It is often found near water because, like other garter snakes, it likes to eat snails, frogs, tadpoles and such, as well as insects and small birds.

As with all garter snakes, the eggs of this snake are held in the female's body until they hatch. The babies look like tiny versions of mom and dad.

WAYNE LYNCH

Plains garter snake
Thamnopphis radix

Plains Garter Snake *(Thamnophis radix)*

This snake is about the same size as the wandering garter snake, but its dorsal stripe (stripe on the back) is orange or orange-tinged rather than yellow. It also has two yellow side stripes. The upper side has no dark spots, and the dark stripes between the light ones are really dark. This snake is found mainly in grassland and parkland areas in the eastern part of the province, so watch for it south of Edmonton and east of Calgary.

Plains garter snakes and wandering garter snakes have similar habits and needs, so it is quite possible you will see them together, cruising the same waterways, looking for the same food.

Up to 40 siblings of this snake are born at the same time and they all look like miniature versions of their parents.

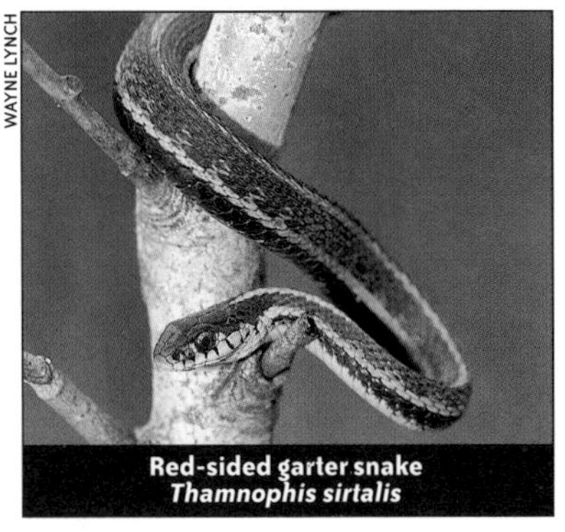

WAYNE LYNCH

Red-sided garter snake
Thamnophis sirtalis

Red-sided Garter Snake (*Thamnophis sirtalis*)

A beautiful species, the red-sided garter snake is distinguished by side stripes that are red instead of yellow. This snake occurs throughout the province but is most often found in the parkland and boreal forest. Although it is widespread, it is less commonly seen than the other gartner snakes.

The red-sided garter snake enjoys the same diet as the province's other garter snakes and gets its food from the same sources. It also hibernates the same way, in large groups, underground.

Red-sided garter snake young are similar to their parents, but labour is probably not too difficult for a momma red-sided—she gives birth to only about 15 young at a time.

5 BASICS
NATURESCAPING FOR REPTILES

1. Keep dogs, cats and children away from an area where you want reptiles.
2. Let the grass grow where you would like reptiles.
3. Build a rock pile.
4. If your property is in an appropriate location, build a snake hibernaculum.
5. Support a child's interest in reptiles.

ACKNOWLEDGMENTS

Larry Powell (Research Associate, Department of Biological Sciences, University of Calgary, Calgary, Alberta)
Anthony P. Russell (Professor, Department of Biological Sciences, University of Calgary, Calgary, Alberta)

SIGNIFICANT REFERENCES

Behler, J.L., and F.W. King. 1979. *The Audubon Society field guide to North American reptiles and amphibians*. Alfred A. Knopf, New York.

Russell, A.P., and A.M. Bauer. 1993. *The amphibians and reptiles of Alberta*. University of Calgary Press, Calgary, and University of Alberta Press, Edmonton.

Stebbins, R.C. 1985. *Western reptiles and amphibians*. Houghton Mifflin Company, New York.

Chapter 9

Butterflies and Butterfly Gardens

TOM WEBB

Clouded sulphur butterfly

Hidden beneath the winged beauty of the mature butterfly we see coursing through our gardens, lies an entirely different world. Butterflies, like many other insects, go through a series of continuous changes (called complete metamorphosis) in order to reach adulthood.

THE BUTTERFLY LIFE CYCLE

Most of the life of a butterfly is spent as an egg, caterpillar and chrysalis, so it is helpful to understand some of the necessities and interesting behaviours of these youthful stages. They are fascinating in their own right, and catching a glimpse of their existence can give you a special thrill of discovery.

Adult

Eggs

Caterpillar

Chrysalis

MOURNING CLOAK BUTTERFLY LIFE CYCLE

The Egg

Life has to start somewhere, and for a butterfly it starts in the egg. Eggs do not show visible behaviour, but there is much to be learned from observing where and how butterflies lay their eggs.

Female butterflies, of course, do the egg laying. To be successful they must recognize appropriate food plants for the caterpillars, and deposit their eggs on or near these plants. Not only does a butterfly species have a preference for a host plant species (see Appendix 2), but also where the egg or eggs are laid on the plant, and whether the egg is laid singly, in small clumps or in large groups.

Egg-laying behaviour is easy to recognize. Usually it involves prolonged fluttering around a particular plant or branch. Sometimes, as with some skippers and the greater fritillaries, it involves walking around on the ground in a jerky, crooked path. You know when an egg is being laid because the female pauses and curls her abdomen underneath her body; the egg is laid the instant the tip of her abdomen touches the leaf. Then the female takes flight.

The Caterpillar (Butterfly Larva)

If you have spent time with children, you have probably also spent time watching caterpillars. Children have a wonderful talent for finding caterpillars and an abundant curiosity about what caterpillars do. On the flip side, if you are a gardener, particularly of vegetables, you may have spent some time and money trying to keep caterpillars from gobbling your cabbages and broccoli. For the ardent gardener

COMPLETE METAMORPHOSIS

Life cycles that include egg, larva, pupa (or chrysalis) and adult are called "development by complete metamorphosis." Metamorphosis is a word derived from ancient Greek that simply means "change in form." Butterflies, moths, beetles, bees, wasps and flies are among the many insects that go through complete metamorphosis.

Great spangled fritillary laying an egg

CATERPILLAR FACTS

Butterflies are not the only insects that have caterpillars or caterpillar-like larvae. If the caterpillar is spiny (not hairy), it is probably a butterfly caterpillar. If the caterpillar is hairy (not spiny), it is likely a moth caterpillar. Caterpillars with a single, large spine on the rear end are also moth caterpillars. Sawfly larvae have more pairs of legs than butterfly caterpillars. They also tend to raise their rear ends when they are disturbed; butterfly caterpillars usually raise their front ends.

CATERPILLAR DEFENCES

Perhaps the best known defence mechanism is that used by the monarch butterfly. The caterpillars of this butterfly feed on a variety of milkweeds, which contain heart-stopping poisons in their leaves and stems. The caterpillars ingest these poisons but are immune to them. They store the poisons and retain them even into adulthood. As a result, the adult monarch butterfly is poisonous, although not poisonous enough to kill a predator. Instead, the predator gets violently sick. The bright orange and black colours of both the adult and caterpillar stages of the monarch are easy to remember—so easy that predators will rarely eat more than one monarch. This chemical poisoning trains predators to leave monarchs alone, and even butterflies that look like monarchs, such as the related queens and the viceroy, receive protection.

There are other ways of using chemicals for defence. Swallowtail caterpillars have a special structure just behind their heads for chemical defence. Normally this structure, called an osmaterium, is not visible. However, when the caterpillar is disturbed, it can rapidly extrude the osmaterium (which is usually orange and often half the size of the caterpillar) and, through it, release a strong odour. At the same time, the caterpillar arches upwards so that the osmaterium has a good chance of coming in contact with, and startling, the predator. This behaviour is usually enough to cause the predator to release the caterpillar.

Many caterpillars are covered with spines that can cause itching and irritation, especially to the lining of the mouth and eyelids. These spines are particularly well developed in the Nymphalids. Although handling these caterpillars will not harm you, rubbing your eyes after handling them can produce a severe reaction. Always wash your hands well after touching spiny caterpillars.

Perhaps the most common defence mechanism is camouflage. Many caterpillars are coloured to blend into the background or into the foliage on which they normally feed—making them particularly hard to locate. The caterpillars of the Satyrids and whites are particularly good at camouflaging themselves.

Other caterpillars, those of Alberta's swallowtails, for example, look like things predators would not like to eat. These tiny caterpillars mimic bird droppings! Some species, notably tiger swallowtails, even crawl out into the middle of a leaf during the day and stay perfectly still, increasing the possibility of being mistaken for bird you-know-what. When these caterpillars get too big to look like real bird droppings, they change their colour pattern completely to the bright colours of warning.

Some caterpillars protect themselves by action. Many will shake the front part of their bodies rapidly to and fro in an attempt, perhaps, to surprise the predator. Some species are only active at night and hide during the day.

Other caterpillars find protection in numbers. Mourning cloak caterpillars, for instance, stay in colonies until they are nearly ready to become chrysalides.

Perhaps the most interesting caterpillar behaviours are related to building artificial, protective "houses." Painted ladies spin webs around their feeding sites making it hard for predators to see them or get at them. Red admirals use their silk to tie leaves into tubes and even tie the tubes together. Milbert's tortoise shells roll the edges of leaves upwards into a tube in which perhaps a half a dozen caterpillars will feed.

The satyr anglewing cuts the midrib of a leaf and pulls the end down to form a kind of umbrella. The larva lives under the umbrella feeding on the leaf until the shelter is too small. Then the caterpillar moves to a new leaf and makes a new shelter. Because the species feeds on stinging nettle, not many predators will try to dismantle the shelter to get at the growing caterpillar within.

herein lies perhaps the most difficult aspect of butterfly gardening—willingly sacrificing some foliage for the betterment of butterfly-kind.

Butterfly caterpillars are at most a few millimetres long when they emerge from the egg. They grow rapidly; the largest ones we see can be as long as an average person's middle finger. This stage is the only one in which butterflies can grow. It is also during this stage that almost all the nourishment needed for developing the eggs of the next generation is acquired. The size of the adult and the number of eggs that can be developed is governed by how much the caterpillar can eat. Therefore, the caterpillar has to be an eating machine.

Except for the caterpillars of a few of our blues (which may eat ant larvae), Alberta caterpillars all eat vegetation, usually leaves, and sometimes flowers and flower buds. This trait makes them vulnerable to attack from predators such as birds, wasps and hornets. In order to reach adulthood, caterpillars have evolved a number of fascinating defence mechanisms (see box to the left).

Most of the butterflies in Alberta complete the caterpillar stage during a single summer and overwinter as chrysalides. A few, like the cabbage butterfly and common sulphur, can do better and have two, three or four generations in one summer. Some, including fritillaries, admirals and checkerspots, overwinter as half-grown caterpillars.

The Chrysalis

After consuming sufficient foliage, all caterpillars that survive produce a pupa, or chrysalis, a quiescent stage in which the caterpillar transforms into a butterfly (pupates). The chrysalis must be able to withstand extremes of weather, including flooding and desiccation, and in some cases an entire winter. It must also be hard to find so that it doesn't become some predator's food.

Very few butterflies spin cocoons. Most spin a small, silk pad that they hold on to with their hind legs. Then they shed their last larval skin, and there appears the chrysalis.

At this stage, all but a few small buds of tissue dissolve. These buds then use the nutrients from the other dissolved tissues to grow into an adult butterfly. At the appropriate time, the chrysalis begins to change colour, taking on the colouration and pattern of the adult butterfly. The wings, in particular, begin to show, as does the pattern on the abdomen.

This whole process can take as little as 10 days or as long as 2 years, although on average, an adult will emerge within 3 weeks unless the chrysalis has to overwinter.

The Adult Butterfly

When an adult butterfly emerges from the chrysalis it does not really look like a butterfly—all the parts are there, but the proportions are wrong. The wings are tiny and floppy; the abdomen extremely large.

Upon emergence, blood from the abdomen is pumped into the wings, expanding them to their proper aerodynamic shape and size. The cuticle that covers the wings is chemically hardened to make the wings functional.

The proboscis (the coiled, hollow drinking tube) is put together, and waste materials from the butterfly's development in the chrysalis are ejected. Now the adult butterfly is able to take to the air. The life cycle is complete.

CREATING A BUTTERFLY GARDEN

In creating a butterfly garden you may want to attract just the adults. Alternatively, you may want to design the "complete" garden, taking into account all the stages of the butterfly life cycle.

Whatever you decide, the process is simple. First, get a good butterfly book (see **Significant References** at the end of this chapter) and pick some butterflies that are found in your area that you would like in your yard. Pay attention to the kind of habitat they like and their habits. If you live in a river valley, you will have a hard time attracting prairie butterflies. If you want to attract a species that enjoys perching, but don't provide perches, you probably won't succeed.

The next step, of course, is to decide to what extent you want to garden for butterflies. In a full butterfly garden you will want to attract adults and provide for all their needs, as well as provide food plants for a number of different caterpillars. See Appendix 1, which has useful information on a variety of butterfly-attracting plants, and Appendix 2, which lists some of the butterflies (adults and caterpillars) that selected plants will attract.

Then follow the process outlined in Chapter 2 for designing a garden. Based on your inventory map, create a bubble diagram. Then draw up a site plan showing what plants you want to include in your garden and where you want to put them. On the following page, we provide two site plans for a butterfly garden—one involving just a few changes and another involving major modifications—using the same urban lot we showed you in Chapter 2. These butterfly gardens are for Calgary and area, but can be altered to suit any region.

As with any NatureScaping project, we encourage you to try new things, take some risks and be patient. Below we describe what butterflies like and how to incorporate these elements into your yard.

Canadian tiger swallowtail on nectar source (lilac)

Nectar Sources

Both sexes of butterflies feed, which is why they visit flowers. The sugars, water and proteins available from flower nectar help augment the supply of nutrients stored by the butterfly during its caterpillar stage. Much of an adult butterfly's life can be spent searching for nectar sources and feeding on them.

So, of all the ways to attract butterflies, planning the right nectar sources for your area is the most important. The popularity of this method stems from the fact that people also like the variety of colours and shapes that flowers provide. Incorporating plants popular with butterflies will ensure that your yard will metamorphose from a still life into an action video.

Butterflies find flowers through the plant's visible colour and ultraviolet reflection. Therefore, you need to pay attention to what colours the butterflies like in the fields and woods around your garden, and plant similarly coloured flowers.

When planting flowers for butterflies, there are some things to remember. First, make sure that your butterfly plants are in the sunniest locations in your yard. A real enthusiast might rearrange the trees and shrubs to increase the amount of sunlight.

SUNLIGHT

Adult butterflies in Alberta love sunlight. It warms them in the morning and on cool, marginal flying days. It enhances their metabolism. It provides guidance and direction in their searches for food and mates. It allows them to spot predators and identify mates. Sunlight in a garden is essential if you want to attract butterflies.

Butterfly garden (minor modifications)

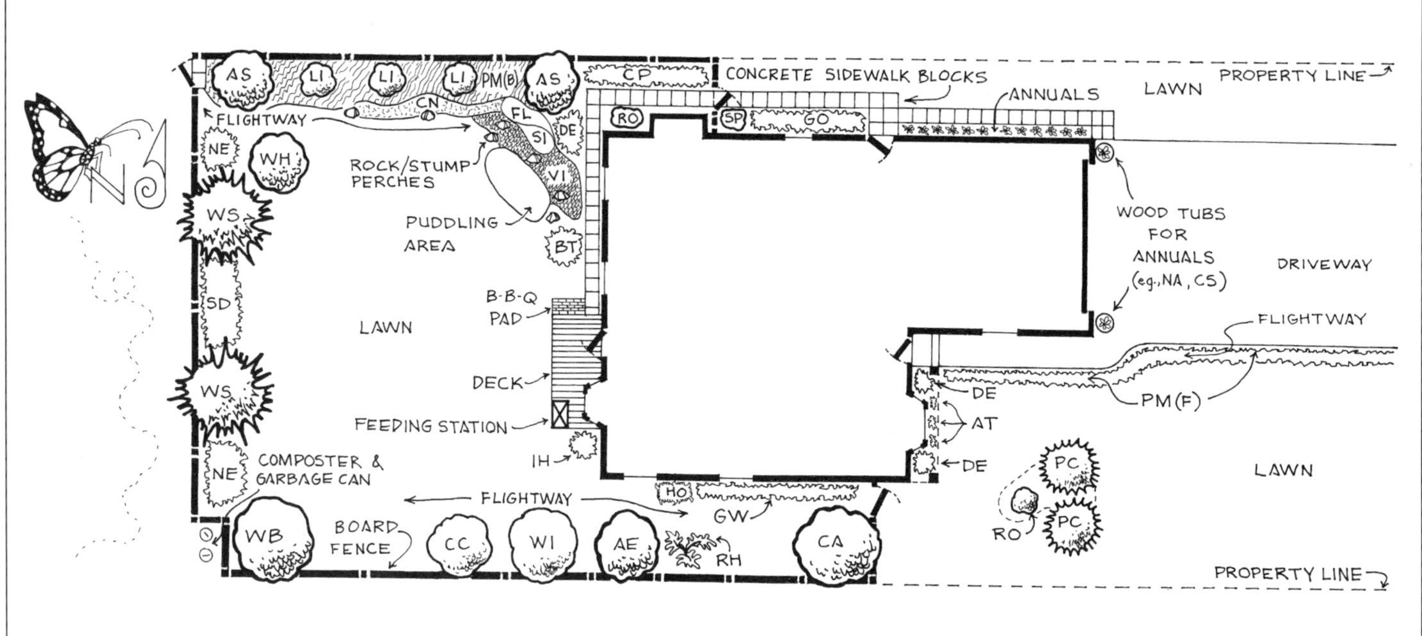

LEGEND

CONIFEROUS TREES AND SHRUBS

PC PYRAMIDAL CEDAR
WS WHITE SPRUCE

DECIDUOUS TREES

AE AMERICAN ELM
AS ASPEN
CA CRAB APPLE
WB WEEPING BIRCH
WH WHITE BIRCH

DECIDUOUS SHRUBS

CC CHOKE CHERRY
LI LILAC
RO ROSE (WILD)
SP SPIREA
WI WILLOW (BEBB'S)

VINES

HO HOPS

GROUND COVERS

GO GOUTWEED

PERENNIALS

AT ASTER
BT BULL THISTLE
CN CANESCENT ASTER
CP COW-PARSNIP
DE DELPHINIUM
FL FLEABANE
GW GUMWEED
IH INDIAN HEMP
NE NETTLE
RH RHUBARB
SD SPREADING DOGBANE
SI SPINY IRONPLANT
VI VIOLET (NATIVE)

PM(B) PERENNIAL MIX (BACK YARD)
AT ASTER
BS BLAZING STAR
FL FLEABANE
GR GOLDENROD
GW GUMWEED
MV MILK-VETCH
SM SHOWY MILKWEED

PM(F) PERENNIAL MIX (FRONT YARD)
BS BLAZING STAR
HY HYACINTH
VI VIOLET (NATIVE)

ANNUALS

CS COSMOS
NA NASTURTIUM

SCALE
2m 6.5ft.

JOHN ACORN

Butterfly garden (major modifications)

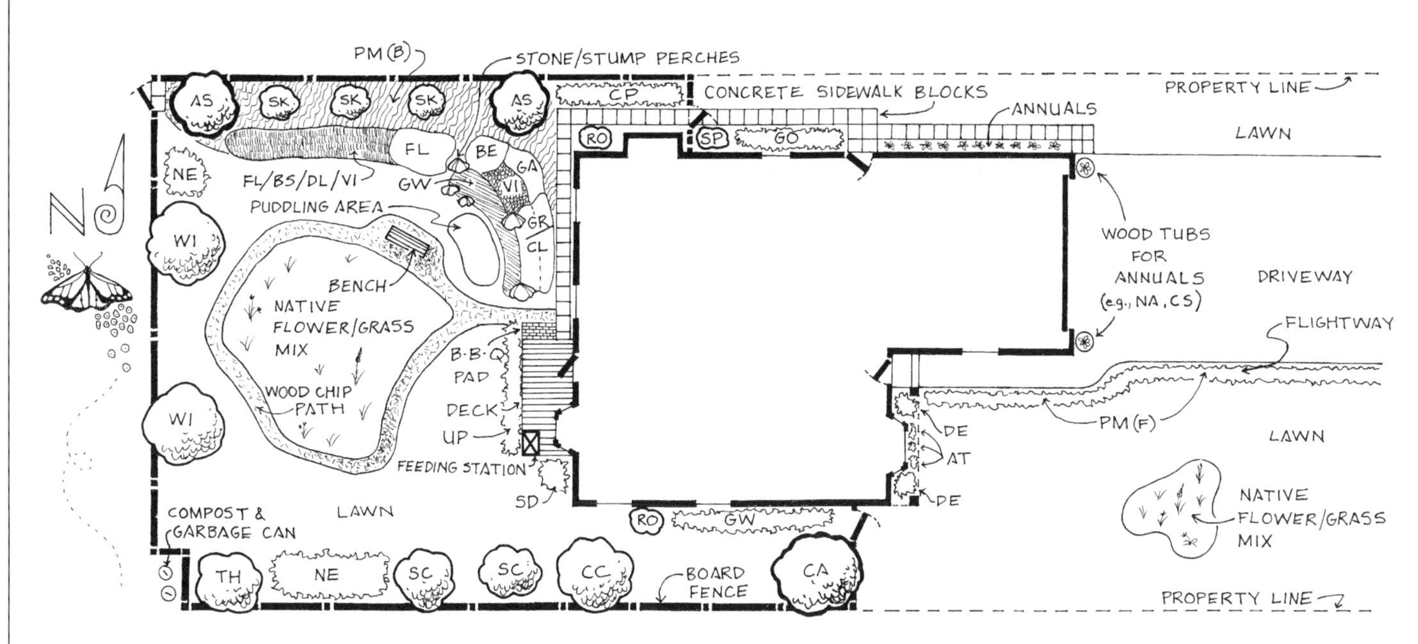

LEGEND

DECIDUOUS TREES

- AS ASPEN
- CA CRAB APPLE

DECIDUOUS SHRUBS

- CC CHOKE CHERRY
- RO ROSE (WILD)
- SC SHRUBBY CINQUEFOIL
- SK SASKATOON
- SP SPIREA
- TH TATARIAN HONEYSUCKLE
- WI WILLOW

GROUND COVERS

- GO GOUTWEED

PERENNIALS

- AT ASTER
- BE BERGAMOT/BEE BALM
- BS BLAZING STAR
- CP COW PARSNIP
- DL DANDELION
- DE DELPHINIUM
- FL FLEABANE
- GA GAILLARDIA

PERENNIALS

- GR GOLDENROD
- GW GUMWEED
- NE NETTLE
- SD SPREADING DOGBANE
- UP UMBRELLA PLANT (YELLOW)
- VI VIOLET (NATIVE)

PM(B) PERENNIAL MIX (BACKYARD)

- AT ASTER
- BE BERGAMOT/BEE BALM
- DE DELPHINIUM
- GA GAILLARDIA
- GR GOLDENROD
- SM SHOWY MILKWEED
- VI VIOLET (UNDERSTORY)

PM(F) PERENNIAL MIX (FRONT YARD)

- BS BLAZING STAR
- HY HYACINTH
- VI VIOLET (NATIVE)

ANNUALS

- CL CLEOME
- CS COSMOS
- NA NASTURTIUM

SCALE

⊢2m⊣ ⊢6.5ft.⊣

Note: In the areas calling for a native flower/grass mix, the species chosen are up to you.

JOHN ACORN

Second, select flowers that will either bloom all season, or choose a variety of species, so that nectar sources will be available throughout the spring and summer.

Third, plant the flowers in groups. Butterflies will choose to visit a clump of flowers rather than single blooms. Flowers in groups can be visited in rapid sequence with little effort. Often, on plants like asters and sneezeweed, butterflies simply crawl from one blossom to another!

Finally, consider the time of day you are likely going to be in the garden. If you are a morning person, plant your butterfly plants in morning sun; an afternoon person should plant them in the afternoon sun. Ignore this factor, and you may attract butterflies, but you won't see them very often.

Milbert's tortoise shell at feeding station

Feeding Stations

Many species of butterflies, including some of the blues and Nymphalids (anglewings, tortoise shells, etc.) will take nourishment from a feeding station, the most commonly used "bait" being a container of fresh or rotten fruit with a little water. You often see these concoctions used in commercial butterfly gardens. Bananas, apples, peaches and grapes are common fare at these stations. Some people add sugar to this potpourri. You can use solid fruits or blended ones, but solid ones are probably better because there is less chance of the butterfly becoming stuck to the food.

Butterflies do not seem to care where you put this type of food as long as it is in a sunny spot. Once they have found a feeding station, they will return every day.

There are two other types of bait that attract butterflies. They are less pleasant than the fruity mixtures but work well for some species of butterflies. The first is carrion (dead animal parts), and the second is animal droppings. Many blues, for example, will enjoy a nice ripe haunch with most of the meat removed, or coyote dung. You probably won't want to put these materials in your garden, but we mention them for the sake of completeness.

We have not tried combined mixtures, but we have the suspicion that the best one would be a solid chunk of horse poop and a soup bone in a large tray with a few slices of fruit. Kept moist. And left in the sun. For a number of days!

Puddling Areas

When a male butterfly mates, he transfers minerals to the female to help supply the eggs and keep her healthy. If he cannot obtain these mineral salts, he cannot mate as successfully as a male that can get them. Male butterflies can only acquire the needed minerals in a dissolved state. Consequently, wet ground with dissolved minerals can attract large numbers of male butterflies. There are locations in the prairies and mountains where you can see clouds of butterflies at these "salt licks." This congregation behaviour is called "puddling."

Butterflies puddling on sand-filled tray, (l) Alexandra sulphur, (m) and (r) Melissa blues

If you can encourage puddling in your garden, you will have an unending supply of butterflies on sunny days throughout the summer. Any mineral source will work. Table salt, moist ashes from a fire, animal (including human) urine, manure from horses (especially good when fresh), and even bear and coyote droppings (for those of you with access to this kind of material) will attract butterflies.

By building a wet area into your garden and adding a mineral source, you can expect to see, sooner or later, butterflies arriving for a nip of water and minerals. The wet area can be a gravel- and sand-filled wood, plastic or metal tray, a low area kept free of vegetation, the edge of stream leading to a water garden, or a water garden beach. If you use a metal tray, make sure the edges are not exposed to the sun or they will become too hot for the butterflies to land. The puddling area should be kept moist as much as possible. The best puddling seems to occur on wet sand, probably because it is easier to obtain the water and salt from sand than from other substrates.

PERCHING BEHAVIOUR

Different groups of butterflies have different perching behaviours. Many skippers bask with their wings held partly open—the hind wing is open all the way, but the fore wing is held at about a 45° angle. Arctics, sulphurs and alpines hold their wings tightly shut most of the time. Fritillaries and admirals prefer to hold their wings fully open unless startled, at which time they close them completely. We do not understand why such variation exists.

Perches

No species of butterfly can stay on the wing all the time. All butterflies need places to rest, to bask in the sun and hide. Many need places from which to look for mates and defend territories (see box below). If you can provide these places, or perches, and make them at least as attractive as those in the wild, the butterflies will come and use them routinely.

Northern pearl crescent on grass stem perch

Some species have definite preferences for the type of perch they will use for basking in the sun. The Mormon fritillary frequently chooses a bare rock low to the ground. The garita skipper prefers a tall, thin grass blade on which it will sit about halfway up. Other fritillaries will perch on flower heads, as will checkerspots and crescents. Admirals most often perch on broad-leaved shrubs and trees, right in the middle of a leaf.

To attract as many butterflies as possible, you will have to provide a number of different types of perches in a variety of places. The best butterfly gardens will contain a few large, flat rocks, some tall grass, flower heads, stumps or old roots and, of course, broad-leaved plants.

Flightways

Many species of butterflies use edges of forests, ravines and coulees as aerial highways, just for flying along or when patrolling for mates (see box below). Therefore, if you can create flightways in your yard, butterflies will be funneled onto your property. You can create a flightway with a hedge, fence, trees, a sidewalk and flowers, or anything else that provides a long, sheltered, sunny path.

NATURAL BUTTERFLY FLIGHTWAYS

In the grassland natural region (the prairies), look for places where the vegetation is greener than usual. Such areas are usually locations where water runs on the surface or underground, and they are a bit lower than the surrounding landscape. Coulees are great flightways, even when choked with saskatoons and thorny buffaloberry. In parkland areas, look for sheltered edges of poplar stands, seismic cuts, pond and stream margins, and ditches. In the foothills, Rocky Mountain and boreal forest natural regions search for forest openings such as glades, marshes and bogs, as well as roadways, powerline rights-of-way and seismic cuts.

FINDING MATES

Among butterflies, mating is almost always initiated by the male. There are two general strategies for mate location that male butterflies use. One is analogous to young guys hanging around the mall waiting for girls. We'll call this behaviour "perching"; it is often coupled with the defence of a territory. The second is more like barhopping. We'll call it "patrolling." A good butterfly garden will take both strategies into account in its design.

The perching strategy is based on the biological assumption that if you have a territory filled with flowers and good oviposition (egg-laying) sites, females will eventually come around looking for either or both. If you are waiting, and alert, you will get your chance. The best place to wait is somewhere with a good range of vision—flower stalks higher than others, branches that stick out, or even logs and rocks. The territory of a perching butterfly can be very complex, with each male having perhaps six to eight favoured perching sites. Each is visited in a regular routine throughout the day.

Therefore, providing a variety of perches will enhance the diversity of butterfly species and behaviour you will be able to observe in your yard. Perching butterflies include most skippers, many blues, coppers, hairstreaks and admirals.

Patrolling is based on a whole different set of assumptions. Presumably, distributions of flowers or egg-laying sites for some species are so continuous, or the plants so abundant, that males have a better chance of finding mates if they search for them. Edges of forests, copses of trees or bushes, small valleys, seismic cuts and forestry roads (areas called flightways) are patrolled by some butterflies in search of mates. This activity tends to concentrate butterflies, increasing the chances of finding an acceptable (or accepting) mate. Patrolling butterflies include the greater and lesser fritillaries, swallowtails, sulphurs and whites.

A special form of patrolling is hilltopping. In this behaviour, males of a few species (notably the Alberta arctic, anise swallowtail and some skippers) congregate on geographical high points. These "hills" may be hundreds of metres tall or just a metre or two above the surrounding landscape. The males chase each other and cruise open areas waiting for females.

Regardless of how they are located, females of the correct species are approached by a male who initiates a complex series of behaviours leading to mating. These intricate mating dances are interesting to watch and are usually unique to each species. They involve much wing fluttering, antennae wiggling and sometimes prancing and dancing. If the male makes all the right moves in the proper way, and the female responds in the appropriate manner, mating will be initiated.

Clouded sulphurs patrolling in a backyard

The most important properties of a flightway are exposure to the sun (the more sun the better) and shelter from wind. Most successful flightways are sheltered by something at least 1.5 m (5 ft.) tall—a fence, hedge or tall vegetation, for example. The best way to get a feeling for flightways is to visit some natural ones in your area.

Host Plants for Caterpillars

To provide host plants for caterpillars you must choose plants that females will use as egg-laying sites. Females recognize correct food plants by smell and taste. The eggs will hatch, the caterpillars will feed and grow, then pupate, and adults will emerge to enjoy the garden as the next generation.

Feeding caterpillars do damage plants. Fortunately, most caterpillars feed in places that are difficult to see. They often stay in the shade or in denser foliage where predators can't easily find them. Therefore, most caterpillars will be able to complete their life cycle without you noticing much impact. (The tent caterpillar, which is highly noticeable, is the larva of a moth.) We suggest you put aside part of your garden to encourage local butterflies and have an area that is especially for caterpillars.

Mourning cloak caterpillar on willow leaf

Remember that the caterpillars of different species are quite specific about what plants they will eat. Mourning cloaks prefer willows, Canadian tiger swallowtails prefer poplars and cottonwoods, and fritillaries must have native violets.

Each butterfly species also has preferences for where they like their host plants. If you plant stinging nettles in the sun, you'll get Milbert's tortoise shells; plant them in the shade and the satyr anglewing will make them home. Willows in the shade will not attract mourning cloaks, and native violets without an overstory of grass or other similar herbaceous vegetation will not please fritillaries. Unfortunately, we need to learn a lot more about the preferences of many butterfly species. When we do, butterfly gardening will get even easier. Please provide us with your observations on the Backyard Watch form (Appendix 6).

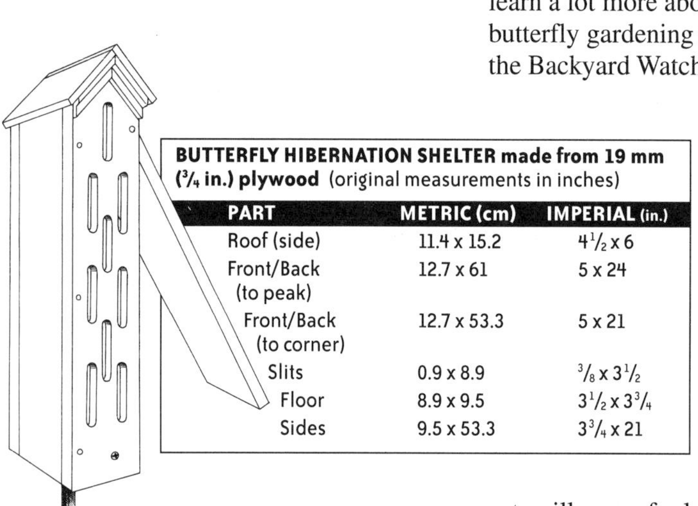

BUTTERFLY HIBERNATION SHELTER made from 19 mm (¾ in.) plywood (original measurements in inches)

PART	METRIC (cm)	IMPERIAL (in.)
Roof (side)	11.4 x 15.2	4½ x 6
Front/Back (to peak)	12.7 x 61	5 x 24
Front/Back (to corner)	12.7 x 53.3	5 x 21
Slits	0.9 x 8.9	⅜ x 3½
Floor	8.9 x 9.5	3½ x 3¾
Sides	9.5 x 53.3	3¾ x 21

Shelter

Most butterflies find shelter wherever they happen to be when it gets too cool for them to keep flying. Some perch in long grass, some on branches and trunks of trees. Any garden will provide adequate shelter for butterflies in the summer as long as you don't overly manicure the vegetation or let the plants get too thick.

Winter, however, is a different matter. Alberta has a number of butterflies that overwinter as adults. To help them hibernate in your yard, leave a pile of branches or a wood pile in a sheltered corner of your lot. Butterflies overwintering as caterpillars prefer leaf litter or mulch. Those that overwinter as chrysalides seem to have no problem finding protected spots, so no extra effort on your part is needed for butterflies in this stage of their life cycle.

Another idea for adult butterflies is to build a butterfly shelter box out of 19 mm (3/4 in.) untreated plywood (see illustration). During warmer months, this box can be put up on its post in your garden, or hung up on a tree, and be a conversation piece or

garden ornament. When fall comes, the box should be placed on its side on the ground. Make sure that leaf litter covers it during a hard frost and snow covers it during the coldest part of the winter. Note that we still don't know if this shelter box actually works, so, if you build or buy a one, let us know of your success or failure on the Backyard Watch form (Appendix 6). Remember to be patient; and even if butterflies don't use the box, other insects might.

NOTE: The source of common and scientific names used in this chapter is Bird et al. (1995). See **Significant References** below.

5 BASICS
NATURESCAPING FOR BUTTERFLIES

1. Put butterfly-attracting plants in your garden.
2. Plant all vegetation in clumps.
3. Provide butterfly perches: tall grass; large, flat rocks; stumps.
4. Have a wood pile for overwintering butterflies.
5. Provide a place for butterflies to puddle: for instance, a moist, sand-filled tray with some table salt added to the sand.

ACKNOWLEDGMENTS

John Acorn (Biologist, writer and broadcaster, Edmonton, Alberta)
Grant Moir (Biologist, and Board Member, Red Deer River Naturalists, Red Deer, Alberta)
Don Wales (Instructor, Red Deer College, Red Deer, Alberta)

MYRNA PEARMAN

A log pile offers shelter to many Alberta butterflies (butterfly hibernation shelter on right)

SIGNIFICANT REFERENCES

Butterflies

Acorn, J. 1993. *Butterflies of Alberta*. Lone Pine Publishing, Edmonton.

Bird, C.D., G.J. Hilchie, N.G. Kondla, E.M. Pike, and F.A.H. Sperling. 1995. *Alberta butterflies.* Provincial Museum of Alberta, Edmonton.

Borror, D.J., and R.E. White. 1970. *A field guide to insects. America north of Mexico.* A Peterson Field Guide. Houghton Mifflin Company, Boston and New York.

Forsyth, A. 1992. *The Equinox guide to insect behaviour*. Camden House, Camden East, Ontario.

Hooper, R.R. 1973. *The butterflies of Saskatchewan*. Saskatchewan Museum of Natural History, Regina.

Milne, L., and M. Milne. 1980. *The Audubon Society field guide to North American insects and spiders*. Alfred A. Knopf, New York.

Mitchell, R.T., and H.S. Zim. 1977. *Butterflies and moths*. Rev. ed. A Golden Guide. Golden Press, New York.

Opler, P., and A.B. Wright. 1996. *Butterflies*. Peterson Flash Guide. Houghton Mifflin Company, New York.

Pyle, R.M. 1981. *The Audubon Society field guide to North American butterflies*. Alfred A. Knopf, New York.

Stokes, D. 1983. *A guide to observing insect lives*. Stokes Nature Guide. Little, Brown and Company, Boston, Toronto and London.

Tilden, J.W., and A.C. Smith. 1986. *Field guide to western butterflies*. Peterson Field Guide. Houghton Mifflin Company, Boston, Massachusetts.

Wright, A.B. 1993. *Peterson first guide to caterpillars: A simplified field guide to the caterpillars of common butterflies and moths of North America*. Houghton Mifflin Company, Boston, Massachusetts.

Butterfly Gardening

Dennis, J.V., and M. Tekulsky. 1991. *How to attract hummingbirds & butterflies*. Ortho Books, Chevron Chemical Company, San Ramon, California.

Potter-Springer, W. 1990. *Grow a butterfly garden*. A Storey Publishing Bulletin, A-114, Storey Communications, Pownal, Vermont.

Stokes, D., L. Stokes and E. Williams. 1991. *The butterfly book: An easy guide to butterfly gardening, identification, and behaviour*. Little, Brown and Company, Boston, Toronto and London.

Tekulsky, M. 1985. *The butterfly garden: Turning your garden, window box or backyard into a beautiful home for butterflies*. Harvard Common Press, Boston, Massachusetts.

Xerces Society and Smithsonian Institution. 1990. *Butterfly gardening — Creating summer magic in your garden*. Sierra Club Books, San Francisco, California.

BUTTERFLY TAXONOMY

FAMILY HESPERIIDAE (SKIPPERS)

Skippers have a rapid, bobbing flight, and many rest with their front wings and back wings at different angles.

JOHN ACORN
European skipper *Thymelicus lineola*

Subfamily Hesperiinae (Branded Skippers)
Most members of this subfamily are brown or yellowish, and the males have a patch or "brand" of scented scales on their front wings. The caterpillars feed on grasses.

JOHN ACORN
Arctic skipper *Carterocephalus palaemon*

Subfamily Heteropterinae
This subfamily is represented by only the arctic skipper (*Carterocephalus palaemon*) in Alberta.

JOHN ACORN
Checkered skipper *Pyrgus communis*

Subfamily Pyrginae (Broad-winged Skippers)
The adults of this subfamily are dark brown or black-and-white checkered. The caterpillars mainly eat leaves from trees (e.g., poplar, birch) or plants of the pea family (Leguminosae).

FAMILY PAPILIONIDAE (PARNASSIANS AND SWALLOWTAILS)

The members of this family of butterflies have a slow, flapping flight. At rest, the front and back wings are at the same angle.

JOHN ACORN
Smintheus parnassian *Parnassius smintheus*

Subfamily Parnassiinae (Parnassians)
These butterflies have wings with a white background and semitransparent borders. Their bodies are hairy, presumably to help keep in the heat in cooler, alpine climates.

JOHN ACORN
Anise swallowtail *Papilio zelicaon*

Subfamily Papilioninae (Swallowtails)
The swallowtails have large wings with a strong black and usually yellow pattern; there are also tails on the back wings. Their flight style is strong and confident.

FAMILY PIERIDAE (WHITES, MARBLES AND SULPHURS)

The colours of the wings of these species are a result of waste products stored during the caterpillar stage. Some Pierids are agricultural and forest pests.

JOHN ACORN
Mustard white *Pieris oleracea*

Subfamily Pierinae (Whites)
The members of this subfamily are mainly black-and-white, with the white predominating. The caterpillars feed on plants in the mustard family (Cruciferae), which includes cabbage and broccoli. The cabbage butterfly (*Pieris rapae*) is a very common urban species that prefers cultivated crucifers as hosts for its caterpillars.

JOHN ACORN
Olympia marble *Euchloe olympia*

Subfamily Anthocharinae (Marbles and Orange Tips)
Marbles have a greenish yellow marbled pattern on the front side of their back wings. Orange tips have this same marbling, as well as an orange patch on the tip of the back side of the front wing.

JOHN ACORN
Pink-edged sulphur *Colias interior*

Subfamily Coliadinae (Sulphurs)
These butterflies have yellow and orange wings, hence their name. The males and females of each species have different wing patterns. The caterpillars feed on Leguminosae (members of the pea family).

FAMILY LYCAENIDAE (GOSSAMER WINGS)

The males of this family of butterflies have reduced forelegs without claws, whereas the forelegs of the females are full-sized and have claws. The caterpillars feed on a variety of plant species and often eat fruit and flowers rather than leaves. The caterpillars are flat and slug-like, not rounded and cylindrical like most other butterfly larvae.

JOHN ACORN

Dorcas copper
Lycaena dorcas

JOHN ACORN

Striped hairstreak
Satyrium liparops

JOHN ACORN

Silvery blue
Glaucopsyche lygdamus

Subfamily Lycaeninae (Coppers)
The top of the wings of members of this subfamily is usually coppery or a brown-gray (one is blue). There are black spots on the underside of both wings, and males have brighter colouration on their backs than the females.

Subfamily Theclinae (Hairstreaks and Elfins)
The front wing of these butterflies has a radial vein with three branches. (Coppers have a radial vein with four branches). The back wings often have delicate, hair-like tails and a black-and-red spot at the bottom (thecla spot).

Subfamily Polyommatinae (Blues)
Blues are small butterflies. The males have blue upper wing surfaces, the females brown. The caterpillars of many species have glands that produce sweet secretions attractive to ants, and the ants will attend the caterpillars. Sometimes the relationship is a simple exchange of food for protection against predators and parasites. Sometimes the caterpillars will eat the ant brood.

FAMILY NYMPHALIDAE (ANGLEWINGS, FRITILLARIES, CHECKERSPOTS AND ADMIRALS)

The members of this family are often called brushfoots because the forelegs are nonfunctioning, furry stumps. The adults are medium to large, and the wings generally have an orange background. Some species have bright blue or silvery spots. The caterpillars tend to be black and spiny, and feed on a wide variety of plants. Many of our most familiar butterflies belong to this family.

JOHN ACORN

Green comma
Polygonia faunus

MYRNA PEARMAN

Mourning cloak
Nymphalis antiopa

CARROL PERKINS

Milbert's tortoise shell
Aglais milberti

Subfamily Nymphalinae (Anglewings)
These butterflies have wings with ragged, angled edges. The mourning cloak and Milbert's tortoise shell, both common butterflies in Alberta, belong to this subfamily.

JOHN ACORN

Silver-bordered fritillary
Boloria selene

JOHN ACORN

Northern pearl crescent
Phyciodes cocyta

JOHN ACORN

White admiral
Limenitis arthemis

Subfamily Argynninae (Fritillaries)
Adult fritillaries are medium to large butterflies that are brown with black spotting on the fore wing (front side). Many species also have silvery spots on the front side of the back wing. The adults nectar on flowers, including thistles and bergamot. The caterpillars of most species feed on native violets. There are lesser (*Boloria* spp.) and greater fritillaries (*Speyeria* spp.)

Subfamily Melitaeinae (Checkerspots)
Most species of this subfamily have squarish, black-outlined, white spots on their front wings. This subfamily includes the crescents or crescentspots (*Phyciodes* spp.), which are black and orange with a white, crescent-shaped spot on the margin of the front of the back wing.

Subfamily Limenitidinae (Admirals)
There are four species of admirals in Alberta. They are quick, strong fliers. Alberta species have a white band on the upper surface, except the viceroy, which mimics the monarch butterfly.

FAMILY SATYRIDAE (SATYRS, WOOD NYMPHS, RINGLETS, ALPINES AND ARCTICS)

The forelegs of the members of this family are much reduced. The vein bases of the fore wings in most, except *Enodia* spp. and *Oeneis* spp., are enlarged. The adults are usually gray or brown with eyespots on the wing margin. The caterpillars eat grasses and sedges. Many species take two or more years to mature. The adults like sap, rotting fruit and flower nectar.

CARROL PERKINS

Northern pearly eye
Enodia anthedon

Subfamily Elymniinae

The two species that represent this subfamily in Alberta have several distinct eyespots on both the front and back of both wings. Both species like wet, grassy areas.

JOHN ACORN

Common wood nymph
Cercyonis pegala

Subfamily Satyrinae

These butterflies have fewer eyespots than members of the Elymniinae, but otherwise they look similar.

FAMILY DANAIIDAE (MILKWEED BUTTERFLIES)

Most butterflies in this family live in the tropics or subtropics, but one species, the monarch butterfly (*Danaus plexippus*), migrates into Alberta. The majority of this family's caterpillars feed on milkweeds and the Solanaceae, which includes potatoes and tomatoes. These butterflies have reduced forelegs, and the males have scent patches on their rear wings.

JOHN ACORN

Monarch
Danaus plexippus

Subfamily Danainae

The monarch butterfly is one of Alberta's largest butterflies (it has a wingspan of 8 cm-10 cm [3-4 in.]). This butterfly is toxic to birds and other vertebrates because of its preference for milkweeds, and is mimicked by the viceroy butterfly.

Adapted from C.D. Bird et al. 1995. *Alberta Butterflies*. The Provincial Museum of Alberta, Edmonton. Please note that there are several different taxonomies of butterflies.

Polyphemus moth

Chapter 10
The Majesty of Moths

We have a concern to voice here. We think our yard and garden bugs, including moths, are fascinating. Unfortunately, we also know that many of our fellow humans are deeply afraid of our six-legged, earthly compatriots, and they're just plain scared silly of moths!

Perhaps this fear grows from the nocturnal habits of most moths, which equates them, in some people's minds, with bats and ghouls and things that go "bump" in the night. Perhaps it is unfamiliarity, or perhaps an unwillingness to share with other beings what we grow in our fields and gardens. Perhaps there are as many reasons for fearing moths as there are people who fear them.

All these fears have no basis whatever in what moths actually do. Moths do not bite (well, except for a small group from tropical southeast Asia). Moths do not sting. Moths do not transmit diseases. Moths do not get tangled in hair or fly up noses (these are the kind of complaints moths get). Moths will not eat your house or your pets or your children. Moths are not ugly. Moths do not cause the dollar to drop or the price of gold to rise. Moths do not threaten the government.

Moths do eat our food (e.g., stored grain). Some moths will eat your fur coats and woollens if you let them. And moths can live in your house if you are careless (or willing).

WHAT IS A MOTH?

Perhaps the most common question asked by people is how to tell the difference between a moth and a butterfly. Moths belong to the Lepidoptera, a group of scaly winged insects that also includes butterflies. There are technical differences between the two, but for our purposes we can say the following: Moths are most often active at night and butterflies always during the day. Moths have a single pair of antennae on their head (their "feelers") and so do butterflies, but moth antennae are feathery or threadlike and those of butterflies tend to be clubbed or hooked. Moths usually have stocky bodies, whereas butterflies are more slender (note, however, the heavy-bodied skippers [butterflies] and the slender-bodied geometrids [moths]). Moth caterpillars are generally hairy; butterfly caterpillars are usually spiny.

WHY NATURESCAPE FOR MOTHS

Moths are extraordinary insects. They are graceful and skilled fliers—at least on par with hummingbirds and helicopters. Their eyes shine with fire, like cats' eyes, at night, and some have eyes that shine with multi-coloured iridescence during the day. Several make sounds to confuse bats, and many can hear the ultrasonic cries of bats hunting at dusk and can react with consummate skill to avoid becoming part of a bat's meal. Some can smell mates kilometres away and follow the scent like a bloodhound to their prospective partner.

Moths provide a significant snack for many species of birds, and of course, bats would not do nearly as well if moths disappeared. Thus, moths are an important

part of the food web. The moths that manage to avoid or evade birds and bats do an excellent job of pollination during the hours when bees, flies and butterflies are not active. Indeed, some plants rely on particular moths for reproduction because only these insects can reach deep enough into the flower to effect fertilization.

Moths, like so many other creatures, need our help. Destruction of habitat threatens a good number of the 110,000 species of moths currently known around the world. Others are in decline due to indiscriminate use of pesticides. Alberta boasts perhaps 1000 to 3000 species of moths, but of all these insects, we know the intimate habits of only a fraction. We do not understand their ecological roles or habitat requirements. We can't identify their caterpillars. We don't know what their feeding preferences are. We are nearly as ignorant of them as they are of us!

NATURESCAPING FOR MOTHS: GENERAL CONSIDERATIONS

Many moths will be nocturnal visitors to your flowers, so what you do for butterflies will often work with moths. Like butterflies, flower-feeding moths prefer their flowers in clumps. They also tend to prefer tall stems so the leaves do not interfere with their wings. Unlike butterflies, these moths keep flying while they feed—they hover and hold on with their front feet as they gather nectar.

Most moths avoid becoming bird feed by hiding. Often the hiding is done in cracks and fissures, sometimes by climbing under things, frequently by holding onto stems of grass and to leaves. They will also choose "safe houses"—places they can fly into but birds cannot, such as under the eaves of houses or garages.

However, most moths hide by "disappearing." In the wild, a creature disappears by looking like something else, and for moths, this something else is usually the bark of trees. Many moths will actually orient themselves to look like snapped twigs or knots where branches have been broken from trunks.

So you can help moths by providing appropriate places where they can hide. See **Shelter for Moths** below.

Many people will have noticed that moths seem to be "attracted" to light. It seems possible that these creatures orient themselves to the moon and use its reflected light for guidance in the dark of night. Because the moon is usually at less than 90 degrees to the horizon, moths will fly with the moon at less than 90 degrees to their line of flight. This characteristic allows them to fly in a single direction under normal circumstances. However, when a light brighter than the moon (like your porch light) appears, the moths will spiral into the light, continually turning towards the closer, brighter light.

It is uncertain how moths navigate when there is a crescent or new moon, but it appears they may find their way using the brightest light available—a planet, star or, perhaps, a street light.

This tendency to come to lights makes it very easy to bring moths into your yard if you want to see what types are living in your area. Leave the porch light on all night, and look around it in the morning. After a warm night, you will find, hanging on window screens, your house siding and nearby branches, a varied selection of what in the moth world is on the dawn and evening prowl.

A SUGARING MIXTURE

You will need about a litre of sugaring solution for the average yard. Mix together a pound of sugar (white or brown—using up your hard, crusty brown sugar is good) and a bottle of beer (it can be stale). Add some denatured ethanol (available from scientific supply houses) or store-bought liquor to make a fairly runny mixture. (You want your concoction to be the consistency of paint.) Some people add blended fruit, especially if the fruit is just past ripe. Bananas and watermelon are popular.

Every moth enthusiast has a secret sugaring formula that he or she swears will bring in moths from as far away as Vancouver. If you've tried a variety of these mixtures, you may have found that they all work just about the same.

Sugaring for Moths

Moths can also be attracted to your yard by "sugaring" for them. The technique is simple. Get a bucket and an old, clean paintbrush. Mix the sugaring solution (see side bar) in the bucket, and at dusk, paint the mixture on trees (rocks and fence posts just don't seem to work as well) at shoulder height. Slop the sweet mixture onto an area about 0.1 m^2 (1 sq. ft.) in size, in a place that will give you a clear view later. Painting a dozen or more trees ensures more success. Prepare to get sticky.

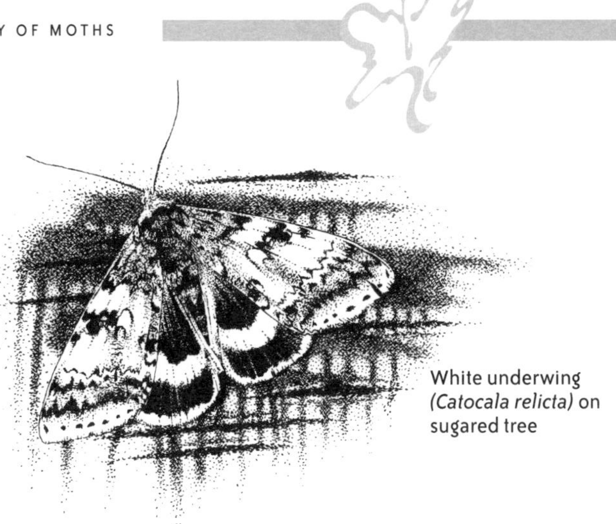
White underwing *(Catocala relicta)* on sugared tree

Do something else for an hour or two, then get a good flashlight and go examine the places you painted. If you are looking in the late summer or early fall, for instance, you should find, resting on the bark, a fine selection of large moths called underwings. You will know why they received that name when the flashlight startles them. The alcohol gets the moths a bit inebriated so you can get a good close look at them; but don't worry, they won't get stuck on your mixture.

If you don't see much the first night, go back a few nights later. You'll probably have better results because the moths learn where the sugaring mixture is and return to it over and over again. During the day, the sugar will also bring in a wide variety of butterflies. Don't sugar for moths where you're likely to attract bears.

PLANTS FOR MOTHS

You or your neighbour might have a fine lilac bush that, in the spring, is studded with fragrant flowers. In some years, at dusk, adults of the bedstraw hawk moth (formerly called the galium sphinx) will swarm the flowers. The larvae of this moth feed on fireweed.

A tiger moth (*Apatensis parthenice*) on bull thistle

A day-flying relative, the snowberry clearwing hummingbird moth, enjoys dandelion flowers and can often be seen buzzing from blossom to blossom during the day. Buzzing is an appropriate term because these moths look, sound and behave like bumble bees. Their caterpillars feed on snowberry.

Many of our brightly coloured tiger moths and our very common miller, or cutworm, moths enjoy thistle flowers at night. Go out in the evening with your flashlight and marvel at the flash of night glow when the beam catches the eyes of these moths. Tiger moth caterpillars feed on a variety of plants, but dandelions and golden bean are frequent choices.

Isabella woolly bear caterpillar (*Pyrrharctia isabella*)

The famous woolly bear caterpillar of the tiger moth *Pyrrharctia isabella*, which in Alberta usually has a black front and rear, and a red band in between, feeds on willow and birch leaves. What we often call woolly bears are caterpillars of the tussock moth *(Lophocampa maculata)*. These caterpillars have black ends with a yellow band in the middle.

Poplars, white birch and willows are all popular foods for the caterpillars of hawk moths and giant silkworm moths. Giant silkworm moth caterpillars will also feed on a variety of trees in the family Rosaceae, including crab apples, some cherries and our native saskatoon.

Spruce trees, pines, poplars and birch provide good camouflage for moths during the day. See Appendix 1 for information on plants that attract moths.

SHELTER FOR MOTHS

We really don't know very much about how to shelter moths. We do know you can shelter larger moths by keeping branches thin in the lower parts of pine and spruce trees. Pruning in this manner gives small perching birds access to shelter but

discourages the larger birds who may want to ingest a juicy moth. Moths can fly in to hide on the bark, but robins and the like tend not to venture into such places.

Moth shelters can be built by stacking large chunks of bark in a shaded area, or by tying a bunch of these bark pieces together and hanging them against a tree trunk or a wall. If you put this type of construction on the ground, it will provide a hibernating area for the winter moths that either hatch or emerge in the fall, then hibernate.

Many moth caterpillars pupate underground and must dig their own way about 10 cm (4-5 in.) down to create their pupal chamber. Keeping your soil loose or incorporating higher than normal amounts of sand into some areas of your garden will allow these caterpillars easier access to underground grottoes.

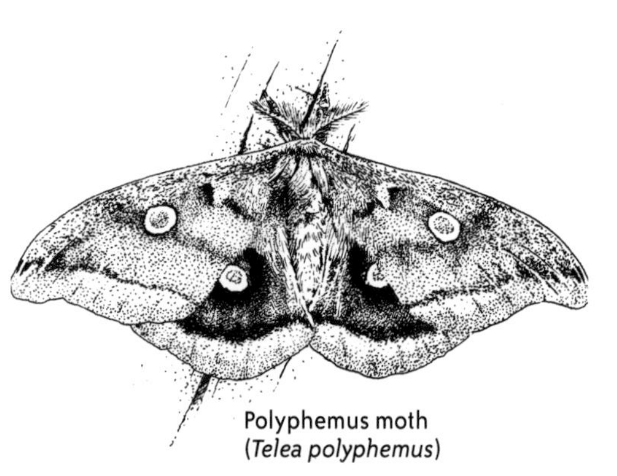

Polyphemus moth
(*Telea polyphemus*)

WS (approximate Wing Span)

MOTHS YOU ARE LIKELY TO SEE

It is impossible to do justice to the many different and interesting moths that you can see in your yard. Therefore, we will describe only a few families and species that you are likely to encounter.

Giant Silkworm Moths (Saturniidae)

Alberta hosts only a half dozen species of these spectacular night beauties. Of the handful we have, the polyphemus moth is the most commonly encountered. The adults of this species do not feed, but its caterpillars feed on saskatoons in Alberta (see illustration on page 5). This species will also eat crab apple and its relatives.

Hawk Moths/Hummingbird Moths (Sphingidae)

Also known as sphinx moths, different species of these large moths can be seen at night or during the day. The "hummingbirds of the night," these moths come in at least a dozen common forms.

If you see a moth with long, thin, pointed fore wings with hind wings less than half the size of the front wings, it is probably a hawk moth. If you see a caterpillar with a single, curved spine on its rear end, it is a hawk moth caterpillar.

One-eyed sphinx
(*Smerinthus cerisiyi*)

WS

The most commonly seen hawk moth as both adult and larva is the bedstraw hawk moth or bedstraw sphinx (formerly galium sphinx). Its bright pink hind wings are hard to see when the moth is at rest because the front wings cover them. The caterpillars of this species come in two forms—a tan brown one and a black one—but both have round, bull's-eye markings on the sides, and both forms feed on fireweed.

Another commonly seen hawk moth is the one-eyed sphinx *(Smerinthus cerisyi).*

Consult *A Field Guide to the Moths of Eastern North America* (the Peterson field guide) for more information about this remarkable family (see **Significant References** at the end of this chapter). If you don't own this book, try your library, as the book is now out-of-print and hard to find.

Tiger moth
(*Apantesis parthenice*)

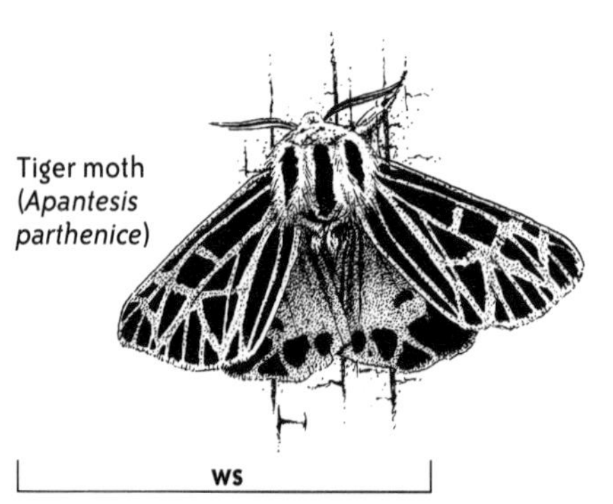

WS

Tiger Moths (Arctiidae, subfamily Arctiinae)

Perhaps Alberta's most colourful moths, tiger moths are named for their bright orange, pink, black and white markings, which warn predators that these moths don't taste very good. We have many species of tiger moth, ranging from quite tiny to over 5 cm (2 in.) across.

Tiger moth caterpillars tend to have long, fuzzy hairs and can be rather attractive in their own right. Sometimes they are called woolly bears, a general term for the caterpillars of a number of North American species. The caterpillar of each species has different-sized and different-coloured bands.

These caterpillars like to burrow before pupating, just like hawk moth caterpillars. It is quite common to see mature larvae or caterpillars of these species crawling around looking for a place to pupate.

Black-rimmed prominent moth (*Pheosia dimidiata*)

WS

Prominent Moths (Notodontidae)
It is unclear why these moths are called prominent moths, but rumour has it that the name comes from a backward extension of the rear margin of the hind wing. We have some very pretty prominent moths in Alberta; some are very common on the prairies, others in the boreal forest.

These moths have long, thin fore wings like the hawk moths, but without the point. Many people like them because they look like they are all huddled up in luxurious fur coats. The caterpillars are usually striped. They feed together, and if frightened, will freeze their bodies with the tail end raised.

Prominent moths are just now getting common names. More people are becoming interested in moths and moth enthusiasts are helping to make information about these insects more accessible to both naturalists and gardeners.

Underwing Moths (Noctuidae, subfamily Catocalinae)
The underwing moths are members of the cutworm or miller moth family and are large, often colourful moths. They are frequently seen in the late summer and fall at lights of fast food restaurants, convenience stores and gas stations. The fore wings are a mottled gray or brown, and the hind wings are a spectacular black and orange or white combination. When disturbed, these moths flash their bright hind wings in the hopes of startling their prospective predator. All Alberta underwings are fond of sugaring mixtures and are easy to attract to your yard if they are around.

Once-married underwing (*Catocala unijuga*)

WS

The larvae of these moths feed on birch, poplar and alder. They have interesting fringes along their sides where they hug the bark. These fringes eliminate shadows and make the caterpillar look like part of the twig on which it is resting.

ACKNOWLEDGMENTS

John Acorn (Biologist, writer and broadcaster, Edmonton, Alberta)
Grant Moir (Biologist, and Board Member, Red Deer River Naturalists, Red Deer, Alberta)
Don Wales (Instructor, Red Deer College, Red Deer, Alberta)

SIGNIFICANT REFERENCES

Borror, D.J., and R.E. White. 1970. *A field guide to insects: America north of Mexico*. A Peterson Field Guide. Houghton Mifflin Company, Boston and New York.

Covell, C.V., Jr. 1984. *A field guide to the moths of eastern North America*. A Peterson Field Guide. Houghton Mifflin Company, Boston.

Forsyth, A. 1992. *The Equinox guide to insect behaviour*. Camden House, Camden East, Ontario.

Holland, W.J. 1968, reprint of 1903 publication. *The moth book: A guide to moths of North America*. Dover Publications, Inc., New York.

Milne, L., and M. Milne. 1980. *The Audubon Society field guide to North American insects and spiders*. Alfred A. Knopf, New York.

Mitchell, R.T., and H.S. Zim. 1977. *Butterflies and moths.* Rev. ed. A Golden Guide. Golden Press, New York.

Morris, R.F. 1980. *Butterflies and moths of Newfoundland*. Canada Research Branch, Minister of Supply and Services Canada.

Stokes, D.W. 1983. *A guide to observing insect lives*. Stokes Nature Guide. Little, Brown and Company, Boston and Toronto.

Wright, A.B. 1993. *Peterson first guide to caterpillars: A simplified field guide to the caterpillars of common butterflies and moths of North America*. Houghton Mifflin Company, Boston, Massachusetts.

5 BASICS
NATURESCAPING FOR MOTHS

1. Plant flowers that will attract nectar-feeding moths.
2. To shelter moths, stack some large chunks of bark in a shady spot.
3. Thin out the lower parts of pine and spruce trees so moths can hide there.
4. Paint trees with a sugaring mixture; then use a flashlight at night to see what moths have been attracted to your "bait."
5. Leave outdoor moths and caterpillars alone.

MYRNA PEARMAN

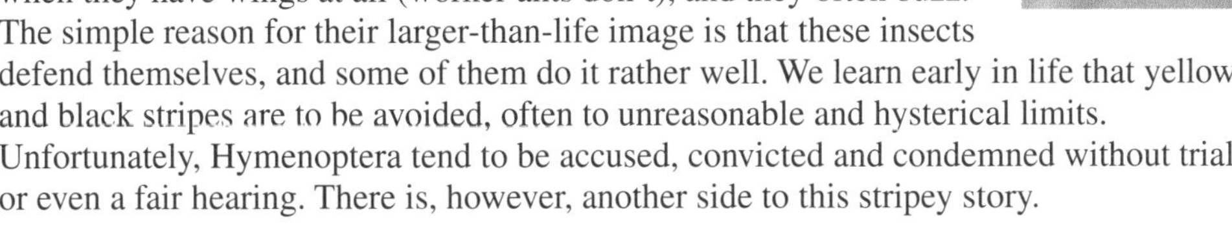

Chapter 11
Helping Hymenoptera

BOB LANE

Bumble bee on sunflower

Of all the insects in our yards, the Hymenoptera (including honey bees, bumble bees, hornets, yellow jackets and ants) are perhaps the most noticeable and most noticed. Everyone knows butterflies and moths, but how often do you remember them in your garden? Now, how about those frisky bees or yellow jackets?

Hymenoptera is an order of insects that usually have four clear wings, when they have wings at all (worker ants don't), and they often buzz. The simple reason for their larger-than-life image is that these insects defend themselves, and some of them do it rather well. We learn early in life that yellow and black stripes are to be avoided, often to unreasonable and hysterical limits. Unfortunately, Hymenoptera tend to be accused, convicted and condemned without trial or even a fair hearing. There is, however, another side to this stripey story.

WHY HELP HYMENOPTERA

Consider what your life would be like without these sometimes aggressive garden "criminals." If you took away the honey bees, you would take away honey and honeycombs. Honey is made from the nectar of flowers—millions of flowers visited over and over by thousands of honey bees.

Honey bee are important pollinators

In gathering nectar, these bees transfer pollen from blossom to blossom, enabling the plant receiving the pollen to set seed and provide the next generation of flowers. The family Apidae (to which honey bees and bumble bees belong) includes insects that are our most important pollinators, and other Hymenoptera pollinate too. Therefore, if you took away these insects, you would not only take away honey, but also most of our crops, wild flowers and a large part of our garden colour. Plants that reproduce by bulbs, corms or tubers would still be around, but many other plants would disappear in no time at all.

One of the most persistent concerns of gardeners relates to keeping leaf-eating insects at bay. We resort to a wide variety of chemical and physical means, and spend a great deal of money, to keep these insects away. But late in the summer, when their populations have built up, hornets, wasps and yellow jackets, perhaps our most feared insects, glean hundreds of leaf-eating insects from the stems and foliage in our yards each day. Many of our ants also spend a great deal of time collecting insects to feed their grub young. Without these insect hunters, our yards would probably look considerably different.

Hidden well below the level of our awareness is a whole pantheon of tiny wasps, sometimes grouped together as the Microhymenoptera. Too small to be seen clearly without a hand lens or a microscope, many of these miniscule creatures spend their larval stage entirely within the body of a caterpillar or aphid, or even inside the egg of another insect. This hidden army of miniature wasps destroys countless eaters-of-green before the latter are hatched or have the chance to mature.

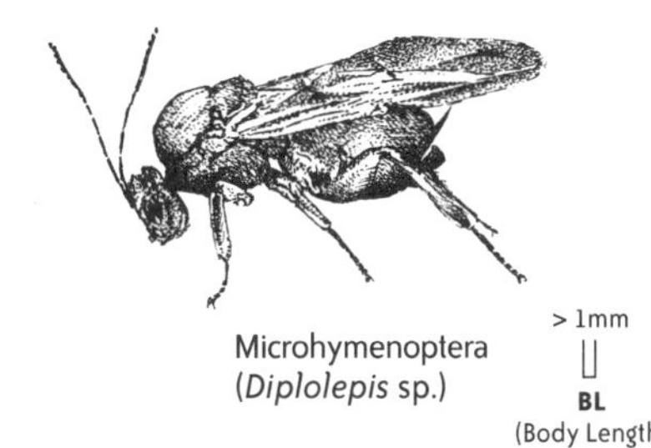

Microhymenoptera (*Diplolepis* sp.)

Note: Body lengths will vary according to species

Considering all the benefits we reap from the Hymenoptera that share our outdoor space, perhaps we can learn to avoid and tolerate the few close encounters we have with these colourful creatures (see Chapter 18.)

ANTS—FRIENDS OF THE SOIL

Whether ants build a large mound or excavate an underground nest, they bring nutrients up to the surface that might otherwise be lost. They also aerate and loosen the soil, enhancing root growth.

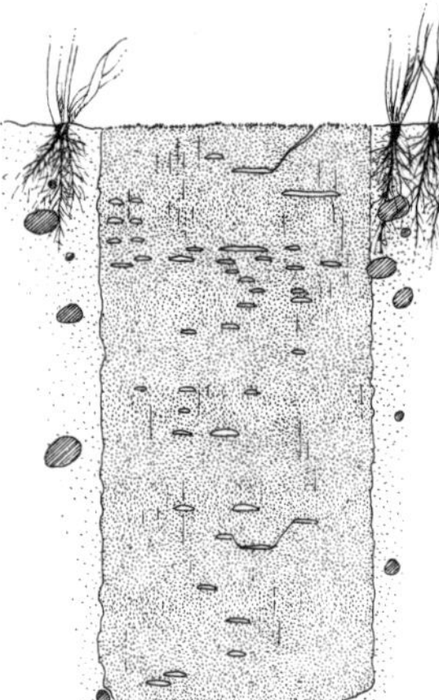

Excavated black ant nest with chambers (for queen[s], food storage and brooding [eggs, larvae and pupae]; tunnels connect the chambers

Yellow jacket–worker (*Vespa* sp.)

BL

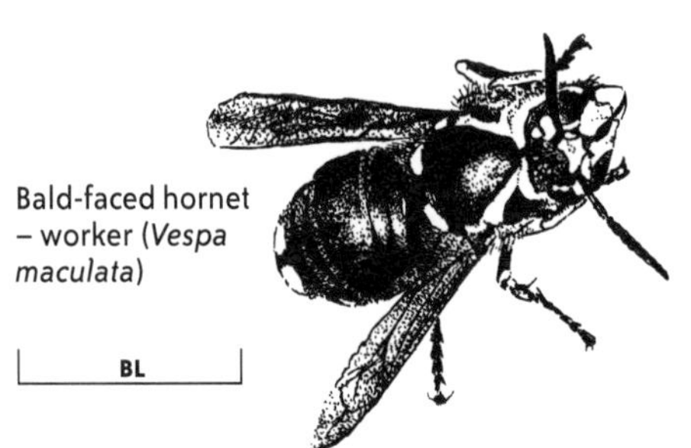

Bald-faced hornet – worker (*Vespa maculata*)

BL

UNDERSTANDING THE HYMENOPTERA

The order Hymenoptera is named for the transparent, unadorned wings that characterize most members of this group of insects ("hymen" [Gk.] membrane; "pteron" [Gk.] wing). The Hymenoptera are often confused with flies and moths that have clear wings, but there are major differences between the two groups: Hymenoptera have mouth parts that chew or are clearly derived from chewing mouth parts, but both flies and moths suck their food. Hymenoptera have two pairs of wings, whereas flies have only one pair. Hymenoptera have simple antennae, but moths have feathered or more complex antennae, and flies often have stubby, almost invisible antennae. Note that there are exceptions to every rule, and knowledge of these general differences may not help you every time.

Perhaps the most encountered garden insect is the ant (supposedly, there are more than 30 species in Alberta). As a child, perhaps you had an "ant farm" built for you by a parent. Now, commercial models are commonly available, which shows how popular these fascinating insects are to children of all ages. The complexity and natural engineering of the underground nest of our various ant species is truly remarkable. An ant farm is a wonderful way to investigate the construction of an ant nest without there being any risk to house or family. Otherwise, our biggest concerns about ants stem from their investigations of our food as we enjoy a sunny summer day. See Chapter 18 for some easy ways to deal with ants who want to share the food you are eating.

Now to the bees and wasps, the Hymenoptera we fear the most. (Yellow jackets and hornets are vespid [social or colonial] wasps. We discuss the difference between these species and "true" wasps on page 96.) It is very important to remember that, when you see these insects, they are only going about their business. If you know that their business consists of a very few activities, and you know what those activities are (generally, nest building and maintenance, eating and gathering food) you can take action to reduce the impact of these creatures on yourself and others (see Chapter 18).

In the spring, a queen bee or wasp has to build her nest. (Nests tend not to overwinter in Alberta, although, occasionally, colonies of feral honey bees in protected parts of buildings such as walls and roofs will successfully make it through, as will protected, commercial hives. Queens do overwinter.) While establishing the nest and until the first workers hatch, a queen is quite passive—her time is taken gathering food and nest materials, and building. (Note that ants have queens too.)

After the first workers emerge, a queen takes to the nest, and the workers, all female, take over the mundane chores of gathering food and fibre for the nest. At this stage, the workers will try to defend a nest, if necessary, but not too vigourously.

After the nest is established, say by midsummer, there can be up to 200 or more workers, depending on the species, and dry conditions can make their need for food more intense. This need, coupled with the problem of there being less food available, can result in workers getting quite aggressive in their food search. Be more wary of bees and wasps at this time.

PLANTS FOR HYMENOPTERA

To encourage all our Hymenoptera, regardless of their stripe, provide lots of flowers; most flowering plants will attract bees, ants and their ilk to some extent. Use these plants to make sure the Hymenoptera are where you want them to be, that is, away from those places where you will be most active. If you put a large clump of bright yellow flowers in a sunny location, you can be sure the bees and wasps will give it their full attention.

Note that many of the nectar-producing plants, such as cotoneaster, aster and caragana, have insect life that is prey for some of the hunting Hymenoptera (e.g., bald-faced hornets, yellow jackets and hunting wasps) so will attract these predators. The leaves of balsam poplar also support many of these prey species.

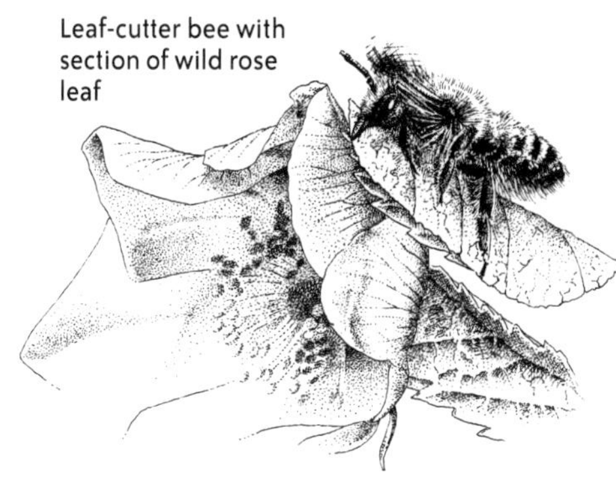

Leaf-cutter bee with section of wild rose leaf

Ants enjoy the sugary fluids produced by aphids that live on the undersides of aster leaves in August and September. These aphids are not the ones that bother you and your car in the fall.

Roses, clover (*Trifolium* spp.), strawberries and alfalfa are preferred by leaf-cutter bees, which use pieces of the leaves to line their egg chambers. Look for circular chunks cut from the leaves to indicate these bees are at work.

SHELTER FOR HYMENOPTERA

Compost heaps provide excellent shelter for ground-dwelling Hymenoptera. Ants, yellow jackets and bumble bees will all build their nests in the loose organic matter. Of course, if you like to turn your compost, you will disturb any nest within, and the tenants will leave (or sting you!). If you want to help out these ground dwellers but still turn your compost, put a pile of grass clippings (about one big plastic garbage bag's worth) in a partially sunny spot where it will not be disturbed. This pile may provide an alternative nest site.

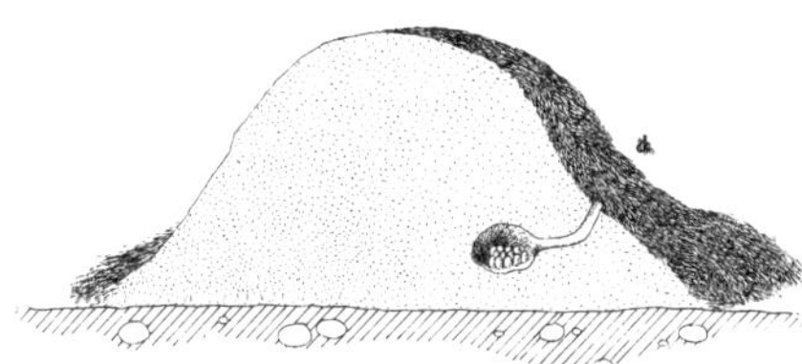

Bumble bee nest in grass clippings

Bumble bee nesting sites can also be made from plastic containers such as one kilogram margarine tubs (bumble bees form small colonies of perhaps 20 to 40 individuals, so can have a small nest). Take the lid off the container, eat the margarine (not necessarily all at once), wash the container, and cut a hole about the size of a bumble bee in its side, at or near the lip. Put leaf litter or grass clippings over the upside-down container, making sure that the entrance hole is visible but the plastic is not. (Research into bumble bee behaviour is done using two-part cement casts very similar to these margarine containers.) Experiment with a variety of hole sizes to see if different species of bumble bees have particular preferences.

An old, clay flowerpot upside down (or laid on its side) and covered with leaf litter will work too. This type of pot already has a hole in the bottom, which must be exposed so the bees have access to the shelter.

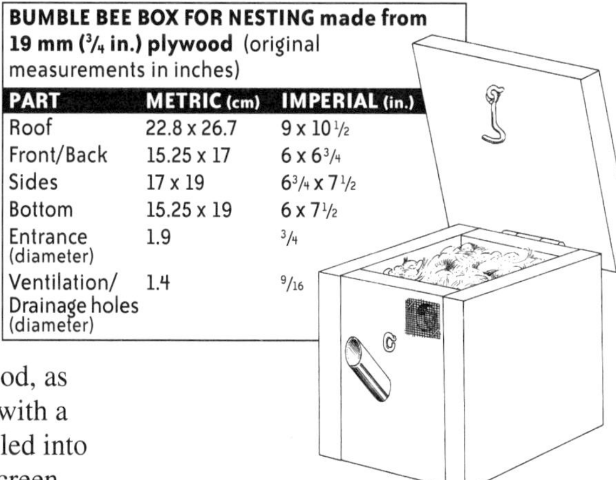

BUMBLE BEE BOX FOR NESTING made from 19 mm (3/4 in.) plywood (original measurements in inches)

PART	METRIC (cm)	IMPERIAL (in.)
Roof	22.8 x 26.7	9 x 10 1/2
Front/Back	15.25 x 17	6 x 6 3/4
Sides	17 x 19	6 3/4 x 7 1/2
Bottom	15.25 x 19	6 x 7 1/2
Entrance (diameter)	1.9	3/4
Ventilation/ Drainage holes (diameter)	1.4	9/16

It is also possible to make a bumble bee nestbox out of 19 mm (3/4 in.) plywood, as illustrated here. The entrance should be drilled down at a 45° angle and fitted with a piece of 2 cm (3/4 in.) PVC water line about 10 cm (4 in.) long. Holes are drilled into the front (for ventilation) and bottom (for drainage), and screened with door screen. The top of the box is fastened with a hinge at the back and secured at the front with a hook and eye. The nestbox should be filled with upholsterer's cotton and then dug into the ground to about half its depth. The end of the PVC hose should be flush with the ground surface. Secure the box firmly. A good place for this kind of box is a partially sunny location, perhaps the east side of a rock pile or hedge.

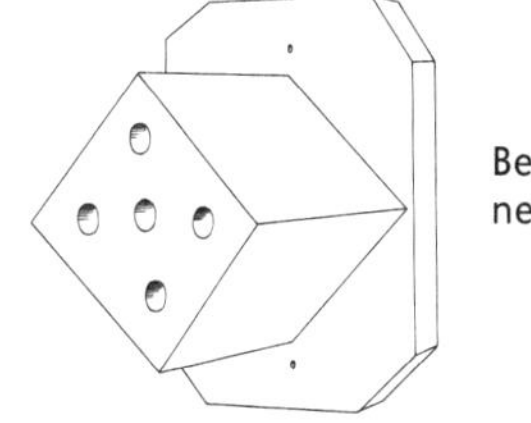

Bee block for nesting

Nesting holes for leaf-cutter bees, orchard bees, and solitary wasps can be produced using pieces of untreated wood and an electric drill. One method is to drill holes into a four-by-four (see illustration) or other piece of wood of a suitable size. Ideally, the holes should be 5 mm-8 mm (7/32-5/16 in.) in diameter and at least 7.5 cm (3 in.) deep—15 cm (6 in.) for leaf-cutter bees. If you have some old logs or a snag in your yard, drill a few holes in them too and see what nests there.

Leaf-cutter bees, orchard bees and solitary wasps can also be attracted by providing drinking straws or glass tubes that are within the size range mentioned above.

MORE HELP FOR LEAF-CUTTERS

Commercial styrofoam nesting materials for leaf-cutter bees are available through the leaf-cutter bee industry. The alfalfa leaf-cutter bee (*Megachile rotundata*) was accidentally introduced into North America from Europe; it is now managed here commercially for alfalfa pollination.

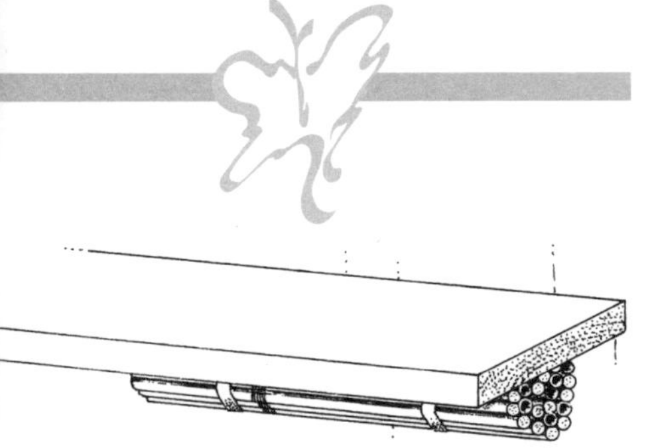

Nest sites made from drinking straws

Raspberry canes work well too. Close one side shut and have openings facing both ways (see illustration). Tape the tubes or straws or stems together into a bundle, and attach them to a window sill or tree in a sunny location. Another option is to put the bundle, with all the openings facing out, into a used aluminum can, and secure the can with the top facing sideways.

Any of these bee and solitary wasp structures with nesting tunnels can be mounted on a post or fence 1m-1.5 m (3-5 ft.) above ground. They should all be near a flower garden.

You can further assist solitary wasps by providing an undisturbed sand pile or sandbox in which they can create their burrows; pieces of sandstone with holes and cracks also make excellent nest sites.

HORNETS, YELLOW JACKETS AND "TRUE" WASPS

There is one species of hornet in Alberta, the bald-faced hornet (*Vespa maculata*), and it is white and black. There are many species of yellow jackets and what entomologists call "true" wasps in Alberta, and the species in the province are all yellow and black or yellow and brown. Yellow jackets have three "dumpy" body segments, but true wasps look long and slender. The legs of true wasps are also longer than those of yellow jackets. (Solitary wasps are parasitic wasps, not true wasps.)

Hornets usually nest underground; above-ground nests are enclosed and very well hidden. Yellow jackets will also nest underground and their above-ground nests are enclosed in "paper." Most of the gray, rounded, papery nests we see hanging from buildings or tree branches are yellow jacket nests. We often attribute them to what we call "paper wasps," but the real paper wasps live only in grassland areas and, like all true wasps, have hanging, open nests with no outer covering.

COMMON HYMENOPTERA

All of us are familiar with the commonly encountered Hymenoptera types, and it is not the purpose of this book to discuss the many views people have about the differences between wasps, hornets and yellow jackets (see side bar). Rather, we will give you some background on honey bees, bumble bees and ants, and we will also introduce you to some of the less familiar but fascinating Hymenoptera groups you can encourage without worrying about adverse encounters.

Honey Bees and Bumble Bees (Apidae, sometimes Bombidae)

Some people who studied these wonderful insects in the recent past separated the bumble bees from the honey bees and put them in their own family (Bombidae). The most recent classification (developed primarily by Canadian scientists, we might add) puts the two groups together as Apidae. Therefore, depending on the age of your reference, you may find either classification in use.

Almost all the honey bees you see are from commercial honey and beeswax operations. Each honey bee colony consists of a queen (who lays all the eggs), female workers and male drones. The nest includes the honeycomb, which consists of hexagonal cells that are used to rear the young and to store honey and pollen. The bees may fly many kilometres in search of nectar and pollen.

The species used in the honey business is the western honey bee, *Apis mellifera*, and no, there are no killer bees in Alberta. Nor are there likely to be any in the future—they don't seem to handle the cold well. It is easy to find books written about bees and beekeeping, so we won't dwell long on the honey bee.

Honey bee–worker (*Apis* sp.)

Bumble bee–worker (*Bombus* sp.)

There are about 20 species of bumble bees in Alberta; the number you come up with depends on how you classify them. Most of these bees are fairly small, and succeeding generations get smaller as the summer progresses. Newly hatched fall workers are typically smaller than newly hatched spring workers. There is a single species that gets quite large (*Bombus nevadensis*) and often startles people because of its size.

Bumble bees normally make small nests, with a few dozen workers. When the nest is disturbed, the workers defend it either by swarming, like honey bees and yellow jackets, or they buzz vigourously and move rapidly around the entrance to the nest.

It is true that honey bees can only sting once. They usually leave their stinger in the skin, fatally injuring themselves when they leave. They do not bite. Bumble bees can sting more than once, and they have a much larger stinger. Consequently, their stings tend to be more painful than the stings of honey bees. There is, however, much debate over whether hornets or bumble bees have the worst sting. We have not conducted the necessary experiments to end the debate.

Leaf-cutter bee (*Megachile* sp.)

BL

Leaf-Cutter Bees (Megachilidae)

There are many native species of leaf-cutters that are having a hard time due to habitat loss and competition with the now abundant agricultural species (the alfalfa leaf-cutter). If they aren't using human-made nest sites, leaf-cutter bees excavate linear burrows in soil, rotting wood or the pithy stems of plants. Then, wherever they are nesting, they build chambers stuffed with pollen. The pollen is wrapped in bits of leaves that the female bee cuts out of plants (see earlier). Each egg chamber becomes a miniature sushi-like package of pollen on which the larva (one egg is laid per chamber) can feed and mature. There are a variety of species of leaf-cutters, each a different size, and with their own preference about where the best place is to build nest chambers.

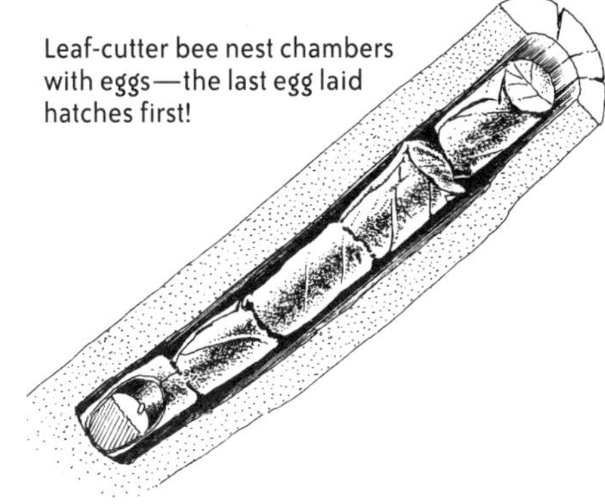
Leaf-cutter bee nest chambers with eggs—the last egg laid hatches first!

Leaf-cutter bees are relatively harmless and can provide many hours of enjoyment, if you can find the time to watch them cut their leaf pieces or stuff their brood chambers. In **Shelter for Hymenoptera**, we described various ways you can provide nesting sites for these bees. Leaf-cutters are solitary, so you don't have to worry about large populations in the fall.

Orchard Bees (Megachilidae)

Orchard bees (also called mason bees) belong to the same family as the leaf-cutter bees and behave in much the same way, with a few twists. They create egg chambers similar to those of leaf-cutter bees, but sometimes they make the chambers of mud and build them under stones, in beetle holes or in the cracks of trees. In Alberta, the nests of these species are easily recognizable because the egg chambers are not lined with leaves, and are separated by plugs of mud, or sometimes sawdust that the bees have chewed from some nearby punky piece of wood. The nesting holes of these bees are always capped with mud. It is a good bet that any solitary bee not carrying leaf bits when seen entering a hole in a piece of wood is an orchard bee.

Orchard bee (*Osmia* sp.)

BL

Orchard bees are present in Alberta, but little is known about their use of human-made nesting sites. You can help us discover more about these bees by using the Backyard Watch form (Appendix 6) to record and report your observations.

Solitary Wasps (Sphecidae, Pompilidae, Mutillidae, etc.)

Usually smaller than most of our colonial wasps, and often more slender in shape, these wasps are superb hunters of a wide variety of insects and spiders. They are usually black, black-and-white or black and yellow striped, the stripes indicating that these insects do indeed sting. (They sting their prey but rarely sting humans.)

Solitary wasps tend to build nest chambers in stems of plants such as raspberries, or in sandy soil. Their sand burrows can be up to 0.5 m (1.5 ft.) in length and rarely branch. At the end of the burrow, there is a small chamber that is filled with paralyzed, but still living, insects (or, perhaps spiders, or caterpillars, etc., depending on the species of solitary wasp). An egg is laid and the burrow sealed. Once a burrow is fully stocked and sealed, a new burrow is started. (The helpless prey provide food for a newly hatched wasp, who eventually digs its way out of the burrow.)

Solitary wasp (*Bembix* sp.)

BL

In **Shelter for Hymenoptera**, we described a few easy ways to provide solitary wasps with nesting opportunities. If you have abundant flowers and foliage in your yard, these wasps will be able to forage for the food they need to "stock their larders."

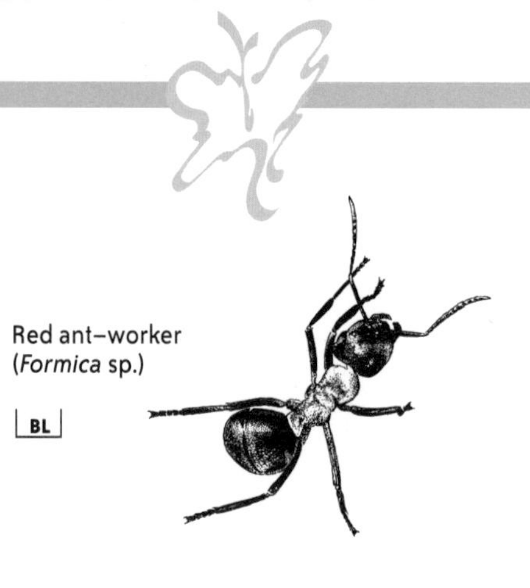

Red ant–worker (*Formica* sp.)

BL

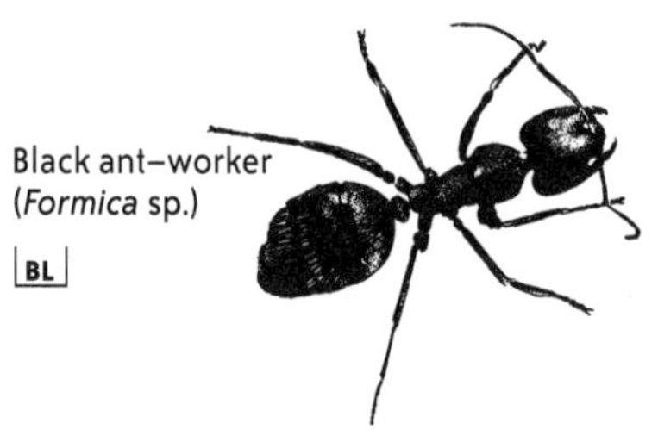

Black ant–worker (*Formica* sp.)

BL

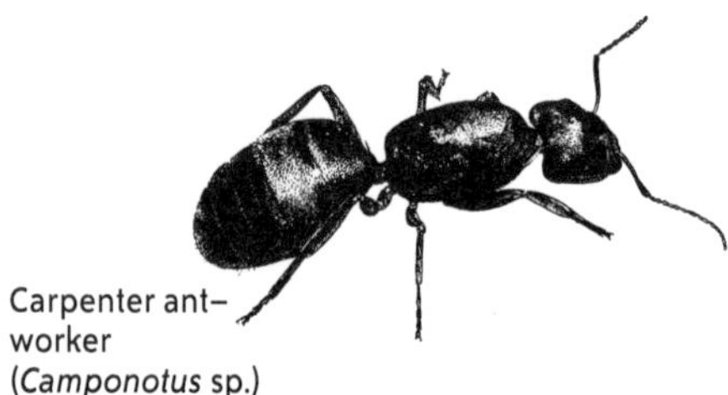

Carpenter ant–worker (*Camponotus* sp.)

BL

Ants (Formicidae)

The benefits of having ant nests in your yard have been described earlier. Most ant nests cause no problem because the nest is an excavation rather than a large mound. Alberta's prominent mound-building ant species include the infamous red ants, although there are black mound builders as well. You are most likely to see excavated nests of the innocuous black ant in your yard, particularly in the lawn, where the soil level may be slightly raised over the nest.

Ants display an incredible variety of size, colour and behaviour. There are three castes in most ant nests—the queen, males (whose main function is to fertilize the queen), and workers. Workers hatch from unfertilized eggs and are females that cannot reproduce. Some ant species tend aphids, some hunt other ants, and some parasitize the nests of other ants. Unfortunately, we don't know very much about ants, and we are only scratching the surface of ant classification and behaviour.

Ant nests are started by single queens after their mating flight. The queen lands, chews off her wings (or they fall off) and searches for a good place to start her nest. Like yellow jackets and bumble bees, she must do all the work herself at the start. But when workers hatch, she takes on the role of egg laying in earnest and may lay millions of eggs in her lifetime. In order to get rid of an ant colony permanently, you must kill the queen; however, disturbing a nest sufficiently, with water or a shovel, is often enough to convince the ants to move.

You will often find ants crawling over your legs, feet or hands while working in the garden. Unless you do something to alarm them, in which case they will run around frantically, and perhaps sting or bite (depending on the species), these ants will just go about their business searching for food. Most of the ants in Alberta are in the subfamily Formicinae, whose female workers (the ants you are most likely to encounter), do not sting. The only time you can really expect to be stung or bitten is if you disturb a nest.

Carpenter ants are members of the genus *Camponotus*. The mound-building ants we see are usually *Formica* or *Polygerus* species. The common black ants of your lawn and garden are members of the genus *Formica*. Identifying most of our ants to the species level requires a great deal of experience with specialized literature.

5 BASICS
NATURESCAPING FOR HYMENOPTERA

1. Plant lots of flowers, especially yellow ones, in a sunny location.
2. Plant roses, strawberries, clover or alfalfa for leaf-cutter bees.
3. Put out a bee block, or tape some straws together with one end shut and attach the bundle beneath a window still (for leaf-cutter bees, orchard bees and solitary wasps).
4. Make a bumble bee nest.
5. Don't destroy an excavated ant nest in your yard.

ACKNOWLEDGMENTS

John Acorn (Biologist, writer and broadcaster, Edmonton, Alberta)
Bert Finnamore (Curator of Invertebrate Zoology, Provincial Museum of Alberta, Edmonton, Alberta)
Dan L. Johnson (Senior Research Scientist, Agriculture and Agri-Food Canada Research Centre, Lethbridge, Alberta)
Grant Moir (Biologist, and Board Member, Red Deer River Naturalists, Red Deer, Alberta)
Ken Richards (Manager, Plant Gene Resources of Canada, Agriculture and Agri-Food Canada, Saskatoon, Saskatchewan)
Don Wales (Instructor, Red Deer College, Red Deer, Alberta)

SIGNIFICANT REFERENCES

Borror, D.J., and R.E. White. 1970. *A field guide to insects: America north of Mexico*. A Peterson Field Guide. Houghton Mifflin Company, Boston, Massachusetts.

Forsyth, A. 1992. *The Equinox guide to insect behaviour*. Camden House, Camden East.

Goulet, H., and J.T. Huber. 1993. *Hymenoptera of the world and identification guide to families*. Canada Communication Group - Publishing, Ottawa.

Milne, L., and M. Milne. 1980. *The Audubon Society field guide to North American insects and spiders*. Alfred A. Knopf, New York.

Stokes, D.W. 1983. *A guide to observing insect lives*. Stokes Nature Guide. Little, Brown and Company, Boston and Toronto.

Wilson, E.O. 1971. *The insect societies*. Harvard University Press, Cambridge, Massachusetts.

Chapter 12
Beetles and NatureScaping

Ground beetle

Many people like beetles, although they may not admit it. Have you ever been startled by, and taken pleasure in, the bright colours of the beetles that visit the flowers in your yard? And have you ever watched the single-minded ramblings of a ground beetle as it tootled around your garden? You might have wondered how the beetle coordinates its six legs during its rapid investigations, or how it can tell where it is going, or why it is going there.

WHY BOOST BEETLES

In spite of this wonderful diversity scooting about in the world, we tend to notice beetles only when they show up where we don't want them. Many are good for the garden, however, and we hope to convince you to look again at these hard-bodied, industrious denizens of your yard.

Alberta's native beetle populations are threatened by the same things that bother our other insects, especially habitat destruction. Because there are so many beetles, a fair amount of research has been done on how they respond to different types of human activity, such as logging. We are learning that these insects can be useful indicators of habitat degradation and change, and that they need our consideration when we NatureScape our yards and gardens.

Beetles are an important part of the food web and form major components of meals for a great many animals. During their nightly forays, bats consume many beetles. Mice often enjoy a juicy, beetle snack. Many insectivorous birds eat beetles and their larvae, and feed both to their young.

LEARNING ABOUT BEETLES

Beetles are those insects that have turned their first pair of wings into hard, protective shells. That's why they are so crunchy. Like butterflies and moths, they undergo complete metamorphosis, starting as eggs and progressing through larval, pupal and adult stages. Some researchers think that the development of hard fore wings has allowed adult beetles to exploit habitats that would rip and shred delicate wings. These habitats include soil, inside logs and under bark, and the space beneath rocks.

There are probably several million species of beetles in the world. Of these, about 200,000 different species have been catalogued by scientists. One in every five known living things is a beetle! Given this tremendous number of beetle-kind you can imagine that they have an incredible range and variety of size, colour and shape. Some are as small as 1/25 of a millimetre long, and others more than fill your hand. Artists have yet to invent a colour that some beetle hasn't already sported for millennia. In fact, J.B.S. Haldane, a great 19th century evolutionary naturalist, when once asked what the study of nature had taught him about his Creator, is reported to have replied that the Creator "has an inordinate fondness of beetles."

These abundant creatures seem to get along well with us and follow us wherever we go. Consequently, there are many common Alberta beetles that originated elsewhere.

Like the ubiquitous house sparrow, they came from afar, but unlike the house sparrow, most of us aren't aware of our beetle hitchhikers. Unfortunately, when these beetles get to a new home they often become insect "pests."

BOOSTING BEETLES: SOME GENERAL CONSIDERATIONS

Beetles need food and shelter just like other living things, but there are so many types it is difficult to say much about how to provide for their needs. No matter what you do, some beetle species will probably benefit. There are, however, a couple of important "don'ts" that we can pass on, as well as a few things we encourage you to think about.

Don't spray. Insecticides are usually non-selective in their killing, and innocent beetles (and other insects) may suffer as a result. Powders for the ground can take out ground beetles, among our best allies in dealing with ground-dwelling pests. Aerial sprays can take down beetles as they disperse from one place to another, or search for mates and food sources. Topical sprays for things like aphids and leaf hoppers kill the larvae and adults of ladybird beetles (ladybugs), which are very helpful in keeping the leaf-eaters under control. Most of the things you might spray for can be controlled in other ways, if you take the time to learn about them (see Chapter 18).

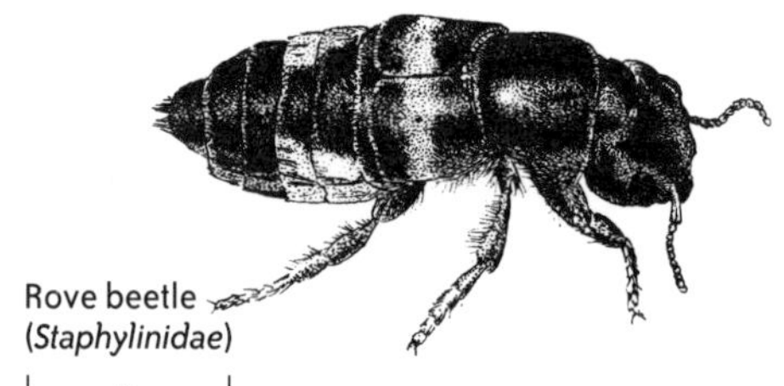

Rove beetle (*Staphylinidae*)

BL (Body Length)

NOTE: Body length will vary according to species

Don't fill your yard with sterile borders and concrete. Red shale looks nice, and it has its place, but such uniform ground cover often precludes beetle survival—it overheats the ground and provides no place for beetle egg laying or feeding. An organic cover such as bark chips doesn't heat up as much during the day and provides shelter and food sources for many beetles.

Encourage loosely packed soils by adding mulch and sand. Many of our common beetles, including the aquatic diving beetles you see under the streetlights in the spring or fall, pupate underground near water. The larvae must be able to dig themselves out of their hibernating and pupal chambers in order to make the transition to the adult stage safely. Furthermore, many adult ground and rove beetles dig about in the soil looking for edibles, which is easier if the soil is fluffed up.

Whirligig beetle (*Gyrinidae*)

BL

Put in a water garden. Streams and ponds make great habitats for a wide variety of beetles. Whirligig beetles spin and dance on the water surface, and diving beetle adults and larvae, which are excellent swimmers and highly predaceous, keep mosquitoes under control. Ground beetles drink from a water garden edge, and many interesting beetle species thrive in the wet soil and ground cover surrounding bodies of water.

Include native plants in your beds and hedges. Native beetles like native plants to feed on and live in; there is a wide variety of bark-loving and wood-boring beetles that will not significantly harm your trees and shrubs. Some beetles crawl around on the bark, never touching the ground. Remember, it is not usually native beetles that cause horticultural or household problems, rather, it's the hitchhikers.

PLANTS FOR BEETLES

Just about any plant you have or put in your garden is going to be helpful to some beetle or other. Therefore, we haven't included beetle information in Appendix 1. However, here is a little information about plants that are particularly attractive to some of the more interesting beetles.

Wild roses (for example, *Rosa acicularis*) support some beautiful beetles. Weevils that are blood-red feed on unopened flower buds, and many longhorn beetle species enjoy the nectar and pollen of the flowers. Ladybird beetles chase aphids on stems and leaves.

Willows, particularly male willows, provide important nectar sources for many small, flower-loving beetles, and brightly coloured leaf beetles, which are often metallic or bright orange and black, feed on the leaves. Some longhorns and larger weevils are also fond of willow.

Leaf beetle (*Chrysomelidae*)

Aspen trees provide homes for one of our largest longhorn (wood-boring) beetles. You may see the soft, white larvae of these beetles fall out of wood when you chop sections for the wood stove or fireplace. These beetles leave interesting, hollow galleries in trees, whose wood, when converted into furniture, commands a higher price than regular wood. Many species of beetles enjoy the sap of opening aspen catkins in the spring.

Spruce and pine trees, particularly white spruce and jack pine, provide wonderful homes for an assortment of bark-loving beetles. Some burrow under the bark, some run around on it, and some dig into the wood. Rarely is a tree killed by these activities until normal senescence (the aging process) takes its toll.

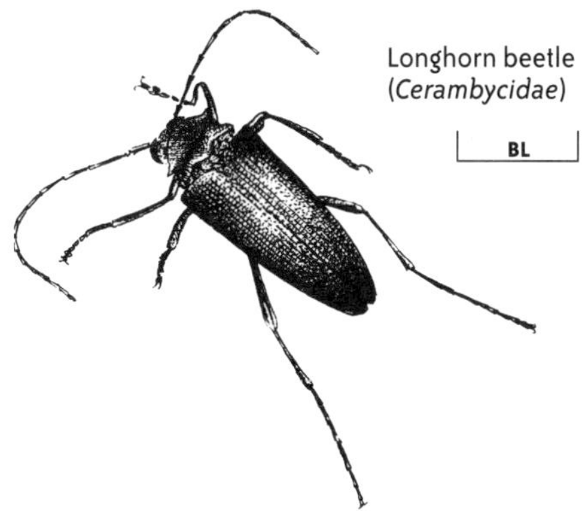

Longhorn beetle (*Cerambycidae*)

Yellow flowers of the Compositae family (e.g., goldenrods, sunflowers, dandelions) will attract many types of beetles that can find there an enjoyable luncheon of pollen and nectar.

Native fleabanes also attract the flower-loving beetles. Bright orange- or yellow-striped clerid beetles will often be found basking in the sun in the centres of fleabane blossoms.

One of the best plants for beetles in the prairies (grassland natural region) is the native prickly pear cactus. The flowers of this cactus become positively packed with a wide variety of beetles, and the stems (or paddles) provide nourishment for some lovely longhorn beetles. The spines can also help keep the local cats out of your yard, or your favourite feline in.

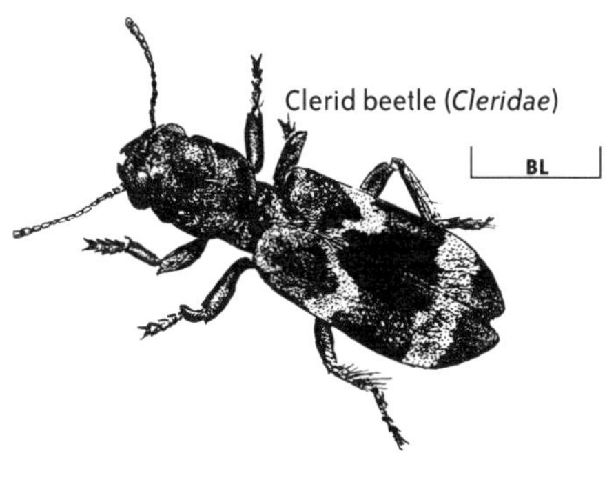

Clerid beetle (*Cleridae*)

Cow parsnip is a native perennial that is particularly attractive to anise swallowtail butterfly caterpillars (*Papilio zelicaon*). An enjoyable sideshow is the variety of beetles that are attracted to this plant's flowers. The blossoms are so large and bright that the beetles are very easy to watch. Tumbling flower beetles really like these flowers and others with similar, umbel-shaped flower heads.

Some other plants that support a few spectacular beetles are the native gaillardia (*Gaillardia aristata*), showy milkweed and spreading dogbane. The latter two plants will sometimes harbour a large, brilliant, metallic green leaf beetle called the dogbane beetle (*Chrysochus auratus)*. Note that spreading dogbane has been declared a noxious weed in Alberta, so has to be controlled.

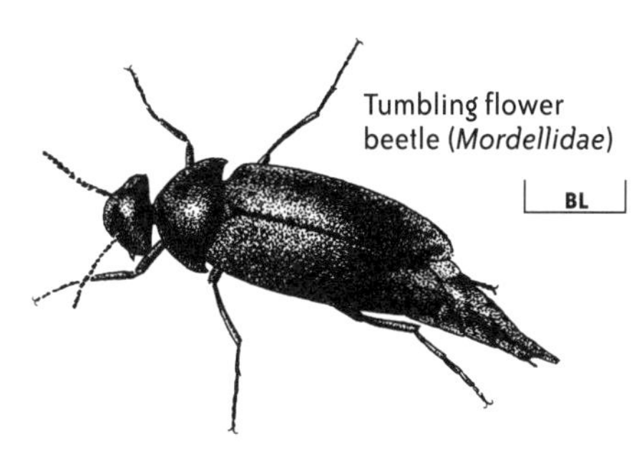

Tumbling flower beetle (*Mordellidae*)

Mayday trees are great for ladybird beetles (and aphids!), and ground beetles like white clover (*Trifolium repens*) planted as a ground cover.

SHELTER FOR BEETLES

Not much has been written about designing shelter for beetles, but here are a few suggestions.

An old, bark-covered log makes an interesting conversation piece to replace the commonly used spruce root or wagon wheel in a front garden. (Logs are great in the backyard too!). As the bark decays, beetles will take to living between the bark and the wood. The bigger the trunk, the better. After a few summers, shelf fungi might begin to grow, making the log even more interesting and providing a whole new living space for the many beetles that enjoy fungi.

Another way to help shelter beetles is to make walkways out of old, flat boards or stones instead of concrete slabs. Some ground beetles take great pleasure in resting and hunting under boards or stones on the ground.

You can also take several rough-cut slices of lumber, maybe acquired from a local logging company, and tie the pieces together, one on top of the other, with baling wire or some stout fibre. If you hang this creation in a tree next to the trunk, you will find that beetles who like close encounters and snug situations will use it as a resting area. Lay the bundle on the ground in the fall, and it will provide some beetles with excellent winter lodging under deep snow. (Maybe butterflies too!)

Ladybird beetle houses, like the one illustrated here, have recently appeared on the market. They can also be made in a home workshop using 19 mm (3/4 in.) plywood.

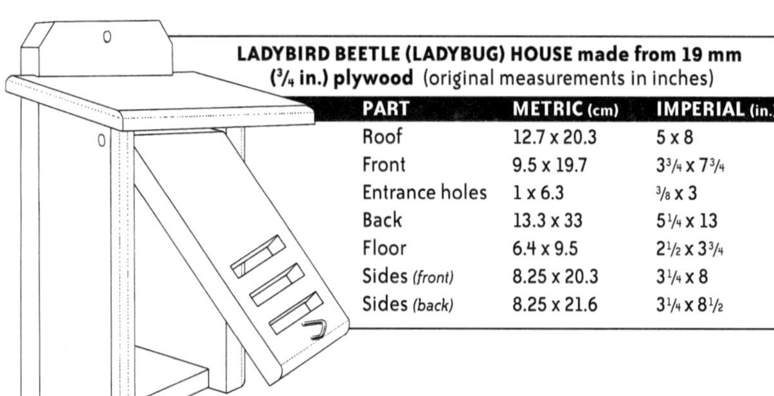

LADYBIRD BEETLE (LADYBUG) HOUSE made from 19 mm (3/4 in.) plywood (original measurements in inches)

PART	METRIC (cm)	IMPERIAL (in.)
Roof	12.7 x 20.3	5 x 8
Front	9.5 x 19.7	3 3/4 x 7 3/4
Entrance holes	1 x 6.3	3/8 x 3
Back	13.3 x 33	5 1/4 x 13
Floor	6.4 x 9.5	2 1/2 x 3 3/4
Sides *(front)*	8.25 x 20.3	3 1/4 x 8
Sides *(back)*	8.25 x 21.6	3 1/4 x 8 1/2

Although this structure will no doubt become a popular garden fixture, few people have experimented with it to see if it actually works. Apparently, it will attract ladybird beetles only if it has a chemical attractant (a "lure" containing the smell of aphids) to invite in the beetles. Unfortunately, the ladybird beetles are unlikely to hang around a structure that promises, but does not deliver, a food source. (If you want ladybugs in your yard, maybe just hang the lure in a tree or put it in a place near where aphids are feeding.)

We suggest that, if you want to try out this ladybird beetle house in the summer, you should use it as you might the butterfly hibernation house—as a garden ornament or conversation piece. In the fall, try filling up the house with leaves and placing it on its side in a sheltered location. Ladybird beetles, or some other insects or small creatures, just might take up residence.

Many species of beetles shelter in ground squirrel holes. You can see them climbing in and out of the holes in the morning or at dusk. If you lay a piece of 7.5 cm (3 in.) or 10 cm (4 in.) PVC tubing in a trench at an angle that mimics a ground squirrel burrow, and make sure that one end reaches below the frost line and the other opens at ground level, you will be able to provide shelter for these insects. The PVC pipe itself or a hole at the bottom will shelter beetles. (Fill in the trench once you have laid down the tubing.)

Many of the beetles that shelter in animal holes probably visit them looking for sustenance rather than refuge. You can spice up your artificial beetle shelter by adding materials that beetles like to eat, such as grass clippings or other decaying vegetation, roots from weeds, or the dead birds that result from collisions with your windows (if you follow the advice in Chapter 17, we expect you will have very few dead birds to give to your beetles).

A large number of beetles also like to shelter in compost heaps and mulch.

Because NatureScaping for beetles is such an unexplored area of gardening, watch your beetle friends. When you become familiar with them, you will develop your own ideas about how to help them establish themselves in your yard. Please send us new information on how you assist beetles on the Backyard Watch form (Appendix 6).

BEETLES YOU ARE LIKELY TO SEE

Most beetle species do not have common names, so when they don't, we'll either use scientific names or make up something interesting (or both).

Ground Beetles (Carabidae)

These beetles got their name because most of them are found running around on the ground. There are two common garden species—both imported—whose common names we made up. The largest, called *Carabus nemoralis*, or the "giant garden marauder," is very fond of caterpillars, slugs and dew worms. It is half the size of your thumb and has large, forward-pointing jaws. Look for a black beetle with a purplish, metallic sheen, running rapidly around on the ground. Second in size in most of our gardens, and far more common, is *Pterostichus melanarius*, the "common garden hunter." A little longer than your thumbnail and shiny black, it is also the most common beetle seen in our basements.

Ground beetle (*Carabidae*)

BL

Weevils or Snout Beetles (Curculionidae)

You are most likely to encounter two types of weevil. The first, the strawberry root weevil (not our name) or *Otiorhynchus ovatus*, is the small, dark beetle with a long snout you find in your house in the fall. You will also see it crawling up the sides of buildings. Its larvae live in the roots of a variety of plants and can be a problem in commercial growing operations of strawberries. Otherwise, these beetles are harmless. Pick them up and put them outside if you find them in your house.

Weevil (*Curculionidae*)

BL

As mentioned earlier, wild rose bushes support a bright red long-nosed beetle we will call the "red rose weevil" (*Rhynchites bicolor*). Look at this lovely insect under a magnifying glass.

Diving Beetles (Dytiscidae)

If you have a water garden, pond or a stream, you will have diving beetles. The big ones (the length of your thumb) you see under the streetlights in the spring and fall, are members of the genus *Dytiscus*, sometimes called predaceous diving beetles. These beetles are really fascinating to watch because their hind legs have become long oars for swimming. There are many different diving beetles of varying size; some with light markings, some with ridges on their streamlined backs.

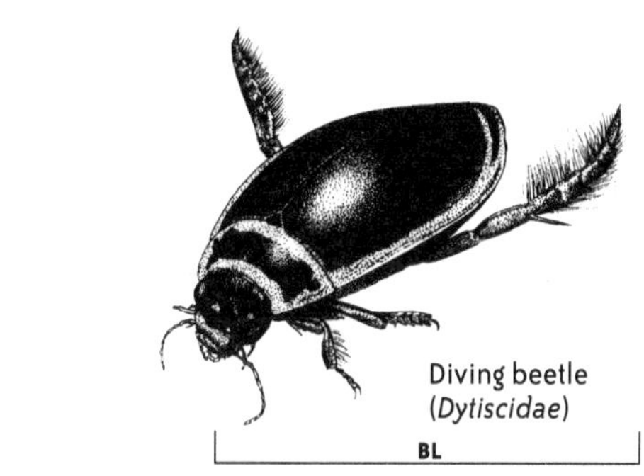

Diving beetle (*Dytiscidae*)

BL

Ladybird Beetles/Lady Beetles/Ladybugs (Coccinellidae)

Everybody recognizes these lovely and charming hunters of aphids (although aphids may not agree!). We have far more species of these insects than you might think, so it is not possible to do them credit. Unfortunately, some of our native species are being displaced by imported varieties. The seven-spotted ladybug we commonly see is imported.

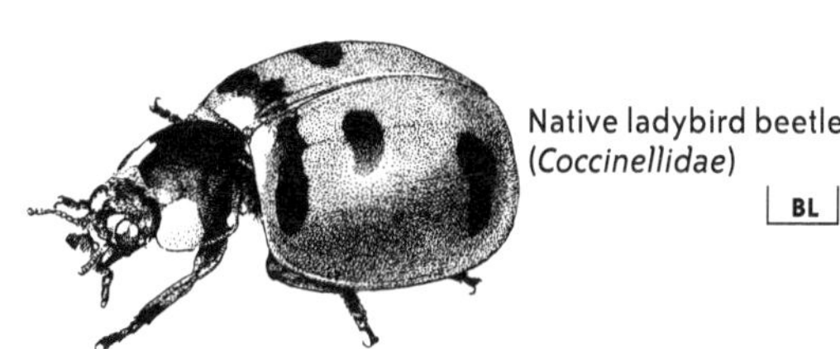

Native ladybird beetle (*Coccinellidae*)

BL

Incidentally, the orange liquid ladybugs squirt on you when you pick them up too roughly is harmless but tastes awful. A quick wash of the hands and it comes off.

TRACKING LADYBIRD BEETLES

Our native ladybugs are orange and black. Sometimes they have bars or other patterns, sometimes no pattern at all, and sometimes spots (up to 14). But none are ever orange with 7 black spots, as is the most common imported species.

If you want to be involved in surveying the ladybugs in your yard or neighbourhood, contact the Canadian Nature Federation about the Canadian Lady Beetle Survey (see Appendix 5).

ACKNOWLEDGEMENTS

John Acorn (Biologist, writer and broadcaster, Edmonton, Alberta)
John and Bert Carr (Beetle afficionados, Calgary, Alberta)
Zoltan Gulyas (Naturalist and gardener, Calgary, Alberta)
Dan L. Johnson (Senior Research Scientist, Agriculture and Agri-Food Canada Research Centre, Lethbridge, Alberta)
Grant Moir (Biologist, and Board Member, Red Deer River Naturalists, Red Deer, Alberta)
Don Wales (Instructor, Red Deer College, Red Deer, Alberta)

SIGNIFICANT REFERENCES

Borror, D.J., and R.E. White. 1970. *A field guide to insects: American north of Mexico*. A Peterson Field Guide. Houghton Mifflin Company, Boston, Massachusetts.

Forsyth, A. 1992. *The Equinox guide to insect behaviour*. Camden House, Camden East.

Jaques, H.E. 1951. *How to know the beetles*. Wm. C. Brown Co., Dubuque, Iowa.

Milne, L., and M. Milne. 1980. *The Audubon Society field guide to North American insects and spiders*. Alfred A. Knopf, New York.

Stokes, D.W. 1983. *A guide to observing insect lives*. Stokes Nature Guide. Little, Brown and Company, Boston and Toronto.

White, R.E. 1983. *A field guide to the beetles of North America*. A Peterson Field Guide. Houghton Mifflin Company, Boston, Massachusetts.

Starcher, A.M. 1995. *Good bugs for your garden*. Algonquin Books of Chapel Hill, Chapel Hill, North Carolina.

5 BASICS
NATURESCAPING FOR BEETLES

1. Build a compost pile.
2. Lay an old log or some flat boards on the ground and leave them there.
3. Use an organic ground cover such as bark chips.
4. Lighten or "fluff up" your soil; one way is to add mulch and sand.
5. Study and enjoy the beetles that you find in your yard.

JAN HEAPS

TOM WEBB

Orb-weaving spider

Chapter 13
Supporting Spiders in Your Yard

We don't often think about spiders unless they appear in our houses, tents or recreational vehicles. Often, we blame spiders for things they could not or would not do. How many times have you heard someone complaining about spider bites when they wake up in the morning? Too often, at least from the spider's perspective. Most of these bites are probably caused by fleas, bed bugs or even ticks. Yes, most spiders can bite, although many would be unable to affect you very much—they would not even be able to break the skin. Most spider bites (in our part of the world) can cause no more harm than a mosquito bite or bee sting, and, although some spiders enjoy living in houses, there are not usually many of these creatures around.

WHY SUPPORT SPIDERS

Spiders are consummate hunters. Each species has its own specialized way of hunting, and most will eat just about anything they catch. Discovering how each species of spider in your yard hunts can be a very interesting and rewarding experience.

Because spiders are such voracious insect hunters, having a healthy population of spiders in your garden will go a long way to keeping unwelcome insects under control. Except for yellow jackets and bald-faced hornets, there isn't much in the insect world some spider won't tackle and consume. On the other hand, spiders are important food for a variety of birds, so having lots of spiders around will help your feathered neighbours.

Spiders are threatened more by habitat destruction and ignorance than anything else. It has been estimated that there are about 170,000 species of spiders in the world, and we are aware of only about a quarter of them. In Alberta, we probably have about 1200 spider species, of which approximately 350 are documented.

Spiders are not usually directly affected by the pesticides used to kill insects in your home or garden. However, it is possible that the loss of insects that results from the use of chemical sprays could cause some spiders to starve, grow more slowly or move away. We strongly suggest you avoid using pesticides under any circumstances in your yard or garden.

THINGS TO KNOW ABOUT SPIDERS

Folks sometimes confuse spiders, members of the class Arachnida and order Araneae, with other spider-like creatures. Spiders are often called insects, but insects have six legs and spiders have eight. Insects also have three basic body divisions, whereas spiders have two. Insects have antennae or feelers, and spiders have none. Insects usually have two large compound eyes, one on each side of their head, and sometimes two or three simple eyes in the centre of their forehead. Most spiders have eight simple eyes.

Another problem is that daddy longlegs (or harvestmen) are thought to be spiders. These creatures are in the same class as spiders (Arachnida) but form a different order (Opiliones). Daddy longlegs do have eight legs, but a close look with your magnifying

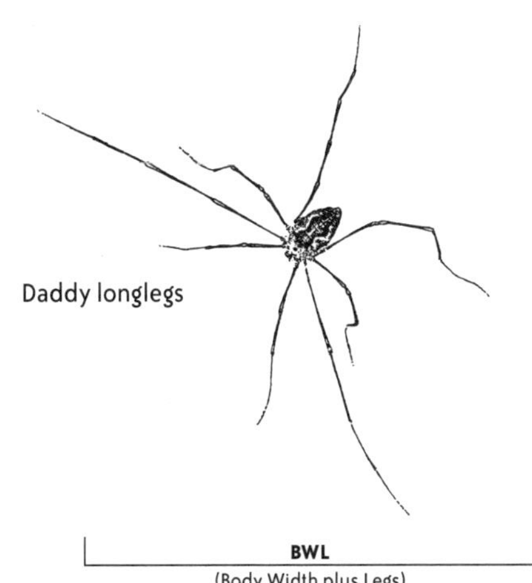
Daddy longlegs

BWL
(Body Width plus Legs)

Note: Body size will vary with species

SPIDER BALLOONING

Ballooning is done during periods of gentle wind (4-10 km/hr. or 2 ½-6 mi./hr.). Young spiders dispersing in this manner can control when they come down.

glass will show you that these creatures have only one body part whereas spiders have two.

Most of the spiders we notice produce elegant webs to trap their insect food, but not all spiders spin webs. Those that don't spin webs may use their silk to line burrows, protect their egg cases and provide a belaying rope (called a "drag line") when they travel. Some young spiders use silk as a parachute to catch the wind and help them disperse to new homes (a process called "ballooning").

The silk itself is very complex, and stronger, by weight, than most of the materials we humans pride ourselves in producing. And we have nothing that combines the strength of spider silk with its elasticity. Much research is being done into the nature of the different spider silks in order to help us mimic their properties.

SUPPORTING SPIDERS: SOME GENERAL CONSIDERATIONS

Variety, or diversity, in a garden will encourage spiders the most. Increase the variety of plant life, particularly native species, and you will enhance the insect fauna, reduce the chance of "pest" problems and supply many spider species with habitat and food resources. Spiders also like areas of higher humidity, which are found close to the ground where there are many low-growing plants.

Increase the variety of ground surfaces—for instance, establish different soils and other planting substrates—and you will encourage spiders to live in your yard. Many spiders are ground dwellers and prefer a rough-textured ground surface. Spiders will search for rough-textured ground when setting their webs and spinning nests. Rough-textured ground also offers them places to hide from predators such as birds and enemy wasps.

Most of Alberta's spectacular and interesting spiders enjoy the sun but not the wind. When roughening up the ground for spiders or designing choice spots for spiders to spin, choose locations that have some sun but are also sheltered.

During the growing season, try to leave spiderwebs (also called snares) alone. Of course, it is not always possible to be non-invasive—sometimes webs are spun in locations we need to pass through, or are between things we need to move. Usually, if we break through a snare, a spider will simply spin a new web in the same location or repair the old one. There is a great investment in spinning webs, so spiders won't easily abandon a damaged one. If you want to ensure that a spider will move its web, either move the spider or destroy the web and nest shelter completely when the spider is not in it.

PLANTS FOR SPIDERS

Although spiders don't eat plants, they do use plants for protection and for anchoring their webs. Some, including crab spiders, use flowers as lures to attract insects. If you grow the following plants, you will have many opportunities to observe interesting spider behaviour.

Water smartweed, which grows in dense mats on sandy or silty soil, as well as in shallow water, provides excellent cover for ground-dwelling spiders. Other spider species use the leaves as cover for their snares and shelters.

The bunchgrasses (e.g., *Festuca* spp.) are very attractive to spiders. Tall grass stems provide anchors for small snares, and last year's leaves and stems provide cover for ground-hunting wolf spiders. The bases of bunchgrasses are especially interesting to wolf spiders for spinning nests and shelters.

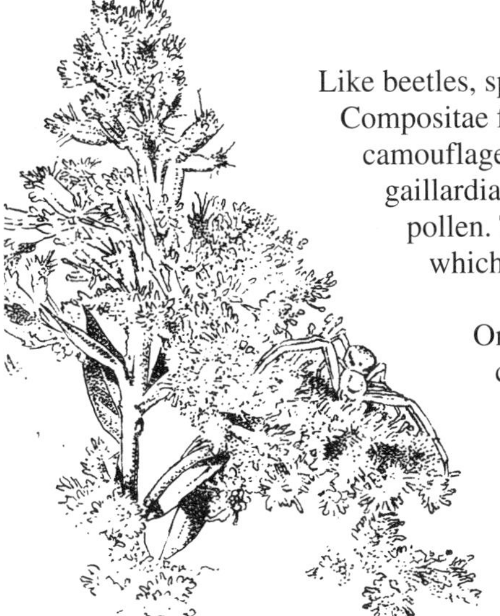
Goldenrod spider on goldenrod blooms

Like beetles, spiders tend to favour yellow flowers of the Compositae family. Certain species of crab spider sit camouflaged on the inflorescences (flower clusters) of gaillardia and snag insects that come by for nectar and pollen. These spiders are wonderfully camouflaged, which is fortunate for them but not their prey.

One yellow composite, goldenrod, is so commonly frequented by a certain species of crab spider that the spider, *Misumena vatia*, is called the goldenrod spider. Many yellow composite flower species support crab spiders, and other spider species frequent the stems and anchor their webs to the tall flower heads.

VERA VHALLIDAY

Spiderweb

SHELTER FOR SPIDERS

Spiders like shelter. Even the big orb-weaving spiders, which we often see in the middle of or near their webs, spin shelters for themselves when they are not attending the web. These shelters are called "retreats."

Spiders can be very opportunistic—for instance, they have been observed living in shelters spun in stinging nettle leaves by butterfly caterpillars! Some species hide in shelters spun in tall grass or in folded leaves. Others, such as the rather rare (in Alberta) trapdoor spiders, dig burrows in the ground and line them with silk. Providing a soft, undisturbed organic soil bed may encourage some of these interesting species to share your yard.

The simplest way to provide protection, nest sites and egg storage sites for ground-dwelling spiders is to lay a few old boards or rotting logs on the ground (especially in tall grass) and leave them there.

Large rocks, particularly flat ones, can be used instead of boards or logs; they will also provide excellent places for jumping spiders to sun themselves and watch for prey.

Leaf litter left untouched is a valuable source of shelter for many spider species. Leaf litter also shelters insects and so provides ground-dwelling spiders with a supply of food.

Lumpy ground is an excellent habitat for many spiders. Take some grass clods and leave them lying around, slightly separated, on a patch of grass. You will have accomplished two things—provided spiders with some diverse habitat and given yourself a part of the yard you will no longer have to mow.

Many spiders search mud flats for food, and use the cracks in dry mud for shelter. Creating an artificial mud flat is quite easy. Build a shallow wooden box, perhaps 5 cm (2 in.) deep, and fill it with mud from a nearby pond or stream bank. Soak the mud, keeping it flat; then let it dry. As it cracks, you can expect to see spiders frequenting the warm earth and hiding in the cracks.

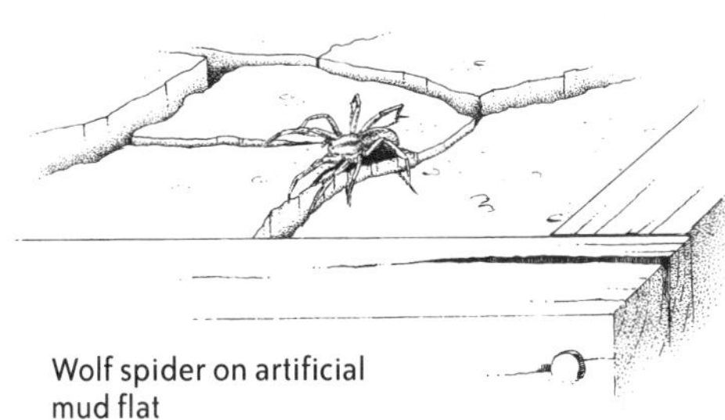
Wolf spider on artificial mud flat

Overhangs of buildings, such as the eaves of roofs, are great places for spiders, particularly the orb weavers. Insects visit overhangs because birds find it difficult to hunt them there (the birds have no place to land or take off). Lots of insects means

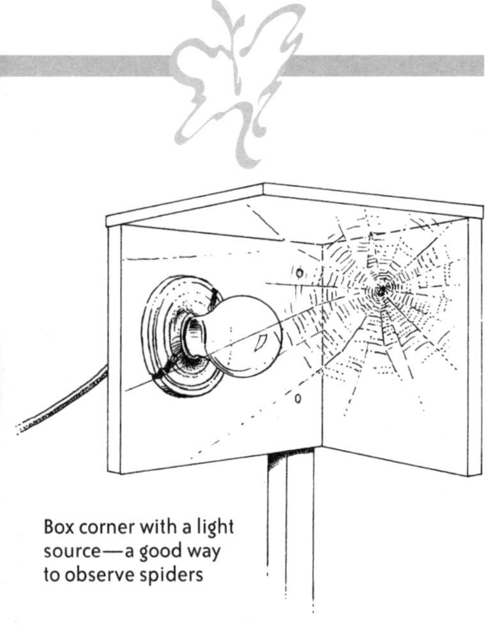
Box corner with a light source—a good way to observe spiders

lots of spiders. To improve your chances of seeing spiders, put a light source under an overhang.

Another idea is to build the corner of a box from three pieces of plywood, and mount your construction on an outside post at about eye level. Put a light socket in the corner formed by the plywood, and wire it to an extension cord you can plug into a nearby outdoor socket. The light attracts insects, and spiders will seek out the insects. The result is a nightly drama of life and death as spider and insect struggle to outwit each other.

SPIDERS YOU ARE LIKELY TO SEE

There is an incredible variety of spiders whose behaviour can hold your interest for hours. Justice cannot be done to them here, but a few of the most common and interesting spider groups are described below.

Jumping Spiders (Salticidae)

Jumping spiders are beautifully coloured, little spider "wolflets." Most species are 5 mm (3/16 in.) or less in size, but some grow to 13 mm (1/2 in.) in length. Frequently seen around window sills, they can be black with white stripes, orange and black, or some variation on these themes. Perhaps the most alert and visually acute of all the spiders, they stalk their prey in slow motion, and at the last second, pounce on their victims. They have two large eyes in the centre of their face—eyes so large they can be seen with the naked eye.

Jumping spider (*Salticidae*)

BWL

Jumping spiders do not spin webs, shelters or places to moult. Their silk is used almost exclusively as a drag line, and to protect eggs and young. Although these spiders seem aggressive when they hunt, they are usually quite passive when handled. Because there is one jumping spider that can give you a good bite (*Phidippus johnsoni*), make sure that you treat any jumping spiders you pick up gently. They won't bite unless they are squeezed or handled harshly. (Any spider you pick up should be handled gently.)

Orb-Weaving Spiders/Garden Spiders (Araneidae)

Just about everyone who has read a fairytale to a child has seen drawings of the large, circular snares spun by the orb weavers. Often seen in calendar photographs covered with early morning dew, the webs give this spider group its name. Spiderling and adult orb-weaving spiders are often quite colourful, and they can usually be found resting on or near their great nets—waiting for some hapless insect to become entangled. One of our most commonly seen orb weavers, *Araneus gemmoides*, is often bright orange with reddish or brownish patterns on the upper abdomen.

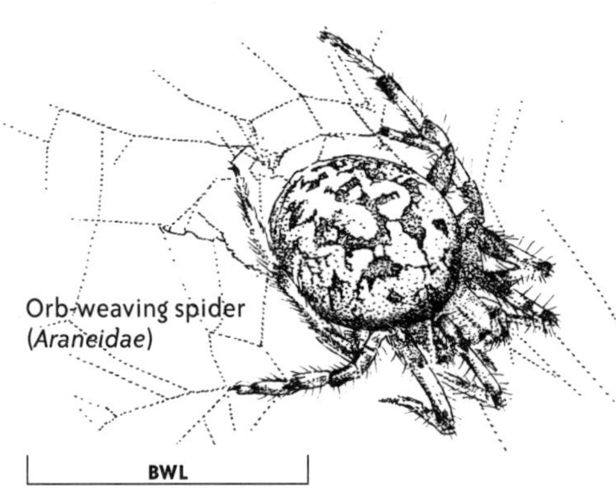
Orb-weaving spider (*Araneidae*)

BWL

In the late summer and fall, female orb weavers attain their largest size and become quite spectacular. They are large because they are full of eggs (which are laid in late August and September). Watching one of these spiders handle a snared insect or repair a web is a wonderful way to pass a few hours on a warm afternoon. A carefully aligned magnifying glass will show details of behaviour without disturbing the spider at its work.

Crab Spiders (Thomisidae)

Less often noticed than other spiders because of their camouflage, the crab spiders that frequent flower heads are easy to find and fun to watch. Sitting unseen on a flower cluster (they are often the colour of the flower they are on!), they grab insects that investigate the flowers for nectar and pollen. Some of these spiders can even change their colour if they change flowers.

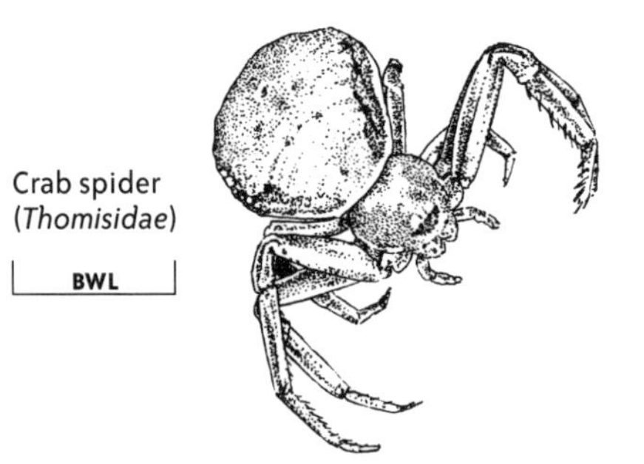
Crab spider (*Thomisidae*)

BWL

Crab spiders got their name because their legs are rotated forward, making the grabbing of prey easier. In other words, these spiders are shaped like crabs and scuttle sideways like crabs.

Wolf Spiders (Lycosidae)

When you see a relatively large spider running for shelter under a board or rock, you are most likely watching a wolf spider. Wolf spiders are among our fastest moving native spiders. Another clue in identifying these spiders is that the females carry their eggs in a large ball. This egg sac is attached to the female's silk spinnerets.

Most wolf spiders do not spin snares. Rather, they spin a silk burrow rather like a funnel (if they spin any shelter at all), and occasionally you will see one hiding in its burrow.

Wolf spider (*Lycosidae*)

BWL

ACKNOWLEDGMENTS

John Acorn (Biologist, writer and broadcaster, Edmonton, Alberta)
Dan L. Johnson (Senior Research Scientist, Agriculture and Agri-Food Canada Research Centre, Lethbridge, Alberta)
Robin Leech (Instructor, Biological Sciences, Northern Alberta Institute of Technology [NAIT], Edmonton, Alberta)
Grant Moir (Biologist, and Board Member, Red Deer River Naturalists, Red Deer, Alberta)
Don Wales (Instructor, Red Deer College, Red Deer, Alberta)

SIGNIFICANT REFERENCES

Comstock, J.H. 1980. *The spider book*. 5th ed., revised by W.J. Gertsch. Cornell University Press, Ithaca and London.

Kaston, J.B. 1978. *How to know the spiders*. 3d ed. Wm. C. Brown Co., Dubuque, Iowa.

Levi, H.W., and L.R. Levi. 1990. *Spiders and their kin*. A Golden Guide. Golden Press, New York.

Milne, L., and M. Milne. 1980. *The Audubon Society field guide to North American insects and spiders*. Alfred A. Knopf, New York..

Preston-Mafham, R., and K. Preston-Mafham. 1984. *Spiders of the world*. Facts on File, Inc., New York.

5 BASICS

NATURESCAPING FOR SPIDERS

1. Put in a variety of plants, especially native species.
2. Grow yarrow, bunchgrasses, water smartweed and the native gaillardia (*Gaillardia artistata*).
3. Lay some old boards or a rotting log on the ground.
4. Leave leaf litter where you can.
5. Wherever possible, leave outdoor webs alone; watch and enjoy the spiders.

ROBIN LEECH

www.naturescape.ab.ca

Pine siskin at feeder

Chapter 14
It's for the Birds (Food, Water and Shelter)

There are three main ways to attract birds to your yard—with food, water and shelter/housing.

PROVIDING FOOD

You can provide food for birds by NatureScaping your yard with food plants appealing to various bird species or by supplying supplemental food (i.e., bird-feeding stations). Bird feeding is definitely a win-win situation: the birds benefit by having access to a reliable food source, and you benefit by having the birds carry out some of their daily activities within viewing distance.

Because vegetation is so important to all wildlife species, we devote all of Chapter 3 to a discussion of how to NatureScape with plants. Appendix 1 has detailed information on how various plants are used by birds for food.

Offering supplemental food to birds can be a seasonal or year-round activity. Some people restrict their feeding program to only one season, whereas others carry out a variety of feeding programs throughout the year.

Although healthy birds do not become dependent on feeder food (see sidebar), they do benefit from having access to a consistent and readily available food supply. The survival rate of birds that have access to feeder food is significantly higher than for those without this access. Feeders are especially important in the early spring and late fall, when there is less natural food available, and in the winter, particularly during and after a heavy snowfall.

BIRD FEEDING MYTHS

Myth 1

Contrary to what is often claimed, healthy birds do not become "addicted to" supplemental food. Birds are opportunistic and will readily eat any suitable food that they find while moving about in their territories or on their migration routes. Because feeding stations are only one of many food sources, birds will simply move to another location with food should a feeder be allowed to go empty, much the same as they would if a supply of cones on a particular tree (for example) were to run out.

Myth 2

Bird-feeding stations do not interrupt normal migration patterns. A bird's natural migration urge, triggered by internal and external cues, is simply too strong to be influenced by the presence or absence of feeders.

Steps to Success

In order for you to attract birds to your feeder(s), you will need to learn what birds you have in your area, what their habits are and their feeder and food preferences (see Table 1 in this chapter, and Appendix 3.) Some bird species, like white-crowned sparrows, will visit a bird feeder temporarily during migration, whereas others, like hummingbirds, rose-breasted grosbeaks and orioles, will use feeding stations for the duration of their stay in Alberta during the breeding season. A few species, such as black-capped and boreal chickadees, may establish permanent territories that encompass a feeding station.

Your bird-feeding program will be more successful if you set up a feeder in an area where there is plenty of cover to provide shelter and protection from predators (see Chapter 17 for information on how to reduce cat predation risk.) Because very few birds like to eat out in the open without nearby shelter, a bird-feeding program in an older, well-treed neighbourhood will be more successful than one started in a new subdivision or area that has been cleared of all trees.

Feeder birds are most comfortable when there are safe and specific routes for them to take to a feeder. Ground-feeding birds, like the native sparrows, prefer to travel low through dense shrubbery. Siskins and chickadees, on the other hand, tend to approach a feeder from the sides and tops of trees.

You will enjoy a feeder more if you put it where you can comfortably see it from the house and where it is easily accessible. To reduce the risk of window strikes, place a feeder 1 m (3 ft.) or less, or more than 4 m (13 ft.) from your window. (For more information on how to prevent window strikes, see Chapter 17).

Seed feeders, especially those that enjoy a lot of year-round activity, have the potential to be transmission sites for both diseases and parasites. To reduce this risk, move your feeding sites periodically and wash all your feeders in hot, soapy water at least once a year. See Chapter 17 for advice on what to do should a disease outbreak occur.

Seed Feeders

Seeds can be dispensed in a variety of ways, and you can choose from a wide assortment of different feeder styles. Most birds are not fussy about what type of feeder they dine at, although they will be more particular about the food they eat, and some feeders are more appropriate for certain kinds of seeds than others.

Ground-feeding Stations

The simplest, although most wasteful, method to feed birds, is to scatter seed on the ground. Many birds, such as redpolls, jays, magpies, doves (including pigeons), native sparrows (including juncos) and grouse are readily attracted to ground-feeding stations. The snow-free area under a coniferous tree is a good place to scatter seed. Just make sure that the feeding area is at least 3 m (10 ft.) from shrubbery and other places where cats can hide.

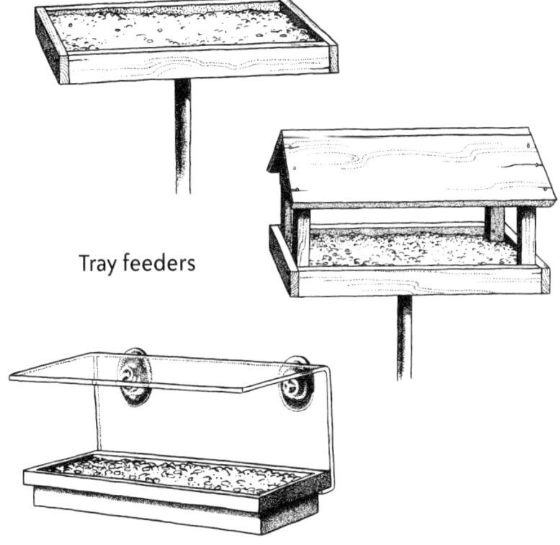

Tray feeders

Tray (Platform) Feeders

This type of feeder is inexpensive, easy to make, simple to fill and clean, and—depending on its size—can accommodate a large number of birds. Placed on or close to the ground (30 cm-45 cm [12-18 in.]), a tray feeder will attract ground-feeding birds (e.g., native sparrows). Placed well off the ground (about 1.2 m-1.8 m [4-6 ft.]), it will be used by species that prefer higher locations (e.g., woodpeckers). Some tray feeders can be attached to a window ledge.

If you live in a windy part of the province, try placing 2.5-cm (6-in.) wooden squares in a tray feeder to help prevent the seeds from blowing out (see illustration). To avoid sodden seeds, make the floor of a tray feeder out of fine screening (use an old window screen) or pieces of soffit. Covering a tray feeder with a roof will help protect the seeds from rain and snow.

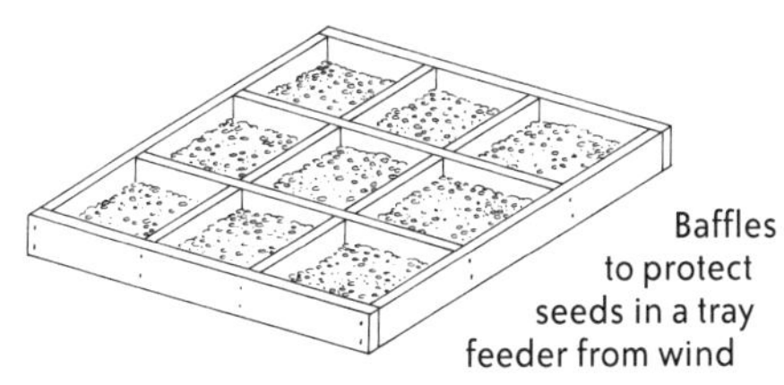

Baffles to protect seeds in a tray feeder from wind

Hopper Feeders

A hopper feeder is an efficient seed dispenser because it can hold a large quantity of seed and offer it (and the birds) protection from the elements. Hopper feeders come in a wide assortment of styles and sizes, and most are easy to construct in a home workshop. You can mount this type of feeder on a post or pole, hang it from a tree or attach it to a balcony.

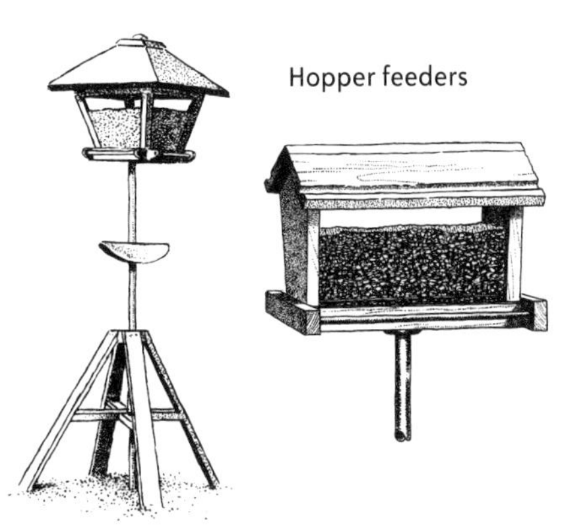

Hopper feeders

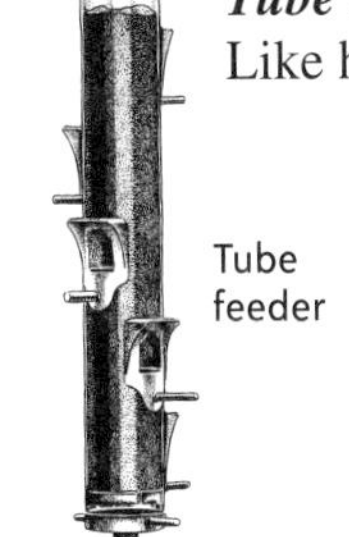

Tube feeder

Tube Feeders

Like hopper feeders, tube feeders protect seeds from the elements, and also come in a variety of shapes and styles. The seeds are clearly displayed in a tube feeder, and there is less waste because the birds have to reach in to get a seed. All types of food can be dispensed from a tube feeder, but most people use them for nygur seed, canola and finch mixes. If you are going to offer the expensive nygur seed or nygur seed mixes, use a tube feeder that has very tiny portals (openings).

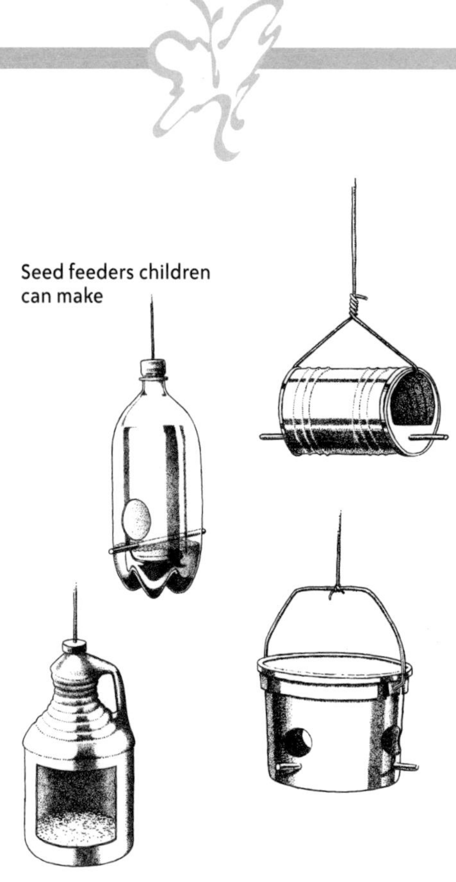
Seed feeders children can make

A tube feeder is usually hung from a bracket or tree branch. Commercial tube feeders are the most popular, although you can easily make this type of feeder from PVC pipe, ABS pipe or a plastic mailing tube.

See Chapter 18 for advice on what to do if house sparrows become a problem at your feeder.

Other Seed Feeders

Seed feeders can be made from such household items as ice-cream pails, coffee cans and plastic jugs (just make sure they're clean before you start!). Avoid using cardboard milk cartons—they deteriorate quickly. Making a bird feeder from household materials is not only an excellent way to reuse materials, it is a wonderful way to involve children in a fun, hands-on activity.

Simply cut holes in the sides of your preferred container (make the holes small if you want to exclude larger birds) and poke a couple of drain holes in the bottom. Because most household bird feeders are made from light materials that can be blown about by the wind, make sure this feeder is securely fastened to a tree or feeder stand.

You can also buy specialty seed feeders, including mesh bags for dispensing nygur seed, squirrel-resistant feeders and corn cob holders.

Feeder Stands

A feeder can be set beside a window, on the corner of a balcony or on the ground, or hung from a tree or stand, depending on your preference and the birds you want to attract. The birds and seed will be most safe if you mount your feeder on a free-standing structure at least 3 m (10 ft.) from the nearest squirrel "launching pad" and put baffles on the stand to prevent cats and other climbing predators from reaching the feeder (see page 157, Chapter 18). You will also need to make sure your feeder is placed a proper distance from your window so that window strikes are avoided (see previous page).

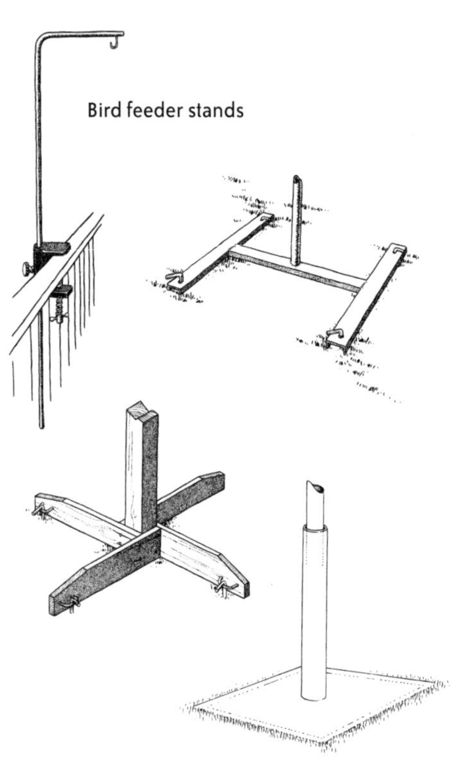
Bird feeder stands

The illustration shows a variety of ideas for feeder stands.

Base of a Seed Feeder

To minimize the unsightly build up of hulls, you can replace the grass around the base of or below a seed feeder with mulch or gravel, and clean the area periodically. Some seeds, including canola and sunflower seeds, will germinate.

Types of Seeds

Seeds attract species whose main summer diet also consists of seeds. There are many type of seeds that can be offered; **sunflower seeds**—of which there are two main types, black oil and striped—are the most sought after.

The small, black oil sunflower seeds contain more oil per gram than the larger, striped variety, and their smaller size and thinner skin make them easier for smaller birds to manipulate. In some areas, birds seem to show a distinct preference for one variety of sunflower seed over the other. Try both types and see what the birds in your yard prefer.

It is economical to buy sunflower seeds in bulk; good quality seeds can be found in such places as wild bird stores, feed stores and nature centres. If the seeds are going to be stored outside, keep them in a cool place in a watertight and squirrel-proof container; a metal garbage can with a tight-fitting lid works very well.

Sunflower seeds can be served shelled (hulled), unshelled (unhulled) or chopped (broken with the shells on and seeds inside) and dispensed by throwing them on the ground, or from a variety of feeders, as described above.

Buying hulled sunflower seeds rather than unhulled seeds is more expensive initially but may be cost-effective in the long run because there is very little seed waste and less mess to clean up. Hulled or lightly chopped sunflower seeds should be dispensed from tube feeders that have small portals.

If you grow sunflowers in your garden, leave some of the seed heads for the birds, squirrels and deer to eat. Seed heads can also be cut off and placed on a tray feeder. In areas with bears, don't serve sunflower seeds anywhere in your yard unless the bears are hibernating (bears love sunflower seeds!)

Be aware that sunflower seed hulls can accumulate on the ground very quickly and can inhibit plant growth (see ***Base of a Seed Feeder*** above). Whole sunflower seeds can germinate, which may or may not appeal to you.

Nygur seed is a tiny, black seed from a tropical thistle (*Guizotia abyssinica*) and is so expensive that you will likely want to dispense it from a fine mesh bag or a tube feeder that has tiny portals. It is a favourite of redpolls, siskins and goldfinches. Nygur seeds will not germinate, but the hulls make quite a mess.

Canola is a popular feeder seed that is eaten by many finches, especially redpolls. Deer will also eat it. Canola is one of those feeder foods that birds seem to ignore in some locations and eagerly devour in others, so experiment! This seed can be dispensed from a tray, although most people use a hopper or tube feeder. Be warned—canola will germinate. Never put out uncleaned seed (you might get noxious weeds) or treated seed (which may be poisonous).

Some canolas and other crop plants have been genetically modified. Until it is certain that birds suffer no negative health effects from eating the seeds of genetically modified plants, you may want to avoid using these products.

Nuts, although expensive, are nutritious and very happily consumed by many birds. Peanuts are the most popular nuts, appealing to many insect- and seed-eating birds. Shelled walnuts are also popular, especially with chickadees.

Corn, which is eaten by several bird species, is rich in carbohydrates and is a good source of vitamin A. Whole kernel corn is a favourite of blue jays, with cracked corn being preferred by house sparrows (so don't serve cracked corn if you don't want to attract house sparrows.)

(White) millet is a good seed to serve alone or mixed with other small seeds, although it is less popular than sunflower seeds. It is a preferred feeder food of the gray-crowned rosy-finch, and when served on the ground during the spring or fall, will attract migrating native sparrows.

Many feeder birds will not eat **cereal grains**, including barley, wheat, oats and buckwheat. However, cereal grains (especially chopped) can be served to waterfowl, members of the grouse family, doves (including pigeons), native sparrows, grackles and blackbirds. If you plan to serve grain, be sure that it is untreated and free of weed seeds.

FEEDER BIRD SEED PREFERENCES
(birds in alphabetical order by common name)

Sunflower seeds (black oil or striped; shelled, unshelled or chopped): American robin, black-billed magpie, blackbirds, brown creeper, chickadees, doves (including pigeons), finches (including American goldfinch, crossbills, evening grosbeak, gray-crowned rosy-finch, pine grosbeak, pine siskin, purple finch, redpolls), gray partridge, house sparrow, jays, native sparrows (including American tree sparrow, dark-eyed junco, Harris's sparrow), nuthatches, ring-necked pheasant, rose-breasted grosbeak, woodpeckers

Nygur seed: finches (including American goldfinch, crossbills, pine siskin, purple finch, redpolls), house sparrow, native sparrows (including chipping sparrow, dark-eyed junco, fox sparrow, Harris's sparrow, white-throated sparrow)

Canola: finches (including American goldfinch, pine siskin, purple finch, redpolls)

Nuts: black-billed magpie, chickadees, European starling, finches (including grosbeaks, redpolls), house sparrow, jays, nuthatches, native sparrows (including chipping sparrow, fox sparrow, white-crowned sparrow, white-throated sparrow), waxwings, woodpeckers

Corn: American robin, blue jay, doves (including pigeons), gray partridge, house sparrow, native sparrows (including dark-eyed junco, fox sparrow), northern flicker, redpolls, ring-necked pheasant, waxwings

Millet: European starling, finches (including gray-crowned rosy-finch, purple finch, redpolls), gray partridge, house sparrow, native sparrows (including American tree sparrow, chipping sparrow, dark-eyed junco, fox sparrow, Harris's sparrow, white-crowned sparrow, white-throated sparrow), ring-necked pheasant

Cereal grain (e.g., oats, barley, wheat, buckwheat): blackbirds, common grackle, doves (including pigeon), gray partridge, native sparrows (including American tree sparrow, dark-eyed junco, white-throated sparrow), ring-necked pheasant

MYRNA PEARMAN

LEGEND

Bird Species

Bird species are in taxonomic order and listed by common name. Although they are common feeder birds, we do not recommend encouraging pigeons, European starlings or house sparrows, all introduced species.

Season Likely to Visit

Spring	Sp
Summer	S
Fall	F
Winter	W

Natural Region

This column shows where the bird species can be attracted to a bird feeder. The Canadian Shield natural region, in northeastern Alberta, has not been included.

Grassland	G
Parkland	P
Boreal Forest	B
Foothills	F
Rocky Mountain	R

Preferred Food

The most preferred foods are in bold-face type.

Sunflower seeds (striped or black oil) can be chopped, shelled or unshelled. What is used depends on the bird species and the birds' preferences in your area.

Peanut butter/cornmeal mixture—to make, mix half and half.

Kitchen scraps should not be salty or spicy.

Cereal grains should be untreated and free of weed seeds.

Feeder Types

This column contains information on what types of feeders can be used to attract a particular species. "Ground" refers to ground-feeding stations (food is left on the ground).

TABLE 1 Common Alberta Feeder Birds

Bird Species	Season Likely to Visit	Natural Region	Preferred Food	Feeder Types
Grouse, Pheasants and Turkey				
Gray partridge	W	G/P/B/F	**Cereal grains (oats, barley)**, sunflower seeds, millet, corn (whole or cracked)	Ground
Doves				
Rock dove (Pigeon)	All	All	**Corn (whole), sunflower seeds, cereal grain**, popcorn, bread	Ground
Hummingbirds				
Ruby-throated hummingbird Rufous hummingbird	Sp/S	Ruby-throated: G/P/B (south) Rufous: F/R	**Sugar water**, suet (usually only during inclement weather)	Hummingbird feeder, suet
Woodpeckers				
Downy woodpecker Hairy woodpecker	All	All	**Suet**, sunflower seeds, bone sawdust, fruit, peanuts, carcasses, mealworms	Ground, suet, tray, hopper, tube
Jays, Crows and Allies				
Gray jay	F/W	B/F/R	**Suet**, sunflower seeds, kitchen scraps, carcasses, peanuts, old wasp nests, mealworms	Suet, ground, tray, hopper
Blue jay	Sp/F/W	P/B/F	**Peanuts (shelled or unshelled), sunflower seeds, corn (whole)**, suet, fruit, mealworms	Suet, ground, tray, hopper
Black-billed magpie	All	All (except extreme northeast)	**Suet, bone sawdust, sunflower seeds, kitchen scraps**, fruit, peanuts, carcasses, old wasp nests, mealworms	Suet, ground, tray, hopper
Chickadees				
Black-capped chickadee	All	All	**Suet, sunflower seeds, peanuts (chopped), walnuts (chopped)**, peanut butter/cornmeal mixture, old wasp nests, mealworms	Suet, ground, tray, hopper, tube
Mountain chickadee	All	F/R	As for black-capped chickadee	
Boreal chickadee	F/W	P/B/F/R	**Suet, bran muffins, sunflower seeds, peanuts (chopped)**, walnuts (chopped), peanut butter/cornmeal mixture, mealworms	Suet, ground, tray, hopper
Nuthatches				
Red-breasted nuthatch White-breasted nuthatch	All	Red-breasted: All White-breasted: P/B(south)/F/R	**Suet, sunflower seeds**, nuts (chopped), peanut butter/cornmeal mixture, old wasp nests, mealworms	Suet, ground, tray, hopper, tube
Creepers				
Brown creeper	W	P/B(south)/F/R	**Bone sawdust, suet**, sunflower seeds (chopped), mealworms	Suet, ground, tray
Starlings				
European starling	All (in some areas)	All (except extreme north)	**Suet**, peanuts (chopped), millet, mealworms, sunflower seeds	Suet, ground, hopper
Sparrows				
American tree sparrow	Sp/F/W	All (during migration) Some overwinter	**Canary seed**, suet, peanut butter/suet mixture, sunflower seeds (shelled or chopped), ground wheat and buckwheat, mixed birdseed, millet	Ground, tray, suet
Chipping sparrow	Sp/F	All (during migration)	**Millet, sunflower seeds (shelled or chopped)**, peanuts (chopped), suet	Ground, tray
White-throated sparrow	Sp/F	All (during migration) A few overwinter	**Sunflower seeds (shelled or chopped), millet, nygur seed**, peanuts (chopped), canary seed, barley (whole or chopped), suet	Ground, tray
White-crowned sparrow	Sp/F	All (during migration) A few overwinter	**Millet (white), sunflower seeds (shelled or chopped)**, peanut butter/suet mixture, walnuts and cornbread), corn bread, walnuts (chopped), peanuts (chopped), suet	Ground, tray
Dark-eyed junco	Sp/F/W	All (during migration) Some overwinter	**Sunflower seeds (shelled or chopped), millet, peanut butter/suet mixture**, canola, corn (fine ground), cereal grain (chopped), suet	Ground, tray (low), suet
Grosbeaks and Buntings				
Rose-breasted grosbeak	S	P/B/F	**Sunflower seeds**	Tray, hopper
Blackbirds and Allies				
Red-winged blackbird	Sp/S/F	All	**Sunflower seeds**, corn (cracked), cereal grain	Ground, tray
Baltimore oriole	Sp/S	P/B(south)/F(south)/R(south)	**Sugar water, grape jelly, orange halves**, apples, watermelon	Oriole feeder, special feeder to hold fruit
Finches and Grosbeaks				
Gray-crowned rosy-finch	W	R (Winter: may be found in G/P/F)	**Millet**, canary seed, sunflower seeds	Ground, tray, hopper
Pine grosbeak	W	All	**Sunflower seeds**, flax	Ground, tray, hopper
Purple finch	Sp	P/B/F/R	**Sunflower seeds, nygur seed**, canola, sugar water	Ground, tray, hopper, tube, large hummingbird feeder
House finch	All	G/P (range is expanding)	**Sunflower seeds (shelled or chopped), nygur seed, wild birdseed mixes**, apples, watermelon, sugar water	As for purple finch
Common redpoll Hoary redpoll	W	All	**Sunflower seeds (shelled or chopped), nygur seed, canola**, corn (finely cracked), peanuts (chopped)	Ground, tray, hopper, tube, nygur seed sack
Pine siskin	All	All	**Sunflower seeds (shelled or chopped), nygur seed, canola**	As for redpolls
American goldfinch	Sp/S	All (rarely overwinters)	**Sunflower seeds (shelled or chopped), nygur seed**, canola	As for redpolls
Evening grosbeak	All	All	**Sunflower seeds**	Ground, tray, hopper, tube
Weaver Finches				
House sparrow	All	All	**Wild birdseed mixes, corn (cracked), sunflower seeds, nygur seed, peanuts (chopped), millet, bread and pastry**, suet, mealworms	Suet, ground, tray, hopper, tube

Safflower seed can be offered, but it is not as popular as other seeds. Gray squirrels don't like it, which may be advantageous if you live in Calgary or Okotoks (see next chapter).

Other seeds that can be offered include **canary seed**, **weed seeds** (excluding noxious and restricted species), and **vegetable and fruit seeds**.

Avoid commercial **seed mixtures** that contain red milo (grain sorghum), which is a filler material ignored by most Canadian bird species. If you want to use a seed mixture, choose ingredients that will appeal to specific species. For example, for chickadees and nuthatches choose a mixture that contains sunflower seeds (the variety will depend on what the birds in your yard prefer), chopped peanuts and sunflower chips (coarsely chopped sunflower seeds). A good blue jay blend would include whole peanuts, shelled peanuts, whole sunflower meats, sunflower seeds and whole corn.

Sugar Water and Sugar-Water Feeders

Feeders with sugar-water solutions put out in the warm months attract many bird species, including hummingbirds, orioles, sapsuckers, tanagers, warblers, purple finches and house finches. These feeders will be most successful if you have yard that offers cover and an assortment of nectar plants (see Chapter 4).

Commercial sugar-water solutions are available, but it is easy and inexpensive to make your own: simply dissolve 100 percent cane sugar (sucrose) in water. Although there is some debate about ratios, we recommend you use four parts water to one part sugar. If you use cold water, add your sugar and gently heat the solution until the sugar is dissolved; then let the solution cool. Boiling the water will sterilize the solution but will make it more concentrated. Add more water to the solution after boiling to dilute it again. If you use warm tap water, the mixture does not have to be heated. Store unused solution in the refrigerator, where it should stay fresh for up to a week.

SUGAR-WATER SOLUTION RATIOS

Solutions stronger than four to one may be eagerly consumed but may not be healthy. Some longtime feeder operators have observed that five to one, or seven to one ratios, are as attractive to birds as the more concentrated mixtures. Yet, some research shows that sugar concentrations in flower nectar can be as high as 35 percent (a ratio of approximately 2:1).

Here are some "no-nos": First, do not use honey, red food colouring or artificial sweeteners in sugar-water solutions. Honey, a dextrose compound, spoils quickly, may produce fungus infections and may contain the toxin that causes botulism. Red food colouring is thought to be unhealthy, and artificial sweeteners have no nutritional value.

Second, never serve old or mouldy solutions. During periods of hot weather, replace the solution every couple of days. If you keep your feeder in a shaded location, the solution will stay fresher a bit longer. Remember that sugar water is not a nutritionally complete food, so use it to supplement, not replace, natural food sources.

INSECTS AND SUGAR-WATER FEEDERS

Ants, bees, hornets and wasps are attracted to sugar-water solutions. If you can find it in your heart to just leave these insects be, you will be contributing to the biodiversity of your yard. If, however, they dominate a feeder or become a problem, you may want to discourage them. Ants can be dissuaded from entering a feeder by hanging it using monofilament fishing line or by "floating" the feeder in a moat of water. Bees and wasps can often be deterred by coating the feeding openings with salad oil, mineral oil or Avon Skin-So-Soft® (there is some concern about how healthy the last ingredient is if ingested by hummers, so you may not want to use it). Commercial bee guards are also available, although they are not always effective.

Hummingbird Feeders

There is a wide assortment of commercial hummingbird feeders available on the market in various designs and styles. Tubular feeders with nozzles at the base are quite popular, as are cup- or bowl-type feeders with feeding portals on top. The latter type performs better in windy areas, but some models are difficult to clean. A hummingbird feeder can also be made from a hamster or poultry watering bottle. Whatever feeder you choose, it should be easy to clean, functional (even when being blown about in the wind), and have parts that are red.

Hummingbird feeder

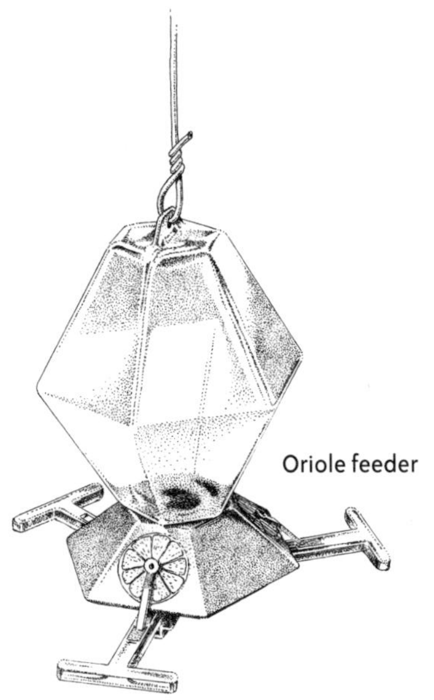
Oriole feeder

To maximize feeder use and minimize waste, start by offering small quantities of solution. Once the birds are coming regularly, set out several feeders, each out of sight of the other. This strategic placement will keep individual hummers, which are very territorial, from dominating more than one feeder.

You will likely want to place a feeder where it can be easily seen, but if it is too close to a window, the hummingbird will fly at its own image reflected in the glass. Some people put out their hummingbird feeders before flowers blossom in order to assist early-returning birds, and keep them up until the end of the fall migration period.

Oriole Feeders

Except for the extreme southern part of the province, where the Bullock's oriole is found, the Baltimore oriole is the common Alberta oriole. The Baltimore oriole is a bird of deciduous trees, so you aren't likely to have it around if your yard or neighbourhood is dominated by conifers.

Sugar-water or commercial oriole nectar solutions can be dispensed using a hanging, open jar, a special oriole feeder or even a hamster water bottle. A hummingbird feeder with large perches and the bee guards removed can also be used. Orioles are not aggressive and tend to leave when more aggressive birds come along. For this reason, you should place several feeders around your yard out of sight of one another. Use a water/sugar ratio of about four to one.

CLEANING A SUGAR-WATER FEEDER

To clean a sugar-water feeder, use 60 ml (1/4 c.) bleach in 4.5 L (1 gal.) of water. Submerge the feeder parts in this solution for 30 minutes. Rinse thoroughly before refilling.

Other Food Offerings and Supplements

Suet is a high-energy winter food eaten by those bird species that eat insects during the summer. The best quality suet is the hard, dense fat found around the kidneys and heart of cattle and sheep, although any type of fat can be used (birds seem to like pork the least). Available at supermarkets or butcher shops, suet can be purchased in its raw form or as lard (which means it has been rendered or melted, and homogenized).

The easiest and most popular way to serve raw suet is to hang it in an onion or other nylon mesh bag. Make sure the bag is kept full to prevent the birds from getting tangled in the strands. Wire mesh dispensers also work well. Most commercial metal dispensers are coated with plastic. The plastic coating is not essential, however, because the birds' feet will not freeze to the metal, and it is unlikely that healthy birds will touch the metal with their tongues or eyes.

Ways to hang suet

If you put out more than one suet feeder, put them out of sight of one another so that one bird can't dominate more than one feeder.

It is easy to render raw suet at home. Simply cut it up into small pieces and melt small quantities at a time in a oven at 120°C (250°F), or in a microwave, frying pan or heavy pot. Scoop out the rind and other "gunk," or strain it out by pouring the liquid through a metal sieve or colander lined with cheese cloth. Then cool the suet. For extra smooth suet, do the melt, strain and cool process twice.

If you want to add some "goodies" to your concoction, start by mixing in peanut butter while the suet is still warm and very runny (the proportions don't really matter). When the mixture cools to the consistency of soft butter, you can add other ingredients—pretty much anything you want, including chopped nuts, cracked corn, chopped fruit, dried ground meat, grit, finely crushed eggshells, rolled oats, cornmeal, wheatlets, wheat germ, crumbled dried or stale pastry, or mashed hard boiled eggs. Don't add seeds or roll the suet mixture around in seeds. The suet makes the seeds greasy and hard for birds to hold onto.

Once you've got your brew all stirred up, spoon it onto pinecones or suet logs (pieces of wood with holes drilled into them), directly onto tree trunks, into muffin tins or cupcake holders. You have to work fast because suet isn't easy to work with once it hardens. (If it does harden, simply warm it up a bit before continuing.) If you have extra suet pinecones, logs, muffins or cupcakes, you can store them in the freezer.

Suet is usually put out in the winter but can be served in any season. Note, though, that rancid suet tends to mat birds' feathers. A good, all-season mix includes vegetable shortening, peanut butter, cornmeal and flour.

Be sure to place a suet feeder high enough off the ground to be out of reach of dogs. Even the fattest and most sedentary of dogs can turn into an Olympian when the prize is a nice, big hunk of suet. An exclusion suet feeder, illustrated here, will exclude cats and dogs. It will also prevent the larger birds from getting in, which might be a good idea if magpies are constantly packing away all your suet.

If you have black bears in your area, they, too, love suet and will climb trees to get it. We suggest you set out a suet feeder only during the winter, when you are sure the bears are hibernating.

Bone sawdust is generated when beef carcasses are cut up, and contains marrow and bits of bone and flesh. It is a favourite of many insect-eating bird species, especially brown creepers. This food rots quickly, so serve it only when temperatures are going to remain below freezing.

Pastry contains ground grains and fat, both of which are attractive to birds. Although boreal chickadees will eat bran muffins, most other **breads** and pastries will attract only house sparrows and European starlings. If you are feeding waterfowl, don't use bread—it can plug their digestive systems.

Fruits and berries, which are appealing to those birds whose summer diet consists of insects or fruit, can be offered year-round. During the winter, cubes of dried or frozen bananas, oranges, apples, pears, plums, peaches, dates or figs, as well as raisins, currants and cherries, are popular with many bird species (especially waxwings). Some people collect mountain-ash berries, crab apples and other fruits in the fall, freeze them spread out on trays, and bag them. This bounty is then set out on tray feeders during the winter and early spring.

If you want to offer larger fruit, impale it on a nail or sharpened dowel to prevent squirrels or larger birds from taking it away. In the summer, fruit, especially orange halves, may attract such birds as blue jays, robins, orioles, tanagers, woodpeckers, warblers, catbirds, sapsuckers and thrashers. Apple halves and watermelon will attract house finches and orioles; orioles will also go for grape jelly.

Other foods that may be offered at a bird feeder include old **wasp nests** (tear them apart so the unhatched eggs and larvae inside are left exposed) and leftover **chicken or turkey carcasses.** Although many bird species will readily eat **pet food** (including cat food, dog food, rabbit pellets and gerbil pellets), its nutritional value for birds has not been established. Until it has, we cannot recommend it. A half-and-half mixture of **peanut butter and cornmeal** is liked by nuthatches and chickadees.

A SUET RECIPE

Pinecone/Suet Log Filling

250 ml (1 c.) melted suet
125 ml (1/2 c.) peanut butter
125 ml (1/2 c.) cornmeal and chopped raisins
125 ml (1/2 c.) rolled oats
125 ml (1/2 c.) wheat germ
125 ml (1/2 c.) crushed walnuts
Small handful of grit

Mix all ingredients together and spoon onto five large pinecones. Store in freezer until needed.

For other recipes, see *Winter Bird Feeding: An Alberta guide* listed in **Significant References** at the end of this chapter.

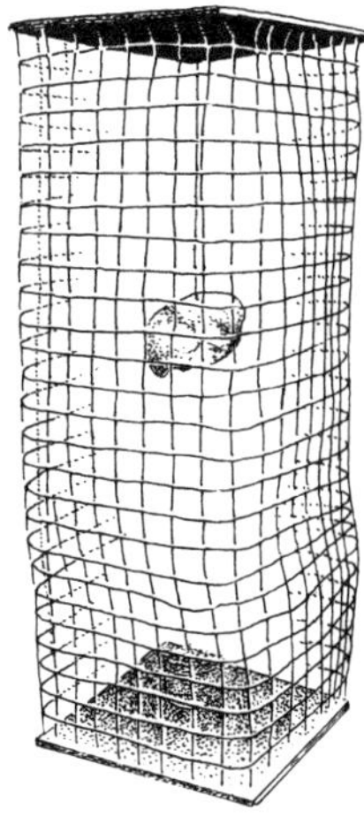

Exclusion suet feeder

During extended periods of bad weather, live **mealworms**, widely available at pet stores, are a high protein offering for insect eaters. If you'd like to grow mealworms (a very easy procedure), contact the Ellis Bird Farm for information (see Appendix 5).

All seed-eating birds require a gizzard full of abrasive material to crush and grind the seeds that they eat. Because grit is often difficult for birds to find in the winter, you may want to offer **commercial grit, beach sand or crushed charcoal** as a feeder food supplement. Put it in a separate feeder or add it directly to seeds or suet.

Calcium supplements can be supplied on a year-round basis by providing ground oyster shell or crushed eggshells. Oyster shell comes ready-to-use. Eggshells can be collected, then set in an oven (use an aluminum can or glass jar) on low heat for about 10 minutes, cooled and pulverized. Oyster shell or eggshells can be served on the ground, in tray feeders, added to suet mixtures, or mixed in with seeds.

Salt is essential for all wildlife species, including birds. Salt is added to the sand used on roads during the winter so is readily available to any bird that wants it (you will often see birds feeding on salt around the sides of parked cars).

Concern is often expressed about providing suet that contains a high concentration of salt. Because salt is so accessible elsewhere, it is a good idea to avoid putting ham fat, bacon grease or other salty drippings in your suet mixture.

PROVIDING WATER

Many different bird species will visit a garden where water is provided. Many birds, even those that are not attracted to supplemental feeding stations, will readily come into a yard where there is a birdbath or pond. In fact, setting out a water source may be the only way you will be able to get some species, especially warblers, to visit.

The two obvious uses of water are for drinking and bathing. Birds drink water all year round, and although the species that overwinter in Alberta are able to secure all the moisture they require from snow, they are readily attracted to open water. They are also ingenious when it comes to finding the liquid stuff—you can see them sipping it from puddles and melting icicles, or at the edges of springs or other open water. Seed-eating birds tend to be a thirstier lot than their insect-eating counterparts.

MYRNA PEARMAN

Bathing is a very popular activity with birds. They bathe to clean their feathers, to remove parasites, to relieve the discomfort associated with the growth of new feathers during moulting, and to cool down. If you've ever watched birds bathing, you'd almost think they were enjoying themselves! Some like the Turkish bath approach—they all bathe together—whereas others prefer to perform this toilet alone. Birds are clever at finding bathtubs too—you'll find them bathing in wet foliage, puddles, the shallows along the edges of water bodies, snow and on lily pads.

Some people are concerned that birds will bathe even when it is too cold for them to do so safely. To date, most reported observations of this phenomenon have been of house sparrows and European starlings bathing in extremely cold temperatures, then dying of hypothermia or freezing to metal fences or other metal perches after leaving a bath. Some feeder operators have also observed mourning doves with frozen toes. If you are concerned about birds bathing during cold weather, cover your water source with wire mesh. The birds will be able to drink but not enter the water.

Birds tend to be less wary when they are drinking, bathing or when they preen themselves after a bath. Less wary means more vulnerable to predators, especially cats. Take precautions to reduce the risk of an attack (see page 147).

Birdbaths

There are dozens of commercial birdbaths available, some equipped with heaters and built-in recirculating pumps. Ideally, a birdbath should be about 45 cm (18 in.) in diameter. It should have a flat bottom, be relatively shallow (no more than 7.5 cm [3 in.] deep) and gradually slope to this depth on at least one side. Medium-sized rocks can be placed in the bath to vary the depth of the water. The surface of the bath should be rough enough to ensure secure footing.

Many people have had success using recycled materials, such as old electric frying pans, cake pans, large flower pot drip trays and garbage can lids, to make birdbaths. The inexpensive, homemade birdbath illustrated here (the Meston bath) keeps water open even at -40°C (-40°F). The only materials needed are 19 mm (3/4 in.) plywood, a shallow dish (e.g., the drip tray from a large flower pot, or a cake pan), an extension cord with a light bulb attachment, some fibreglass insulation, a large aluminum can and a 25-watt (for milder weather) or 50-watt (for very cold temperatures), "rough service" light bulb.

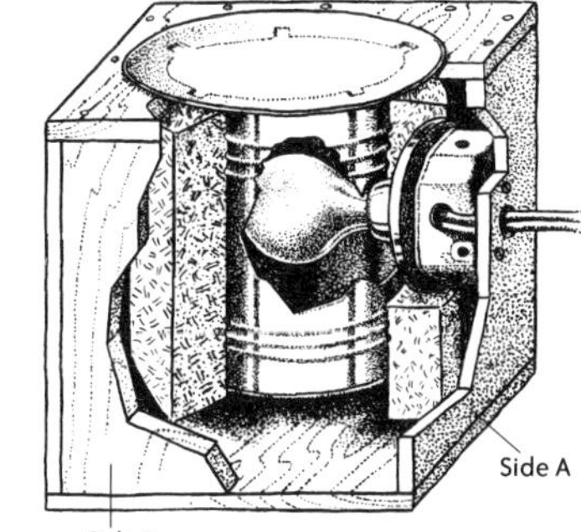

MESTON BATH made from 19 mm (3/4 in.) plywood (original measurements in inches)

PART	METRIC (cm)	IMPERIAL (in.)
Roof	34.3 x 34.3	13 1/2 x 13 1/2
Hole in roof (diameter)	27.9	11
Floor	34.3 x 34.3	13 1/2 x 13 1/2
Side A	33 x 34.3	13 x 13 1/2
Side B	30.5 x 33	12 x 13
Bulb	Place 15 cm (6 in.) below the bottom of the water dish	

The most popular and safe birdbaths are located near shrubbery (about 1 m [3 ft.] away). Birds look for safe approaches to a drinking or bathing area, and their well-used routes will thread to and fro through surrounding trees and overhanging branches. If you are landscaping a new yard, plant shrubs and shade plants close to at least one side of a water source.

A bath can be mounted on a pedestal or set on the ground. Mounting it at least 1 m (3 ft.) off the ground will offer your birds some safety from cats. If you set your bath on the ground near shrubbery, be sure to encircle it with mesh or ornamental fencing.

Many birds are attracted to the sound and motion of moving water, so try to incorporate these elements into your birdbath, designing it so that the water drips or splashes. The simplest way to provide this effect is to suspend a bucket, into which has been punctured a small hole, over a pedestal birdbath. The hole should be placed on the side of the bucket, near the bottom, and should have a piece of cloth or wick inserted into it to reduce the drip rate. The moving-water effect can also be provided by hanging a dripping garden hose over the bath or by using a commercial dripper. Most bird and wildlife specialty stores offer a wide variety of commercial drippers and misters.

Birdbath with American robin

A birdbath should be cleaned regularly—squirt it with a garden hose every week or so. Occasionally, give the bath a thorough scrubbing. If you have a plastic or fibreglass bath, scrub it clean using warm, soapy water. A ceramic or metal bath should first be scrubbed with steel wool, then washed with bleach. Do a second wash with rubbing alcohol, then leave the surface to dry. After the bath has dried, rinse it with clean water.

If the area around the base of a your birdbath becomes excessively muddy (remember that many creatures like mud!), dig a shallow trench at the base of the pedestal and fill it with gravel or small rocks.

Water Gardens

If you are installing a water garden, be sure to include some shallow bathing and drinking areas for birds. If you have a steep-sided water garden, make it more bird-friendly by installing rocks in one corner or by placing a shallow bathing dish just below the water. If these procedures are not feasible, place a birdbath adjacent to your water garden. A stream or waterfall incorporated into a water garden is very attractive to birds. We discuss water gardens in Chapter 5.

PROVIDING SHELTER AND HOUSING

Shelter

If there is sufficient habitat in your yard, most species of birds will find their own shelter, and will choose a site to build their own nest. However, they won't come to your yard unless they feel secure and safe; and to feel secure and safe, they need to have lots of protective cover.

You can provide this cover by planting trees and shrubs, as described in Chapter 3. Trees with densely packed branches furnish the best hiding, nesting and roosting sites. Conifers offer the most thermal protection during the winter, whereas deciduous trees and shrubs are an important source of shelter during the spring and summer. Vines, such as Virginia creeper, will also provide cover.

WHY BIRDS DON'T FREEZE IN WINTER

In order to survive the Alberta winter, birds have to eat lots of high energy food, and their blood has to maintain high levels of glucose. At nightfall, once the birds have all the food they need, they seek out shelter. A few birds cope with the cold by snuggling up together in dense coniferous trees. Others, especially the small ones, seek out natural cavities, where a group of them will sleep together. Larger birds, like woodpeckers, also seek out a natural cavity but usually sleep alone.

Some birds (e.g., grouse, chickadees) will plunge into the snow to keep warm on extremely cold winter nights.

Most birds maintain a protective layer of fat during the winter. Their thick coat of feathers, made even more efficient with a thick layer of down feathers next to the body, traps body heat and helps keep the bird warm.

Additional shelter can also be offered by setting out brush piles. To construct a brush pile, simply heap tree branches into a large pile, with the larger branches on the bottom and smaller-sized ones on top. You can provide temporary coniferous cover in the winter by setting out your old Christmas tree next to one of your bird feeders. Dead and dying trees (snags) are also a very important source of shelter for many birds (for more details about snags, see Chapter 3).

During inclement weather, birds will often huddle together in nestboxes. Roosting boxes are often recommended, but there is little evidence that they actually attract birds. We suggest you try insulating a few nestboxes in your yard to see if the birds will roost in them. If you have a wren nest, leave it full of sticks for the winter—it has been observed that chickadees and nuthatches will sometimes use this type of abode for roosting. And make sure there are plenty of other sheltered areas in your yard, such as snags and brush piles, in which they can roost. If birds do use roosting boxes on your property, let us know using the Backyard Watch form (Appendix 6).

Nestboxes

Nestboxes provide nesting sites for birds that require a hole, or cavity, in which to nest. Some birds are called "primary cavity nesters." These birds (for example, woodpeckers) make their own cavities by excavating holes in tree trunks. "Secondary cavity nesters," like house wrens and tree swallows, also require cavities for nesting, but because they lack the carpentry skills necessary for excavating, they rely on pre-existing cavities.

In the wild, an old woodpecker hole is the usual cavity picked by a secondary cavity nester, but natural tree cavities, pockets in rock cliffs, holes in mud banks and nestboxes are also used. Some species (for example, chickadees, nuthatches and flickers) sometimes excavate their own cavity; other times they choose secondhand housing.

It is the secondary cavity nesters that will take to a human-built nestbox; the primary cavity nesters will find their own nest site in your yard if there is suitable natural habitat or "planted" snags.

Unfortunately for our native cavity nesters, two introduced species—the house sparrow and the European starling—also nest in cavities. These two aggressive and persistent species are abundant throughout Alberta. Although some people don't mind them taking up residence in their nestboxes, ecologists warn that these birds have contributed to the decline of some of our native bird species. We recommend that you exclude these birds from your nestboxes. If you would like more information on how to reduce the problems posed by sparrows and starlings in nestboxes, see below and/or contact the Ellis Bird Farm (Appendix 5).

Nestboxes for Smaller Secondary Cavity Nesters

Of the approximately 15 species of smaller secondary cavity nesters in Alberta, only 8 are likely to be attracted to an urban or acreage backyard. Of these 8, the mountain bluebird rarely comes into urban areas, and only the tree swallow will commonly use a box in a treeless yard. Purple martins will nest only if they have adequate open space adjacent to their house (see discussion below) and the other species—house wren, black capped chickadee, boreal chickadee, white-breasted nuthatch and red-breasted nuthatch—all require substantial tree and shrub cover.

Some other small species, like the brown creeper and American dipper, will, on rare occasions, use a nestbox, but require specialized nesting structures. Contact the Ellis Bird Farm (see Appendix 5) for information.

Nestbox Design for Smaller Secondary Cavity Nesters. There is no one perfect nestbox for smaller secondary cavity nesters, but all the criteria listed in the sidebar have to be met. As long as the birds are safe, dry and warm, they don't really care what type of house you offer them.

The two nestbox plans, shown on the following page, will work for all smaller cavity nesters. You can use an entrance hole size of 38 mm (1 1/2 in.) in diameter, unless you are on an acreage and want to attract mountain bluebirds, in which case a 40-mm (1 9/16-in.) hole should be used. Never use a 42-mm (1 5/8-in.) or larger hole, because European starlings will be able to enter. If house sparrows are present, use boxes that have a 29-mm (1 1/8-in.) entrance hole. This small size will exclude house sparrows but allow wrens and chickadees to nest. The specific entrance hole sizes needed by each species are listed in Table 2.

If house sparrows take up residence in a nestbox, we recommend you remove their nesting material. If the sparrows persist, try a McEwan box (illustrated here) or move the box to a more suitbale, sparrow-free location.

The best materials for nestbox construction are 19-mm (3/4-in.) pine or exterior grade plywood. Thick wood provides insulation against early spring chills and summer heat; thinner material provides less insulation and deteriorates more quickly. Never use treated lumber because it may contain harmful chemicals. Do not try to convert milk cartons or other waxed cardboard containers, or plastic jugs into nestboxes. However, aluminium containers, as long as they are adequately ventilated, will provide reasonable nesting sites (see side bar on the next page).

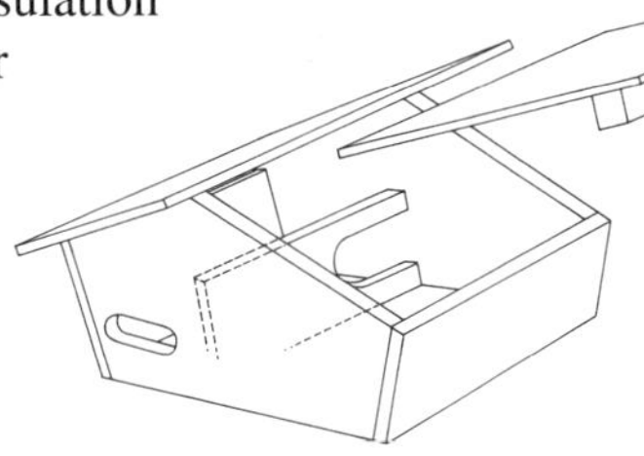

Charles McEwan nestbox

NESTBOXES FOR SMALLER SECONDARY CAVITY NESTERS: THE NECESSITIES

All nestboxes must have

- one panel (top, front or side) that opens easily to allow for observation and cleaning;
- ventilation holes near the top of each side board—small holes can be drilled on an upward angle to provide ventilation without allowing rain to blow in;
- adequate drainage—small holes can be drilled in the floor, or the corners of the floor can be cut off;
- a roof that has an overhang extending at least 5 cm (2 in.) to provide shade, protect the entrance hole from driving rain and to discourage magpies, crows and other predators from reaching in to capture young;
- shallow saw slashes (saw kerfs) on the inside of the front panel to help the young exit the box.

Do not put perches on the front of small nestboxes—they allow house sparrows and predators to enter.

All smaller secondary cavity nesters bring in their own nesting material.

Mount your bird nestbox on a fence post or, if you have cats or raccoons in your neighbourhood, on free-standing posts (e.g., galvanized pipe or rebar). Additional protection can be offered by placing metal baffles or pieces of stovepipe below the box. An alternative is to rub car wax or axle grease on smooth poles. On an acreage with horses, put your box on top of a tall post (at least 2.5 m [8 ft.] high) and wrap the post with barbed wire.

Always face the entrance hole away from the prevailing wind.

To monitor a nestbox, approach it quietly from the side. Open it slowly, check inside, then close it up quickly and leave. Never open a box in cold or rainy weather.

Except for wren boxes that might be used by chickadees and nuthatches for roosting in the winter, boxes can be cleaned out after the young have fledged. Although secondary cavity nesters will readily use a nestbox with an old nest, removing the old nest will ensure that nesting material does not build up in the box (exposing the occupants to predators). Use gloves for this rather messy job, and be sure to avoid inhaling any dust. In areas where keen-scented raccoons are becoming a problem, collect the old nesting material in a plastic bag and dispose of it in your regular garbage.

THE MCEWAN BOX

To deter house sparrows, you might try using the oval entrance-holed box shown here, designed by Charles McEwan in New Brunswick. The entrance slot on this box, which measures 24 mm x 76 mm (15/16 x 3 in.), is intended to exclude the plump house sparrow but allow entry by the slimmer tree swallow. If you put up this box, please give us some feedback on its success, which, so far, in Alberta, has been mixed (use the Backyard Watch form [Appendix 6]). For detailed box plans, contact the Ellis Bird Farm (see Appendix 5).

MYRNA PEARMAN

ALUMINUM NESTBOXES

In the TELUS Feather Care® program, the orange aluminum markers for buried cable are converted into nestboxes. For more information, contact TELUS at 1-800-667-1125.

In a small, urban backyard, one or two nestboxes is plenty. If you live on an acreage that provides adequate habitat, you may be able to set out several boxes. On larger acreages, where both tree swallows and mountain bluebirds might be attracted, place two boxes side-by-side (1.5 m-7.5 m [5-25 ft.] apart), so both species can nest together peaceably.

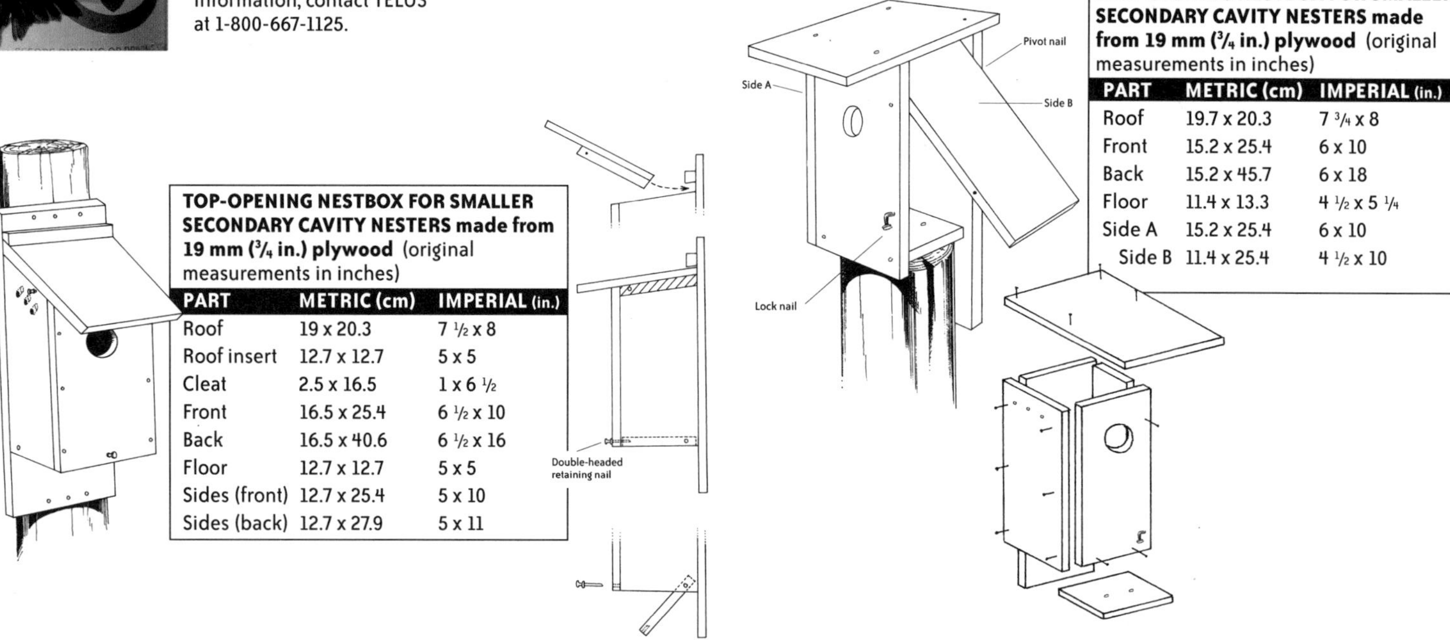

TOP-OPENING NESTBOX FOR SMALLER SECONDARY CAVITY NESTERS made from 19 mm (3/4 in.) plywood (original measurements in inches)

PART	METRIC (cm)	IMPERIAL (in.)
Roof	19 x 20.3	7 1/2 x 8
Roof insert	12.7 x 12.7	5 x 5
Cleat	2.5 x 16.5	1 x 6 1/2
Front	16.5 x 25.4	6 1/2 x 10
Back	16.5 x 40.6	6 1/2 x 16
Floor	12.7 x 12.7	5 x 5
Sides (front)	12.7 x 25.4	5 x 10
Sides (back)	12.7 x 27.9	5 x 11

SIDE-OPENING NESTBOX FOR SMALLER SECONDARY CAVITY NESTERS made from 19 mm (3/4 in.) plywood (original measurements in inches)

PART	METRIC (cm)	IMPERIAL (in.)
Roof	19.7 x 20.3	7 3/4 x 8
Front	15.2 x 25.4	6 x 10
Back	15.2 x 45.7	6 x 18
Floor	11.4 x 13.3	4 1/2 x 5 1/4
Side A	15.2 x 25.4	6 x 10
Side B	11.4 x 25.4	4 1/2 x 10

TABLE 2 Information about Smaller Secondary Cavity Nesting Birds and Their Nestboxes

Species	Nest Description	Usual Clutch Size	Egg Colour	Incubation Period	Nestling Period	Size of Nestbox Entrance Hole	Height of Nestbox off Ground	Attach Nestbox To	Last Date to Set Out Nestbox	NatureScape Habitat
Chickadees										
Black-capped chickadee	ALL SPECIES: Base of nest is moss, lined with plant down, hair, wool, feathers	ALL SPECIES: 6-8	ALL SPECIES: Reddish-brown speckled	12-14 days	16 days	ALL SPECIES: 29 mm-32 mm 1 1/8-1 1/4 in.	ALL SPECIES: 1.2 m-3 m (4-10 ft.)	ALL SPECIES: Fence post or tree	ALL SPECIES: Early March	ALL SPECIES: Within or at the edge of mixed woods, poplar or spruce woods
Boreal chickadee				About 14 days	About 19 days					
Mountain chickadee				14 days	Unknown					
Nuthatches										
White-breasted nuthatch	Bark shreds, fur, wool, cow hair, feathers, grass	5-9	White or pinkish	12 days	14-17 days	38 mm-40 mm (1 1/2-1 9/16 in.)	2 m (6.5 ft.)	Tall post or tree	Mid-April	Urban or acreage areas with poplar or mixed poplar-spruce woods
Red-breasted nuthatch	Grass, rootlets, moss, shredded bark, plant fibres	5-6								
Wrens House wren	Sticks or twigs, lined with hair and feathers	6-8	Reddish speckled	13-15 days	12-18 days	25 mm-32 mm 1-1 1/4 in.	1.2 m-1.5 m (4-5 ft.)	Fence post or tree	Late April	Urban or acreage areas with trees and shrubs
Swallows Tree swallow	Grass nest lined with feathers (prefers white)	4-6	White	13-16 days	21 days	38 mm-40 mm 1 1/2-1 9/16 in.	1.2 m-1.5 m (4-5 ft.)	Fence post or free-standing post	Early-April	Urban areas, acreages with open areas, adjacent to wetlands
Bluebirds All species	Tidy grass nest	5-6	Blue (rarely white)	13-14 days	18-21 days	40 mm 1 9/16 in.	1.2 m-1.5 m (4-5 ft.)	Fence post or free-standing post	Early March	Acreages with open areas, low-cut grass and scattered trees

Nestboxes for Larger Secondary Cavity Nesters

Not surprisingly, you need a big yard with specific habitat or to live adjacent to a natural area to attract any of the larger secondary cavity nesters. Of the approximately 14 species of larger secondary cavity nesters in Alberta, only 4 are likely to take up residence in a large backyard or acreage where appropriate habitat is offered: common goldeneye, bufflehead, American kestrel and northern saw-whet owl. The northern flicker, which is a primary cavity nester, will also accept a nestbox designed for a larger secondary cavity nester.

Nestbox Design for Larger Secondary Cavity Nesters. One basic design can be used for all the larger secondary cavity nesters (see illustration). Construct the box from 19-mm (3/4-in.) untreated, exterior grade plywood. The different hole sizes required by different species are shown in the accompanying table. Boxes for the larger cavity nesters should be mounted as high as possible (1.8 m-3.5 m [6-12 ft.] is ideal) on a tree or pole.

TABLE 3 Information about Larger Secondary Cavity Nesting Birds and Their Nestboxes

Species	Usual Clutch Size	Egg Colour	Incubation Period	Nestling Period	Size of Nestbox Entrance Hole	Last Date to Set Out Nestbox	NatureScape Habitat
Bufflehead	8-12	Creamy white	29 days	24-36 hours	7.6 cm (3 in.) wide 6.3 cm (2.5 in.) high	Mid-March	Small, wooded lakes and ponds
Common goldeneye	6-14	Greenish	27-32 days	24-36 hours	10.2 cm (4 in.) wide 7.6 cm (3 in.) high	Late March	Wooded ponds and lakes or along rivers
American kestrel	3-5	White, creamy or pale pink, brownish spotted	28-32 days	25-31 days	7.6 cm (3 in.) diameter	Mid-April	Open meadows or grassy areas, edges of poplar groves
Northern saw-whet owl	3-6	Whitish	21-28 days	28-33 days	7.6 cm (3 in.) diameter	Mid-March	Areas of mixed spruce and poplar in the north, poplar groves in parkland areas, and wooded coulees and river valleys in the grassland region
Northern flicker	6-8	White	11-12 days	25-28 days	6.3 cm (2.5 in.) diameter	Late March	Open areas near deciduous groves or mixed poplar-spruce woods

OTHER LARGER SECONDARY CAVITY NESTERS

If you live along the rivers running through Calgary or Medicine Hat, you may be able to attract wood ducks. Farther north, the common merganser might take up residence in a nestbox. In western Alberta, Barrow's goldeneye may also use a nestbox. For more information on these and other larger secondary cavity nesting species, we recommend you read *Nestboxes for Prairie Birds* (see **Significant References** at the end of this chapter).

Unlike the smaller secondary cavity nesters, cavity-nesting ducks, kestrels, owls and flickers do not bring in their own nesting material. Provide a 5 cm (2 in.) layer of wood shavings or sawdust for ducks and owls, a 2.5 cm (1 in.) layer for kestrels, and fill the box with shavings for flickers. (Filling the nestbox up with shavings will prevent flickers from "excavating" the front of the box; they will "excavate" the shavings and leave the box intact.)

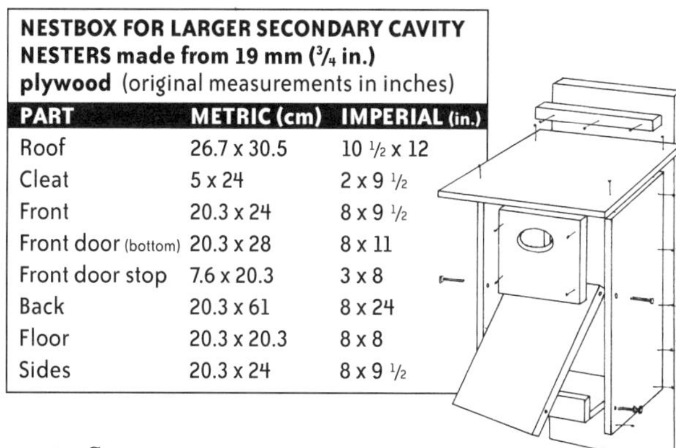

NESTBOX FOR LARGER SECONDARY CAVITY NESTERS made from 19 mm (3/4 in.) plywood (original measurements in inches)

PART	METRIC (cm)	IMPERIAL (in.)
Roof	26.7 x 30.5	10 1/2 x 12
Cleat	5 x 24	2 x 9 1/2
Front	20.3 x 24	8 x 9 1/2
Front door (bottom)	20.3 x 28	8 x 11
Front door stop	7.6 x 20.3	3 x 8
Back	20.3 x 61	8 x 24
Floor	20.3 x 20.3	8 x 8
Sides	20.3 x 24	8 x 9 1/2

Boxes for larger cavity nesters do not have to be cleaned out every year, but an annual inspection should be done to check nesting success, remove eggshells and add shavings.

The habitat requirements for the larger cavity nesters are fairly specific. Duck boxes, for instance, must be placed close to a permanent water body. Because ducklings are vulnerable to predation until they are old enough to fly, they rely on the protection offered by water.

We encourage waterfront property owners to set out duck boxes on their property. Snags and dying, cavity-bearing trees are usually the first to fall prey to the developer's blade or new landowner's chain saw, and because natural cavities are often in short supply to begin with, the removal of these wildlife trees has resulted in duck housing shortages in some areas.

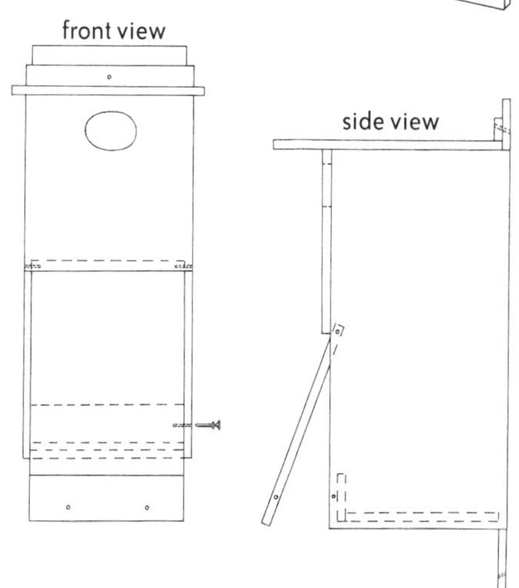

Nestboxes for ducks can be placed quite close together because the males defend territories on the water, not around the nest site. The number of boxes placed will be determined by the amount of "brood water" available (the depth and size of the water body on which the young spend their preflying youth). On a large lake or along a river, boxes can be placed as close as 1 m (3 ft.) apart; on smaller ponds, one or two boxes are usually all that is feasible.

If you have both buffleheads and goldeneyes, put at least one box out for each species, to ensure all the ducks have nesting sites (female goldeneyes outcompete female buffleheads for nesting spots). The Alberta Conservation Association (ACA) has had success placing one box directly above the other on the same tree or pole. For more information, contact the ACA (see Appendix 5).

American kestrels

American kestrels are quite readily attracted to nestboxes. These delightful little falcons are found throughout Alberta, including in urban areas. They will devour the occasional bird but eat mostly rodents and grasshoppers. Kestrels will nest at almost any height, but placing their nestboxes 3 m-3.5 m (10-12 ft.) high will reduce vandalism and predation. These birds like open hunting areas near their nest site, and they prefer to have a tall tree, pole or wire within 100 m-200 m (330-650 ft.) of their nest, as a place to perch or from which to hunt.

Northern saw-whet owls occur throughout the central part of the province. They prefer forested areas and will not likely be attracted to your property unless there is a significant amount of habitat available for them.

Northern flickers are rather tame, brownish woodpeckers that are often seen feeding on the ground, even in urban areas. Two forms, the yellow-shafted and the red-shafted, occur in Alberta. Flickers seem to prefer boxes that resemble natural cavities, so make their box out of wood cut from tree stumps, or cover the front of a regular box with a slab of rough wood.

COLLECTING NESTBOX INFORMATION

You may want to collect information on your nestbox occupants. A sample recording form can be found on the NatureScape Alberta website or can be obtained from the Ellis Bird Farm (see Appendix 5). Send completed forms to NatureScape Alberta .

Other Nesting Structures

Purple Martin Condo Housing. Purple martins are North America's largest swallows and one of the most sought-after and adored backyard birds. Ironically, their initial popularity can be attributed to the false claim that they consume massive quantities of mosquitoes. However, unlike the smaller, mosquito-eating swallows, martins focus on the larger insects, including adult dragonflies and damselflies. Because the nymphs of these insects eat vast quantities of mosquito larvae, it is possible that having a martin colony could result in an increase, rather than a decrease, in the number of mosquitoes nearby!

Some martin sites attract breeding pairs soon after they are erected; others remain empty for years, or never do attract them. Here are some tips for increasing your chances of success.

- Make sure your martin condo is within or very close to their known breeding range (see illustration). Your chances of occupancy will greatly increase if you place a new house near a neighbouring colony site.
- Martins prefer to nest within 3 km (1.8 mi.) of a sizeable pond or other water body and within 9 m-30 m (30-100 ft.) of a human dwelling.
- Martins require at least 12 m (40 ft.) of unobstructed air space for turning and landing. Keep tall shrubs and vines away from the support pole.
- Mount the house 4.5 m-5 m (15-16 ft.) off the ground, and make sure the pole is planted firmly enough to withstand high winds. Winch-style poles are preferable to pivoting ones because they can be easily raised and lowered for box monitoring and maintenance.
- Although martins will use condos and gourds painted various colours, they seem to be most attracted to white. Painting a house white may also prevent it from overheating.
- A martin condo should have at least four compartments. All compartments should be adequately ventilated and easily accessible. Each compartment should be 15 cm (6 in.) high and have minimum floor dimensions of 18 cm x 20 cm, 25 cm or 30 cm (7 x 8, 10 or 12 in.). Most plans call for a floor size of 15 cm x 15 cm (6 x 6 in.), a size now proven to be too small. If you have a martin house with small compartments, contact the Purple Martin Conservancy (PMC) for information on how to remodel it (see Appendix 5 for the address). The PMC should also be contacted for detailed construction plans if you're starting from scratch.

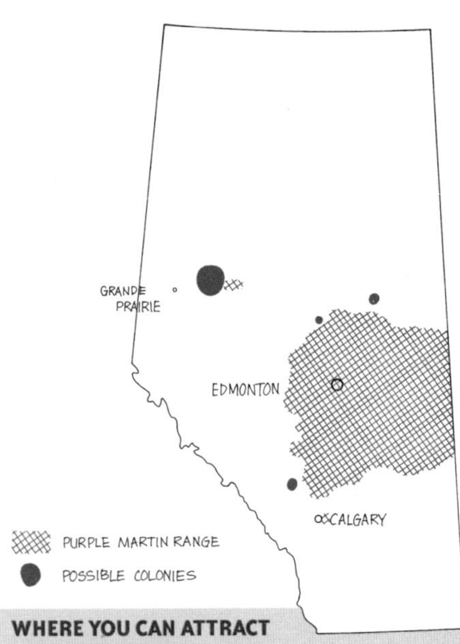

WHERE YOU CAN ATTRACT PURPLE MARTINS

In Alberta, martins are most common in the parkland natural region—north to the Cold Lake area, south to about Carstairs, west to Drayton Valley, and east to the Saskatchewan border. There are now confirmed records of them breeding in the Peace River District, which was a historical breeding location, and in the Calgary area. If you know of purple martins breeding outside of the rough range described here and illustrated by our map, contact the Purple Martin Conservancy (see Appendix 5).

- Each entrance hole should be 5.4 cm (2 1/8 in.) in diameter and placed about 2.5 cm (1 in.) above the compartment floor.
- Martins prefer used nests, so try nest "seeding" by placing a 2.5-cm (1-in.) layer of coarse grass (not lawn grass cuttings), leaves and small twigs in each compartment.
- Play dawn-song tapes of martin calls in the spring. Contact the PMC for the tapes and details on how to use them.
- The ideal time to erect a house is in the spring; martins will take up residence between late April and the end of June. Even if no martins use the condo, continue to maintain the site until the end of August because it might be discovered by migrants moving back south.
- Provide extra perching spots in a neutral location away from the defended, private areas in front of each individual compartment. Perching rods attached to the roof of your house or adjacent to the nest site will be used by the martins. Even old TV antennas work.
- Supply calcium to breeding martins by offering crushed eggshells or oyster shell in a safe location (on a shed roof or from a feeder made by attaching a perforated aluminum pie plate atop a 1.5-m [5-ft.] post).
- Supply nesting materials, including mud, straw and small, scattered twigs in a safe area.
- If you want to keep nest records, contact the PMC for details on box registration, monitoring and data collection.
- Clean all compartments after the martins have left for the season. Before removing nest contents, saturate the entire cavity with a bleach solution (one part bleach to ten parts water). Remove the soaked contents, or wait until the material has dried before proceeding. A clean condo can then be stored until spring, or placed back on the pole with the holes plugged (it will last longer if it is stored).

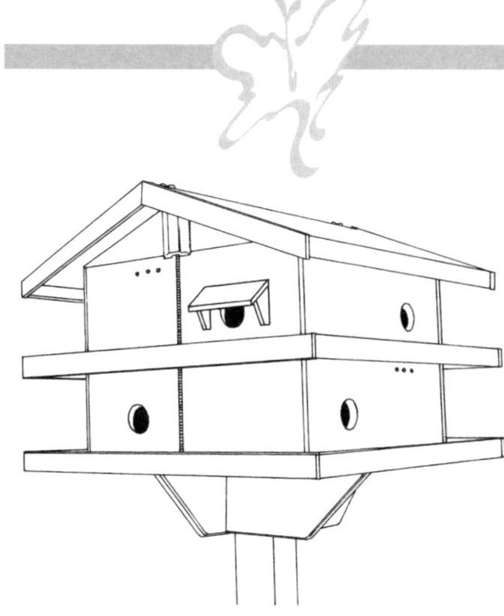
Two-tiered purple martin apartment housing (designed by Purple Martin Conservancy)

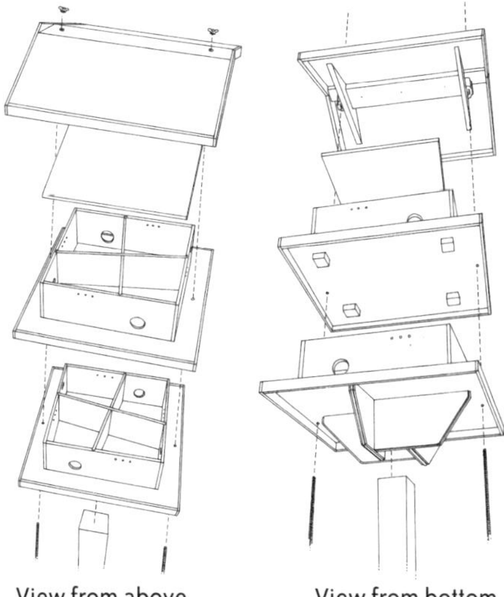
View from above　　View from bottom

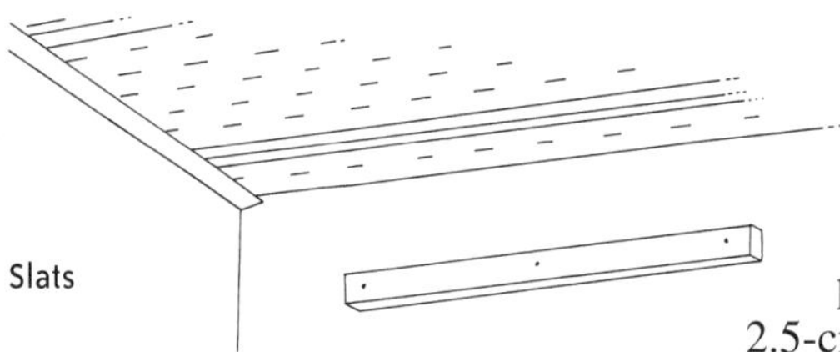
Slats

Cliff Swallow Nests. Cliff swallows are colonial nesters. If you have a bridge or a large outbuilding on your property, you may be able to encourage these swallows to nest by providing a nesting base or substrate—2.5-cm x 5-cm (1- x 2-in.) slats nailed flat against a wall. To minimize rain damage, place the slats 15 cm (6 in.) or less below the eaves or overhang.

You can also make more elaborate nesting frames for these birds. For instructions, we recommend you read *Nestboxes for Prairie Birds* (see **Significant References** at the end of this chapter).

Nesting Nails and Nesting Shelves. Nails and shelves or brackets will supply sites on which American robins, barn swallows and eastern phoebes can build their nests. These structures can also be used to encourage these species to relocate from above your backdoor or beside your kitchen window to a more acceptable site.

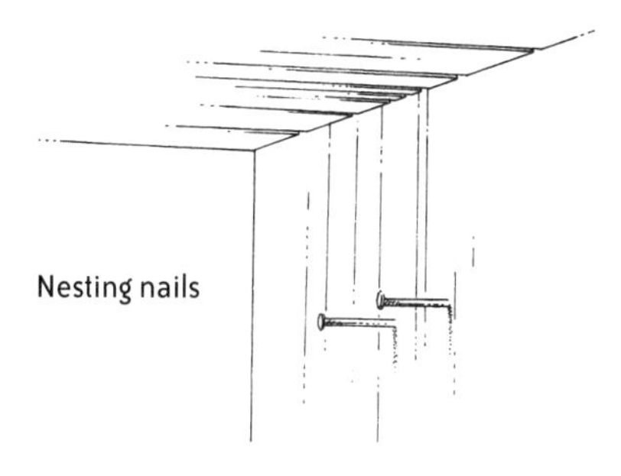
Nesting nails

Nesting nails are the easiest to provide: simply pound two small spikes, about 2.5 cm (1 in.) apart, into a beam or wall so that they protrude out about 3.8 cm (1 1/2 in.). Place them 11.5 cm-12.5 cm (4 1/2 - 5 in.) below an eave or overhang.

Small, triangular, plywood shelves (sides about 5 cm [2 in.] in length) work well for barn swallows. The distance from the floor of the shelf to the top of the overhang above it (e.g., soffit of a building) should be the same as for the nesting nails. The birds will then build a nest approximately 5 cm (2 in.) high, leaving a gap of about 6.5 cm (2 1/2 in.) for the adults to fly in and out, and to feed the young.

Nesting shelf

Larger shelves may attract robins and eastern phoebes. The larger shelves should have sides about 15 cm (6 in.) in length and will provide the most protection if placed under the eaves of a building (about 15 cm [6 in.] below). Phoebes are most likely to use a bracket located near water, whereas robins and barn swallows will nest in a variety of habitats.

If birds choose an inappropriate spot to nest and you need to deal with their droppings, place a 25-cm x 25-cm (10- x 10-in.) shelf about 30 cm (12 in.) under the nest to intercept the droppings.

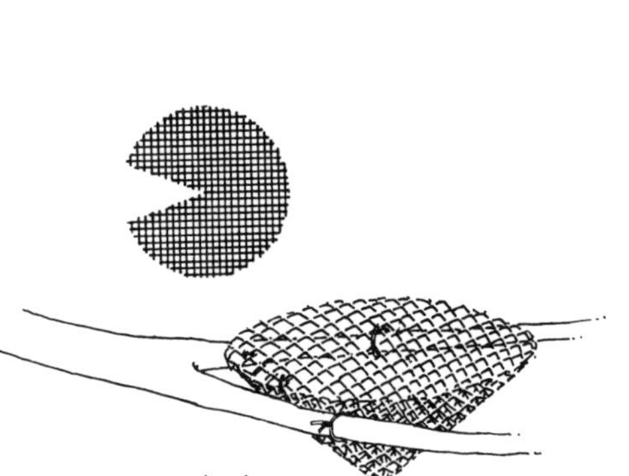
Dove nesting basket

Baskets. Mourning doves and great horned owls will nest in baskets placed in the appropriate habitat, as long as they are given a reasonable amount of solitude.

Mourning doves like to nest in a treed area that has water nearby and an adjacent open meadow or cultivated field for foraging. Dove baskets can be constructed from 6.5-mm or 13-mm (1/4-in. or 1/2-in.) wire mesh. Place the basket in the crotch of a tree limb about 2 m (6 1/2 ft.) off the ground and fasten it down with wire.

To construct a great horned owl basket, use a 1 m^2 (10 3/4 sq. ft.) piece of chicken wire lined with a piece of tar paper the same size. Cut a drain hole in the bottom and make a nest base by weaving small branches into the wire. Set the basket out in the fall, secured into a tree crotch 3 m-6.5 m (10-22 ft.) off the ground.

Wetland Nesting Sites

Several different types of structures can be used in wetland areas, provided there is adequate marginal habitat.

Nesting Islands. Nesting islands increase the diversity of a wetland by providing breeding and loafing sites. Although they do not offer protection from bird predators, islands are secure from most predatory mammals. Rock islands are the least difficult to install because they are typically made by dumping a large pile (15 m^2 [20 cu. yd.]) of pit run gravel on the frozen surface of a shallow wetland. Other types of islands, including push-up islands and nesting mounds, require technical expertise. For more information, contact your nearest Ducks Unlimited or Alberta Environment, Natural Resources Service [Fish and Wildlife] office (see Appendix 5).

Nesting Platforms. Some bird species, including Canada geese, will use nesting platforms placed in or near permanent water. If placed in the water, make sure the platform is about 1 m (3 ft.) above the high water level.

Floating Nesting/Loafing Structures. Floating structures are suitable for wetlands with fluctuating water levels, or where the water is too deep to install other structures. They are not suitable on water bodies where motorized boats are used. Because a Licence of Occupation may be required before one of these structures can be installed, be sure to consult Alberta Environment before an installation. Grebes, shorebirds and ducks may be attracted to floating structures, either to loaf or to nest.

There are several different styles of floating nesting structures that can be built. For ideas on constructing floating nests, contact the Ellis Bird Farm (see Appendix 5) or your nearest Ducks Unlimited office. Innovative plans can also be found at http://members.aol.com/Tjacmc/.

MYRNA PEARMAN

Nesting Tunnels. Nesting tunnels provide secure nesting sites for such duck species as mallard, redhead and gadwall. Because they have a roof, nesting tunnels offer protection from crows, hawks and other bird predators. Tunnels are useful in small (less than 8-ha.[20-a.]) permanent or semi-permanent water bodies that are not subject to moving ice during spring runoff. Small potholes (sloughs) with a cattail fringe are ideal. The nesting tunnels now used by Ducks Unlimited consist of a 25-cm (10-in) round geotex tube fastened to a 2.5-m (8-ft.) steel pole, as shown in the illustration. When placing a tunnel, be sure its bottom is above the spring high water level. For more details, contact your nearest Ducks Unlimited office.

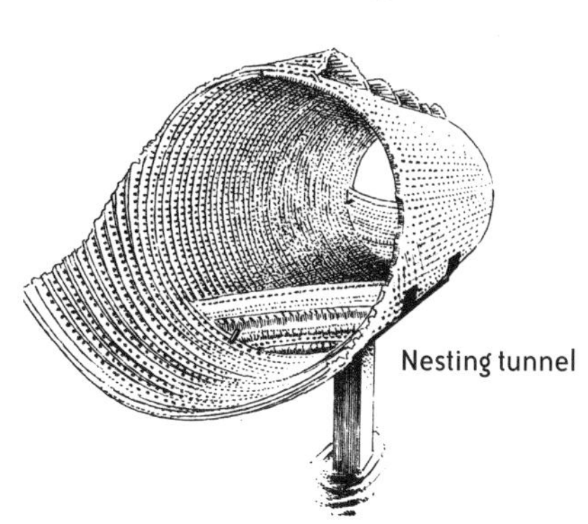

Nesting tunnel

OTHER OFFERINGS

Perches

Birds perch for many different reasons—to hawk for food, rest, sing, preen and guard a territory. Tree swallows are particularly fond of sitting on a perch near their nestboxes. Flycatchers and even hummingbirds might also rest on a perch if it is provided in a convenient location. Birds that are fed mealworms (e.g., bluebirds, robins) especially appreciate having a perch close to their feeding site. Never place a perch directly on a nestbox.

Perches can easily be made from narrow posts or two-by-twos. Install a post or a two-by-two as you would a fence post, then secure a 35-cm (14-in.) piccc of 13 mm (1/2 in.) dowling to the top. To convert a perch made with a post or two-by-two into an eggshell dispenser, simply remove the dowling and replace it with an aluminum pie plate.

Mud

A patch of moist soil might be visited by barn swallows, cliff swallows and robins, all of which use mud to construct their nests.

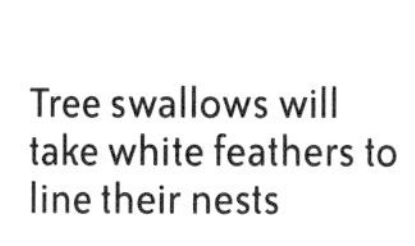

Tree swallows will take white feathers to line their nests

Nest Liners

Many bird species, including waxwings, orioles, robins, vireos, goldfinches and some sparrows, appreciate the provision of nesting materials, such as short lengths (about 15 cm [6 in.]) of yarn and string. Avoid long pieces, which can become tangled. Drape the string on a clothesline or over branches, scatter it on the ground or serve it from mesh bags. Orioles can untie single knots, so yarn set out for these species can be loosely tied.

Tree swallows love to line their nests with white feathers. If you have these birds around, you can either throw the feathers up into the air for the birds to snatch up, or hold the feathers between your fingers and let the birds pull them out.

Other nesting materials you can offer include cotton batting, animal hair, human hair, moss, mattress stuffing and dried grass. Don't use lint from a clothes drier because it swells when it gets wet. Hang these offerings out in an onion bag.

Dust Beds

Many bird species regularly dust bathe; apparently, a good roll in a dust pile will reduce annoying external parasites. Place a dust bath in a sheltered corner of your yard (protect it from cats if necessary). The ideal size is about 1 m^2 (10 3/4 sq. ft.), and the ideal ingredients are sand, loam and ashes, in equal parts.

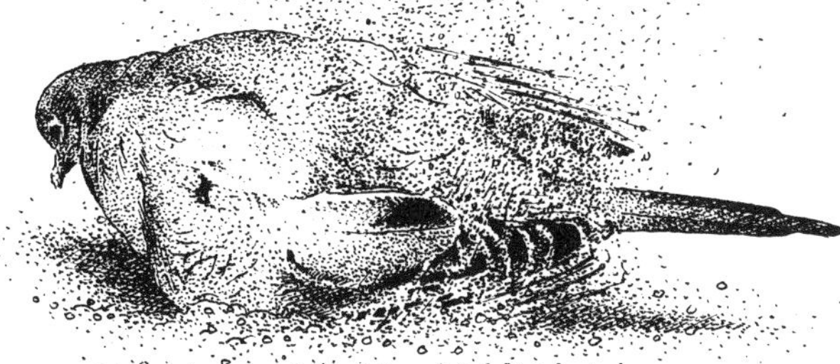

Mourning dove taking a dust bath

Ruffed Grouse Drumming Log

If you live on a large acreage or are adjacent to a natural area that is dominated by ungrazed or lightly grazed aspen or mixed spruce-aspen forest, you may attract a pair of ruffed grouse. In a perfect grouse world, the male uses two trees that are spaced about 3 m (10 ft.) apart—a downed log for drumming and a standing live tree for guarding his drumming spot. You can either haul in a drumming log, or provide one by felling a tree about 1 m-2 m (3-6 1/2 ft.) above the ground. Fell it so that it falls not more than 0.3 m (1 ft.) from the guard tree.

NOTE: The source of bird scientific names used in this chapter is the American Ornithologists' Union (1998).

Ruffed grouse drumming

ACKNOWLEDGMENTS

Jack Clements (Owner, The WildBird General Store, Edmonton, Alberta)
Kaye Detomasi (Owner, Birds in Your Garden store, Cochrane, Alberta)
Zoltan Gulyas (Designer of barn swallow nesting shelf, Calgary, Alberta)
Jocelyn Hudon (Curator of Ornithology, Provincial Museum of Alberta, Edmonton, Alberta)
Robert Kreba (Interpretive Specialist, Royal Saskatchewan Museum, Regina, Saskatchewan)
George Loades (Member, Sarcee Fish and Game Association, Calgary, Alberta)
Del & Debra McKinnon (Purple Martin Conservancy, Mulhurst Bay, Alberta)
Bruce McGillivray (Assistant Director, Provincial Museum of Alberta, Edmonton, Alberta)
Pat Marklevitz (Bird expert, and graduate student [Conservation Biology], University of Alberta, Edmonton, Alberta)
Doug Meston (Designer of homemade birdbath, Rocky Mountain House, Alberta)
Jack Park (Coordinator, Alberta Breeding Bird Survey, Edmonton, Alberta)
Jim Potter (Wildlife Technician, Alberta Conservation Association, Red Deer, Alberta)
Howard Troughton (Provincial Compiler, Alberta Christmas Bird Count, Calgary, Alberta)
Tom Webb (Veteran backyard bird feeder operator, Turner Valley, Alberta)

Thanks to Ellis Bird Farm Ltd., Lacombe, Alberta, for permission to use Gary Ross's illustrations in *Winter Bird Feeding: An Alberta Guide and Nestboxes for Prairie Birds*.

SIGNIFICANT REFERENCES

General

American Ornithologists' Union. 1998. *Check-list of North American birds*. 7th ed. American Ornithologists' Union, Washington, D.C.

Ehrlich, P.R., D.S. Dobkin and D. Wheye. 1988. *The birder's handbook: A field guide to the natural history of North American birds*. Simon & Schuster Inc., New York, London, Toronto, Sydney, Tokyo and Singapore.

Gadd, B. 1995. *Handbook of the Canadian Rockies*. 2d. ed. Corax Press, Jasper.

Semenchuk, G.P., ed. 1992. *The atlas of breeding birds of Alberta*. Federation of Alberta Naturalists, Edmonton.

Stokes, D. 1979. *A guide to bird behavior*. Volume I. Stokes Nature Guides. Little, Brown and Company, Boston, New York, Toronto and London.

————. 1989. *A guide to bird behavior*. Volume III. Little, Brown and Company, Boston, New York, Toronto and London.

Terres, J. 1991. *The Audubon Society encyclopedia of North American birds*. Wings Books, New York.

Welty, J.C. 1975. *The life of birds*. W.B. Saunders Co., Philadelphia, Pennsylvania.

Field Guides

Bovey, R. 1990. *Birds of Calgary*. Rev. ed. Lone Pine Publishing, Edmonton.

————. 1990. *Birds of Edmonton*. Rev. ed. Lone Pine Publishing, Edmonton.

Fisher, C. 1997. *Birds of the Rocky Mountains*. Lone Pine Publishing, Edmonton.

Fisher, C., and J. Acorn. 1998. *Birds of Alberta*. Lone Pine Publishing, Edmonton.

Harrison, C. 1984. *A field guide to the nests, eggs and nestlings of North American birds*. Collins Publishers, Don Mills.

McGillivray, W. B., and G.P. Semenchuk. 1998. *The Federation of Alberta Naturalists field guide to Alberta birds*. Federation of Alberta Naturalists, Edmonton.

Peterson, R.T. 1990. *Western birds*. A Peterson Field Guide. Houghton Mifflin Company, Boston and New York.

Robbins, C.S., B. Bruun and H.S. Zim. 1983. *Birds of North America*. Golden Press, New York.

Salt, W.R., and J.R. Salt. 1976. *The birds of Alberta with their ranges in Saskatchewan & Manitoba*. Hurtig Publishers, Edmonton.

Scott, S.L. 1987. *Field guide to the birds of North America*. 2d ed. National Geographic Society, Washington, D.C.

Scotter, G.W., T.J. Ulrich and E.T. Jones. 1999 (first published in 1990). *Birds of the Canadian Rockies*. Fifth House Publishing, Calgary.

Attracting Birds

Butler, E. 1991. *Attracting birds*. Lone Pine Publishing, Edmonton.

Dennis, J. 1986. *Beyond the bird feeder*. Alfred A. Knopf, New York.

Dennis, J., and M. Tekulsky. 1991. *How to attract hummingbirds & butterflies*. Ortho Books, Chevron Chemical Company, Ramon, California.

Dion, A. 1988. *A garden of birds*. Quebec Adgenda Inc., Quebec.

Henderson, C.L. n.d. *Woodworking for wildlife: Homes for birds and mammals*. Nongame Wildlife Program, Minnesota Department of Natural Resources, St. Paul, Minnesota.

————. 1995. *Wild about birds. The DNR bird feeding guide*. Nongame Wildlife Program - Section of Wildlife, Minnesota Department of Natural Resources. Minnesota's Bookstore, St. Paul, Minnesota.

Kress, S. 1985. *The Audubon Society guide for attracting birds*. Scribner, New York.

Mahnken, J. 1998. *The backyard bird-lover's guide*. Storey Communications, Pownal, Vermont.

Needham, B. 1995. *Beastly abodes*. Sterling Publishing Co., New York.

Newfield, N., and B. Nielsen. 1996. *Hummingbird gardens*. Chapters Publishing Ltd., Shelburne, Vermont.

Pearman, M. 1993. *Nestboxes for prairie birds*. Ellis Bird Farm Ltd., Lacombe.

————. 1989. *Winter bird feeding: An Alberta guide*. Ellis Bird Farm Ltd., Lacombe.

Proctor, N. 1985. *Garden birds*. B. Mitchell, Rexdale.

Schneck, M. 1989. *The bird feeder guide: How to attract and identify birds in your garden*. New Burlington Books, London, England.

Stelfox, H., and C. Fisher, comps. 1998. *A winter birding guide for the Edmonton region*. Edmonton Natural History Club, Edmonton.

Stokes, D., and L. Stokes. 1987. *The bird feeder book*. Little, Brown and Company (Canada), Toronto.

————. 1989. *The hummingbird book. The complete guide to attracting, identifying, and enjoying hummingbirds*. Little, Brown and Company, Boston, New York, Toronto and London.

————. 1990. *The complete birdhouse book*. Little, Brown and Company (Canada), Toronto.

Stokes, D., L. Stokes and J.L. Brown. 1997. *Stokes purple martin book: The complete guide to attracting and housing purple martins*. Little, Brown and Company, Boston, New York, Toronto and London.

Waldon, B. 1990. *A prairie guide to feeding winter birds*. Western Producer Books, Saskatoon.

5 BASICS
NATURESCAPING FOR BIRDS

1. Provide habitat and cover by planting a wide variety of plants; try to provide for the birds' needs year-round.
2. Supplement natural food with seeds and suet.
3. Provide a water source: birdbath, water garden, water mister, waterfall or mud.
4. Put out nestboxes wherever suitable.
5. Use preventative measure to reduce bird injuries (e.g., from window strikes, cats).

MYRNA PEARMAN

www.naturescape.ab.ca

SOME COMMON ALBERTA BIRDS

BETTY FISHER
Canada goose
Branta canadensis

BETTY FISHER
Mallard
Anas platyrhynchos

WAYNE LYNCH
Bufflehead
Bucephala albeola

GORDON COURT
Common goldeneye
Bucephala clangula

GORDON COURT
American kestrel
Falco sparverius

GORDON COURT
Merlin
Falco columbarius

COURTESY OF THE PROVINCIAL MUSEUM OF ALBERTA
Gray partridge
Perdix perdix

WAYNE LYNCH
Rock dove (Pigeon)
Columba livia

COURTESY OF THE PROVINCIAL MUSEUM OF ALBERTA
Mourning dove
Zenaida macroura

RUSS AMY
Great horned owl
Bubo virginianus

MYRNA PEARMAN
Northern saw-whet owl
Aegolius acadicus

COURTESY OF THE PROVINCIAL MUSEUM OF ALBERTA
Ruby-throated hummingbird
Archilochus colubris

MYRNA PEARMAN
Yellow-bellied sapsucker
Sphyrapicus varius

RUSS AMY
Downy woodpecker
Picoides pubescens

RUTH STEWART
Hairy woodpecker
Picoides villosus

RUSS AMY
Northern flicker
Colaptes auratus

RUSS AMY
Least flycatcher
Empidonax minimus

COURTESY OF THE PROVINCIAL MUSEUM OF ALBERTA
Eastern phoebe
Sayornis phoebe

RUSS AMY
Eastern kingbird
Tyrannus tyrannus

COURTESY OF THE PROVINCIAL MUSEUM OF ALBERTA
Warbling vireo
Vireo gilvus

MYRNA PEARMAN
Gray jay
Perisoreus canadensis

GORDON COURT
Blue jay
Cyanocitta cristata

DOUG LEIGHTON
Clark's nutcracker
Nucifraga columbiana

DOUG LEIGHTON
Black-billed magpie
Pica pica

WAYNE LYNCH
American crow
Corvus brachyrhynchos

SOME COMMON ALBERTA BIRDS . . . CONTINUED

GORDON COURT
Common raven *Corvus corax*

JAMES R. HILL III
Purple martin *Progne subis*

MYRNA PEARMAN
Tree swallow *Tachycineta bicolor*

MYRNA PEARMAN
Barn swallow *Hirundo rustica*

WAYNE LYNCH
Cliff swallow *Petrochelidon pyrrhonota*

MYRNA PEARMAN
Black-capped chickadee *Poecile atricapillus*

WAYNE LYNCH
Mountain chickadee *Poecile gambeli*

MYRNA PEARMAN
Boreal chickadee Peocile hudsonicus

JEAN McCULLOUGH
Red-breasted nuthatch *Sitta canadensis*

RUSS AMY
White-breasted nuthatch *Sitta carolinensis*

COURTESY OF THE PROVINCIAL MUSEUM OF ALBERTA
Brown creeper *Certhia americana*

GORDON JOHNSON
House wren *Troglodytes aedon*

MYRNA PEARMAN
Mountain bluebird *Sialia currucoides*

MYRNA PEARMAN
American robin *Turdus migratorius*

MYRNA PEARMAN
European starling *Sturnus vulgaris*

WAYNE LYNCH
Bohemian waxwing *Bombycilla garrulus*

COURTESY OF THE PROVINCIAL MUSEUM OF ALBERTA
Cedar waxwing *Bombycilla cedrorum*

RUSS AMY
Yellow warbler *Dendroica petechia*

MYRNA PEARMAN
American tree sparrow *Spizella arborea*

WAYNE LYNCH
Chipping sparrow *Spizella passerina*

WAYNE LYNCH
Savannah sparrow *Passerculus sandwichensis*

WAYNE LYNCH
Song sparrow *Melospiza melodia*

COURTESY OF THE PROVINCIAL MUSEUM OF ALBERTA
White-throated sparrow *Zonotrichia albicollis*

WAYNE LYNCH
White-crowned sparrow *Zonotrichia leucophrys*

BETTY FISHER
Dark-eyed junco *Junco hyemalis*

SOME COMMON ALBERTA BIRDS . . . CONTINUED

WAYNE LYNCH
Rose-breasted grosbeak
Pheucticus ludovicianus

RUSS AMY
Red-winged blackbird
Agelaius phoeniceus

WAYNE LYNCH
Baltimore oriole
Icterus galbula

DOUG LEIGHTON
Gray-crowned rosy-finch
Leucosticte tephrocotis

GORDON COURT
Pine grosbeak
Pinicola enucleator

COURTESY OF THE PROVINCIAL MUSEUM OF ALBERTA
Purple finch
Carpodacus purpureus

DOUG LEIGHTON
House finch
Carpodacus mexicanus

GORDON COURT
Red crossbill
Loxia curvirostra

GORDON JOHNSON
Common redpoll
Carduelis flammea

MYRNA PEARMAN
Hoary redpoll
Carduelis hornemanni

MYRNA PEARMAN
Pine siskin
Carduelis pinus

GORDON JOHNSON
American goldfinch
Carduelis tristis

MYRNA PEARMAN
Evening grosbeak
Coccothraustes vespertinus

DOUG LEIGHTON
House sparrow
Passer domesticus

The birds are listed in taxonomic order according to the American Ornithologists' Union (1998).

Chapter 15

Mammals and the Natural Garden

Red squirrel

Mammals are the crowning touch to a NatureScaping project. These creatures, whether large or small, add interest to a NatureScaped yard, and their presence means that your yard provides a welcoming space for them. Unfortunately, joy can quickly turn to dismay when they cause property damage or turn their attention to your vegetable garden, backyard pond or flower garden. In this chapter we describe some ways to provide habitat for mammals. If you have attracted these animals and they become a problem, you may find some information that will be of assistance in Chapter 18.

PROVIDING FOOD FOR MAMMALS

Most mammals prefer to find their own food, and if you provide them with habitat that offers a selection of food sources, it is possible you will attract a wide variety of them. The species that come will depend to a large extent on where you live, the size of your lot, as well as the nature of the surrounding habitat.

For most mammals, food and shelter go hand-in-hand. For this reason, the ideal NatureScape habitat for woodland mammals is a copse of trees with a thick understory of shrubs. A few snags, a few downed logs, a large brush pile and a rock pile add even more habitat value. Herbivores (e.g., mice, voles, hares, deer) will find plants to their liking in this habitat, and they, in turn, will attract predators such as weasels, coyotes, hawks and owls. Remember, a healthy ecosystem depends on a wide prey base for those animals further up the food chain.

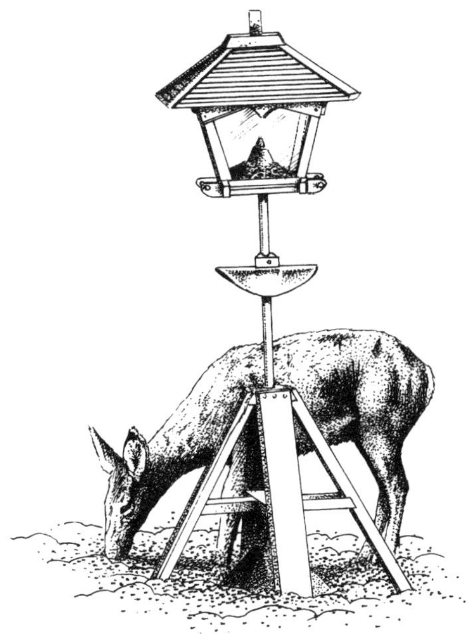

White-tailed deer at sunflower seed feeder in winter

If you want to put in flowers that attract mammals, try sunflowers—many species of mammals, from mice to deer, will dine on the seeds. (Be cautious about growing sunflowers where there are bears!) Other plantings that are attractive to a wide range of mammals include alfalfa, timothy and clover.

Supplemental Food

Many mammal species will be attracted by supplemental food. For example, several will avail themselves of seeds spilled beneath bird feeders. Squirrels, rabbits, hares and mice eagerly eat sunflower seeds, grain, corn or nuts. To prevent these animals from getting up on your bird feeders, use baffles or other guards (see page 157, Chapter 18). If you are concerned about attracting deer mice (*Peromyscus maniculatus)*, which can carry hantavirus, make sure your bird-feeding stations are well away from your house.

SALT LICKS

A salt lick is an alternative to a salt block and can be created by putting salt into a burlap sack, then hanging the sack from a tree branch. Over time, rain will leach the salt into the soil.

Deer often visit yards that offer grain, sunflower seeds, alfalfa pellets or even piles of dried leaves. Deer may also come to a yard if there is a salt block or salt lick. Porcupines and snowshoe hares also appreciate a salt source.

Scavenging

Some mammals, such as skunks, foxes and coyotes, may come in to your yard to scrounge through your garbage or glean other foodstuffs that have been left outside. If you don't want to encourage this behaviour, keep all garbage and other eatables in

metal garbage cans with secure lids. Attach the cans securely to a post or fence so they can't be pushed over. And don't feed your pets outside!

SNOW AND MAMMALS

Some mammal species, like snowshoe hares, have large, soft feet that are well adapted to "snowshoeing." Deer, which are heavy and have relatively small feet, move with great difficulty through deep snow.

Many species of small mammals (e.g., mice, voles, shrews) depend on snow for their survival because they remain active throughout the winter, moving about in the *pukak* layer (the interface between the earth and snowpack above).

SHELTER AND HOUSING FOR MAMMALS

As is the case with food, most mammals will find their own shelter, roosting sites and denning sites, as long as you offer them enough habitat. The smaller species, such as rabbits, hares, mice, voles, shrews, squirrels, chipmunks, woodchucks, foxes, ground squirrels and weasels, are the mammals most likely to take up residence. Raccoons, which are becoming more common in southern Alberta, may also find a home in appropriate habitat.

Because the larger species, such as deer, moose, foxes and coyotes, have territories that are larger than most yards, you are likely to see these animals only when they are passing through. However, if you have a large enough yard, these creatures may find a denning site or a bedding-down area.

Many mammals overwinter in Alberta, and for them, snow is a fact of life.
To ensure animals dependent on snow have lots of safe habitat, especialy those that depend on an intact *pukak* layer (see sidebar), try to protect at least one area of your yard from being trampled during the winter.

Brush Piles and Rock Piles

Brush piles and rock piles are easy to build and can add great habitat value to your yard. They provide mammals with nesting sites, denning sites and shelter from both predators and the elements, and are especially attractive to these animals if they are near sources of food and other types of cover.

ROCK PILE BURROW MADE WITH A BUCKET AND PVC PIPE

Bucket on ground

Bucket covered with rocks

If you decide to add a brush pile to your yard (a whole lot easier than packing away all those branches after fall pruning), try to build it so that it is about 1.2 m-2.4 m (4-8 ft.) high and 3 m-4.5 m (10-15 ft.) in diameter.

Rock piles are simple to make, but a bit more work than brush piles, because you will probably have to haul rocks. Use larger rocks (18 cm-20 cm [7-8 in.] in diameter) on the bottom and pile smaller rocks on top.

The value of a brush or rock pile to mammals can be greatly enhanced if large internal spaces are incorporated. These areas will be used as denning sites and travel tunnels. You can maximize the amount of internal space by strategic placement of the branches or rocks, or by placing 15-cm (6-in.) PVC pipe, flex hose, weeping tile or sections of hollow logs within the structure.

Try to lay tunnel material in a zigzag fashion and make sure that the entrance and exit holes are well supported so they won't collapse. If you want to provide burrows, lay the tunnel material in at a low angle (especially important if you use PVC pipe or some other slippery material). Construct the tunnel so that one end is at the edge of the structure, the other buried into the rock or brush pile.

You can also create a burrow or central nesting structure inside a brush or rock pile by using an overturned bucket with holes cut into the rim, and sections of 15-cm (6-in.) PVC pipe. The bucket forms the central chamber, and the PVC pipe is used to make access tunnels radiating out from the bucket to the edge of the mound (see illustration).

Roost Boxes and Nestboxes

Bats

Bats—the creatures that once conjured up images of Dracula, Halloween and ghosts—are now gaining the public respectability and popularity they deserve. Bat houses, which bats use for roosting and raising young, have played a large part in helping to educate people about these creatures of the night. The houses have been provided for more than 60 years in Europe and have recently become popular in North America.

In Alberta, two bat species, little brown bat (*Myotis lucifugus*) and big brown bat (*Eptesicus fuscus*), will use a bat house.

The ideal material to use in box construction is 25-mm (1-in.) boards or 19-mm (3/4 in.) exterior grade plywood. Do not use wood that has been chemically treated. All the contact points between the sides, front, back and roof should be caulked to eliminate cross ventilation.

Although relatively little research has been done on bat houses in Canada, it is thought that there are several factors crucial to their success. These factors are the distance from the bat house to drinking and feeding areas; the daily temperature profile of the bat house; the size and shape of internal roosting spaces; the roughness of the surfaces to which the bats must cling; and placement.

Distance. It seems bat houses are most likely to be successful if they are located 0.4 km (1/4 mi.) or less from a water source. Bats have been observed drinking from sources as diverse as lakes, ponds, streams, rivers, birdbaths and livestock waterers.

Temperature. Bats' roost requirements vary widely according to species and social group. Smaller bats, for example, seem to prefer hotter roosts (32-43°C [90-110°F]) than the larger species, which prefer temperatures of 27-32°C (80-90°F). Bachelor groups (males) tend towards cooler roosts, whereas most nursery colonies are warmer.

Roosting needs also vary according to climate, so the challenge in Alberta is to build a box that will accommodate a wide range of temperatures. Recent research conducted by the Bat Conservation Society of Canada (BCSC) indicates that, in the prairie climate, internal box temperatures can be maximized by painting or staining bat boxes black. Alternatively, you can cover the boxes with tar paper or dark shingles.

Internal roosting space. It has been suggested that bat boxes in Alberta should have several long chambers, which will allow more bats to cluster near the ceiling where body heat can be trapped. With a black exterior, the front chambers will readily absorb outside heat while the rear chambers will remain slightly cooler.

The size of the internal roosting space is also important—it should be between 19 mm (3/4 in.) and 32 mm (1 1/4 in.) wide. Little brown bats prefer the smaller space; big brown bats, the larger. With enough internal space and differentially heated chambers, the bats can move around and find the ideal roosting spot.

Roughness of surface. All inner surfaces of the house must be rough or horizontally grooved so that the bats can get a firm foothold. One way to provide this rough surface is to etch the back board and roosting partitions with 1.6-mm (1/16-in.) saw kerfs at 13-mm(1/2-in.) intervals. Alternatively, you could cover these areas with fiberglass or plastic insect screening cloth. Metal mesh is too abrasive and also decomposes quickly because of urine.

BATS IN ALBERTA

Little brown bat *(Myotis lucifugus)*
Northern bat *(Myotis septentrionalis)*
Long-eared bat *(Myotis evotis)*
Long-legged bat *(Myotis volans)*
Western small-footed bat *(Myotis ciliolabrum)*
Silver-haired bat *(Lasionycteris noctivagans)*
Big brown bat *(Eptesicus fuscus)*
Hoary bat *(Lasiurus cinereus)*
Eastern red bat [accidental] *(Lasiurus borealis)*

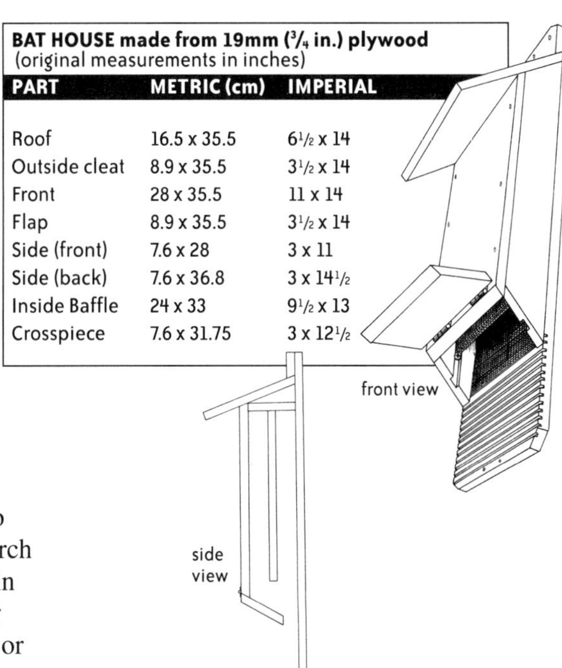

BAT HOUSE made from 19mm (3/4 in.) plywood
(original measurements in inches)

PART	METRIC (cm)	IMPERIAL
Roof	16.5 x 35.5	6½ x 14
Outside cleat	8.9 x 35.5	3½ x 14
Front	28 x 35.5	11 x 14
Flap	8.9 x 35.5	3½ x 14
Side (front)	7.6 x 28	3 x 11
Side (back)	7.6 x 36.8	3 x 14½
Inside Baffle	24 x 33	9½ x 13
Crosspiece	7.6 x 31.75	3 x 12½

BAT BOX INSULATION

One unknown in the bat house department is how box insulation might affect bat use. Bat Conservation International (BCI) recommends that interested individuals experiment with insulation by testing insulated versus non-insulated boxes, and by testing boxes with insulated attics and central chambers (which would divide a single house into a relatively hot and a cooler area). If you are interested in participating in these experiments, contact the Bat Conservation Society of Canada (BCSC) or BCI (see Appendix 5 for addresses).

HELPING OUT BATS

According to BCI, houses that are properly constructed and erected can be expected to attract occupants within two seasons. Both the BCSC and BCI welcome any information from experiments (successful or unsuccessful) and experiences with bat houses. BCI is looking for volunteer Research Associates to assist with the North American Bat House Research Project. (See Appendix 5 for BCI's address.)

Placement. Bat boxes should be mounted 3.5 m-6 m (12-20 ft.) off the ground. They can be mounted on poles, on the sides of buildings or on trees, with trees being the least preferred. One suggested mounting arrangement is to place two boxes back-to-back on a pole, one facing east and the other facing west. Single houses should be placed facing south or southeast. Because it is the length of daily sun exposure that is important, try to position the boxes so that they receive a minimum of six hours of direct sun per day.

Bat house use appears to be higher when a bat house is placed on a heat sink, such as the south or east side of a building. If bats are roosting in or on a building, a bat house should be placed in a suitable location on that building.

An alternative bat roost can be provided with the use of a 45 cm (18 in.) wide piece of thick tar paper wrapped around a tree trunk so that it is tight at the top and flares out about 5 cm (2 in.) at the bottom. Attach this roost as high up a tree as possible, and make sure it is protected from predators such as squirrels and cats. The bats climb up into the shelter from the bottom and can choose a comfortable roosting spot according to weather and temperature.

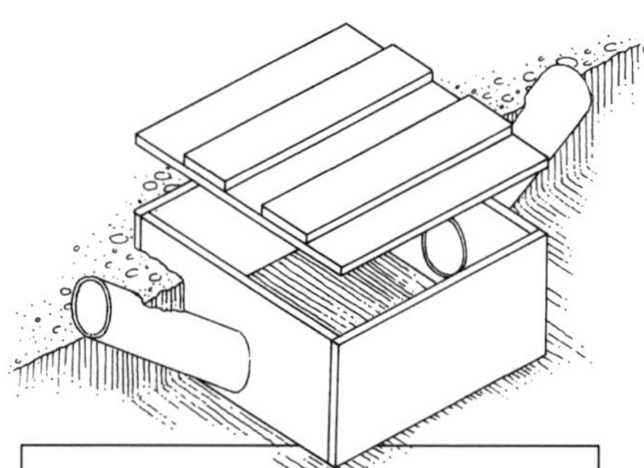

RABBIT/HARE HOUSE

PART	METRIC (cm)	IMPERIAL (in.)
Top	60 x 60	24 x 24
Sides	30 x 60	12 x 24
Entrance diameter	15	6
(No bottom)		

Rabbits and Hares

We have three species of leporids (rabbits and hares) in Alberta—the white-tailed jackrabbit (*Lepus townsendii*), which inhabits grassland and open meadows; the mountain cottontail/Nuttall's cottontail (*Sylvilagus nuttallii*), which is restricted to grasslands; and the snowshoe hare (*Lepus americanus*), a forest dweller.

Some rabbits and hares might be attracted to an artificial shelter. Rabbit/hare houses can be constructed from rough, untreated wood. They should measure about 60 cm x 60 cm (24 x 24 in.) and should be approximately 30 cm (12 in.) deep. Concrete drain pipe, PVC pipe or flex hose (15 cm [6 in.] in diameter) can be used for entrance tunnels. The box should have a lid but no floor, and should be buried in an area with good drainage. The lid can be covered with rocks, brush or soil. This type of house is more likely to be occupied if it is placed next to a treed fence row or wooded/bushy area.

Squirrels

We have two native species of tree-dwelling squirrels in Alberta: the red squirrel (*Tamiasciurus hudsonicus*) and the northern flying squirrel (*Glaucomys sabrinus*). The red squirrel is the more aggressive of the two and has the habit of caching great quantities of food, a problem, perhaps, if the squirrel's food source is your bird feeder. The delicate flying squirrel, which is active only at night, often eats seeds from bird feeders but does not pack away food.

Flying squirrel young in nestbox

An introduced species, the eastern gray squirrel (*Sciurus carolinensis*), is now well established in the city of Calgary and nearby Okotoks, but there are no confirmed reports of breeding populations elsewhere in the province. Some of these squirrels were offered to the Calgary Zoo in 1937 or 1938, but because there was no place to house them, they were set free. From the original five came the population of today. Most individuals seen are the black-phase form; the gray-phase form of this creature is more typical elsewhere in Canada.

Both native squirrel species will use a box for nesting; red squirrels may also use one for food storage. These squirrels are attracted to boxes that are located in wooded areas. They aren't fussy about the size or style, so just offer them a standard nestbox for a smaller secondary cavity nesting bird (see page 122) with an entrance hole at least 41 mm (1 5/8 in.) in diameter. If they find the hole size cramps their style, they will chew it bigger. Attach a squirrel nestbox to a tree at a height of 1.2 m-3 m) 4-10 ft.

If you are having trouble with squirrels, see Chapter 18.

See Appendix 4 for details on several Alberta mammals, their habitats and what will attract them to your yard.

NOTE: The scientific names used in this chapter are based on Jones et al. (1997). See **Significant References** below.

5 BASICS
NATURESCAPING FOR MAMMALS

1. Have lots of trees and a dense understory of shrubs.
2. Do what is necessary to avoid potential conflicts with mammals.
3. Build a rock pile or brush pile.
4. Build roost boxes and nestboxes for native mammals.
5. Put out supplemental food and plant sunflowers.

ACKNOWLEDGMENTS

Jim Burns (Curator, Quaternary Paleontology, and (Acting) Curator of Mammalogy, Provincial Museum of Alberta, Edmonton, Alberta)
Robert Kreba (Interpretive Specialist, Royal Saskatchewan Museum, Regina, Saskatchewan)
Margo Pybus (Wildlife Diseases Specialist, Natural Resources Service, Alberta Environment, Edmonton, Alberta)
Bob Young (Founder, Bat Conservation Society of Canada, Calgary, Alberta)

SIGNIFICANT REFERENCES

Banfield, A.W.F. 1977. *The mammals of Canada*. University of Toronto Press, Toronto.

Burt, W., and R. Grossenheider. 1976. *A field guide to the mammals*. Houghton Mifflin Company, Boston, Massachusetts.

Gadd, B. 1995. *Handbook of the Canadian Rockies*. 2d. ed. Corax Press, Jasper.

Grassy, J., and C. Keene. 1998. *Mammals*. National Audubon Society First Field Guide. Scholastic Inc., New York.

Hartson, T. 1999. *Squirrels of the West*. Lone Pine Publishing, Edmonton.

Henderson, C.L. 1987. *Landscaping for wildlife*. Non-game Wildlife Program - Section of Wildlife, Minnesota Department of Natural Resources. Minnesota's Bookstore, St. Paul, Minnesota.

Jones, C., R.S. Hoffman, D.W. Rice, R.T. Baker, M.D. Engstrom, R.D. Bradley, D.D. Schmidly and C.A. Jones. 1997. *Revised checklist of North American mammals north of Mexico, 1997*. Occasional Paper No. 173, Museum of Texas Tech University, Lubbock, Texas.

Marriott, J. 1997. *Central Rockies mammals*. A 'Pack-It' Pocket Guide. Luminous Compositions, Banff.

Pattie, D., and C. Fisher. 1999. *Mammals of Alberta*. Lone Pine Publishing, Edmonton.

Pybus, M. n.d. *Bats of Alberta, "the real story . . ."*. Alberta Forestry, Lands and Wildlife and Alberta Agriculture, Edmonton. (Booklet)

Smith, H. 1993. *Alberta mammals: An atlas and guide*. Provincial Museum of Alberta, Edmonton.

Soper, J.D. 1964. *The mammals of Alberta*. Hamly Press Ltd., Edmonton.

Whitaker, J.O., Jr. 1989. *The Audubon Society field guide to North American mammals*. 6th ed. Alfred A. Knopf, New York.

SOME ALBERTA MAMMALS

CY HAMPSON
Masked shrew *Sorex cinereus*

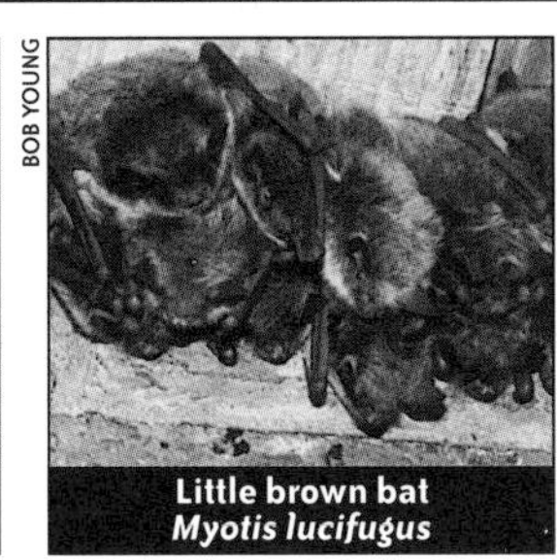
BOB YOUNG
Little brown bat *Myotis lucifugus*

GORDON COURT
Snowshoe hare *Lepus americanus*

RUSS AMY
White-tailed jackrabbit *Lepus townsendii*

SOME ALBERTA MAMMALS . . . CONTINUED

RUSS AMY — **Least chipmunk** *Eutamias minimus*

RUTH STEWART — **Woodchuck (Groundhog)** *Marmota monax*

MYRNA PEARMAN — **Richardson's ground squirrel** *Spermophilus richardsonii*

WAYNE LYNCH — **Eastern gray squirrel** *Sciurus carolinesis*

WAYNE LYNCH — **Red squirrel** *Tamiasciurus hudsonicus*

MYRNA PEARMAN — **Northern flying squirrel** *Glaucomys sabrinus*

RUSS AMY — **American beaver** *Castor canadensis*

DOUG LEIGHTON — **Deer mouse** *Peromyscus maniculatus*

GREG OHM — **Meadow vole** *Microtus pennsylvanicus*

COURTESY OF THE PROVINCIAL MUSEUM OF ALBERTA — **Common muskrat** *Ondatra zibethicus*

RUSS AMY — **Coyote** *Canis latrans*

RUSS AMY — **Red fox** *Vulpes vulpes*

KEVIN BERNER — **Common raccoon** *Procyon lotor*

RUSS AMY — **Long-tailed weasel** *Mustela frenata*

RUSS AMY — **Striped skunk** *Mephitis mephitis*

RUSS AMY — **Mule deer** *Odocoileus hemionus*

RUSS AMY — **White-tailed deer** *Odocoileus virginianus*

RUSS AMY — **Moose** *Alces alces*

The mammals are listed in taxonomic order according to Jones et al. (1997).

Chapter 16

Wildlife Habitat and School Yards

MYRNA PEARMAN

Students at Joseph Welsh Elementary School, Red Deer, Alberta

Schools are like a second home to many young people. By the time they're out of grade six, children have spent approximately 260 full days on their school grounds. Although these grounds are functional and provide open spaces for children to recreate, most are sterile, hard-packed playing surfaces.

The application of NatureScape principles can transform these grounds into more interesting, healthy, vibrant and educational landscapes. NatureScaping can bring the natural world close and even, into, the classroom. Students can learn, through active participation, about their local environment and landscapes, and integrate academic and hands-on activities.

GODO STOYKE

Children involved in NatureScaping learn to care about their natural environment, and hopefully will carry the values, knowledge and experiences gained with them throughout their lives. As society becomes increasingly urbanized, school yard NatureScaping can be a vital link connecting individuals to the natural world.

NatureScaped school grounds can also benefit neighbourhoods—by providing aesthetically pleasing and biologically diverse community spaces. Encouragement of a sense of community among participants in a NatureScaping project is another tangible benefit to a neighbourhood.

TIPS FROM THE CALGARY ZOO: HOW TO NATURESCAPE A SCHOOL GROUND

Tip 1: Develop a Common Vision

- Develop a shared vision of the end product. Be sure that curriculum relevance and student involvement, not the end product of a small, natural site, drive every stage of the project.

Tip 2: Branch Out

- Once the educational, environmental and social goals are addressed, decide on the type of natural environment you would like to create.
- Involve other community members in the project. Although most projects are initiated by a few enthusiastic and dedicated people, the success of the project depends on the support of a wide selection of people with a range of backgrounds. People interested could be involved in the following ways: as Project Coordinator, Human Resource Coordinator, Outreach Coordinator, Design Coordinator, Resource/Financial Coordinator, Graphics Coordinator or Education Coordinator.
- Obtain local school board regulations regarding naturalization projects.
- Conduct surveys to determine the knowledge, attitude and behaviours of students, teachers and members of the local community towards the environment and existing planted areas on the school grounds. This kind of surveying will give a good indication of the level of support for the project.

Tip 3: Site Survey and Selection

- Obtain a detailed map of the school yard, then inventory existing natural and built components, as well as exposure, wind, soil, drainage, traffic and use patterns, view lines, utility lines and historic uses. (See Chapter 2.)
- Keep written records of the project as well as photographic documentation of the entire process.

Tip 4: Plan and Design

- After determining the main project goals (and priorities, if it is a multi-staged project), produce a rough idea of what you want to end up with and a tentative cost estimate.
- Compile a list of human resources, equipment, hard landscaping materials and plants required for the project. Consider how to get materials and services you need free of charge or at low cost.
- Work with local experts to draw up a site design.
- Determine what grants to apply for and their deadlines.
- Obtain approval from the school board or other authorities.
- Broadcast your intentions to the local community (showing your planting plans) and seek assistance from its members. Make sure students do a short community presentation.
- Develop a three-year rotating task calendar with the third year added annually to include fresh ideas and new people.

Tip 5: Planting Days

- Order plants and materials at appropriate times, and have appropriate tools and water available. Label all your plants.
- Have horticulture experts, such as Master Gardeners, on hand to assist. Have multiple copies of the planting plan available for reference.
- Assume nothing! Demonstrate how to do each task.
- Try to keep volunteers busy for a three hour maximum. Include fun children's tasks, such as a water bucket brigade, and provide refreshments when undertaking a task.

Tip 6: Celebrate!

- Have an official opening celebration for the community and the media.
- Thank all participants and funding agencies, and honour all other requirements that funders may have requested.
- Enjoy the naturalized site and all of the curriculum-related chances to explore.

Adapted from the Calgary Zoo's *Grounds for Change - Schoolyard Naturalization Project*. Contact the Calgary Zoo, Calgary, Alberta for more information (see Appendix 5).

MYRNA PEARMAN

SCHOOL YARD NATURESCAPING PROJECT IDEAS

Bird-feeding station
Butterfly garden
Climbing trees
Compost bin
Conversation area
Cultivated native wildflower/shrub border
Ecosystem garden
Greenhouse or cold frame project
Herb garden
Historic use of native plants
Hummingbird garden
Multi-sensory plantings
Native plant nursery
Natural habitat garden (montane, sub-alpine, foothills, grassland, parkland, boreal forest)
Nature trail
Nesting structures
Outdoor classroom setting
Planting for specific seasonal effect
Plantings that stress biological diversity
Pond
Quiet, reflective space
Rock and brush pile habitat
Shade plantings
Succession type of planting (showing an environmental gradient)
Vegetable/food garden
Weather station
Wildflower meadow
Wildlife observation station
Wildlife-attracting trees and shrubs
Woodland
Xeric plantings

MYRNA PEARMAN

WHAT IT TAKES

NatureScaping a school ground is a complex and multi-faceted challenge that requires the long-term commitment and shared vision of teachers, parents, administrators, school boards, students, maintenance staff and the community. Careful planning and design, realistic budgeting, clear lines of communication, and written agreements between the participating parties are cornerstones of a successful project.

Students need to be involved from the beginning, and should take part in project design, development and maintenance. A project should encompass curriculum-related activities and accommodate different grade levels.

A NatureScaped school ground should be designed to be easily maintained, and to minimize safety risks and vandalism potential.

A successful project will also demand patience: transformation does not happen overnight. School gardens require a minimum of two years to reach their potential.

SOME SUCCESSFUL PROJECTS AND PROGRAMS

In Alberta, the Calgary Zoo is taking a lead role in promoting school yard stewardship through a program called *Grounds for Change - Schoolyard Naturalization Project*. One of the main purposes of the project is to increase awareness of the ecological, educational and social value of habitat restoration and biological diversity on school sites. The Zoo is working with individual schools to promote and assist with the organized development of school yard habitat restoration projects, provide workshops on curriculum-related activities, and promote long-term stewardship of natural areas. Through its work with various schools, the Zoo has developed a workable process for completing a successful school yard NatureScaping project (see previous page).

In Red Deer, Joseph Welsh Elementary School has transformed an old courtyard into an Outdoor Environmental Classroom (OEC). Two of the purposes of this project have been to provide an area where students can be involved in hands-on environmental projects that extend and enhance the science curriculum, and to create a natural environment that could become a haven for wildlife.

Spearheaded by teachers and well supported by the community, the project began in the spring of 1997. It now boasts several wildlife habitat features, including a butterfly garden and a pond (see bubble diagram on the next page). Each grade is involved in curriculum-based activities in the OEC. Despite some of the challenges presented by the project (e.g., site security, pond evaporation), it promises to be an ongoing success.

The University of Alberta Devonian Botanic Garden near Edmonton has produced an excellent reference book entitled *Environmental School Program: A Teacher's Guide* (1996). This book covers all aspects of creating a wildlife school yard, and we recommend it highly to schools that are considering a NatureScaping project. The Botanic Garden is also developing a demonstration wildlife school yard for public viewing.

Elsewhere in Alberta, other school yard naturalizing projects have taken root. Check the NatureScape Alberta web site for a list of schools that have completed or are undertaking NatureScaping projects on their school grounds.

The *Greening Schoolgrounds* program has recently been implemented in British Columbia. This program promotes several NatureScaping activities, such as the use of large canopy trees to provide shade and protection from ultraviolet (UV) sun rays.

The Evergreen Foundation, an organization based in Ontario, sponsors a school ground naturalization program called *Learning Grounds*.

For information on any of these projects and programs, contact the organizations and schools listed in the NatureScaped School Grounds section of Appendix 5.

If your school has embarked on a school ground naturalization project, please let us know. Simply fill in the NatureScape Alberta Yard Certification Application form (Appendix 7) and mail or fax it to NatureScape Alberta. We'll add your school to the NatureScaped School Grounds list on our website and provide you with an attractive NatureScape participant sign to display at your school. You will receive our free newsletter too!

SOME IDEAS FOR SCHOOL YARD NATURESCAPING

Wild creatures require a safe place within which they can find food, water and shelter. As with a residential NatureScaping project, a school ground naturalization project should take all of these requirements into account. See previous chapters for general NatureScaping principles and techniques. Here are some ideas that can be applied to school yards.

Space

It is always better to start off with a small area and expand, rather than begin with an overly ambitious project that is difficult to maintain. Try to retain existing natural features, rather than trying to create something completely different.

As with a NatureScaped residential yard, trees likely will be the first item to consider. If the school ground is adjacent to an existing natural area, complement that area with additional clump plantings. Strategically locate large trees to provide shade, but make sure they are far enough away from athletic fields so as not to interfere with activities. Be sure to take neighbouring property into consideration, and don't block views or plant trees that might interfere with septic fields or utility lines.

Given the intensive use of school grounds and the potential for vandalism, most NatureScaping projects (especially ponds, gardens and built structures) are best confined to areas that can be secured with protective fences.

Food

Food can be provided by way of plantings or by setting out such attractants as bird-feeding stations. See Chapter 3 for ideas about how to use plants to attract wildlife. Ideas for hummingbird gardening are outlined in Chapter 4; butterfly gardening in Chapter 9. Appendix 1 lists wildlife-attracting trees, shrubs, perennials, annuals, vines and ground covers. Bird feeding is covered in Chapter 14. The process of establishing a school yard wildflower garden can be hastened by transplanting plants that have been grown by students or purchased from a nursery, greenhouse or native plant growers.

Water

Water gardens and their construction are discussed in Chapter 5. Given the safety risk posed by deep water, a school pond will have to be shallow. Although a shallow pond is less desirable than a deeper one in

Bubble diagram for a naturalized school courtyard, Joseph Welsh Elementary School, Red Deer, Alberta *(with permission from Joseph Welsh Elementary School)*

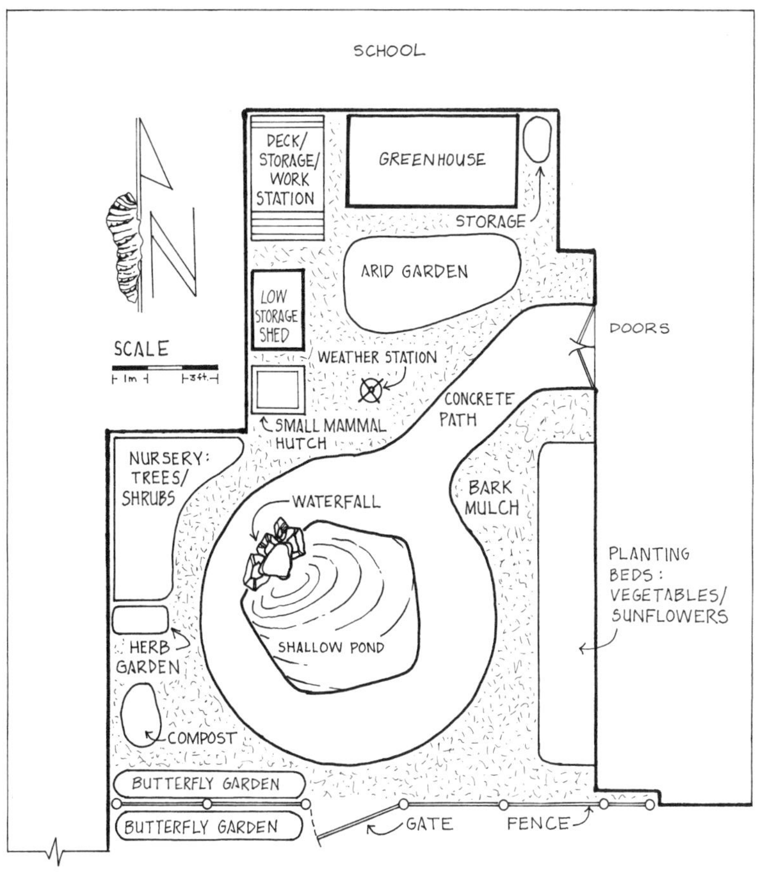

Bubble diagram for a demonstration naturalized school ground *(with permission from the Devonian Botanic Garden, Edmonton, Alberta)*

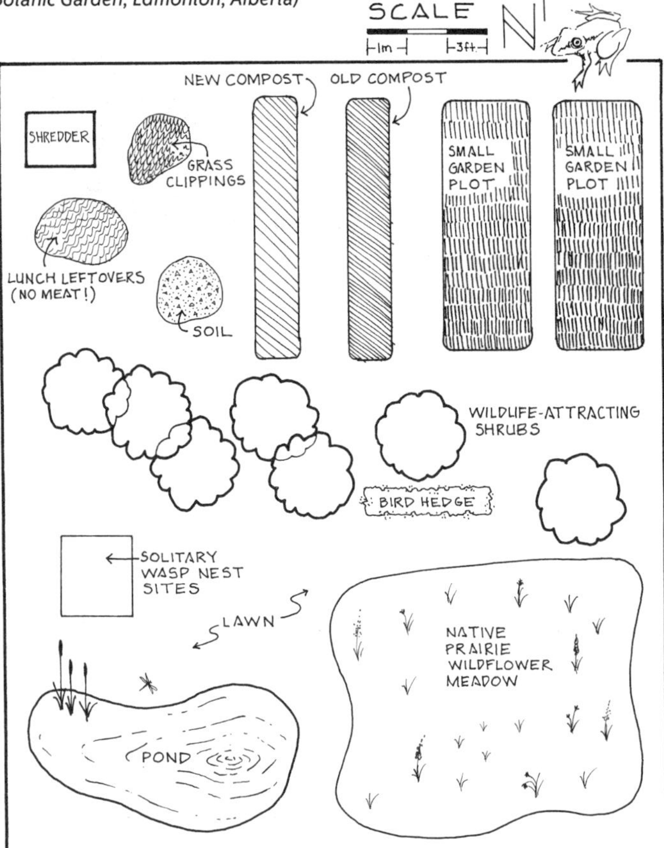

terms of wildlife value, shallow ponds and boggy areas can attract a surprising diversity of wild creatures. Small ponds can have a depth of 45 cm (18 in.) and larger ones can be 60 cm (24 in.) deep.

Be sure to take all necessary safety precautions (fencing, signage, supervision) if you create a water garden. Container water gardens, birdbaths and mud puddles can be used to complement, or to replace, a pond. See Chapter 14 for information on birdbaths.

Shelter

Shelter can be provided either through plantings or by constructing and erecting structures such as bird nestboxes, bat houses or bee blocks. We provide information on how to build and install different nesting structures and shelters for wildlife in a number of chapters.

NOTE: This chapter is based on the booklet *Grounds for Change*, written by Sue Arlidge and published by the Calgary Zoo.

ACKNOWLEDGMENTS

Sue Arlidge (Education Programmer, Calgary Zoo, Calgary, Alberta)
Sheila Spence and Rick Moore (Outdoor Classroom Coordinators, Joseph Welsh Elementary School, Red Deer, Alberta)
Godo Stoyke (formerly, Director of Environment, Devonian Botanic Garden, Edmonton, Alberta)

5 BASICS — NATURESCAPING SCHOOL YARDS

1. Involve students and the whole community in your planning and activities.
2. Start simple.
3. Plant wildlife-attracting trees, shrubs and flowers.
4. Provide supplemental food, water and shelter for wildlife.
5. Make sure the location is made safe from vandalism.

SIGNIFICANT REFERENCES

Boulton, D., comp. 1998. *Native plants for school naturalization projects*. Calgary Zoo, Calgary. (Booklet)

Calgary Zoo. n.d. *Grounds for change - Schoolyard naturalization project*. Calgary Zoo, Calgary. (Booklet)

Cheskey, E.D. 1993. *Habitat restoration: A guide for pro-active schools*. Waterloo County Board of Education, Waterloo.

(The) Evergreen Foundation. 1994. *A guide to school ground naturalization: Welcoming back the wilderness*. Prentice Hall Canada, Scarborough.

Hunken, J., and The New England Wild Flower Society. 1993. *Botany for all ages: Discovering nature through activities for children and adults*. Globe Pequot Press, Chester, Connecticut.

Jurenka, N., and R. Blass. 1996. *Beyond the bean seed: Gardening activities for grades K-6*. Teacher Ideas Press, Englewood, Colorado.

Pearce, T. 1990. *Butterflies: A practical guide to their study in school grounds*. Pergamon Press Canada Ltd., Willowdale.

Schiff, P., and C. Smith-Walters. 1993. *Wild school sites: A guide to preparing for habitat improvement projects on school grounds*. Project WILD, Bethesda, Maryland.

Stoyke, G. 1996. *Environmental school program: A teacher's guide*. Friends of the Garden, Devonian Botanic Garden, Edmonton.

Chapter 17

Helping Sick and Injured Wildlife

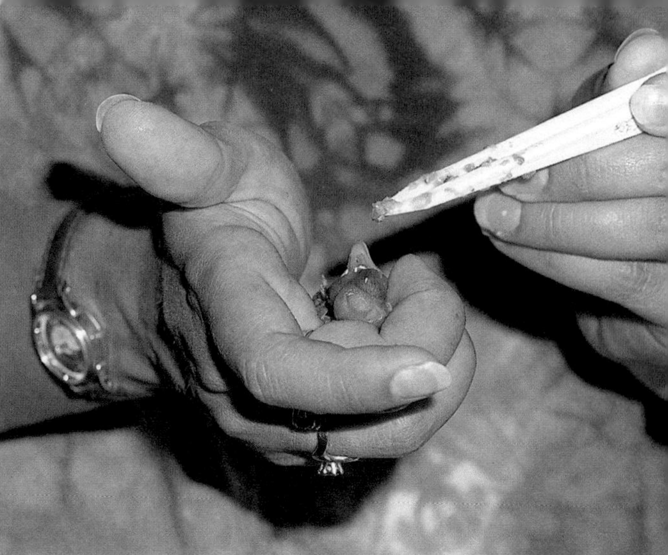

MEDICINE RIVER WILDLIFE REHABILITATION CENTRE

Feeding injured baby bird

Although injury and sickness among wild creatures are inevitable, it is important to take as many preventative measures as possible to minimize these problems in a yard or garden situation. We discuss some of the more common problems and their prevention below, as well as what to do if you come across a sick or injured animal.

COMMON INJURIES

Most injuries to wildlife are caused by collisions with vehicles, as well as barbed wire, domestic predators (cats, dogs) and window strikes. In a typical urban or acreage setting, the latter two are the most problematic.

Domestic Predators

Try to contain your cats and dogs and keep them away from wildlife in your yard. Cats, in particular, are major predators of all small wild animals. If an animal has been injured by a cat or dog, remove the injured creature and administer first aid, as described below. For information on reducing cat problems, see later on in this chapter.

Window Strikes

It is estimated that a billion or more birds die in North America each year by colliding with windows. Collisions occur for only one reason—sheet glass is essentially invisible to birds.

Window strikes usually occur because birds see an expansive scene reflected in a window, or they see through aligned windows to the other side of a building and attempt to fly through. Window strikes can also happen as birds scatter from a feeding station when they are disturbed.

In late spring and summer, some breeding birds may also repeatedly hit residential windows as they attempt to defend their territory against their reflected image. This type of strike can be annoying to a homeowner but is usually harmless to the bird, although there have been rare reports of birds killing or injuring themselves while fighting their reflections.

The only way to prevent window strikes is for the birds to recognize that a window is an obstacle so they can avoid it. One rather drastic measure is to hang a barrier, such as garden netting, about half a metre outside your windows. The disadvantages of this line of action are that your house can look a little bizarre and the view from your windows will be obscured.

An alternative is to transform the glass itself into a visible barrier by placing objects on the outside surface (see sidebar). The shape of the objects you place on a window doesn't matter—hawk silhouettes, triangles or other geometric designs will work equally well. Although some manufacturers claim that static-cling, plastic spider webs are the answer, they may be less effective than strategically placed solid silhouettes.

BIRDS, WINDOW STRIKES AND NIGHT-LIT BUILDINGS

Adding to the problem of residential windows are brilliantly lit skyscrapers. During the fall and spring, nighttime migrants are attracted to, and confused by, these lit buildings. Some strike the building walls, while others flutter to the street exhausted. Once on the ground, the birds may be killed by gulls, cats and other predators.

One way to deal with this difficulty is for skyscraper lights to be turned out at night during fall and spring migration.

A national organization, Fatal Light Awareness Program (FLAP), is working to prevent birds from being killed as a result of skyscraper lights (see Appendix 5 for contact information).

WINDOWS AS BARRIERS

Because a clear pane of glass will reflect like a mirror, objects placed on windows must be put on the outside surface—not the inside—to prevent strikes. Simply closing the curtains will not work if the exterior reflection is not eliminated.

A glass surface will be recognized and avoided by birds junco-sized and larger if the objects are uniformly spread over the surface and separated by a distance of 12.5 cm-25 cm (5-10 in.). One object by itself on a window will not significantly reduce strike rates. The strike rate drops proportionately to the number of objects added to the window surface.

In addition to making the glass surface visible, there are a number of things to do to protect your feeder birds from window strikes (see sidebar).

TO MAKE YOUR BIRD FEEDERS SAFE

- Feeders should be placed a safe distance away from a window to avoid window strikes. Place them 1 m (3 ft.) or less, or more than 4 m (13 ft.) from your window. The short distance is the least deadly because, when the birds scatter from the feeder, they haven't gained enough momentum by the time they hit to harm themselves. The deadliest distance is 4 m (13 ft.). From this distance, the birds are able to fly fast enough to kill themselves, and the feeder is close enough that the birds are likely to choose a flight path that heads directly to the window. Window strikes are more likely to occur when the birds (especially flock species like redpolls and grosbeaks) are frightened from a feeder by a predator, human or a loud noise.
- If you turn a hopper feeder away from the window, strikes will be reduced because, when the birds scatter from the feeder, they have to make a turn, a move which forces them to slow down.
- A frame of 2.5 cm (1 in.) chicken wire can be placed on the house side of tube and open-sided feeders. The birds will veer to miss this obstruction, which will both slow them down and encourage them to fly off in a direction away from the house.

A chicken wire frame between a feeder and a house can save bird lives

Window Strike First Aid

Birds that collide with windows seldom die of a broken neck. Instead, they usually die from swelling and the resulting brain damage (the blood-brain barrier is broken). Although many birds seem fine shortly after the collision, it is thought that about 50 percent of them eventually die. The mortality of those not fatally wounded by the strike is also high because cats, hawks and other predators quickly learn that a stunned bird makes an easy meal.

A bird found in a stunned condition should be put into a small cardboard box that is covered with a towel, or has a lid into which a few air holes have been punched. Try to make sure the bird is sitting upright to aid normal respiration. If the bird can't stand on its own, put in a doughnut made of tissue to help keep it upright. Give fluids to the bird (see page 147) using water (sterile is best) or a half-and-half mixture of water and Gatorade®. A few drops of Rescue Remedy® put in the liquid may help the bird recover (see side bar).

GOOD MEDICINE FOR WILDLIFE

At the Medicine River Wildlife Rehabilitation Centre, in central Alberta, 10 drops of Rescue Remedy® is mixed with 30 ml of sterile water or Lactated Ringers, and this solution is used to rehydrate injured birds. (Rescue Remedy® is a homeopathic product, available at many health food stores, that is now widely used by wildlife rehabbers.) Try to use these proportions (10 drops of Rescue Remedy® to 30 ml of water or a half-and-half water/Gatorade® mixture) if you are going to try to help a bird or other animal at home.

Place the box in a quiet, warm location for a few hours. If the bird revives, release it near dense shrubbery, or on top of a garage or shed, away from cats. Handle the bird as little as possible (handling causes stress), and if you must hold the bird to release it, just open your hands to let it go. Do not "launch" a bird, or it may get disoriented. Always wash your hands after handling a bird.

If the bird's condition continues to worsen, contact your local wildlife rehabilitation centre, nature centre or Alberta Environment, Natural Resources Service [Fish and Wildlife] office (see Appendix 5).

DISEASES

Disease and illness are realities among wild creatures. Information on two wildlife-related human health concerns (hantavirus and rabies) is provided in Chapter 18.

Birds

In some cases, precautions can be taken to reduce disease-related problems in a yard or garden, especially among feeder birds (see sidebar). Contagious avian diseases are sometimes harboured and spread at crowded feeders through contaminated droppings, mould and diseased birds.

SALMONELLA AND BIRDS

To minimize the risk of salmonella, use feeders (i.e., tube and hopper) that prevent the birds from defecating in the seeds. To reduce the risk of infection, clean your feeders at least once a year with hot, soapy water.

The most common cause of death among wild birds is infection by the salmonella bacterium, and the species most affected are those that flock together in large numbers. The extent of the problem may not be obvious because many infected birds remain healthy. Still, these birds are capable of passing the disease, usually through infected feces.

Salmonella causes birds to contract pneumonia when they are stressed with cold or hunger. Sick birds are quite easy to spot because they become lethargic, fluff out their feathers and may stand with their mouths open or their heads tucked under their wings. Death can quickly follow the onset of pneumonia.

Sick common redpoll

If sick or dead birds are found near a feeder, stop the feeding immediately, and rake up and remove all discarded seed hulls and other debris. This contaminated material can be bagged and sent with your regular garbage. Report the problem to your nearest Alberta Environment, Natural Resources Service [Fish and Wildlife] office. To stop the spread of an infection, thoroughly clean and disinfect all feeders with a mixture of bleach and hot water.

Mammals
Do not attempt to handle or treat a diseased mammal. Call your local wildlife rehabilitation centre or appropriate government agency (see Appendix 5). The legal responsibility for most wildlife in Alberta is split between the Canadian Wildlife Service (federal) and Alberta Environment (provincial).

Other Animals
Call your local wildlife rehabilitation centre or appropriate government agency for advice (see Appendix 5).

FIRST AID

Immediate and proper treatment can often save a life. Once basic first aid has been administered, a call should be made to the closest wildlife rehabilitation centre or the appropriate government agency (see Appendix 5).

The Capture

Birds

Before capturing an injured wild bird, be absolutely sure that it does need help. If the problem is obvious—it cannot stand; is entangled in fishing line, barbed wire or other human-made material; has one leg or wing dangling; is unable to fly; has been mauled by a cat; has a damaged beak; has oil on it; is frozen in ice; or is caught in a trap—the bird requires assistance. An injured bird should be placed in a suitably sized cardboard box (rather than an open cage) with bedding of some sort and kept quiet, dark and warm.

Small Birds. Small birds are usually easy to catch. If the bird runs too quickly to be caught by one person, simply have two or three people approach it from different directions. This tactic usually confuses the bird and enables it to be caught, either by hand or by throwing a cloth over it.

Raptors. Raptors, such as hawks and owls, can be dangerous to handle so care should be taken to avoid a beak strike, talon clasp or talon raking. In capturing a raptor, use leather gloves, and a fish net, towel, jacket or blanket to throw over the bird. Should an injury result from handling a raptor, seek immediate medical attention.

Shorebirds. Larger shorebirds, especially grebes and herons, can inflict serious wounds with their beaks and may not strike out until they are approached closely. To avoid getting struck in the face, grab these birds behind the neck, or reach for and hold their beak, before attempting to grasp their legs. Wear leather gloves and safety glasses.

Always wash your hands after handling a bird.

Mammals

Small Mammals. Injured small mammals should be treated much the same as raptors because they can kick, claw and bite. Although injured, they may still have an amazing amount of strength and energy.

Bats. Bats are not aggressive animals! Even the rare, rabid bat that is found is seldom aggressive. If handled, however, bats will bite to defend themselves. A bat bite should be washed and medical attention sought immediately.

Although a bat found on the ground may be diseased, it is more likely to be injured or a juvenile that has become tired, disoriented or weak from hunger. As long as the bat will not be found by children or pets, leave it alone. If you need to move it, place it on a nearby tree (using leather gloves, a dust pan or jar). If the bat doesn't leave after 24 hours, call your nearest Alberta Environment, Natural Resources Service [Fish and Wildlife] office or wildlife rehabilitation centre (see Appendix 5) for further instructions.

If the animal dies, call your local Alberta Environment, Natural Resources Service [Fish and Wildlife] office for information on how to submit a dead bat for a rabies analysis. Do not freeze a dead bat that is to be turned in for analysis.

Large Mammals. Do not attempt to capture a large mammal because it may inflict serious injury. Call the appropriate government agency or your local wildlife rehabilitation centre.

THE PROBLEM OF CATS

Domestic cats (*Felis catus*) are descendants of the wild cat of Africa and southwestern Asia. They were domesticated in Egypt approximately 4000 years ago and introduced into North America by European settlers. Large numbers were brought over during the latter part of the nineteenth century, when rodent populations increased following the spread of agriculture.

Although some people feel that cats provide a beneficial service by killing mice in and around farmyards, it is important to remember that small mammals form the prey base for predatory animals such as great horned owls, red-tailed hawks and coyotes. Cats are very efficient predators and compete with their native counterparts for this prey base.

MYRNA PEARMAN

It is estimated that domestic and feral cats (which can exist at very high densities) kill hundreds of millions of birds and more than a billion small mammals (e.g., rabbits, chipmunks, squirrels, voles, shrews) in North America each year. Extensive studies show that 60-70 percent of cat kills are mammals, 20-30 percent are birds, and up to 10 percent are amphibians, reptiles and insects. The number and types of animals killed by cats vary, depending on the individual cat, time of year and availability of prey. Some free-roaming domestic cats kill more than 100 animals each year.

Although cats take a serious toll on the nestlings and fledglings of many bird species, it is the ground-nesting species, such as ground-nesting sparrows, that are regularly targeted. Cats are also significant predators at bird feeders.

Habitat loss is the most significant cause of bird species declines worldwide, but predation (including killing by cats) ranks second. And the problem of population decline is being exacerbated by the increasing fragmentation of our forests and wild areas. Islands of habitat (e.g., suburban and urban parks, bird sanctuaries, green spaces) are usually surrounded by urban, agricultural or industrial development. Cats that live in settled areas roam into the natural areas, predating the birds and small mammals that inhabit them.

Here is some information about predation by cats that everyone should know.

Well-fed cats do kill. Well-fed cats kill birds and other small wildlife because the urge to kill is independent of the urge to eat. The instincts to kill and to eat are triggered by different parts of the cat brain.

Cats with bells on kill. Bells are not effective at saving wildlife because animals don't associate the sound of a bell with danger, and cats with bells learn how to stalk without ringing the bell. Once the cat pounces and the bell rings, it is usually too late for an animal to escape. Bells offer no protection at all to nestlings, fledglings and small mammals in a nest.

De-clawed cats kill birds. Cats are adept at batting birds out of the air and killing them, even with their claws removed.

Animals that escape usually die anyway. Wildlife rehabilitation centres report that most small animals they see that are injured by cats die from either internal injuries or from diseases transmitted by the cat.

The problem of feral cats is not solved. The problem of what to do with feral cats is very controversial. Some people advocate managing colonies of stray cats though a practice called TTVAR (trap, test, vaccinate, alter [neuter], release). Theoretically, this practice should reduce feral cat populations, and cat advocates feel that this goal can be achieved if given widespread support from city councils, SPCAs, local vets and concerned citizens.

However, from a wildlife conservation point of view, the practice of TTVAR is not an adequate solution to the problem. Feral cats, whether fed or not, still kill birds and small mammals. Although the TTVAR program may help prevent the spread of disease and ensures feral animals are neutered, it does not address the issue of encouraging responsible pet ownership (see next page).

Other Animals

Call your local wildlife rehabilitation centre or appropriate government agency for advice (see Appendix 5).

Always wash your hands after handling an animal.

Administering First Aid

To minimize stress and increase their chance of survival, sick and injured wildlife should receive a suitable first aid treatment as quickly and as quietly as possible.

Although it may seem the logical thing to do, feeding a creature that is sick or injured is not usually advisable. Most injured animals are suffering from shock and are often emaciated and dehydrated. Keep them warm and stress-free, and, if feasible, administer fluids as described under **Window Strikes**. Try to keep some sterile or distilled water, Gatorade® and Rescue Remedy® on hand.

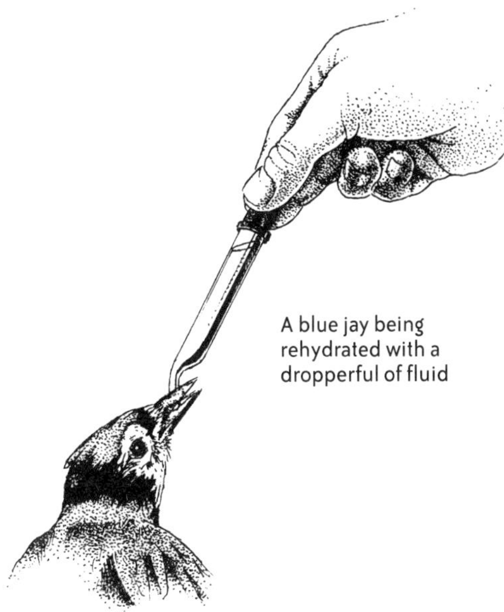

A blue jay being rehydrated with a dropperful of fluid

Small birds are most easily given fluids by an eyedropper held to the end of the beak. Judge the amount to give by what the bird will swallow and not spit back up. Larger birds will need the expert care of a wildlife rehabilitator. A small mammal can be offered fluids in a low dish. If it is unable to drink, try to dribble fluids down the back of its throat. Don't administer anything to a large mammal!

For other animals, contact your local wildlife rehabilitation centre or appropriate government agency for assistance.

THE PROBLEM OF CATS . . . continued

Keeping Cats Under Control

The obvious solution to the cat problem is for cat owners to keep their animals indoors, or to have control over their pets' outdoor activities. Cats could be put in a cat run, kept in a screened back porch or put on a cat harness and leash. These actions would prevent widespread wildlife predation and also be advantageous for cats.

Although many people still feel that it is more "natural" for a cat to be outdoors, free-roaming cats face serious hazards, including a variety of diseases (e.g., rabies, feline distemper, parasites), as well as other risks—motor vehicles, poisoning, other animals, human abuse, etc. Outdoor cats live, on average, three to five years, whereas indoor cats commonly live seventeen years.

It is possible to turn an outdoor cat into a well-adjusted indoor cat. The key is to undertake the conversion gradually and to provide plenty of attention and stimulation for the cat while it is indoors.

If you feel strongly about giving your cat(s) outdoor space or your cat doesn't want to be indoors, build a cat run. A cat run can be made interesting through the provision of tree limbs, tires, toys hanging from branches and multi-level condos. A cat run (also a screened back porch or the use of a cat harness and leash) will enable a cat to enjoy the outdoors but still be contained within your yard.

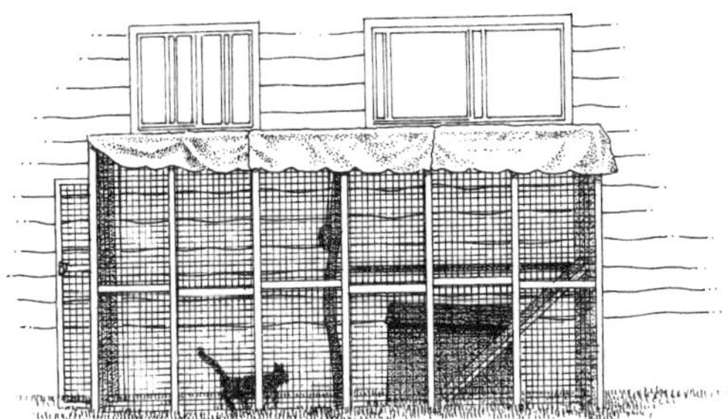

Build a cat run for cats who like to be outdoors

In recognition of how keeping cats indoors can be in the best interest of both cats and birds, the American Bird Conservancy (ABC) has sponsored a program entitled *Cats Indoors! The Campaign for Safer Birds and Cats* (see Appendix 5 to contact the ABC).

To Discourage a Wandering Cat

If your neighbours have cats that tresspass, talk to them and try to arrive at an amicable solution. Encourage them to keep litter boxes in their houses and yards so the cats will be less likely to undertake their toiletries in your yard. If you can't come to an agreement, you may want to obtain the services of a mediator (available in Edmonton and Calgary, and soon, possibly, in Red Deer).

There are several techniques that you can use to try to discourage cats from coming into your yard. What works in one area may not work in another, and what works for one cat may not work for another. So, you may have to experiment and try different methods before you find one (or more) that works well for you.

One technique to deter a cat is to spray it with water (summer only). A high-powered water gun or a garden hose can be used. Just spray long enough to discourage the cat.

If a cat is being particularly annoying around a bird feeder, pond or birdbath, set the lawn sprinkler adjacent to where it likes to hang out. As the cat draws near, turn on the sprinkler. Be sure that you are not visible when the sprinkler is turned on, or the cat will associate you with the soaking. If it doesn't see you, it will learn to associate its approach with the soaking and will avoid it. A motion-activated sprinkler, if you can get one, will also work well.

You can also try laying prickly things down where a cat likes to walk. Prickly, dry juniper branches, dry raspberry canes and chicken wire can all be used. Chicken wire is particularly effective because cats dislike walking on it and it will prevent them from digging.

If you keep your garden soil moist, cats are less likely to bother it. In dry areas, place wooden chopsticks or short plant stakes at 20 cm (8 in.) intervals to prevent a cat from digging or scratching. Other options include spreading orange and lemon peel, using citrus-scented sprays, and sprinkling cayenne pepper, coffee grounds or pipe tobacco in areas that cats like to frequent. Old towels or rags that have been soaked with stale perfume and hung near a favourite haunt may also be a deterrent. Cat repellent (available at pet stores) sprayed around the perimeter of your yard, near a cat's favourite sunning spot and along the top of a fence will also discourage them. Cats also dislike rue (*Ruta graveolens*), a foul-smelling annual that can be planted in strategic locations around your yard. Marigolds are also said to keep cats away.

If you have any other ideas on how to humanely, yet effectively, prevent cats from trespassing, please send them to us using the Backyard Watch form (Appendix 6).

Wound Management

Should a bird or animal be found with a fracture of the wing or leg, it is extremely important that the area be immediately cleaned, placed in a normal position and lightly bandaged. This task is not easy, so it is usually more realistic to take the animal directly to a veterinarian or a wildlife rehabilitation centre for care.

DEALING WITH ORPHANS

Birds

It is important to assess whether or not a seemingly orphaned animal has indeed been abandoned by both of its parents. Many young birds, for example, may hop around on the ground for several days before becoming skilled flyers. Although it may seem like they are on their own, they are still being cared for.

One can safely assume, however, that a featherless, young bird is orphaned if it is found on the ground or out of its nest. A young bird can also be considered orphaned if, after several hours, it has not been fed, is continually begging for food or appears to be weak.

If it is known that a nest containing young has been destroyed by a storm or an animal, construct another nest of grass inside an appropriately sized container and return the nestlings, in their new home, to the nest site. In most cases, the parents will resume feeding. It is not true that parent birds will abandon their young if the young have been handled by humans. Most birds have a very poorly developed sense of smell and, thus, do not detect human scent.

Young, orphaned birds must be kept in a warm, moist environment and require frequent feeding. Do not attempt to look after them for an extended period of time—administer first aid, then transport the orphan(s) to a local zoo, government wildlife office or wildlife rehabilitation centre. In some cases, a foster nest can be found to which the orphan can be added. A qualified government agency or wildlife rehabilitation centre should be contacted for further information about fostering (see Appendix 5).

Mammals

Before attempting to capture what appears to be an orphaned mammal, be sure that it is indeed orphaned. Deer, rabbits and hares will leave their young by themselves, so a youngster alone may still be under parental care. If the animal is still alone after 24 hours and is showing signs of being cold or hungry, you can assume that it is without parents.

FAWNS FOUND ALONE

Although a doe frequently will leave her offspring for several hours at a time, she is well aware of where her young have been left and will return to them when she is ready to do so. The best you can do is to protect a fawn from dogs.

If you happen upon a doe that has been killed, then discover one or more fawns nearby, transport the young to safety and contact a wildlife rehabilitation centre for further instructions.

TRANSPORTATION

When transporting any wild creature, care must be taken not to cause it damage or stress. A sturdy cardboard box with little room for movement provides a secure and safe cage for transporting most animals. Air holes in a cardboard box are not usually needed unless the box has a tight lid.

Aggressive and chewing mammals should be transported in a metal or plastic container (punch a few air holes in the lid). Metal garbage cans work well. Pet cages can also be used, but cover the cage with a blanket to keep the animal dark and quiet, and line the bottom with bedding such as straw, blankets or paper towels.

HEALTH CONCERNS

In most cases, good hygiene and avoiding direct contact with wild animals or their droppings are sufficient precautions to prevent the transmission of wildlife-related diseases or parasites. If you are bitten by a wild animal or raked by the talons of a bird, especially a bird of prey, seek immediate medical attention.

EUTHANASIA

When an attempt is made to save a life, it is sometimes unthinkable to destroy it. There are times, however, when an animal is so sick or so badly injured that to let it live would mean dooming it to pain and misery. As difficult as the decision may be, the only reasonable option in such cases is euthanasia. Euthanasia can be performed by a veterinarian or at a wildlife rehabilitation centre.

5 BASICS

HELPING SICK AND INJURED WILDLIFE

1. Take action to prevent injuries to wildlife (e.g., from window strikes, dogs, cats).
2. When you find a sick or injured animal, administer first aid if possible, and call a wildlife rehabilitation centre or the appropriate government agency.
3. If you have sick or dead birds at your feeder, stop feeding the birds, clean up all the hulls beneath the feeder, and clean out your feeder with hot, soapy water and bleach.
4. Always wear thick gloves when handling sick or injured wildlife.
5. If you're bitten or scratched by a wild animal, seek medical attention immediately.

ACKNOWLEDGMENTS

Dick and Marlys Hjort (Veteran backyard bird feeder operators, Chigaso City, Minnesota)
Hugh Johnston (Interpretive Coordinator, Medicine River Wildlife Rehabilitation Centre, Spruce View, Alberta)
Carol Kelly (Executive Director and founder, Medicine River Wildlife Rehabilitation Centre, Spruce View, Alberta)
Daniel Klem, Jr. (Professor of Biology, Muhlenberg College, Allentown, Pennsylvania)
Kathleen Sheppard (Research Assistant, Medicine River Wildlife Rehabilitation Centre, Spruce View, Alberta)
Joan White Calf (formerly, Hospital Coordinator, Medicine River Wildlife Rehabilitation Centre, Spruce View, Alberta)

SIGNIFICANT REFERENCES

American Birding Conservancy. 1997. *Cats Indoors! The campaign for safer birds and cats.* American Birding Conservacy, Washington, D.C. (Education kit)

The California Center for Wildlife, with D. Landau and S. Stump. 1994. *Living with wildlife: How to enjoy, cope with, and protect North America's wild creatures around your home and theirs.* Sierra Club Books, San Francisco, California.

RUSS AMY

Moose in Red Deer, Alberta, water garden

Chapter 18 Co-existing with Wildlife

In most cases, "pest" species are the ones that cause grief in a yard or garden. However, even "desirable" species can overrun and damage property and habitat.

"PEST" SPECIES

Most of the animals that are likely to become pests in urban areas share common traits: they reproduce rapidly, have flexible food requirements, are very tolerant of variable environmental conditions, are adept at avoiding predators and, in the case of birds, have flexible nesting needs.

LIVETRAPPING A WILD ANIMAL

Livetrapping an offending animal (almost always a mammal) and transporting it away to a natural area should be used only as a last resort. Removing an animal often just creates a vacuum that is quickly filled by another individual; and, animals not taken far enough away often return. As well, animals translocated to unfamiliar, and sometimes already overcrowded, habitat are at a disadvantage when they have to compete with other species, or others of their own kind, for food and shelter.

INSECT OUTBREAKS

Although some insect outbreaks are part of a natural cycle, most of the large populations of insects we notice are due to our own mishandling of their environment.

WHEN WILDLIFE BECOMES A PROBLEM

The most effective approach to reducing the potential for human-wildlife conflict is to "animal-proof." It is always easier to discourage animals before or soon after they move into an area than to eliminate or deter them after they become established.

Physical barriers, which exclude animals, are usually the most effective method to protect property from wildlife damage. Such barriers include fences, walls, screens, wire mesh and netting. Porcupine cloth (cloth with sharp points sticking out from it) and sloped ledges will deter birds from landing. Repellents, which are materials that are loathsome to one or more of an animal's senses, can also be used. Some repellents can be applied directly to vegetation, whereas others can be placed or used adjacent to an area you want to protect.

If you find yourself in a situation where it appears that livetrapping is your only recourse, contact your local Alberta Environment, Natural Resources Service [Fish and Wildlife] office for information on local livetrapping regulations and procedures.

Cautions and Concerns

It is best to avoid direct contact with a wild animal. However, if physical contact is necessary and you cannot access the services of an expert, be sure to take precautions—if necessary, wear thick leather gloves and safety glasses. Don't inhale fecal dust, and never touch fecal material. Protect any cuts or sores, and wash your hands thoroughly after contact. Never touch your eyes or mouth before washing your hands. If you are bitten or scratched, seek medical advice immediately. Teach children to follow these guidelines.

DEALING WITH PROBLEM AMPHIBIANS AND REPTILES

Amphibians and reptiles seldom pose problems. Should any become too numerous, individuals can be captured and relocated to a nearby natural area. If handled roughly, toads and salamanders release poisonous (but not very dangerous) toxins from the glands in their skin. Always wash your hands after handling these animals.

Garter snakes may sometimes be a nuisance if they decide that your basement would make a good hibernaculum. This problem usually occurs when a new building is erected on or near a traditional denning site, or if a traditional site has been destroyed, causing the snakes to search for a new winter den. To prevent snakes from entering a house, ensure the foundation and basement are perfectly sealed and crack-free. Installing a snake hibernaculum may also help (see Chapter 9).

DEALING WITH PROBLEM INSECTS

We strongly urge you to deal with yard and garden insect problems using the safest and most environmentally responsible methods possible. Before you take any action at all, be sure to identify the "offending" insects. Many a gardener has recoiled in

horror at the sight of one of the most vicious looking of all "bugs"—the larva of the beneficial, beloved ladybird beetle! And let's keep insect problems in perspective—only about two percent of all insect species can be considered pests.

Using the Hose and Your Fingers

One of the easiest ways to dislodge insects is to simply hose them down from plants. If you water in the morning instead of in the evening, slugs, which are active at night, will have a harder time moving around (because the vegetation will be dry).

If you don't have too many unwelcome insects, you can also pick off individuals manually. Drop the offenders in a jar of water with a few drops of dish soap to kill them.

Some Common Sense Ideas

Unwanted plants ("weeds") should be kept in check—any plant monoculture is a trigger for insect populations to grow rapidly. Insects living on weeds can transfer to your other, more valued plants. If certain insects really bother you, don't put in the plant species that you know will attract them (e.g., mayday trees, if you don't like aphids).

REMOVING WEEDS

The most ecologically sound method of removing plants you don't want is to handpick them. If you do this job when the plants are small and the soil is moist, the task will be relatively easy. Remove weeds from your lawn by handpicking them or by digging them out individually with a knife or appropriate garden tool. For larger weeds, remove the flowers or seeds and put the remainder of the plant in your compost pile.

Generally, we advocate planting in clumps to increase the chances of attracting wildlife to your yard. However, in situations where insect pests might be a problem, try planting a large variety of plant species, with only a few of each type, or widely space the individuals of a given species. This strategy makes it less likely that insects will transfer from one plant to another without being eaten by something on the way.

If you are planting annuals or vegetables, vary the locations of these plantings each year. Insects that feed on a given plant often spend the winter in the soil beneath that plant, so replanting the same species in the same location will ensure your six-legged friends an easy target.

MYRNA PEARMAN

Open soil can be turned in the fall or spring to expose underground insect pupae to predators and killing frosts. This practice kills both harmful and beneficial insects.

As your garden matures, watch the common insects that you would like to discourage. Keep notes on when they first appear, what they feed on and when their populations reach their height. With a little experience, a good gardener can learn to cut back perennials at just the right time to prevent insect population outbreaks. Annuals and biennials can be planted after a pest species has run its course.

Biological Controls

Bats and birds are excellent biological insect controllers. A typical colony of little brown bats, for example, can eat up to 50 kg (110 lb.) of insects during a summer! Native sparrows eat ground-dwelling insect pests, and swallows devour large quantities of aerial insects. Encourage these animals to take up residence (see Chapters 14 and 15).

Predatory and parasitic insects will also help. Predatory insects such as ladybird beetles, green lacewings, antlions, dragonflies and damselflies eat unwanted insects. Parasitic insects lay their eggs on or inside a host insect (egg, larva, pupa or adult). When they hatch, the parasitic larvae get their nourishment from the host. See Chapter 5 on establishing a water garden (which will encourage dragonflies and damselflies), Chapter 11 on how to help solitary wasps (which are parasitic insects), and Chapter 12 on how to encourage beetles.

Bt

A bacterial control, Bt (*Bacillus thuringiensis*), is sometimes used to control insects. Although Bt is not harmful to humans, it affects all moth and butterfly caterpillars, so should not be used in butterfly gardens. Expert advice on its use is advised.

The field of biotechnology is expanding rapidly, and new biocontrols are always being developed. Garden centres should have up-to-date information on new products and techniques.

BUG ZAPPERS

The use of bug zappers should be avoided. Not only are these zappers ineffective at controlling biting insects, but they also destroy all nocturnal insects, many of which are beneficial.

A NATURAL PESTICIDE

If you have a very serious insect problem, here is a gross (but effective) way to make up your own fairly specific insect spray. When an insect population begins to take charge, collect as many of the problem insects as you can in 30 minutes, put them in an old blender with a cup or two of water, and give them a good blending. Filter the bits and pieces out with a rag or an old dish towel, and put the solution in a hand spray bottle. Use this spray on the affected plants. If the sample of insects you use to make the spray is large enough, at least some of them will be carrying disease or parasites, which will be sprayed on, and will reduce, the offending population.

STINGS

Although being stung by a bee is not a pleasant experience, most incidents involving stings or "bee bites" are usually stings by yellow jackets, which are quite aggressive and can sting repeatedly. Usually honey bees and bumble bees sting only when pinched or accidentally stepped on. Most stings do not hurt for very long and need no special treatment (rubbing a raw onion or mud on the site may help relieve discomfort). However, people with allergies or sensitivities to bee and wasp venom can die from anaphylactic shock if they do not receive immediate treatment.

Mechanical Controls

Mechanical controls, such as the use of diatomaceous earth or traps, can also reduce the problem of insect pests. A saucer of beer will lure slugs to their death. Commercial slug guards for enclosing gardens are also available.

Spraying

Many scientists and health officials are becoming increasingly concerned about the deleterious health effects of common lawn and garden pesticides (see page 6, Chapter 2). Avoid chemical spraying, if at all possible.

Most insect outbreaks are quickly followed by an increase in natural predators and parasites that quickly check the population growth. Spraying kills these beneficial insects as well as the pests. Invariably, the problem insects get a fresh head start because their populations are never completely eliminated by sprays and they breed more rapidly than their predators.

If you feel you must spray, and you don't like the idea of blending up insects (see side bar), choose a product very carefully. Research the ingredients so you can choose the least toxic, use the product only according to instructions, and take all precautions necessary.

Although they are often recommended, even "natural" pesticides such as rotenone and pyrethrum are toxic and should be handled accordingly. You might want to consider other alternatives, like Safer's® Insecticidal Soap or a homemade solution using a teaspoon of detergent in 4.5 L (1 gal.) of water, although these products can harm the leaves of some plants and thus cause as much damage as the bugs!

"Teas" brewed from cedar chips, rhubarb leaves, tomato leaves or hot peppers (add dishwashing detergent to the pepper tea so it will adhere to the plants) will control several insect pests. (See *The Naturalist's Garden* in **Significant References** at the end of this chapter for more information on these solutions.)

Wasp Visits, Bee Stings and other Annoyances

The easiest way to reduce the annoyance of wasps (including yellow jackets and hornets) trying to share your picnic or gardening is to place a dish containing a small amount of fruit or a sugar-water solution a short distance from where are eating or working. The insects will find this food and turn their attention to collecting it. When there are lots of wasps around, don't wear yellows and bright oranges (they make you look like a big flower) or bright blues and reds (they make you look like a source of nesting material).

The nest locations of yellow jackets and hornets can be easily shifted in early spring. Up until about mid-May, the queens search out new nest sites and build their nests. If you disturb a queen's chosen site by plugging up the hole or putting a rock over the entrance, or destroying what she has built, she will look for another spot.

Both bees and wasps will defend their hives and nests from intrusion. By moving slowly around nests and hives, the potential for getting stung can be minimized. Should a bee swarm be encountered, stay calm. Phone a local beekeeper to have the swarm removed.

Ants know where they are going, or where they are, by the invisible chemical trails they leave as they journey to and from their nest. Once a food source has been found, the chemical trails intensify, leading more ants to gather the nourishment. Break the trail and you reduce the ants' ability to find the food. Trails can be broken by washing them with water, glass cleaner or weak solutions of vinegar.

Moths

The only moths that can cause a real problem are those species that go through cyclic population changes (e.g., tent caterpillars). The population changes that cause large numbers of caterpillars to appear are usually natural events, and there is little that you can or should do about them.

When mature, many moth caterpillars will begin to travel. Mellow out and be patient—this stage of moth life usually lasts only a week or so.

TOUCHING MOTH CATERPILLARS

Be careful when handling fuzzy caterpillars because the hairs can be irritating to the mucus membranes of human eyes and mouths. Never touch your eyes, and always wash your hands with soap and water, if you handle these creatures.

DEALING WITH SPIDERS

Unwanted webs or snares of the orb-weavers are probably the most common spider annoyance. The easiest way to deal with them is to just leave them be—watch and admire!

If you need to move a web, do so with a stiff broom, making sure you don't hurt the spider. You may find a spider will get frightened by what you're doing and will try to run away or hide, so don't be standing directly under the broom (if you're brushing a web away from high up) unless you are willing to tolerate an excited spider dancing around your face and shoulders.

Often the web will probably reappear from where it was removed, or close by, unless you destroy both the web and the spider's silk nest. If you can get a spider on a stick or broom, and put it in a new location, it won't return to its original nest site.

Occasionally, spiderling (baby spider) hatches cause people tension. When spiderlings hatch, hundreds of the tiny creatures show up on an egg mass and quickly disperse. Seeing so many spiderlings in one place and watching them as they spread themselves out is fascinating to an open-minded naturalist but can look like something from a bad science fiction movie to someone else.

If a hatch begins in an unsuitable location, use a putty knife to gently pry the egg mass from where it is attached and slowly move it to a place where you will not be bothered. Don't shake the egg mass, or the spiderlings will jump off and slide down their anchoring silks to the first surface they touch.

DEALING WITH PROBLEM BIRDS

Pigeons (Rock Doves)

Domestic pigeons are introduced birds usually found in association with human-built environments. Although some people enjoy feeding them, and they are one of the main food sources for overwintering merlins and gyrfalcons, pigeons can become overly abundant and may need to be discouraged (see side bar).

DISCOURAGING PIGEONS

Here are some ways to exclude pigeons from their perching and roosting sites.

- String monofilament line or stainless steel wire a few centimetres above the top of a ledge or balcony.
- Use netting, mesh or porcupine cloth on a landing surface. Make your own porcupine cloth by pounding two-and-a-half inch nails, spaced 19 mm (3/4 in.) apart, through an appropriately sized piece of 13 mm (1/2 in.) plywood.
- Apply a sticky material (e.g., axle grease) to a landing surface.
- Retrofit a landing surface with caps that have been cut to at least a 60° angle.
- Use an owl decoy (move it frequently).
- Drive the birds from roosting sites at night by hosing them down with water from a garden hose (summer only).
- Livetrap and translocate them (contact Alberta Environment, Natural Resources Service, first).

House Sparrows

House sparrows were introduced into North America from England in the 1800s and have since spread throughout the continent. Permanent residents, they are especially ubiquitous in urban areas and around farm buildings, where they may be attracted to bird -feeding stations and nestboxes.

To discourage these birds from dominating all bird feeders, set up a feeding station especially for the sparrows using a feeder filled with one of their preferred foods (e.g., wild birdseed mix or millet). Set this feeder apart from your regular feeders. Other ideas include offering less-preferred foods, such as canola, or offering nygur seed or sunflower chips from tube feeders with tiny portals (a sparrow's large beak prevents it from taking the seeds). Tube feeders with their perches cut short (to 13 mm [1/2 in.]), and tube feeders with portals below the perches will not likely be used by house

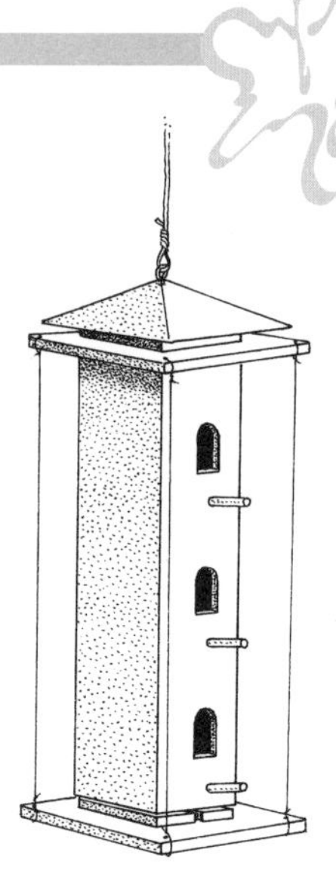

Monofilament line on a tube or hopper bird feeder will help keep house sparrows away

HOUSE SPARROWS AND STARLINGS

An effective way to reduce both house sparrows and starlings around your property is to eliminate nesting and roosting sites. To keep sparrows out of buildings, seal all nooks, crannies and holes, and keep the doors closed (especially during the winter).

Trapping programs are sometimes used to reduce local house sparrow and starling numbers. Contact the Ellis Bird Farm (see Appendix 5) for trap plans. Wildlife rehabilitation centres will often take sparrows to feed to their rehabilitating hawks and owls.

HELP FOR WOODPECKERS

In many cases, woodpeckers end up damaging buildings because there is a lack of natural snags in the area. If you preserve or install snags in your backyard, you will reduce the potential for damage. Hanging out large quantities of suet for woodpeckers to eat will encourage them to spend less time hunting for bugs on or in your house.

sparrows. Stringing monofilament (fishing) line from each corner of a tube or hopper feeder (see illustration) also deters these determined birds.

See Chapter 14 for tips on how to discourage house sparrows from using nestboxes.

European Starlings

Like house sparrows, European starlings were introduced into North America in the nineteenth century and have spread throughout the continent. Although mostly migratory in Alberta, starlings are sometimes attracted to winter bird-feeding stations that provide suet, millet, chopped peanuts or sunflower seeds.

One way to deter starlings from a feeding station offering suet is to use an exclusion feeder (see page 117) or to dispense the food from an upside down feeder. Starlings also have trouble feeding from a wire suet cage.

Starlings can be excluded from nestboxes with entrance holes that measure 40 mm (1 9/16 in.) or less. They are less easily deterred from using larger nestboxes, but frequent nest clean-outs early in the season usually discourage them.

Woodpeckers

Woodpeckers are attracted to houses for two reasons—drumming and food. Drumming activity does not usually result in serious damage to a house; however, if a woodpecker persists at drumming on your building, hang surveyor's tape or strips of cloth that flutter in the wind to scare it away.

When a woodpecker actually drills holes in a building, it is seeking insects. If it continues to excavate small holes, your house is likely infested. To discourage a bird from excavating, cover the affected area with plastic (i.e., black garbage bags) or netting. Another method is to paint it with one or two coats of wood preservative or ST-138® (a commercial woodpecker deterrent). If the bird is persistent and extensive damage results, contact your local Alberta Environment, Natural Resources Service [Fish and Wildlife] office for further advice.

Yellow-bellied and red-naped sapsuckers are interesting woodpeckers that can contribute to the biodiversity of your yard (see Chapter 3 for details). On the downside, sapsucker wounds on a tree can attract unwelcome insects or hungry squirrels and chipmunks, and provide a place for disease and fungi to enter.

If you need to deter sapsuckers, hang wind chimes or some other fluttering, noisy device around the sap well site. Damaged areas can be wrapped with burlap, or duct tape (sticky side out). Wounds can also be treated with pruning dressing to seal them against insects and disease.

If you have problems with other bird species, contact your local Alberta Environment, Natural Resources Service [Fish and Wildlife] office (see Appendix 5).

DEALING WITH PROBLEM MAMMALS

The most serious problem mammal in urban yards is the domestic house cat, which we have discussed in the previous chapter.

The key to minimizing conflict with non-domestic mammals is to keep things in perspective—are the mammals that prowl around your yard really causing harm? If they aren't, leave them be. If they are, take preventative measures to minimize the potential for damage. Do not cause them undue stress or suffering, and do not take actions that will result in orphaned young.

Bats

Bats are an important component of the ecosystem and are important predators of flying insects. Because they hibernate for six to seven months each year and are inactive for up to 20 hours each day during the summer, your chances of having direct contact with a bat are quite slim. If bats take up residence in your house or an outbuilding, they will not chew wood, insulation or electrical wire, and their presence in your house will not result in the spread of any disease. However, they do make noises, and the odour from their urine and excrement is not exactly pleasant. Eviction and exclusion, together with erecting a bat house for alternate housing (see Chapter 15), are the only safe and permanent ways to deal with them.

Little brown bats consume many insects

In order to exclude bats from a building, watch where they emerge at dusk to feed. These entry and exit holes can be confirmed during the day because they will have small, dark brown oil smears around them. Cover each of these entrance/exit holes with 13 mm (1/2-in.) wire mesh. The mesh should be attached directly above the hole and should extend at least 6-mm (1/4 in.) below and to each side of it. The top and sides of the mesh can be attached with staples or duct tape, but the bottom should be allowed to hang free. The bats will climb out the hole, then drop down and out when they leave, but cannot fly in when they want to re-enter. Leave the mesh in place for a few nights to ensure that the bats have all left, then seal the hole.

Do not attempt to remove bats during June or July, when the young are not yet old enough to fly. Don't kill individual bats, and don't use chemical poisons (they're toxic) or ultra-high frequency repellents (they don't work). The ideal time to bat-proof your house is in the fall, after the bats have left. (Little brown bats are migratory, and big brown bats don't usually use human-inhabited buildings to hibernate.)

For how to deal with bats that get inside your house, see the sidebar; for bats you might find outside, see the section on bats in Chapter 17.

BAT-PROOFING

To completely bat-proof your house, put 6-mm (1/4 in.) mesh hardware cloth over known entry and exit points, all louvres, vents, chimneys and large ventilation openings; seal small cracks in the eaves and rafters with caulking; nail down loose shingles or facings; and seal the joint between the roof and the chimney.

IF A BAT GETS INSIDE YOUR HOUSE

Sometimes, bats get confused when they attempt to exit a building and end up flying around the inside. If a bat ends up in your house, stay calm. It doesn't want to be there, either, and will not chase or attack you. The easiest way to assist the errant bat to get out is to confine it to one room, then open a window or outside door and leave it open until the bat leaves. Another option is to just sit down and wait a few minutes for the bat to land and go back to sleep. Put on some thick leather gloves, gently pick up the snoozing bat, take it outside and place it on a tree or shed roof. Alternatively, take a large can or jar and place it over the bat. Slip a piece of paper up between the can and the wall, and let the bat shuffle into the can. Take the can outside, tip the bat out in a safe place, and leave it be.

Coyotes and Foxes

Coyotes and foxes are wily, adaptable creatures that survive in surprisingly close association with humans, even in more urban settings.

If a female fox or coyote takes up residence under a building, it is best to leave her to raise her family in peace. If you need to evict her, walk around the den site, leaving human scent and making noise. She will likely move her young to another location.

Coyotes and foxes will quickly avail themselves of handouts and can become quite bold. Do not feed these animals, and do not leave pet food or garbage outside overnight. See Chapter 15 for more information on how to prevent scavenging. Should you have specific problems, contact your local Alberta Environment, Natural Resources Service [Fish and Wildlife] office.

Deer

Deer and humans have co-existed for millennia, and they (the deer) are usually welcome visitors to your yard until they develop an appetite for your flowers, shrubs and garden vegetables, or the sunflower seeds in your bird feeder.

If the deer persist in eating your garden plants, the only sure-proof way to exclude them is to fence them out (see side bar). In order to protect small shrubs, encircle each of them with wire mesh or bird netting. Make mesh excluders large enough to allow for the summer's growth, and, if you use netting, be prepared to move it frequently to accommodate plant growth.

DEER FENCES

If you have a garden or large flower bed that you need to protect, encircle it with a mesh or board fence. If you choose mesh, use 15 cm x 30 cm (6 x 12 in.) mesh. Both board and mesh fences should be 2.5 m (8 ft.) high and should have 0.6 m (2 ft.) of barbed wire at the top. The bottom of board fences should touch the ground and mesh fences should be buried beneath ground level.

A HOMEMADE TASTE REPELLENT
In *The Naturalist's Garden* (1993), Ruth Ernst Shaw suggests how to make a taste-repelling solution that can be applied to vegetation. It consists of an onion, a garlic bulb and red pepper flakes, mixed with water in a blender, strained, then added to 4.5L (1 gal.) of water. Adding a bit of soap helps make this solution adhere.

Noise makers and taste repellents (commercial or home-made) can also be tried.

Hares and Rabbits

Hares and rabbits can make a welcome addition to a backyard sanctuary. If you would like to attract them, see Chapter 15. Unfortunately, hares and rabbits have an appetite for garden vegetables in summer and tree or shrub bark in winter. They generally feed to a maximum of 45 cm (1.5 ft.) above ground or snow level. Burlap, poultry wire or commercial tree wrap (a type of fabric) wrapped around trunks and lower limbs will protect trees during the winter. Be sure to wrap your trees high enough to accommodate the highest expected snow level. Seedlings and small plants can be protected by cylinders of wire or plastic mesh.

KEEPING HARES AND RABBITS OUT OF YOUR GARDEN
Hares and rabbits can be excluded from garden areas by using 25 mm-38mm (1-1 1/2in.) poultry netting that is 1 m (3 ft.) wide. Bury the bottom 15 cm (6 in.) below ground level. A strand of electric fencing around the fence base can be tried, as can taste repellents and noise makers.

Mice and Voles

With the exception of deer mice, which will enter houses, most native mice seldom cause problems in urban or acreage homes. However, they can cause serious damage to trees (especially young ones) during the winter by girdling the portions adjacent to the ground, beneath the snow. As a precaution, wrap all young trees with mesh or plastic sleeves (as for **Hares and Rabbits**, above).

Deer mice are the only Alberta rodents found to carry hantavirus (see side bar). Mice are an important link in the food chain, so they should not be subject to widespread eradication efforts. However, always take precautions to minimize contact and reduce the risk of infection. To discourage deer mice (and house mice) from living in or around buildings, remove food and nesting material sources, mouse-proof your buildings and set traps as required.

Voles, which look like stubby mice with small eyes and short tails, are adept at making impressive under-snow tunnels during the winter. In the spring, these tunnels may leave rather garish looking tubes of black soil on your lawn. Although the soil tubes are a bit unsightly, the grass will soon grow back. Voles will girdle young trees; protect your trees as described under **Hares and Rabbits**.

HANTAVIRUS
Although hantavirus has been recently identified as a human health concern in North America, the virus has probably been in existence for thousands of years. In Alberta, transmission to humans is through contact with the feces, urine or saliva of infected deer mice or by breathing air contaminated with infected deer mouse droppings.

Infections in humans are extremely rare but often fatal. To prevent infection, do not handle live deer mice, and wear gloves and an approved half-mask respirator with a HEPA (high efficiency particulate) cartridge when cleaning or working in mouse-infested areas.

The virus is easily killed with common household disinfectants, and feces, dead mice, nests, food or other tainted items can be decontaminated by spraying them with a disinfectant.

If you find deer mice or a deer mouse nest in a bird nestbox, spray down the nesting material with a disinfectant before removing the material, and be sure to stand upwind from the box when cleaning it out. As long as these precautions are taken, a mask is not needed.

A website with information on hantavirus is www.cdc.gov/ncidod/diseases/hanta/hps/noframes/consumer.htm .

Skunks

Skunks are omnivorous, night-dwelling creatures that consume large numbers of harmful insects. They should be considered friends, not foes!

To prevent skunks from settling down where you don't want them (usually under porches and outbuildings), try running water into their den-to-be. These animals can be excluded from burrows by either sealing the burrow or by installing a one-way door over the exit site after they have left to feed at dusk. Do not shut out a skunk from a burrow that may have offspring. Instead, cover up the exit hole each day with loose dirt. The mother will eventually abandon the den site and move her family elsewhere.

If a skunk gets into a basement, hole or other accidental location, place a "ladder" down into the hole for it. The ladder should not be at more than a 45° angle, and cleats should be at 15-cm (6-in.) intervals. If you need to livetrap a skunk, contact your nearest Alberta Environment, Natural Resources Service [Fish and Wildlife] office.

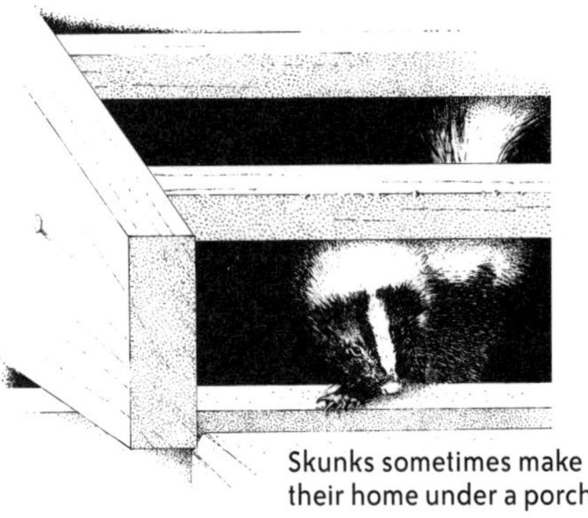

Skunks sometimes make their home under a porch

GETTING RID OF SKUNK ODOUR
Skunk odour can be removed or reduced with tomato juice, vinegar, gasoline or ammonia followed by soap and water. Glass cleaner can be sprayed on clothes before laundering to reduce odour. Using bleach in the wash will also help.

Squirrels

Red and eastern gray squirrels can be problems when they dominate bird-feeding stations, dig up garden bulbs or chew their way into nestboxes.

Squirrels can be discouraged from visiting a bird-feeding station if the feeder is placed on a free-standing pole placed 2 m-3 m (6 1/2-10 ft.) high and at least 3 m (10 ft.) away

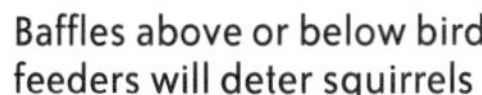

from the nearest access point from which a squirrel can leap or drop on to the feeder. Baffles should be placed above and/or below the feeder. Commercial baffles are widely available. Alternatively, baffles can be constructed at home using large pop bottles, plastic salad bowls or sheet metal. Commercial, squirrel-proof feeders are available at wild bird specialty stores.

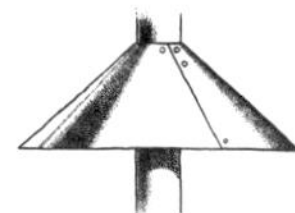

Baffles above or below bird feeders will deter squirrels

Squirrels will readily use nestboxes (see Chapter 15 for details). If you want to keep them out of your bird nestboxes, place the boxes well away from squirrel habitat, or construct them from 19-mm (3/4-in.) fir plywood, which squirrels can't chew through. Squirrels can also be prevented from chewing nestbox entrance holes if a 6 cm x 6 cm (2 1/2 x 2 1/2-in.) aluminum or plastic laminate protector plate, into which has been drilled the appropriate-sized hole, is tacked onto the front of the box.

Mothballs, moth flakes or cayenne pepper scattered over a bulb bed (reapply after each rain) should discourage squirrels from digging up bulbs. Commercial repellents are also available. Livetrapping and removal is an effective way to evict problem individuals but will likely be of only short-term benefit, as others will move in to fill the void.

SQUIRRELS AND CAPSAICIN

The addition of capsaicin (the chemical ingredient that makes hot peppers "hot") to birdseed is sometimes recommended to deter squirrels. However, we caution against using this substance because it may cause pain to the mammals that ingest it and may cause serious harm if it gets in birds' eyes.

If you are considering livetrapping or have problems with other mammal species, contact your local Alberta Environment, Natural Resources Service [Fish and Wildlife] office.

DISEASES AND PARASITES

Occasionally, wild animals are afflicted with diseases or parasites that can infect people. Hantavirus and rabies, two diseases transmitted by wild creatures, are of concern to Albertans. The risk of contracting a disease or parasite in this province is low, yet NatureScapers should be aware of the problem and take adequate precautions. See **Cautions and Concerns** (page 150).

For more information on wildlife-transmitted diseases, contact a government wildlife agency (see Appendix 5) or call the Canadian Cooperative Wildlife Health Centre at 1-800-567-2033.

RABIES

Rabies is a viral disease that is spread in saliva and thus is passed on when an infected animal bites another animal. Once quite common among dogs and cats, rabies is now found primarily in foxes, skunks and bats (bat rabies is uncommon). Human infection in Alberta can be prevented by avoiding direct contact with these animals. Anyone bitten by any wild animal should contact a physician immediately.

DEALING WITH PROBLEM PLANTS

Although plants are obviously not wildlife, they could potentially cause some problems for the NatureScaper.

Weeds

We suggest that as NatureScapers we need to reexamine our widely held views about "weeds"—basically what we call plants that we don't like. The exception are those rapid-growing, noxious and restricted weeds (see definitions on page 23), whose rampant spread we ignore to our peril. Purple loosestrife (see side bar) is an example of such a plant.

As you may have noted from earlier chapters, wild creatures find many widely reviled plants much to their liking. Many species of weeds are important for native bees and butterflies, and provide an

THE SPECIAL CASE OF LOOSESTRIFE

Purple loosestrife (*Lythrum salicaria*) is now considered to be a serious noxious weed in North America. Brought from Europe to North America in the early 1800s, this purple-spiked, very hardy, horticultural perennial poses a serious threat because of its ability to spread quickly and displace most native vegetation in wetland habitats.

Growing to heights of 1 m-2 m (3-6 1/2 ft.), the plant spreads primarily by seeds, which can remain dormant for years, then germinate once conditions become favourable.

In Alberta, infestations of this plant are presently small and scattered. The areas with the highest densities are around Edmonton, Calgary, Lethbridge and Medicine Hat.

To help abate the rapid spread of this plant, it is best to remove all *Lythrum* plants from your property (see below). If you know of neighbours that still have plants, explain the problem to them and suggest that they dispose of the plants. Although individual plants pose no threat to a typical yard, they may add to the overall problem by cross-pollinating with cultivars or naturalized plants. (*Lythrum* cultivars are not sterile, as originally thought.) Seeds can be spread in various ways, including with storm water runoff, and on the bottom of running shoes or on car tires.

To remove *Lythrum* from your yard, dig out the plant (including the roots) with a shovel, seal the plant in a plastic garbage bag, and take the bag to a sanitary landfill site for disposal. Alternatively, the plant can be dried and, where permitted, burned. Because purple loosestrife and its cultivars can regenerate from roots and stems, they should not be composted.

If you are uncertain about the identification of purple loosestrife or its cultivars, consult a plant identification book. Alternatively, you can take a sample to your local nursery or Alberta Agriculture, Food and Rural Development office. In Alberta, only two other plants—blazing star/gayfeather and fireweed—resemble purple loosestrife.

Report any purple loosestrife or *Lythrum* cultivars in the wild by contacting your local Weed Inspector or district Alberta Agriculture, Food and Rural Development office.

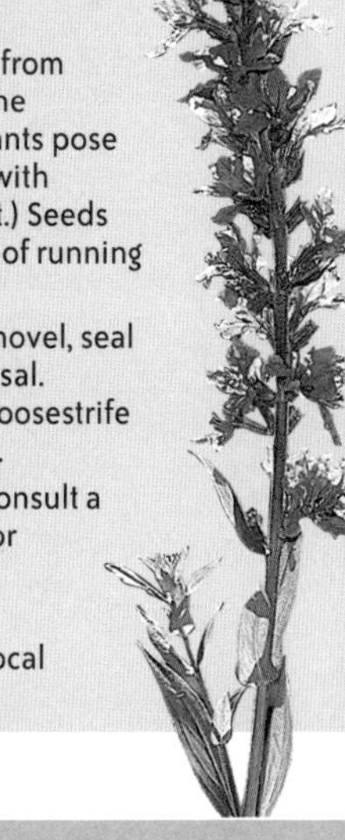

Red admiral butterfly on nettle plant

important food source for birds, especially during the winter, when seed stalks protrude above the snow.

For the benefit of wildlife, we suggest that you at least provide a small patch of non-noxious weeds in the corner of your backyard. This weed patch could include plants such as dandelions, knotweeds and lamb's-quarters. Stinging nettles, which are popular with several species of butterflies, could be part of a yard where children don't play.

To have an effective weed patch, you need to have a variety of plant species, such as the ones noted above, and you need to keep the edges hoed to prevent the plants from spreading into adjacent garden or lawn areas. Weed patches should be tilled every couple of years because natural succession will eventually favour such species as goldenrod, asters and perennial grasses.

Invasive Plants

Not all invasive plants have been designated as noxious or restricted weeds. Keep control of invasive ground covers (see Appendix 1) and all other invasive plants. The suckers of invasive shrubs, such as caragana, should be kept pruned off.

5 BASICS
CO-EXISTING WITH WILDLIFE

1. Try to avoid potential conflicts before they occur (e.g., animal-proof an area using physical barriers such as fences, screen or wire mesh).
2. Look at your yard as an ecosystem, with all the elements (including you) connected together.
3. Avoid direct contact with wild animals and their droppings.
4. Don't assume all insects are harmful—most aren't.
5. Use environmentally responsible methods to deal with unwanted insects and plants; avoid chemical sprays if at all possible.

ACKNOWLEDGMENTS

Shaffeek Ali (Provincial Weed Specialist, Plant Industry Division, Alberta Agriculture, Food and Rural Development, Edmonton, Alberta)
Jim Allen (Wildlife Biologist, Natural Resources Service, Alberta Environment, Rocky Mountain House, Alberta)
Elisabeth Beaubien (Research Associate, Devonian Botanic Garden, c/o University of Alberta, Edmonton, Alberta)
Jerome Jackson (Professor, College of Arts and Sciences, Florida Gulf Coast University, Fort Myers, Florida)
Margo Pybus (Wildlife Diseases Specialist, Natural Resources Service, Alberta Environment, Edmonton, Alberta)
Ruth Staal (Manager, Golden Acre Garden Sentre South, Calgary, Alberta)
Bob Young (Founder, Bat Conservation Society of Canada, Calgary, Alberta)

SIGNIFICANT REFERENCES

Alberta Purple Loosestrife Action Committee. 1994. *Control of purple loosestrife in Alberta*. N.p. (Booklet)

California Center for Wildlife, with D. Landau and S. Stump. 1994. *Living with wildlife: How to enjoy, cope with, and protect North America's wild creatures around your home and theirs*. Sierra Club Books, San Francisco, California.

Ernst, R.S. 1993. *The naturalist's garden: How to garden with plants that attract birds, butterflies, and other wildlife*. The Globe Pequot Press, Old Saybrook, Connecticut.

Fenton, B. 1983. *Just bats*. University of Toronto Press, Toronto.

Gill, D., and P. Bonnett. 1973. *Nature in the urban landscape: A study of the city ecosystem*. York Press, Baltimore, Maryland.

Hodge, G., ed. 1991. *Pocket guide to the humane control of wildlife in cities and towns*. The Humane Society of the United States, Washington, D.C.

Knowles, H., and E. Mengerson. 1989. *Insect pests for the prairies*. Lone Pine Publishing, Edmonton.

Pearman, M. 1992. *Nestboxes for prairie birds*. Ellis Bird Farm, Lacombe.

Pybus, M. n.d. *Bats of Alberta, "the real story . . . "*. Alberta Forestry, Lands and Wildlife and Alberta Agriculture, Edmonton. (Booklet)

Tuttle, M. 1988. *America's neighborhood bats*. University of Texas Press, Austin, Texas.

Appendixes

APPENDIX 1
NATURESCAPING WITH PLANTS

These tables provide information on the wildlife value of plants, and plant characteristics (whether or not a plant is a native species, where it grows, its sun and moisture preferences, and height/spread, if relevant). Native plant scientific names follow Moss (1983). See **Significant References** in Chapter 3.

LEGEND

PLANT SPECIES
All plants are listed in alphabetical order by their botanical or scientific name; common names are also given.

WILDLIFE VALUE

Winter Shelter (CONIFEROUS TREES AND SHRUBS)
The ability of a conifer to provide winter thermal protection or shelter to wildlife is rated as follows:
- **1** - Excellent
- **2** - Good
- **3** - Fair

Availability of Fruit/Seeds (CONIFEROUS TREES AND SHRUBS, DECIDUOUS TREES, DECIDUOUS SHRUBS, VINES)
The season in which fruit/seeds of various plants are available is as follows:
- **Sp** - Spring
- **S** - Summer
- **F** - Fall
- **W** - Winter

In other tables (GROUND COVERS, PERENNIALS, ANNUALS), the availability of fruit/seeds to birds is noted without season.

Type of Seed (CONIFEROUS TREES AND SHRUBS)
Most conifers have cones, but a few have berries.
- **C** - Cone
- **B** - Berry

Type of Fruit (DECIDUOUS TREES, DECIDUOUS SHRUBS)
Birds often eat the fruit/seeds of deciduous trees and shrubs. We've provided information on the type of fruit displayed by the listed plants. See Chapter 3 for descriptions and illustrations of common fruits.

Nectar/Larval Food - Insects (ALL TABLES EXCEPT CONIFEROUS TREES AND SHRUBS)
These columns indicate if bees, butterflies or moths use a plant for nectar or larval food. Note that all bees except leaf-cutter bees collect both nectar and pollen from flowers; leaf-cutters collect only pollen.

Nectar (for Hummingbirds), Buds, Sap, Snag, Thorns, Dense Nesting Cover, Nesting Material
In these columns, there is information about which plants provide nectar for hummingbirds (ALL TABLES EXCEPT CONIFEROUS TREES AND SHRUBS, GROUND COVERS). We also tell you which plants provide buds (DECIDUOUS TREES), supply sap (CONIFEROUS TREES AND SHRUBS, DECIDUOUS TREES), make good snags (CONIFEROUS TREES AND SHRUBS, DECIDUOUS TREES), have thorns (DECIDUOUS SHRUBS), provide dense nesting cover (DECIDUOUS SHRUBS) and supply nesting material (PERENNIALS), all for birds. Some coniferous trees provide sap (mugo pine too) and make good snags for a wide variety of wildlife species, as well as birds.

Browse/Graze - Mammals (ALL TABLES EXCEPT CONIFEROUS TREES AND SHRUBS AND VINES)
If mammals use a plant for food, it is noted in this column.

PLANT CHARACTERISTICS (including horticultural requirements)

Origin (ALL TABLES)
The origin of a listed plant is indicated as follows:
- **N** - Native to Alberta
- **I** - Introduced to Alberta
- **C** - Cultivars of native or introduced species are available

Natural Region (ALL TABLES)
Where a plant can easily be grown in Alberta is indicated in this column. If the natural region has an asterisk, the plant is native to that region. The Canadian Shield natural region, in the northeast corner of the province, has not been included.
- **G** - Grassland
- **P** - Parkland
- **B** - Boreal Forest
- **F** - Foothills
- **R** - Rocky Mountains

See Chapter 3 for a map of Alberta's natural regions.

Plant Type (VINES, GROUND COVERS)
Vines and ground covers are classified as annuals, perennials or shrubs.
- **A** - Annual
- **P** - Perennial
- **S** - Shrub

Sun Exposure (ALL TABLES)
This column shows the amount of sunlight needed by a plant for optimum growth.
- **F** - Full sun
- **P** - Partial shade
- **S** - Shade

Moisture Preference (ALL TABLES)
The amount of water needed by a plant for best growth and development is indicated as follows:
- **D** - Dry
- **M** - Moist
- **W** - Wet

Height/Spread (ALL TABLES)
In some tables (CONIFEROUS TREES AND SHRUBS, DECIDUOUS TREES, DECIDUOUS SHRUBS), average height and spread (in metres) are provided. Average height is given for VINES; maximum height for GROUND COVERS. For the PERENNIALS and ANNUALS, a height range is given, as follows:
- **L** - Low (< 30 cm)
- **M** - Medium (30 cm-60 cm)
- **T** - Tall (> 60 cm)

Flower Colour (PERENNIALS, ANNUALS)
Flower colour is particularly important when you are planting annuals and perennials
- **W** - White
- **Y** - Yellow
- **O** - Orange
- **R** - Red
- **P** - Pink
- **V** - Violet (includes all purples)
- **B** - Blue
- **G** - Green

Bloom Period (PERENNIALS)
We have noted the bloom period of NatureScaping perennials, as follows:
- **Ap** - April
- **M** - May
- **J** - June
- **Ju** - July
- **A** - August
- **S** - September
- **O** - October

NOTE: The information in these tables was both summarized from the available literature and provided by experts; it represents the best data available to us at the time of writing. Regional variations are to be expected, as are variations that reflect different growing conditions. New or different information should be brought to our attention; please use the Backyard Watch form (Appendix 6) to share your observations with us.

Species Common Name *Botanical (Scientific) Name*	Wildlife Value: Winter Shelter 1-Excellent • 2-Good • 3-Fair	Availability of Seeds Sp-Spring • S-Summer F-Fall • W-Winter	Type of Seed C-Cone • B-Berries	Sap	Snag	Plant Characteristics: Origin N-Native to Alberta I-Introduced species C-Cultivars of native or introduced species available	Natural Region *(where the plant can be grown; an asterisk indicates where native in Alberta)* G-Grassland • P-Parkland B-Boreal Forest • F-Foothills R-Rocky Mountain	Sun Exposure F-Full Sun • P-Partial Shade S-Shade	Moisture Preference D-Dry • M-Moist • W-Wet	Average Height/ Average Spread (m)	Comments
Balsam fir *Abies balsamea*	1	W	C	X		N/C	*B/*F/R	F/P/S	M	10-15 4-5	Shade-tolerant
Junipers *Juniperus* spp. (Tree or shrub—usually grown as shrub; common juniper [*J. communis*] and creeping juniper [*J. horizontalis*] are native shrubs; see also Ground Covers)	2	W	B			N/I/C	G/P/B/*F/*R	F/P	D	0.15-6 (shrub/tree) 1.5-3 (shrub/tree)	Avoid planting in damp, clay soils; some cultivars borderline hardy in chinook areas; some grown as ground covers
American larch/Tamarack *Larix laricina*	3		C			N/C	P/*B/*F/R	F/P	M/W	10-15 4	Not evergreen; in autumn needles turn yellow and fall off
Siberian larch *Larix sibirica*	3		C			I/C	All	F/P/S	D/M	10-15 5	Not evergreen; in autumn needles turn yellow and fall off
Norway spruce *Picea abies*	2	F/W	C			I/C	G/P/B/F	F/P	D/M	15-20 8	Borderline hardy in chinook areas; thins out as ages
White spruce *Picea glauca*	1	W	C	X	X	N/C	*All except southern Grassland	F/P	D/M	15-20 5-8	
Colorado spruce *Picea pungens*	1	W	C		X	I/C	All	F/P	D/M	15-20 5-10	Sharp, blue-green needles
Bristlecone pine *Pinus aristata*	3	W	C	X	X	I/C	All	F/P	D	6 3	Grows very slowly; prefers loose, gravelly soil; may need protection
Jack pine *Pinus banksiana*	3	W	C	X		N/C	P/*B/F/R	F/P	D/M	10-15 5	Prefers acid soil
Swiss stone pine *Pinus cembra*	1	F W	C	X		I/C	G/P/B	F	M	10-15 3	Slow-growing; borderline hardy in chinook areas
Lodgepole pine *Pinus contorta* var. *latifolia*	3	W	C	X		N/C	G/P/*B/*F/*R	F	M	15-20 4	
Mugo pine *Pinus mugo* (Tree or shrub—usually grown as shrub; includes dwarf mugo pine [*P. mugo* var. *pumilio*])	2	W	C	X		I/C	All	F	D/M	0.3-3.5 0.6-2	Good for stabilizing slopes; very hardy
Scots pine *Pinus sylvestris*	3	W	C	X		I/C	G/P	F	M	10-15 6	Liked by porcupines and sapsuckers; can live in poor soil
Cedar *Thuja* spp. (Usually planted as shrub in Alberta)	1	W	C			I/C	G/P/B/F	F/P/S	M	0.3-6 0.5-4	Moderately shade-tolerant; not always hardy in chinook areas; need lots of water

Species	Wildlife Value								Plant Characteristics					
	Insects		Birds					Mammals						
Common Name *Botanical (Scientific) Name*	**Nectar** Be-Bee • B-Butterfly • M-Moth	**Larval Food** B-Butterfly • M-Moth	**Sap**	**Availability of Fruit/Seeds** Sp-Spring • S-Summer F-Fall • W-Winter	**Type of Fruit**	**Nectar** (for hummingbirds)/ **Buds**	**Snag**	**Browse**	**Origin** N-Native to Alberta • I-Introduced species • C-Cultivars of native or introduced species available	**Natural Region** (where the plant can be grown; an asterisk indicates where native in Alberta) G-Grassland • P-Parkland B-Boreal Forest • F-Foothills R-Rocky Mountain	**Sun Exposure** F-Full Sun • P-Partial Shade S-Shade	**Moisture Preference** D-Dry • M-Moist • W-Wet	**Average Height/ Average Spread** (m)	**Comments**
Amur maple *Acer ginnala/Acer tataricum* ssp. *ginnala*	B		X	F	Samara				I/C	All	F/P	D/M	4-6 4	Abundant seedlings; red foliage in fall
Manitoba maple/Box elder *Acer negundo*	B	M	X	F/W	Samara		X		N/I/C	*G/*P/*B	F/P	D/M	10-14 10-12	Fast-growing and short-lived; weak branches; abundant seedlings; yellow foliage in fall
White birch/Paper birch Betula papyrifera		B/M	X	W	Winged nutlet in catkin		X	X	N/C	*All	F/P	M	12 6	Especially liked by pine siskins; susceptible to drought
European white birch *Betula pendula* (Weeping birches are cultivars of this species)			X	W	Winged nutlet in catkin				I/C	All	F/P	M	5-15 6-10	Some cultivars borderline hardy in chinook areas—need lots of moisture before hard frost in these areas; yellow foliage in fall
Hawthorn *Crataegus* spp. (Black hawthorn/Douglas hawthorn [C. douglasii] and round-leaved hawthorn [C. rotundifolia] are native species)				F/W	Pome	N			N/I/ C	*G/*P/B/ *F(south)/R	F	D/M	3-6 3-4	Some have thorns; some not completely hardy in chinook areas; white flowers
Russian olive *Elaeagnus angustifolia*				W	Drupe				I/C	G(south)/ P	F	D/M	4-6 6	Good shelterbelt species; not completely hardy in Calgary area
Manchurian ash *Fraxinus mandshurica*				F/W	Samara				I/C	G/P	F	M	8 5	Very compact; good size for small yard
Black ash *Fraxinus nigra*				F/W	Samara				I/C	G/P/B/F	F	M/W	10 5	Most commonly planted in grassland and parkland; yellow foliage in fall
Green ash *Fraxinus pennsylvanica* var. *subintegerrima*		M	X	F/W	Samara		X	X	I/C	All	F	D/M	12 8	Most commonly planted in grassland and parkland; transplants easily; flowers eaten by some birds
Crab apple and apple *Malus* spp. and cultivars	Be/B/ M	M		F/W/Sp	Pome	N/B	X	X	I/C	All	F	D/M	3-6 4	Pomes of some varieties eaten by deer and coyotes; rabbits eat the bark; prefer well-drained soil
Balsam poplar *Populus balsamifera*	Be/B	B/M	X	Sp	Capsule	B	X	X	N	*All	F	M/W	25 15	Competitive root system
Plains cottonwood *Populus deltoides*	Be/B	B/M	X	Sp	Capsule	B	X	X	N/C	*G/P/B/F/R	F	M/W	30 20	Tough tree but short-lived, and brittle in high winds; competitive root system
Aspen *Populus tremuloides*	Be/B	B/M	X	Sp	Capsule	B	X	X	N/C	*All	F	M	10 6	Bright yellow foliage in fall; reproduces by suckers, therefore may not suit small yard
Mayday tree *Prunus padus* var. *commutata*	Be/B/ M	M		F/W	Drupe				I/C	G/P/B/F	F	D	10 10	Wide tree that needs lots of room to grow; showy, white flowers in spring
Ussurian pear *Pyrus ussuriensis*	Be/B/ M			F/Sp	Pome				I/C	G/P/B	F	D 5	8	Needs two different varieties for pollination; red-orange foliage in fall; beautiful, white flowers but fruit barely edible for humans
Bur oak *Quercus macrocarpa*		M	X	F/W	Acorn (nut)		X	X	I	G/P	F/P	D/M/ W	10-15 10	Blue jays and squirrels like acorns; has taproot, therefore difficult to transplant; likes acidic soil; is moderately shade-tolerant
Willow *Salix* spp. (Most are shrubs; see Deciduous Shrubs)	Be/B	B/M	X	Sp	Capsule			X	N/I/C	*Varies with species All	F/P/S	M/W	4-15 3-15	Some borderline hardy in chinook areas
American mountain-ash *Sorbus americana*				F/W	Pome				I/C	All	F/P	D/M	6-8 4-6	Clusters of red berries in fall/winter; germinates readily in mulched, protected area
European mountain-ash *Sorbus aucuparia*				F/W	Pome				I/C	All	F/P	D/M	8-12 8-10	Clusters of orange-red berries; does not grow well in wet locations; subject to sun scald
Showy mountain-ash *Sorbus decora*				F/W	Pome				I/C	All	F/P	D/M	6 4	Clusters of red berries; has largest fruit of mountain-ashes
Western mountain-ash *Sorbus scopulina*				F/W	Pome				N	G/*P/*B/*F	F/P	D/M	5 4	Not generally sold in nurseries
American elm/White elm *Ulmus americana*		B	X	Sp	Samara		X	X	I/C	G/P/B	F	D/M	15-25 10-15	Subject to Dutch elm disease, therefore vigilant maintenance is required
Manchurian elm/ Siberian elm *Ulmus pumila*				Sp	Samara			X	I/C	G/P/B	F	D/M	10 8	Resistant to Dutch elm disease; grows very quickly

Pin cherry *(Prunus pensylvanica)* • **Choke cherry** *(Prunus virginiana)* – **see Deciduous Shrubs**

Species Common Name *Botanical (Scientific) Name*	Wildlife Value: Insects Nectar Be-Bee • B-Butterfly • M-Moth	Larval Food B-Butterfly • M-Moth	Birds Availability of Fruit/ Seeds S-Summer • Sp-Spring • F-Fall • W-Winter	Type of Fruit	Nectar (for hummingbirds)	Thorns	Dense Nesting Cover	Mammals Browse	Plant Characteristics Origin N-Native to Alberta • I-Introduced species • C-Cultivars of native or introduced species available	Natural Region (where the plant can be grown; an asterisk indicates where native in Alberta) G-Grassland • P-Parkland B-Boreal Forest • F-Foothills R-Rocky Mountain	Sun Exposure F-Full Sun • P-Partial Shade S-Shade	Moisture Preference D-Dry • M-Moist • W-Wet	Average Height/ Average Spread (m)	Comments
Green alder/American alder *Alnus crispa*		M	F/W	Winged nutlet				X	N	G/*P/*B/ *F/*R	F/P/S	M/W	3 3	Borderline hardy in chinook areas; shallow-rooted
Saskatoon/Serviceberry *Amelanchier alnifolia*	B/M	M	S/F/W	Pome				X	N/C	*All	F/P	D/M	2-5 1-2	White flowers in spring; blue fruit edible for humans and other animals; suckers
Choke berry *Aronia* spp.			F/W	Pome				X	I/C	P/B	F/P	M/W	1.5-2 1-2	Edible fruit for humans
Dwarf birch/Bog birch *Betula glandulosa/Betula nana*			S/F/W	Samara				X	N/C	*P/*B/*F/*R	F	M/W	1-2 1-2	Fall leaf colour a deep orange to russet
Common butterfly bush/ Summer-lilac *Buddleja davidii*	B/M			Capsule?					I/C	G/P	F	M	1.5 0.75	Blue, purple or white flowers; blooms late in year (August and September); needs winter protection; usually doesn't produce seed in Alberta
Caragana/Siberian pea tree *Caragana arborescens*	B		F	Capsule	X	X	X		I/C	All	F	D	0.5-3 1-3	Yellow flowers; can be invasive; some cultivars don't sucker and are therefore not invasive; do not plant where wet; can tolerate poor soil; often used in hedges or shelterbelts
Tatarian dogwood *Cornus alba*			S/F/W	Drupe				X	I/C	All	F/P/S	M/W	1-2 1-2	White flowers and blue fruit; shade-tolerant; borderline hardy in chinook areas
Red-oiser dogwood *Cornus stolonifera/Cornus sericea*		B	S/F/W	Drupe				X	N/C	*All	F/P/S	M	2 3	White flowers and fruit; shade-tolerant
Beaked hazelnut *Corylus cornuta*			S/F/W	Nut			X	X	N	G/*P/*B	F/P	M	2 2	Not usually sold in nurseries; borderline hardy in chinook areas
Cotoneaster *Cotoneaster* spp.	Be		F/W	Berry			X		I/C	G/P	F/P	D/M	0.5-3 1.5-2 (ground covers 0.15-0.3)	Some species borderline hardy in chinook areas; some species shade-tolerant; usually seen in hedges; liked by wasps
Yellow dryas/Yellow dryad/ Yellow mountain avens *Dryas drummondii* (See also Ground Covers)	Be/B		F/W	Achene					N	*F/*R	F/P	D/M	0.2 (forms mat)	Yellow or white flowers; likes gravelly soil
Wolf-willow/Silverberry *Elaeagnus commutata*	Be/B	M	W	Drupe					N/C	*All	F	D/M	2-3 2	Flowers yellow and fragrant; can be invasive
Burning bush *Euonymus* spp. (Includes Turkestan burning bush [*E. nanus* 'Turkestanica' or *E. nanus* var. *turkestanicus*])			F/W	Capsule					I/C	G/P	F/P/S	D/M	0.6-3 1-3	Has deep red or pink autumn leaf colour; may need protection
Sea buckthorn *Hippophae rhamnoides*			W	Drupe		X	X		I/C	G/P	F	D	3 3	Attractive silvery-green foliage and orange berries; both male and female plants needed for fruit production (dioecious); tolerates poor soil; invasive
Bracted honeysuckle/ Black twinberry/ Twinberry honeysuckle *Lonicera involucrata*	B/M	B	S/F	Berry					N	G/*P/*B/*F	P/S	D/M/ W	2 1.5	Berries inedible for humans
Tatarian honeysuckle *Lonicera tatarica*	B		S/F/W	Berry	X				I/C	G/P/B	F/P/S	D/M	2.5-3 2-2.5	Flowers pink or red and fragrant; red berries inedible for humans; cultivar 'Arnold Red' recommended
Mockorange/Lewis mockorange *Philadelphus lewisii* (Includes Waterton mockorange [*P. lewisii* 'Waterton'])	Be/B		F/W	Capsule				X	N/C	G/P/*F/*R	F/P	M	1.5-3 1.5-3	Showy, white flowers
Ninebark *Physocarpus opulifolius*	Be/B		F	Capsule				X	I/C	G/P	F/P	M	1-2.5 1-2	Some have yellow foliage and red seed pods; do not plant in high lime soil
Shrubby cinquefoil/Potentilla *Potentilla fruticosa*	Be/B/ M		F/W	Achene				X	N/C	*All	F/P	D/M	0.6-1 0.6-1	Yellow flowers; some cultivars borderline hardy in chinook areas
Cherry prinsepia *Prinsepia sinensis*			S/F/W	Drupe		X			I	G/P/B	F/P	D/M	2 1.5	Early, fragrant flowering; gold fall colour and red berries; berries edible for humans; borderline hardy in northern areas; usually seen in hedges and shelterbelts
Western sandcherry *Prunus besseyi*	Be/B/ M		S/F/W	Drupe					I/C	G/P	F	D/M	0.7 2	Black cherry astringent for humans; borderline hardy in chinook areas

Hawthorn *(Crataegus* spp.*)* • **Mountain-ash** *(Sorbus* spp.*)* – see Deciduous Trees

	Wildlife Value								Plant Characteristics					
	Insects		Birds					Mammals						
Species **Common Name** *Botanical (Scientific) Name*	**Nectar** Be-Bee • B-Butterfly • M-Moth	**Larval Food** B-Butterfly • M-Moth	**Availability of Fruit/ Seeds** Sp-Spring • S-Summer • F-Fall • W-Winter	**Type of Fruit**	**Nectar** (for hummingbirds)	**Thorns**	**Dense Nesting Cover**	**Browse**	**Origin** N-Native to Alberta • I-Introduced species • C-Cultivars of native or introduced species available	**Natural Region** (where the plant can be grown; an asterisk indicates where native in Alberta) G-Grassland • P-Parkland B-Boreal Forest • F-Foothills R-Rocky Mountain	**Sun Exposure** F-Full Sun • P-Partial Shade S-Shade	**Moisture Preference** D-Dry • M-Moist • W-Wet	**Average Height/ Average Spread** (m)	**Comments**
Mongolian cherry *Prunus fruticosa*	Be/B/M		F	Drupe					I/C	G/P	F	D/M/W	1 1	Bright red, sour cherry; suckers
Pin cherry *Prunus pensylvanica*	Be/B/M	M	F/W	Drupe				X	N/C	*P/*B/*F	F/P	D/M	3-5 2-3	Profuse, white flowers in spring; red cherries edible for humans; orange and yellow foliage in fall
Nanking cherry *Prunus tomentosa*	Be/B/M		S/F	Drupe					I/C	G/P	F/P	D/M	2 2	Fragrant, white blossoms in spring; bright red cherries edible for humans; easy to start from seed
Choke cherry *Prunus virginiana* (Schubert choke cherry is *P. virginiana* 'Schubert')	B	B/M	F/W	Drupe				X	N/C	*G/*P/*B/*F/R	F/P	D/M	5 3 (Schubert choke cherry - 5/5)	White flowers in spring; Schubert cherry fruits heavily and is a favourite of robins; black cherries edible for humans
Currant and Gooseberry *Ribes* spp. (Includes golden currant [*Ribes aureum*], a native species)	Be/B	B	S/F	Berry	X	X			N/I/C	*Varies with species All	F/P/S	D/M	1-2 1.5-2.5	Shade-tolerant; *R. aureum* is drought-resistant; not all varieties have thorns
Rose *Rosa* spp. (*R. acicularis* is the Alberta floral emblem)	Be		W	Rose hip		X		X	N/I/C	*Varies with species All	F	D/M	0.3-2 1-2	Native species have pink flowers; leaf-cutter bees like to line egg chambers with parts of rose leaves
Raspberry *Rubus* spp.	Be		S	Berry with druplets		X			N/I/C	*Varies with species All	F	D/M	1-2 Variable	Roots invasive; can grow flowering raspberry (*R. odoratus*) in shade—most raspberries like sun
Willow *Salix* spp. (Includes pussy willow [*S. discolor*], a native species; see also Deciduous Trees)	Be/B	B/M	Sp	Capsule			X	X	N/I/C	*Varies with species All	F/P/S	M/W	0.5-3 1-2	Some borderline hardy in chinook areas; pussy willow (*S. discolor*) has large catkins very early in spring
American elder *Sambucas canadensis*			S/F/W	Drupe					I/C	All	F	D/M	2-3 2	White flowers and purple fruit; will grow in all areas where there is adequate moisture; humans can eat fruit
Red elderberry/ European elderberry *Sambucus racemosa*			S/F/W	Drupe				X	N/C	G/P/*B/*F	F/P	D/M	2-4 2-3	White flowers and red fruit; fruit not edible for humans but eaten by birds
Thorny buffaloberry/ Silver buffaloberry *Shepherdia argentea*			F/W	Berry		X			N/C	*G	F	D/M	3-4 3-4	Good xeriscape plant; will grow in poor soil; deep red fruit, edible for humans
Canada buffaloberry/ Russet buffaloberry/Soapberry *Shepherdia canadensis*	B		F/W	Berry					N	*G/*P/*B/*F	F	D/M	1-2 1-2	Will grow in poor soil; orange or red fruit—very bitter for humans
Spirea/Spiraea *Spiraea* spp.	Be/B			Follicle					N/I/C	G/*P/*B/*F/R	F/P	D/M/W	0.4-2 0.4-2	
Common snowberry/ Few-flowered snowberry *Symphoricarpos albus*	Be	M	W	Drupe				X	N	*G/*P/*B/*F	F/P	D/M	1 1	White berries not edible for humans; can sucker
Buckbrush/Western snowberry/ Wolfberry *Symphoricarpos occidentalis*	Be/B	M	W	Drupe				X	N	*G/*P/*B/*F/R	F	D	1 1	White berries not edible for humans
Lilac *Syringa* spp. and cultivars (Includes common lilac [*S. vulgaris*] and Meyer's or dwarf Korean lilac [*S. meyeri* 'Palabin'])	Be/B/M		W	Capsule	X				I/C	G/P/B	F	D/M	1-5 1.5-3	Many cultivars; flowers white, pink or purple; common lilac suckers; dwarf Korean lilac best for hawk moth and Canadian tiger swallowtail butterfly; birds eat seeds in capsules
Blueberry *Vaccinium* spp.		B	S	Berry					N/C	*P/*B/*F/*R	F/P	M	0.5 Variable	Need acidic soil
Wayfaring tree *Viburnum lantana*	B		W	Drupe					I	G/P	F/P/S	M	1.5-3 1.5-3	Showy, white flowers; black berries edible for humans; more fruit if several planted in vicinity; prefers sun
Nannyberry *Viburnum lentago*			W	Drupe					I	G/P/B	F/P/S	M	4 3	White flowers in spring; blue-black berries edible for humans; glossy foliage turns purplish red in fall; roots will sucker if disturbed
Sargent's viburnum *Viburnum sargentii*			W	Drupe					I/C	G/P/B	S/P	M	4.5 3	Needs acidic soil
High-bush cranberry/ American highbush *Viburnum opulus* ssp. *trilobum*/*V. trilobum*			W	Drupe					N/C	G/*P/*B	F/P/S	M	1-3 1-2	White flowers and red fruit; fruit edible but sour for humans

Species Common Name *Botanical (Scientific) Name*	Wildlife Value: Insects **Nectar** Be-Bee • B-Butterfly • M-Moth	Wildlife Value: Insects **Larval Food** B-Butterfly • M-Moth	Wildlife Value: Birds **Availability of Fruit/Seeds** Sp-Spring • S-Summer F-Fall • W-Winter	Wildlife Value: Birds **Nectar** (for hummingbirds)	Plant Characteristics **Origin** N-Native to Alberta • I-Introduced species • C-Cultivars of native or introduced species available	Plant Characteristics **Natural Region** (where the plant can be grown; an asterisk indicates where native in Alberta) G-Grassland • P-Parkland B-Boreal Forest • F-Foothills R-Rocky Mountain	Plant Characteristics **Plant Type** A-Annual • P-Perennial • S-Shrub	Plant Characteristics **Sun Exposure** F-Full Sun • P-Partial Shade S-Shade	Plant Characteristics **Moisture Preference** D-Dry • M-Moist • W-Wet	Plant Characteristics **Average Height** (m)	**Comments**
American bittersweet *Celastrus scandens*	B		W	X	I/C	G/P/B	S	F	D/M	4	Male and female plants needed for fruit (dioecious); showy, orange fruit on female plants; not completely hardy in grassland region
Western clematis/ Western virgin's bower *Clematis ligusticifolia*	B		F/W		N	*G/*F	P	F/P	M	4-5	White flowers; dioecious; not usually sold in nurseries
Purple clematis/Blue clematis *Clematis verticillaris/ Clematis occidentalis*			F/W		N	*G/*P/*B/ *F/R	P	F	M	2-3	Purple or blue flowers; climbs trees; not usually sold in nurseries
Yellow clematis/Golden clematis/ Golden virgin's bower *Clematis tangutica*	B		F/W		I/C	G/P	P	F/P	D/M	3	Yellow flowers; introduced escapee in several areas, including Calgary, Stettler and Edmonton; can be weedy in small gardens
Wild morning glory/ Hedge bindweed *Convolvulus sepium*	B?			X?	N	*G/*P	P	F/P/S	M	2-3 (variable)	Flowers white to pinkish; grows in waste places
Chilean glory flower *Eccremocarpus scaber* (Perennial grown as annual)				X	I/C	P/F	A	F	D/M	1.5-2	Yellow, orange-red or pink flowers; will bloom through October
Wild cucumber vine/ Mock cucumber *Echinocystis lobata*			F		I	G/P/B	A	F	D	4	White flowers; weedy; will grow in poor soil
Hops *Humulus lupulus*	Be/B				I/C	All	P	F/P	D/M	6	Flowers not showy; very fast growing
Morning glory *Ipomoea purpurea* and *Ipomoea tricolor*				X	I/C	G/P	A	F	D	2.5	White, red, pink, purple or blue flowers; will grow in poor soil
Perennial sweet pea *Lathyrus latifolius*			F/W		I/C	P/B/F/R	P	F	D/M	2.5	White, red and pink flowers; often escapes and naturalizes
Creamy peavine/ Cream-coloured vetchling *Lathyrus ochroleucus*	Be	B	S/F	X	N	*P/*B/*F/*R	P	F/P	D/M	1	Yellowish white flowers; not usually sold in nurseries
Sweet pea *Lathyrus odoratus* (Also in Annuals)	Be		F		I/C	All	A	F/P	M	1.5	Flowers white, yellow, red, pink, violet and blue; also fragrant
Scarlet trumpet honeysuckle/ Dropmore scarlet honeysuckle *Lonicera* x *brownii* 'Dropmore Scarlet'/ *Lonicera* x *brownii* 'Dropmore Scarlet Trumpet'			F/W	X	I/C	All	S	F/P	D/M	3	Flowers orangey-red and trumpet-shaped; fruit not edible for humans
Twining honeysuckle *Lonicera dioica/Lonicera glaucescens*	B?/M		F/W	X	N/C	*P/*B/*F/*R	S	F/P	D/M	3	Flowers yellow to reddish
Virginia creeper *Parthenocissus quinquefolia*			W		I/C	All	S	F/P	D/M	3-10+ (0.3 as ground cover)	Shade-tolerant; beautiful fall colour
Scarlet runner bean *Phaseolus coccineus*				X	I/C	All	A	F	D/M	2.5	Needs a lot of water; red flowers; beans edible for humans
Canary bird vine/Canary bird flower *Tropaeolum peregrinum*			F	X	I	All	A	F/P	D	3	Yellow flowers; self-seeds but may not set seed in cooler areas
Riverbank grape *Vitis riparia*			S/F		I/C	G/P/B	P	F	D	4-6	Usually used to cover arbours or walls; borderline hardy in chinook areas; fruit used in jams and jellies

Species	Wildlife Value				Plant Characteristics						
	Insects		Birds	Mammals							
Common Name *Botanical (Scientific) Name*	**Nectar** Be-Bee • B-Butterfly	**Larval Food** B-Butterfly • M-Moth	**Fruit/Seeds** F-Fruit • S-Seeds	**Graze/Browse**	**Origin** N-Native to Alberta • I-Introduced species • C-Cultivars of native or introduced species available	**Natural Region** (*where the plant can be grown; an asterisk indicates where native in Alberta*) G-Grassland • P-Parkland B-Boreal Forest • F-Foothills R-Rocky Mountain	**Plant Type** A-Annual • P-Perennial • S-Shrub	**Sun Exposure** F-Full Sun • P-Partial Shade S-Shade	**Moisture Preference** D-Dry • M-Moist • W-Wet	**Maximum Height** (m)	**Comments**
Goutweed *Aegopodium podograria*					I/C	All	P	F/P/S	D/M/W	0.45	Good as understory planting; invasive
Bearberry/Kinnikinnick *Arctostaphylos uva-ursi*					N/C	*All	S	F/P	D	0.3	Evergreen; needs snow cover
Snow-in-summer *Cerastium tomentosum*				X	I/C	All	P	F	D	0.25	White flowers; can be invasive; good xeriscape plant
Lily-of-the-valley *Convallaria majalis*					I/C	All	P	P/S	D/M	0.25	White flowers; invasive; will grow in poor soil
Yellow dryas/Yellow dryad/ Yellow mountain avens *Dryas drummondii* (See also Deciduous Shrubs)	Be/B		F/S	X	N	*F/*R	P	F/P	D/M	0.25	Yellow or white flowers; forms a mat; likes gravelly soil
Bishop's hat/Barrenwort *Epimedium* spp.					I/C	All	P	P/S	D/M	0.3	Does not form a thick mat in northern areas
Strawberry *Fragaria* spp.			F/S	X	N/I/C	*Varies with species All	P	F/P	M	0.25	White flowers; leaf-cutter bees use leaves to line egg chambers
Common juniper *Juniperus communis*					N/C	P/B/*F/*R	S	F/P	D	1	Avoid planting in heavy, damp, clay soils
Creeping juniper *Juniperus horizontalis*					N/C	G/P/B/*F/*R	S	F/P	D	0.5	Avoid planting in heavy, damp, clay soils
Yellow archangel *Lamiastrum galeobdolon*	Be				I/C	G/P/ B(south)/F	P	P/S	D/M	0.2	Yellow flowers; fast-growing
Lamium/Deadnettle *Lamium maculatum*					I/C	All	P	F/P/S	M/W	0.45	Can suffer winter kill in severe winters; can be invasive
Creeping Jenny/Moneywort *Lysimachia nummularia*					I/C	G/P/B/F	P	F/P/S	M/W	0.10	Golden flowers in spring; good for wet areas; forms mat; invasive
Ostrich fern *Matteuccia struthiopteris*					N/I/C	P/*B/F	P	P/S	M/W	1.0	Can suffer winter kill in severe winters; can be invasive
Variegated creeping Charlie/ Ground ivy *Nepeta hederacea/Glechoma hederacea*					I/C	All	P	F/P	M	0.1	Blue flowers; very invasive
Cliff green/Pachistima *Paxistima canbyi*					I/C	P/B/F/R	P	F/P/S	D/M	0.4	Not hardy in northern areas; needs snow cover
Pulmonaria/Lungwort *Pulmonaria* spp.					I/C	All	P	P/S	D/M	0.35	Purple or blue flowers
Thyme *Thymus* spp. (Includes woolly thyme [*T. pseudolanuginosus*] and creeping thyme/mother-of-thyme [*T. serpyllum*/*T. praecox*])	Be				I/C	All	P	F/P	D/M	0.1	Woolly thyme has pink flowers; creeping thyme has red, pink or purple flowers
Western Canada violet *Viola canadensis*					N	*All	P	P/S	D/M	0.4	White to violet flowers, yellow at base
Stonecrop/Sedum (*Sedum* spp.) – see Perennials											

Species	Wildlife Value					Plant Characteristics							
	Insects		Birds		Mammals								
Common Name *Botanical (Scientific) Name*	**Nectar** Be-Bee • B-Butterfly • M-Moth	**Larval Food** B-Butterfly • M-Moth	**Nectar** (for hummingbirds)/ **Seeds**	**Nesting Material**	**Graze**	**Origin** N-Native to Alberta • I-Introduced species • C-Cultivars of native or introduced species available	**Natural Region** (*where the plant can be grown; an asterisk indicates where native in Alberta*) G-Grassland • P-Parkland B-Boreal Forest • F-Foothills R-Rocky Mountain	**Sun Exposure** F-Full Sun • P-Partial Shade S-Shade	**Moisture Preference** D-Dry • M-Moist • W-Wet	**Height Range** L-Low (<30 cm) M-Medium (30 cm-60 cm) T-Tall (>60 cm)	**Colour** W-White • Y-Yellow O-Orange • R-Red • P-Pink V-Violet • B-Blue • G-Green	**Bloom Period** Ap-April • M-May • J-June • Ju-July A-August • S-September O-October	**Comments**
Yarrow *Achillea* spp. (Common yarrow [*A. millefolium*] is most common native species; includes woolly yarrow [*A. tomentosa*])	B				X	N/I/C	*All	F	D/M	M/T (woolly yarrow L)	W/Y/R/P (native species W/P)	J/Ju/A/S	Invasive; snowshoe hares graze yarrow
Giant hyssop *Agastache foeniculum*	Be/B		N			N/C	G/*P/*B	F	D/M	T	W/Y/R/P/V/B (native V/B)	Ju/A	Plant has anise fragrance
Hollyhock *Alcea rosea* (Can be annual, biennial or short-lived perennial; see Annuals)	Be/B		N/S			I/C	All	F	D/M	T	W/Y/R/P/V	Ju/A/S	Single cultivars much hardier than double; can self-seed; edible flowers
Allium/Ornamental onions, garlic, chives *Allium* spp.	Be/B		N			N/I/C	*All	F	D/M	L/M/T	W/P/V	J/Ju/A	
Angelica *Angelica gigas* (Biennial)	Be/B					I	P/B/F/R	S	M	T	R	J/Ju/A/S	May be difficult to find; generally, needs rich, moist soil and cool conditions
Spreading dogbane *Apocynum androsaemifolium*	Be/B		N			N	*All	F/P	D/M	L/M/T	P	J/Ju	Noxious weed, so has to be controlled; fruit is poisonous to humans
Indian-hemp *Apocynum sibiricum/Apocynum cannabinum* var. *hypericifolium*	Be/B					N	*G/*P/*B	F	D	M/T	W	Ju	
Columbine *Aquilegia* spp.	Be		N			N/I/C	G/*P/*B/*F/*R	F/P	M	L/M/T	W/Y/R/P/V/B (native species Y/B)	M/J/Ju/A	Self-seeds; often seen on rocky slopes
Rockcress *Arabis* spp. (Some biennial)	B	B				N/I/C	*Varies with species All	F/P	D	L	W/P	M/J	If snow cover is inadequate in spring, some winterkill can occur; good xeriscape plant
Sea thrift *Armeria* spp.	Be					I/C	All	F	D	L	W/P	M–S	
Swamp milkweed *Asclepias incarnata*	B					I	All	F	M	T	P	A/S	Monarch butterflies are attracted to this plant
Showy milkweed *Asclepias speciosa*	Be?/B	B				N	*G/*P	F/P	D/M	T	P/V	J/Ju	Monarch butterflies are attracted to this plant
Butterfly weed *Asclepias tuberosa*	B	B				I/C	G/P	F/P	D/M	M/T	Y/O/R	Ju/A	Not always hardy
Aster *Aster* spp.	Be/B	B	S		X	N/I/C	*Varies with species All	F	D/M	L/M/T	W/R/P/V/B/O	Ju/A/S/O	If possible, use native species; wasps are attracted to some asters
Astilbe/False spirea *Astilbe* spp.	B		N?/S			I/C	G(north)/P/B/F/R	P/S	M	L/M/T	W/R/P/V	Ju/A	Hardy if have enough moisture; prefer rich soil
Milk-vetch *Astragalus* spp.	B	B			X	N	*Varies with species All	F/P	D/M	L/M/T	W/Y/V/B	M/J/Ju/A	Most common in grassland; a few species poisonous to livestock; not usually available from nurseries
Basket-of-gold *Aurinia* spp.	Be					I/C	All	F	D	L	Y	M/J	
Bellflower *Campanula* spp. (Some biennial; includes Carpathian bellflower [*C. carpatica*]; for Canterbury bells, see Annuals)	Be					I/C	All	F/P	M	L/M/T	W/V/B	J/Ju/A/S	Creeping bellflower (*C. cochlearfolia*) good for ground cover but can be invasive
Harebell/Common bluebell *Campanula rotundifolia*	Be					N/C	*All	F	D/M	L/M	V/B	J/Ju	Sometimes used as ground cover
Yellow bachelor button/ Yellow hardhead *Centaurea macrocephala*	Be/B		N/S			I/C	All	F	D/M	T	Y	Ju/A/S	
Mountain bluet/Perennial cornflower *Centaurea montana*	Be/B					I/C	All	F/P	D/M	M/T	W/B	J/Ju/A/S	Self-seeds
Bull thistle *Cirsium vulgare*	B/M	B	S	X		I	G/P/B/F	F	M/W	T	P	J/Ju	Don't confuse with Canada thistle (*C. arvense*), a noxious weed
Coreopsis/Tickseed *Coreopsis* spp. (Some Coreopsis are annuals; see Annuals)	B		S			I/C	G/P	F/P	D/M	M	Y	Ju/A/S	
Delphinium *Delphinium* spp. (Includes *D. elatum*)	Be/M		N			I/C	All	F	M	M/T	W/P/V/B	J/Ju/A	'Bright Butterfly' is very attractive to hummingbirds
Tall larkspur *Delphinium glaucum*	Be/B/M		N			N	*P/*B/*F/*R	F/P/S	M	T	W/B	J/Ju	Poisonous to livestock

Species Common Name *Botanical (Scientific) Name*	Wildlife Value: Insects **Nectar** Be-Bee B-Butterfly • M-Moth	Insects **Larval Food** B-Butterfly • M-Moth	Birds **Nectar** (for hummingbirds)/ **Seeds**	Birds **Nesting Material**	Mammals **Graze**	Plant Characteristics **Origin** N-Native to Alberta • I-Introduced species • C-Cultivars of native or introduced species available	**Natural Region** *(where the plant can be grown; an asterisk indicates where native in Alberta)* G-Grassland • P-Parkland B-Boreal Forest • F-Foothills R-Rocky Mountain	**Sun Exposure** F-Full Sun • P-Partial Shade S-Shade	**Moisture Preference** D-Dry • M-Moist • W-Wet	**Height Range** L-Low (<30 cm) M-Medium (30 cm-60 cm) T-Tall (>60 cm)	**Colour** W-White • Y-Yellow O-Orange • R-Red • P-Pink V-Violet • B-Blue • G-Green	**Bloom Period** Ap-April • M-May • J-June • Ju-July A-August • S-September O-October	**Comments**
Pink/Dianthus *Dianthus* spp. (Includes sweet William [*D. barbatus*], which can be annual, biennial or short-lived perennial)	B/M		N			I/C	All	F	D/M	L/M/T	W/Y/R/P/V	M/J/Ju	Many have clove scent; some have evergreen foliage
Yellow foxglove *Digitalis grandiflora*	Be		N?			I/C	G/P	P	M	M/T	Y	Ju/A	
Purple coneflower *Echinacea purpurea* (*E. angustifolia* is narrowleaf echinacea)	Be/B					I/C	G/P/B/F	F/P	D	M/T	W/V	Ju/A	Both *E. purpurea* and *E. angustifolia* used in herbal medicine; flowers edible; good xeriscape plant
Globe-thistle *Echinops ritro*	Be/B		S			I/C	G/P/B/F	F	D	T	V/B	Ju/A/S	Good xeriscape plant
Fireweed *Epilobium angustifolium*	Be/B	M	N		X	N	*All	P	D/M	M/T	P/V	Ju/A	Can be invasive; deer graze the flowers; not usually sold in nurseries
Fleabane *Erigeron* spp.	B/M					N/I/C	*Varies with species All	F/P	D/M	L/M	W/Y/P/V/B	J/Ju/A	
Yellow umbrella plant *Eriogonum flavum*	B	B				N	*G/*P/*F(along river valleys)	F	D	L	Y	J/Ju	Found most often in grassland and parkland
Sea holly *Eryngium* spp.	Be		S			I/C	All	F	D	M/T	B	J/Ju/A	Can be invasive; good xeriscape plant; attractive to wasps
Spotted Joe-pye weed *Eupatorium purpureum* var. *maculatum*/ *Eupatorium maculatum*	B					N/I? (may not be native to Alberta)	G/P/*B/F	F/P	M/W	T	P/V	A/S	
Gaillardia/Blanket flower/ Brown-eyed Susan *Gaillardia* spp. (*G. aristata* is native species)	Be/B					N/I/C	*All	F	D	M/T	Y/O/R	J/Ju/A	*G. aristata* is especially attractive to butterflies; fragrant flowers; will grow in poor soil; good xeriscape plant
Gentian *Gentiana* spp.			N			N/I/C	*G/P/B/*F/*R (not southern Grassland)	P/S	M	L/M	W B	Ju/A/S	Evergreen foliage; native species often found in montane habitats
Sticky purple geranium *Geranium viscosissimum*	Be/B					N	*G/*P/*F	F/P	M	M/T	W/P/V	J/Ju	
Grasses, native spp. (See text for species names)		B	S		X	N	*Varies with species All	F/P	D/M/W	L/M/T		J/Ju	Some species very invasive
Gumweed *Grindelia squarrosa*	B		S			N	*G	F	D	M	Y	Ju/A	
Spiny ironplant *Haplopappus spinulosus*	B					N	*G	F	D	L	Y	J/Ju	
Northern hedysarum/ Northern sweetvetch *Hedysarum boreale*	Be	B				N	G/P/*B/ *F/*R	F	D/M	M	V	M–A	
Sneezeweed *Helenium autumnale*	Be/B/M		S			N/C	*G/*P/*B	F/P	M	M/T	Y/O/R	Ju/A	Tolerates dry conditions
Sunflower *Helianthus* spp. (Some are annual; see Annuals)	Be/B	B	S		X (seeds)	N/I/C	*G/*P/*B(mostly south)/*F/R	F/P	D	M/T	Y/O	Ju/A/S	Will grow in poor soil
Day lily *Hemerocallis* spp.	B		N			I/C	All	F/P/S	D/M	L/M/T (usually M/T)	Y/O/R/P	J/Ju/A	Usually disease-free; edible flowers; dwarf varieties available
Cow parsnip *Heracleum lanatum*	Be/B	B	S		X	N	*All	P/S	M/W	T	W	J/Ju	
Sweet rocket/Dame's rocket *Hesperis matronalis*	B/M					I/C	G/P	F/P/S	D/M	M/T	W/P/V	J/Ju	May be invasive; fine evening scent
Golden aster/Hairy golden aster *Heterotheca villosa*	Be/B/M					N	*G	F	D	L/M	Y	Ju/A/S	Very attractive to bees
Coral bells *Heuchera* spp. (Native species include Richardson's alumroot [*H. richardsonii*])	Be/B		N			N/I/C	*Varies with species All	F	D/M	L/M/T	W/Y/R/P/V/G	J/Ju/A/S	Disease-resistant; do not do well in clay soils
Hosta/Plantain lily *Hosta* spp.	Be		N			I/C	All	P/S	M/W	L/M	W/P/B	Ju/A/S	Can be grown as ground cover; fragrant
Hyacinth *Hyacinthus orientalis*	Be/B/M		S			I/C	All	F	D/M	L/M	W/R/B/V	M	Bulb planted in fall
Colorado rubberweed *Hymenoxys richardsonii*	Be/B		S			N	*G/*P	F	D	L	Y	J/Ju/A	
Hyssop *Hyssopus officinalis*	Be/B					I/C	All	F	D	M/T	W/P/V/B	J/Ju/A	Herb

Species	Wildlife Value					Plant Characteristics							
	Insects		Birds		Mammals								
Common Name *Botanical (Scientific) Name*	**Nectar** Be-Bee B-Butterfly • M-Moth	**Larval Food** B-Butterfly • M-Moth	**Nectar** (for hummingbirds)/ **Seeds**	**Nesting Material**	**Graze**	**Origin** N-Native to Alberta • I-Introduced species • C-Cultivars of native or introduced species available	**Natural Region** (where the plant can be grown; an asterisk indicates where native in Alberta) G-Grassland • P-Parkland B-Boreal Forest • F-Foothills R-Rocky Mountain	**Sun Exposure** F-Full Sun • P-Partial Shade S-Shade	**Moisture Preference** D-Dry • M-Moist • W-Wet	**Height Range** L-Low (<30 cm) M-Medium (30 cm-60 cm) T-Tall (>60 cm)	**Colour** W-White • Y-Yellow O-Orange • R-Red • P-Pink V-Violet • B-Blue • G-Green	**Bloom Period** Ap-April • M-May • J-June • Ju-July A-August • S-September O-October	**Comments**
Perennial candytuft *Iberis sempervirens* (Annual varieties available; see Annuals)	Be/B					I/C	All	F/P	D	L/M	W	J	Some cultivars are fragrant; evergreen
Lavender *Lavandula spp.*	Be					I/C	All	F	D/M	T	V	J/Ju/A	Plant very fragrant
Daisy *Leucanthemopsis* spp.; formerly, *Chrysanthemum* spp. (Includes shasta daisy [*L.* x *superbum* or *L. superbum*])	Be/B					I/C	All	F/P	D/M	M/T	W/Y/O/ R/P/V (shasta W)	J/Ju/A	Can be invasive; ox-eye daisy is noxious
Lovage *Levisticum officinale*	Be					I/C	All	F	D/M	T	W/G	J/Ju/A	Herb; very fragrant
Blazing star/Gayfeather *Liatris* spp. (Native liatris are dotted blazing star [*L. punctata*] and meadow blazing star [*L. ligulistylis*])	B/B		S			N/I/C	*G (*L. punctata*) *P (*L. ligulistylis* and *L. punctata*) All	F	D/M	M/T	P/V	Ju/A/S	Sometimes will self-seed
Lily *Lilium* spp. (Western wood lily [*L. philadelphicum*] is native)			N			N/I/C	*G/*P/*B	F/P	M	M/T	W/Y/O/ R/P/V (western wood lily O/R)	J Ju A	See *Alberta Yards...*for hardy species
Statice/Sea lavender *Limonium* spp. (Some statice are annuals; see Annuals)	Be					I/C	G/P	F/P	D/M	M/T	B	J/Ju/A	Large tap root, so don't disturb plant once it's planted
Dwarf yellow flax *Linum flavum* 'Compactum'	B					I/C	G/P	F	D	L	Y	J/Ju/A	May have to treated as annual in some areas
Yellow puccoon/Woolly gromwell *Lithospermum ruderale*	B					N	*G/*P	F	M	M	Y	J	
Lupine *Lupinus* spp.	Be/B	B	N			N/I/C	*G/*P/*F/*R (native in southern Alberta only)	F/P	D/M	M/T	W/Y/O/ R/P/V/B (natives W/P/V/B)	M/J/Ju	Can self-seed
Maltese cross/Scarlet lychnis *Lychnis chalcedonica* (Other *Lychnis* [e.g., *L. alpina*, *L.* x *haageana*, *L. viscaria*, *L. coronaria* also seed/nectar plants)			N/S			I/C	All	F/P	D/M	M/T	W/R/P	J/Ju	
Canescent aster *Machaeranthera canescens* (Biennial)	Be/B	B/M				N	*G	F	D	L/M	B	A	Not usually available from nurseries; reseeds
Malva/Mallow *Malva* spp. (Malva has annual, biennial and perennial forms; perennials include musk mallow [*M. moschata*]; see Annuals)		B	N			I/C	All (naturalized species found in agricultural areas up to north of Edmonton)	F	D/M	T	P/V	J/Ju/A/S	Can be short-lived but reseeds; some are good xeriscape plants
Alfalfa *Medicago sativa*	Be/B/ M	B				I/C	All	F/P	D/M	L/M	Y/V/B	J/Ju/A	Leaf-cutter bees use leaves to line egg chambers
Sweet clover *Melilotus* spp. (Includes white sweet clover [*M. alba*] and yellow sweet clover [*M. officinalis*])	Be		S			I	All	F/P	D/M	M/T	W/Y	J/Ju/A	
Lemon balm *Melissa officinalis*	Be					I/C	All	F	D/M	L/M/T	W	J/Ju/A	Herb; wards off mosquitoes and ants
Mint *Mentha* spp. (*M. arvensis* is native species)	B	B				N/I/C	*All	P	M/W	L/M/T	W/P/V	Ju/A/S	Can be used as ground cover; tends to be invasive
Bergamot/Bee balm/Monarda *Monarda* spp. (Includes *M. didyma* and native species *M. fistulosa*)	Be/B/ M		N			N/I/C	*G/*P/*B(very occasional)/*F/R All	F	M	M/T	W/R/P/V	Ju/A/S	Fragrant and edible flowers; *M. fistulosa* has sharper, mintier aroma than *M. didyma*; source of Earl Grey tea flavour
Evening primrose *Oenothera* spp.	Be/B/ M		S			N/I/C	*G/*P	F/P	D	M/T	W/Y/P	J/Ju	Yellow sundrops (*O.tetragona*) is especially attractive to butterflies; can grow in poor soil
Prickly pear cactus *Opuntia* spp. (Includes *O. polyacantha* and *O. fragilis*)	Be/B/ M		S			N	*G	F	D	L	Y	J/Ju	Sometimes used as ground cover
Oregano/Wild marjoram *Origanum vulgare* (Often grown as annual)	Be					I/C	All	F	D	M/T	P/V		Herb
Loco-weed *Oxytropis* spp.	Be		S		X	N	*G/*F/*R	F	D	L/M	Y/V/B	M/J/Ju/A (some early; some midsummer)	Some species poisonous to livestock
Peony *Paeonia* spp.	B					I/C	All	F/P	D/M	M/T	W/Y/R/P	J/Ju	Attractive to ants
Penstemon/Beard-tongue *Penstemon* spp.	Be/B/ M		N/S			N/I/C	*Varies with species All	F	D	M/T	W/P/V/B	J/Ju/A	

Species	Wildlife Value					Plant Characteristics							
	Insects		Birds		Mammals								
Common Name *Botanical (Scientific) Name*	**Nectar** Be-Bee B-Butterfly • M-Moth	**Larval Food** B-Butterfly • M-Moth	**Nectar** (for hummingbirds)/ **Seeds**	**Nesting Material**	**Graze**	**Origin** N-Native to Alberta • I-Introduced species • C-Cultivars of native or introduced species available	**Natural Region** *(where the plant can be grown; an asterisk indicates where native in Alberta)* G-Grassland • P-Parkland B-Boreal Forest • F-Foothills R-Rocky Mountain	**Sun Exposure** F-Full Sun • P-Partial Shade S-Shade	**Moisture Preference** D-Dry • M-Moist • W-Wet	**Height Range** L-Low (<30 cm) M-Medium (30 cm-60 cm) T-Tall (>60 cm)	**Colour** W-White • Y-Yellow O-Orange • R-Red • P-Pink V-Violet • B-Blue • G-Green	**Bloom Period** Ap-April • M-May • J-June • Ju-July A-August • S-September O-October	**Comments**
Purple prairie clover *Petalostemon purpureum/Dalea purpurea*	Be/B	B				N	*G/*P	F	D	M/T	P/V	J/Ju/A	
Arrow-leaved coltsfoot *Petasites sagittatus*	Be/B/M					N	*All	F/P	M/W	M	W	M	Aggressive spreader
Hood's phlox/Moss phlox *Phlox hoodii* (*P. subulata* is also called moss phlox; it is an introduced species)	Be/B					N	*G	F	D	L	W	Ap/M	Hot sun ground cover; not available from nurseries
Summer phlox/Garden phlox/ Carolina phlox *Phlox paniculata*	B/M					I/C	All	F/P	D/M	M/T	W/R/P/V	Ju/A	
Obedient plant/False Dragonhead *Physostegia virginiana*	Be					I/C	All	F/P	M	M/T	W/P	J/Ju/A	Can be grown as ground cover
Polygonum/Knotweed *Polygonum* spp. (Includes fleeceflower [*P. bistorta*])	Be/B	B	S			N/I/C	*G/*P/*B/F/R	F/P	D/M	L/M	P	M/J	Some native species prefer dry conditions, others moist; *P. bistorta* likes moist soil
Pasque flower/Prairie crocus *Pulsatilla* spp. (Native is *Anemone patens/P. patens*)	Be				X (flower)	N/I/C	*G/*P/*B/ *F/R	F	D	L/M	W/Y/R/ P/V/B (*A. patens* W/V/B)	Ap/M/J	*A. patens* most common in grassland and parkland; its flowers are eaten by elk, deer and ground squirrels
Prairie cone-flower/ Longhead cone-flower *Ratibida columnifera*	Be/B					N	*G	F	D	M/T	Y (occasionally purplish brown)	Ju/A/S	
Black-eyed Susan/Gloriosa daisy/ Coneflower *Rudbeckia hirta* (Can be treated as annual because will bloom the first year from seed)	Be/B		S			I/C	G/P/B	F/P	D/M	L/M/T	Y/O/R	Ju/A/S	
Dock/Sorrel *Rumex* spp.		B	S			N	*All	F	M/W	M/T	G	J/Ju/A	
Salvia *Salvia* spp. (Many salvias are annual; see Annuals)	Be/B					I/C	All	F	D	M/T	W/V/B	Ju/A	
Saxifrage *Saxifraga spp.*	Be/B					N/I/C	*F/*R	P	D/M/W	L	W/R/P	J/Ju/A	
Pincushion flower/Scabious *Scabiosa* spp. (Some are annuals; see Annuals)	Be/B					I/C	All	F	D/M	L/M/T (usually M/T)	W/Y/P/ V/B	Ju/A/S	Some dwarf varieties grown as ground cover; will grow in poor soil
Stonecrop/Sedum *Sedum* spp. (Some now *Hylotelephium* spp.)	Be/B	B				N/I/C	*G/P/B/*F/*R	F	D	L/M/T	W/Y/O/ R/P/ V (natives Y/V)	J/Ju/A/S	Will grow in poor soil; native species usually found in foothills and mountains
Moss campion *Silene acaulis*	Be/B					N	G/*R	F	D	L	P/V	M	
Goldenrod *Solidago* spp.	Be/B	S			X	N/I/C	*All	F	D/M	L/M/T	Y	Ju/A/S	Invasive; ragweed, not goldenrod, causes allergies
Scarlet mallow *Sphaeralcea coccinea*	B	B				N	*G/*P	F	D/M	L	R	Ju/A	Needs good drainage
Woolly lamb's ears *Stachys byzantina*	Be/B					I/C	G/P/B	F/P	D/M	M	P/V	J/Ju/A	Soft, woolly leaves; sometimes grown as ground cover
Dandelion *Taraxacum officinale*	Be/B/M	M	S	X	X	I	All	F/P	D/M	L	Y	Ap–O	
Meadow rue *Thalictrum* spp. (Most common native species is veiny meadow rue [*T. venulosum*])	B					N/I/C	*Varies with species All	F/P	M/W	M/T	W/Y/P/ V/G (native species V/G)	M/J/Ju	
Golden bean *Thermopsis rhombifolia*	Be/B	B/M				N	*G/*P	F	D/M	L	Y	M/J	Sometimes called buffalo-bean; seeds and flowers mildly poisonous to humans
Clover *Trifolium* spp. (Some are annual, e.g., *T. incarnatum*)	Be/B	B	S			I	All	F/P	D/M	L	W/Y/P/R	J/Ju/A	Leaf-cutter bees use leaves to line egg chambers
Nettles *Urtica* spp. (Includes stinging nettle [*U. dioica*])		B				N/I	*All	F/P	M/W	M/T	G	J/Ju	
Mullein *Verbascum* spp.	Be		S			I/C	All	F	D	T	W/Y	Ju/A/S	Good xeriscape plant
Speedwell/Veronica *Veronica* spp. (Includes longleaf speedwell [*V. longifolia*]; both annuals and perennials)	Be		N			N/I/C	*Varies with species All	F/P	D/M/W	L/M/T	W/P/V/B	J/Ju/A	Native species need very moist conditions; dwarf varieties available
Wild vetch *Vicia americana*	Be	B				N	*All	F	M	M/T	V	J/Ju	Sometimes grown as ground cover
Violet *Viola* spp.		B				N	*Varies with species All	F/P/S	D/M/W	L	W/Y/P/ V/B	M/J	Sometimes grown as ground cover; use only native species

Species	Wildlife Value				Plant Characteristics						
	Insects		Birds	Mammals							
Common Name *Botanical (Scientific) Name*	**Nectar** Be-Bee • B-Butterfly • M-Moth	**Larval Food** B-Butterfly • M-Moth	**Nectar** (for hummingbirds)/ **Seeds**	**Graze**	**Origin** N-Native to Alberta • I-Introduced species • C-Cultivars of native or introduced species available	**Natural Region** *(where the plant can be grown; an asterisk indicates where native in Alberta)* G-Grassland • P-Parkland B-Boreal Forest • F-Foothills R-Rocky Mountain	**Sun Exposure** F-Full Sun • P-Partial Shade S-Shade	**Moisture Preference** D-Dry • M-Moist • W-Wet	**Height Range** L-Low (<30 cm) M-Medium (30 cm-60 cm) T-Tall (>60 cm)	**Flower Colour** W-White • Y-Yellow O-Orange • R-Red • P-Pink V-Violet • B-Blue • G-Green	**Comments**
Ageratum/Floss flower *Ageratum houstonianum*	Be/B/ M				I/C	All	F/P	D/M	L/M	W/P/V/B	
Hollyhock *Alcea rosea* (Hollyhock has annual, biennial and perennial forms; see Perennials)	Be/B		N/S		I/C	All	F	D/M	T	W/Y/R/P/V	Edible flowers
Amaranth/Pigweed *Amaranthus* spp. (Only possible native is California amaranth [*A. californicus*])			S		N/I/C	*G/P/B	F	D	L/M/T	R/P/V/G	Many amaranths are introduced weeds and are invasive
Dill *Anethum graveolons*	Be				I/C	All	F	D	T	Y/G	Herb; self-seeds
Snapdragon *Antirrhinum* spp. and cultivars	Be		N		I/C	All	F	D/M	L/M/T	W/Y/O/R/P/V/B	Prefer rich soil
Borage *Borago officinalis*	Be	B	N		I/C	All	F	D	M/T	W/R/V/B	Herb; self-seeds; does not transplant easily
Calendula/Pot marigold *Calendula officinalis*	B				I/C	All	F/P	D	M	W/Y/O	Good xeriscape plant; edible flowers; self-seeds
Canterbury bells *Campanula medium* (Biennial planted as annual)	Be				I/C	All	F	M	M/T	W/P/V/B	
Bachelor button/Cornflower *Centaurea cyanus*	Be/B		S		I/C	All	F	D	L/M/T	W/R/P/V/B	Self-seeds; can be grown in dry conditions
Lamb's-quarters *Chenopodium album*			S		I	G/P/B/F	F	D	M/T	G	Prolific; viewed as garden weed; young leaves edible for humans but should be eaten in moderation
Spider flower/Cleome *Cleome hasslerana/Cleome hassleriana*	Be/B		N/S		I/C	All	F/P	D	T	W/Y/P/V	Good xeriscape plant; fragrant
Cleome/Pink bee plant *Cleome serrulata*	Be/B		N		N	*G/*P	F/P	D	M	W/P/V	Grows well in dry, sandy soil
Coreopsis/Tickseed *Coreopsis* spp. (Native species is *C. tinctoria*; some coreopsis are perennial; see Perennials)	B				N/I/C	*G All	F	D	M/T	Y/O/R	
Cosmos *Cosmos* spp. (Includes *C. bipinnatus* and *C. sulphureus*)	B		S		I/C	All	F/P	D/M	M/T	*C. bipinnatus* W/R/P/V *C. sulphureus* Y/O/R	Good xeriscape plant; some will grow in poor soil
Pink/Dianthus *Dianthus* spp. (Annual, biennial or perennial; includes sweet William [*D. barbatis*] which can be annual, biennial or short-lived perennial; also China pink [*D. chinensis*]; see Perennials)	B		N		I/C	All	F	D/M	L/M/T	W/Y/R/P/V	Good xeriscape plant; some will grow in poor soil
Foxglove/Common foxglove *Digitalis purpurea* (Biennial grown as annual)	Be		N		I/C	P	F/P/S	D/M	M/T	W/Y/P/V	Poisonous for humans
Fuchsia *Fuchsia* spp./*Fuchsia* x hybrida			N		I/C	All	P/S	M	L	W/R/P/V	Best in hanging baskets or planter boxes; need shade and moisture; edible flowers
Sunflower *Helianthus* spp. (Some are perennial; see Perennials)	Be/B		S	X (seeds)	N/I/C	*G/*P/*F(south) All	F/P	D	M/T	Y/O	Good xeriscape plant; will grow in poor soil
Heliotrope *Heliotropium arborescens*	Be/B/ M				I/C	All	F/P	D/M	M/T	W/P/V/B	Fragrant flowers; likes rich soil
Candytuft/Globe candytuft *Iberis umbellata* (Perennial varieties of *Iberis* also available; see Perennials)	Be/B				I/C	All	F	D	L/M	W/R/P/V	
Impatiens *Impatiens* spp.	Be				I/C	All	P/S	M	L/M	W/Y/O/R/P/V	
Himalayan orchid/ Policeman's helmet *Impatiens glandulifera/Impatiens roylei*			N		I	G/P/B	P/S	M	T	P/V	Noxious weed in eastern Canada; self-seeds readily; avoid planting near wetland or other natural area

Species	Wildlife Value				Plant Characteristics						
	Insects		Birds	Mammals							
Common Name *Botanical (Scientific) Name*	**Nectar** Be-Bee • B-Butterfly • M-Moth	**Larval Food** B-Butterfly • M-Moth	**Nectar** (for hummingbirds)/ **Seeds**	**Graze**	**Origin** N-Native to Alberta • I-Introduced species • C-Cultivars of native or introduced species available	**Natural Region** (where the plant can be grown; an asterisk indicates where native in Alberta) G-Grassland • P-Parkland B-Boreal Forest • F-Foothills R-Rocky Mountain	**Sun Exposure** F-Full Sun • P-Partial Shade S-Shade	**Moisture Preference** D-Dry • M-Moist • W-Wet	**Height Range** L-Low (<30 cm) M-Medium (30 cm-60 cm) T-Tall (>60 cm)	**Flower Colour** W-White • Y-Yellow O-Orange • R-Red • P-Pink V-Violet • B-Blue • G-Green	**Comments**
Sweet pea *Lathyrus odoratus* (Also under Vines)	Be				I/C	All	F/P	M	L/M/T	W/Y/O/R/P/ V/B	Fragrant flowers
Lavatera *Lavatera* spp.			N		I/C	All	F/P	D/M	T	W/P	
Statice/Sea lavender *Limonium* spp. (Some are perennials; see Perennials)	Be				I/C	All	F	D/M	L	W/Y/P/V/B	
Sweet alyssum *Lobularia maritima*	B				I/C	All	F/P	D/M	L	W/P/V	Fragrant flowers; will grow in poor soil
Malva/Mallow *Malva* spp. (Malva has annual, biennial and perennial forms; see Perennials)			N		I/C	All	F/P	D/M	M/T	W/R/P/V	Escapees have become local wildflowers; self-seeds
Stock *Matthiola* spp. (*M. longipetala* is evening-scented stock, and *M. incana* has several varieties, including ten-weeks stock)	M				I/C	All	F/P	M	L/M	W/Y/R/P/V	Need abundant water and prefer rich soil; fragrant flowers (in evening or on dull days for evening-scented stock)
Four o'clock/Marvel-of-Peru *Mirabilis jalapa*			N		I/C	All	F	M	M	W/Y/R/P/V	Fragrant flowers; self-seeds readily
Forget-me-not *Myosotis sylvatica* (Biennial treated as annual)	Be				I/C	All	F/P/S	M	L/M	B	Early blooming; self-seeds; often believed to be perennial; sometimes grown as ground cover
Nicotiana/Flowering tobacco *Nicotiana spp.*	Be/M		N		I/C	All	F/P	D/M	M/T	W/Y/R/P/V/G	Flowers all season; hummingbirds like red ones
Sweet marjoram *Origanum majorana* (Perennial grown as annual)	Be				I/C	All	F	D/M	L/M	W/P	Herb
Oregano/Wild marjoram *Origanum vulgare*		(Herb; perennial sometimes grown as annual; see Perennials)									
Opium poppy *Papaver somniferum*	Be/B		S		I/C	All	F	D/M	M/T	W/R/P/V	
Petunia *Petunia* x hybrida	Be/M		N		I/C	All	F/P	M	L/M	W/Y/O/R/P/ V/B	Need full sun at least three hours a day; need abundant water
Polygonum/Knotweed *Polygonum* spp. (Some are perennials; see Perennials)	Be/B	B	S		N/I/C	*G/*P/*B/F/R	F/P	D	L/M	P	
Black-eyed Susan/Gloriosa daisy/ Coneflower *Rudbeckia hirta*		(Can be treated as annual because will bloom the first year from seed; see Perennials)									
Salvia *Salvia spp.* (Includes scarlet sage [*S. splendens*]; some salvias are perennial; see Perennials)	Be/B?		N		I/C	All	F/P	D	L/M/T	W/R/Y/P/V/B	Prefer rich soil; excellent for hummingbirds (scarlet sage is a favourite)
Pincushion flower/Scabious *Scabiosa spp.* (Some are perennials; see Perennials)	Be/B				I/C	All	F	M	M/T	W/R/P/V/B	Self-seeds
Marigold *Tagetes* spp. or *Tagetes* x hybrida	Be/B		S	X (seeds)	I/C	All	F	D	L/M	W/Y/O/R	Good xeriscape plant
Nasturtium *Tropaeolum majus*	B		N		I/C	All	F/P	D	L/M/T	W/Y/O/R/P	A favourite of the cabbage butterfly; likes sandy soil; edible flowers; tart fragrance
Verbena *Verbena* spp. and cultivars (Common verbena usually listed as *Verbena* x hybrida or *Verbena hybrida*; is perennial treated as annual)	Be/B				I/C	All	F	D/M	L/M/T	W/R/P/V/B	Need rich soil
Zinnia *Zinnia elegans*	Be/B		S		I/C	All	F	D	L/M/T	W/Y/O/R/P/V	Good xeriscape plant

APPENDIX 2

Selected Butterfly Plants and Some Butterflies They Attract

Butterflies are listed according to the order given in Bird et al. (1995). Butterfly scientific names of butterflies also follow Bird et al. (1995).
Plants are listed in alphabetical order by scientific name. Scientific names of native plants follow Moss (1983).

N-Nectar Food Source

L-Larval Food Source

Butterflies	Trees and Shrubs							Vines	Perennials																				Annual
	Saskatoon *Amelanchier alnifolia*	**Wolf-willow/Silverberry** *Elaeagnus commutata*	**Aspen** *Populus tremuloides*	**Shrubby cinquefoil** *Potentilla fruticosa*	**Choke cherry** *Prunus virginiana*	**Willow** *Salix* spp.	**Lilac** *Syringa* spp.	**Western clematis** *Clematis ligusticifolia*	**Common yarrow** *Achillea millefolium*	**Spreading dogbane** *Apocynum androsaemifolium*	**Showy milkweed** *Asclepias speciosa*	**Aster** *Aster* spp.	**Bull thistle** *Cirsium vulgare*	**Purple coneflower** *Echinacea purpurea*	**Fleabane** *Erigeron* spp.	**Gaillardia/Brown-eyed Susan** *Gaillardia aristata*	**Gumweed** *Grindelia squarrosa*	**Sneezeweed** *Helenium autumnale*	**Blazing star** *Liatris* spp.	**Lupine** *Lupinus* spp.	**Canescent aster** *Machaeranthera canescens*	**Alfalfa** *Medicago sativa*	**Bergamot/Bee balm** *Monarda* spp.	**Purple prairie clover** *Petalostemon purpureum*	**Goldenrod** *Solidago* spp.	**Dandelion** *Taraxacum officinale*	**Stinging nettle** *Urtica dioica*	**Violets** *Viola* spp.	**Cleome/Pink bee plant** *Cleome serrulata*
SKIPPERS																													
Delaware skipper *Atrytone logan*										N	N		N																
Common branded skipper *Hesperia comma*													N	N			N		N		N	N							N
Uncas skipper *Hesperia uncas*																	N		N		N								
Afranius duskywing *Erynnis afranius*													N				N	N	N		N								N
Dreamy duskywing *Erynnis icelus*																	N	N	N							N			
Persius duskywing *Erynnis persius*										N			N				N	N	N							N			N
Checkered skipper *Pyrgus communis*				N						N	N	N	N		N		N	N	N		N	N		N		N			N
SWALLOWTAILS																													
Canadian tiger swallowtail *Papilio canadensis*	N	N	L		N	L	N				N															N			
WHITES																													
Cabbage butterfly *Pieris rapae*							N				N				N		N	N			N	N/L		N		N			N
Western white *Pontia occidentalis*							N				N				N		N	N				N	N	N	N	N			N
SULPHURS																													
Alexandra sulphur *Colias alexandra*								N							N	N	N	N	N				N		N				N
Alfalfa butterfly *Colias eurytheme*		N				N	N	N		N	N	N	N	N	N		N	N			N	N/L	N	N	N				N
Clouded sulphur *Colias philodice*	N	N			N	N	N	N		N	N	N	N	N	N	N	N	N	N		N	N/L	N	N	N	N			N
COPPERS																													
Purplish copper *Lycaena helloides*				N				N		N		N					N	N			N	N			N				N
Great gray copper *Lycaena dione*								N				N						N				N			N				
HAIRSTREAKS																													
Coral hairstreak *Harkenclenus titus*	N				L					N															N				
Striped hairstreak *Satyrium liparops*	N				L					N																			
BLUES																													
Spring azure *Celastrina ladon*						N																							
Silvery blue *Glaucopsyche lygdamus*	N	N			N	N														N/L									
Melissa blue *Lycaeides melissa*		N							N	N								N			N	N		N/L					N
Greenish blue *Plebejus saepiolus*	N	N		N	N				N	N												N		N		N			N
TORTOISE SHELLS																													
Milbert's tortoise shell *Aglais milberti*			N			N	N					N	N				N									N	L		
Mourning cloak *Nymphalis antiopa*			N			N/L	N					N	N													N			
Compton's tortoise shell *Nymphalis vaualbum*			N			N/L																				N			
ANGLEWINGS																													
Green comma *Polygonia faunus*			N			N/L						N	N													N			
Hoary comma *Polygonia gracilis*						N						N														N			
Gray comma *Polygonia progne*			N			N						N														N			
Satyr anglewing *Polygonia satyrus*			N			N						N	N													N	L		
Zephyr *Polygonia zephyrus*			N			N						N	N													N			

Butterflies are listed according to the order given in Bird et al. (1995). Butterfly scientific names of butterflies also follow Bird et al. (1995).
Plants are listed in alphabetical order by scientific name. Scientific names of native plants follow Moss (1983).

N -Nectar Food Source
L -Larval Food Source

	Trees and Shrubs							Vines	Perennials																				Annual
Butterflies	**Saskatoon** *Amelanchier alnifolia*	**Wolf-willow/Silverberry** *Elaeagnus commutata*	**Aspen** *Populus tremuloides*	**Shrubby cinquefoil** *Potentilla fruticosa*	**Choke cherry** *Prunus virginiana*	**Willow** *Salix* spp.	**Lilac** *Syringa* spp.	**Western clematis** *Clematis ligusticifolia*	**Common yarrow** *Achillea millefolium*	**Spreading dogbane** *Apocynum androsaemifolium*	**Showy milkweed** *Asclepias speciosa*	**Aster** *Aster* spp.	**Bull thistle** *Cirsium vulgare*	**Purple coneflower** *Echinacea purpurea*	**Fleabane** *Erigeron* spp.	**Gaillardia/Brown-eyed Susan** *Gaillardia aristata*	**Gumweed** *Grindelia squarrosa*	**Sneezeweed** *Helenium autumnale*	**Blazing star** *Liatris* spp.	**Lupine** *Lupinus* spp.	**Canescent aster** *Machaeranthera canescens*	**Alfalfa** *Medicago sativa*	**Bergamot/Bee balm** *Monarda* spp.	**Purple prairie clover** *Petalostemon purpureum*	**Goldenrod** *Solidago* spp.	**Dandelion** *Taraxacum officinale*	**Stinging nettle** *Urtica dioica*	**Violets** *Viola* spp.	**Cleome/Pink bee plant** *Cleome serrulata*
RED ADMIRAL AND LADIES																													
Red admiral *Vanessa atalanta*							N						N									N					L		
Painted lady *Vanessa cardui*							N				N		N/L								N	N				N			N
FRITILLARIES																													
Meadow fritillary *Boloria bellona*																												L	
Purple fritillary *Boloria chariclea*				N								N											N						
Aphrodite fritillary *Speyeria aphrodite*								N	N	N	N	N	N	N		N	N		N		N	N	N		N	N		L	N
Atlantis fritillary *Speyeria atlantis*								N	N	N	N	N	N			N	N		N		N	N	N		N	N		L	N
Northwestern fritillary *Speyeria electa*								N		N	N	N	N	N		N	N		N		N	N	N		N	N		L	N
Callippe fritillary *Speyeria callippe*								N	N	N	N	N	N			N	N		N		N	N	N		N			L	N
Great spangled fritillary *Speyeria cybele*								N		N						N			N			N	N					L	N
Edwards' fritillary *Speyeria edwardsii*								N		N	N					N												L	N
Mormon fritillary *Speyeria mormonia*								N	N	N	N	N	N			N	N		N		N	N	N		N			L	N
Zerene fritillary *Speyeria zerene*								N		N						N						N						L	N
CHECKERSPOTS																													
Acastus checkerspot *Charidryas acastus*										N		N									N/L								
Northern checkerspot *Charidryas palla*										N		N/L			N										N				
CRESCENTS/CRESCENTSPOTS																													
Tawny crescent *Phyciodes batesii*									N			N/L			N		N	N			N				N				
Northern pearl crescent *Phyciodes cocyta*									N			N/L			N		N	N			N				N	N			
Field crescent *Phyciodes puichella*									N			N/L			N														
Pearl crescent *Phyciodes tharos*									N			N/L			N		N	N			N				N	N			
ADMIRALS																													
Viceroy *Limenitis archippus*						L		N		N	N		N																
White admiral *Limenitis arthemis*	N		L					N		N	N		N																
WOOD NYMPHS																													
Dark wood nymph *Cercyonis oetus*									N		N		N			N			N			N	N		N				N
Common wood nymph *Cercyonis pegala*									N		N		N			N			N			N	N		N				N
RINGLETS																													
Inornate ringlet *Ceononympha inornata*									N		N		N			N							N		N				N
ALPINES																													
Common alpine *Erebia epipsodea*	N	N			N																					N			
MONARCH																													
Monarch *Danaus plexippus*											N/L																		

APPENDIX 3
Some Alberta Birds

This table has information on some of the more common birds that might be seen in a yard or garden in Alberta. Only a few wetland species have been included.

LEGEND

BIRD SPECIES
The birds are listed in taxonomic order according to the American Ornithologists' Union (1998). The order to which the species belongs is in full capitals and boldface type; the common name of the family is in boldface type following the order. The common name and scientific name of the species are below the order and family names. The source of the scientific and common names is the American Ornithologists' Union (1998).

STATUS
The status noted here applies to Alberta as a whole; regional variations will occur.

- **SR:** Summer Resident - present and breeding over the summer months
- **PR:** Permanent Resident - found year-round and breeding
- **M:** Migrant - generally only seen on migration in the spring and/or fall
- **WR:** Winter Resident - generally only present during the winter

NATURAL REGION
This section indicates in which natural region(s) the species may be observed.

Grassland **P**arkland **B**oreal Forest
Foothills **R**ocky Mountain

See Chapter 3 for more information on the province's natural regions. The Canadian Shield natural region, in the province's northeast, has not been included here.

BREEDING OR OVERWINTERING HABITAT, PLANTINGS
The native habitat and plantings are the same except where noted otherwise. "All habitats" refers to those habitats found within the species' range.

ATTRACTANTS
There are four sections:
Supplemental **F**ood (if this section has an ✪, the information is in the **Common Alberta Feeder Birds** table in Chapter 14) – **W**ater – **S**helter/Housing – **O**ther.

Bird Species Common Name • *Scientific Name*	Status SR-Summer resident • M-Migrant PR-Permanent resident • WR-Winter resident	Natural Region G-Grassland • P-Parkland • F-Foothills B-Boreal Forest • R-Rocky Mountain	Breeding or Overwintering Habitat, Plantings	Attractamts F-Supplemental Food W-Water S-Shelter/Housing O-Other ✪-Refer to Chapter 14—*Common Alberta Feeder Birds*
ANSERIFORMES – Ducks, Geese and Swans				
Canada goose *Branta canadensis*	SR	All	Grazes/feeds on lawns, parks, fields, golf courses, grain fields; nests in wetland areas of ponds, marshes, city parks	**F:** Grain (chopped), corn (cracked) **S:** Nest platform, nesting island, floating structure for nesting/loafing
Mallard *Anas platyrhynchos*	SR (some overwinter)	All	Grazes/feeds on lawns, parks, fields, golf courses, grain fields; nests in ponds, marshes, lakes, rivers, city parks, dugouts	**F:** Grain, buckwheat, millet **S:** Nesting tunnel, nesting island, floating structure for nesting/loafing; some may come in to a large water garden
Bufflehead *Bucephala albeola*	SR (some overwinter)	All	Small ponds and lakes	**S:** Nestbox, nesting island, floating structure for nesting/loafing
Common goldeneye *Bucephala clangula*	SR (some overwinter)	All (except extreme south of province)	Lakes, ponds, rivers	**S:** Nestbox, nesting island, floating nesting/loafing structure
FALCONIFORMES – Hawks and Eagles				
Northern harrier *Circus cyaneus*	SR (some overwinter)	All (rare in R)	Open meadows and marshes	
Red-tailed hawk *Buteo jamaicensis*	SR (some overwinter)	All	Wooded areas	
FALCONIFORMES – Falcons				
American kestrel *Falco sparverius*	SR	All	Open or semi-open areas	**S:** Nestbox
Merlin *Falco columbarius*	PR	All	Open woodlands, wooded areas in cities; nests in tall coniferous trees	
GALLIFORMES – Grouse, Pheasants and Turkey				
Gray partridge *Perdix perdix*	PR (introduced)	G/P/ B (south)	Open grassland, acreages	**F:** ✪ **O:** Dust bath
Ring-necked pheasant *Phasianus colchicus*	PR (introduced)	G/P/ B (south)	Grassland with adjacent tree and shrub cover	**F:** Cereal grain (cracked), sunflower seeds, millet, corn (whole or cracked)
Ruffed grouse *Bonasa umbellus*	PR	P/B/F/R	Aspen woods, mixed woods; likes to eat cotoneaster	**O:** Drumming log for male
CHARADRIIFORMES – Plovers				
Killdeer *Charadrius vociferus*	SR	All	Open areas, close-cropped pastures, ploughed fields, golf courses, parks	**S:** Nesting island, gravel bar by water or small gravelled area in open field
COLUMBIFORMES – Doves and Pigeons				
Rock dove (Pigeon) *Columba livia*	PR (introduced)	All (except extreme north)	Cities, towns, farms	**F:** ✪

Bird Species Common Name • *Scientific Name*	**Status** SR-Summer resident PR-Permanent resident • M-Migrant WR-Winter resident	**Natural Region** G-Grassland • P-Parkland B-Boreal Forest • F-Foothills R-Rocky Mountain	**Breeding or Overwintering Habitat, Plantings**	**Attractamts** F -Supplemental Food W-Water S -Shelter/Housing O -Other ✪ -Refer to Chapter 14—*Common Alberta Feeder Birds*
Mourning dove *Zenaida macroura*	SR	G/P/F/ B (south)	Woodlands, grasslands	**F:** Grain (cracked), corn (cracked), sunflower seeds, millet **W:** Birdbath **O:** Dust bath
STRIGIFORMES – Owls				
Great horned owl *Bubo virginianus*	PR	All	Wooded areas in both cities and rural areas	**F:** Frozen mice/ground squirrels **S:** Nesting basket
Northern saw-whet owl *Aegolius acadicus*	PR	P/F/B	Wooded areas, including parks and ravines	**S:** Nestbox
APODIFORMES – Hummingbirds				
Ruby-throated hummingbird *Archilochus colubris*	SR	G/P/ B (south)	Woodland clearings, gardens; nests in spruce; feeds at sapsucker sap wells and nectar-producing flowers	**F:** ✪ **W:** Birdbath, water mister, waterfall in water garden
Rufous hummingbird *Selasphorus rufus*	SR	F/R	Open areas, meadows, gardens; nests in spruce; feeds at sapsucker sap wells and nectar-producing flowers	**F:** ✪ **W:** As for ruby-throated
PICIFORMES – Woodpeckers				
Yellow-bellied sapsucker *Sphyrapicus varius* **Red-naped sapsucker** *Sphyrapicus nuchalis*	SR	All (except extreme south)	Poplar or mixed spruce-poplar woodlands; sap well trees including alder, birch, saskatoon	**F:** Sugar-water solution **O:** Plantings (for sap wells)
Downy woodpecker *Picoides pubescens* **Hairy woodpecker** *Picoides villosus*	PR	All	Poplar and mixed spruce-poplar woodlands	**F:** ✪
Northern flicker *Colaptes auratus*	SR (some overwinter)	All	In and around clearings in poplar, mixed and coniferous woods	**F:** ✪ **S:** Nestbox **O:** Snags
Pileated woodpecker *Dryocopus pileatus*	PR	All	Mature poplar and mixed woods (requires large tracts of woodland)	**F:** Suet, sunflower seeds, bone sawdust
PASSERIFORMES – Flycatchers				
Western wood-pewee *Contopus sordidulus*	SR	All	Open mixed or poplar woods	
Least flycatcher *Empidonax minimus*	SR	All	Poplar or mixed spruce-poplar woods	
Eastern phoebe *Sayornis phoebe*	SR	G/P/B/F	Wooded areas near a stream or river	**S:** Nesting shelf
Eastern kingbird *Tyrannus tyrannus*	SR	G/P/B/F	Edge of wooded areas	**S:** Modified nesting bracket
PASSERIFORMES – Vireos				
Warbling vireo *Vireo gilvus*	SR	All	Shrubby poplar woods	
Red-eyed vireo *Vireo olivaceus*	SR	All	Mature poplar woods	
PASSERIFORMES – Jays, Crows and Allies				
Gray jay *Perisoreus canadensis*	PR	B/F/R	Dense spruce or mixed spruce-poplar woods	**F:** ✪ **W:** Birdbath
Blue jay *Cyanocitta cristata*	PR	P/B/F	Mixed and coniferous woods, urban areas	**F:** ✪ **W:** Birdbath
Clark's nutcracker *Nucifraga columbiana*	PR	R	Coniferous forests (open or broken stands)	**F:** Sunflower seeds, suet, kitchen scraps
Black-billed magpie *Pica pica*	PR	All (except extreme northeast)	All habitats	**F:** ✪
American crow *Corvus brachyrhynchos*	SR (some overwinter)	All (except extreme northeast)	All habitats	**F:** Suet, bone sawdust, sunflower seeds, kitchen scraps, fruit, peanuts, carcasses, old wasp nests, mealworms **W:** Birdbath
PASSERIFORMES – Jays, Crows and Allies continued				
Common raven *Corvus corax*	PR	All (except southeast)	Forested areas	**F:** As for crow **W:** Birdbath **S:** Will sometimes nest on power poles
PASSERIFORMES – Swallows				
Purple martin *Progne subis*	SR	P	Open areas, near humans	**S:** Apartment-style nestboxes **O:** Eggshells (crushed), perching areas near nestbox
Tree swallow *Tachycineta bicolor*	SR	All	Open or treed areas, near water	**S:** Nestbox **O:** White feathers, perches
Barn swallow *Hirundo rustica*	SR	All	Anywhere near human-built structures	**S:** Nesting shelf, nesting nails **O:** Eggshells, mud, white feathers
Cliff swallow *Petrochelidon pyrrhonota*	SR	All	Near wetlands, prefers bridges, rock cliffs, buildings	**S:** Slats, nest frame, nestbox **O:** Eggshells, mud
PASSERIFORMES – Chickadees				
Black-capped chickadee *Poecile atricapillus*	PR	All	All habitats; nests in rotting birch and poplar	**F:** ✪ **W:** Birdbath **S:** Nestbox **O:** Roosting box (e.g., nestbox containing old house wren nest)
Mountain chickadee *Poecile gambeli*	PR	F/R	As for black-capped	As for black-capped
Boreal chickadee *Poecile hudsonicus*	PR	P/B/F/R	Coniferous and mixed woods	As for black-capped
PASSERIFORMES – Nuthatches				
Red-breasted nuthatch *Sitta canadensis*	PR	All (G–river valleys only)	Coniferous and mixed woods	**F:** ✪ **W:** Birdbath? **S:** Nestbox **O:** Roosting box
White-breasted nuthatch *Sitta carolinensis*	PR	G (winter only)/ P/B (south)/ F/R	Poplar or mixed woods	**F:** ✪ **W:** Birdbath? **S:** Nestbox **O:** Roosting box
PASSERIFORMES – Creepers				
Brown creeper *Certhia americana*	PR	P/B (south)/ F/R	Coniferous and mixed woods	**F:** ✪ **S:** Modified nestbox
PASSERIFORMES – Wrens				
House wren *Troglodytes aedon*	SR	All (except NE Boreal)	Poplar woods, thickets, shrubby areas	**F:** Mealworms **W:** Birdbath **S:** Nestbox
PASSERIFORMES – Kinglets				
Ruby-crowned kinglet *Regulus calendula*	SR	P/B/F/R	Mixed woods with lots of conifers	**F:** Suet, sunflower seeds
PASSERIFORMES – Bluebirds and Thrushes				
Mountain bluebird *Sialia currucoides*	SR	All (except extreme north)	Open poplar woods, short-grass areas with scattered trees; likes to eat saskatoon berries	**F:** Mealworms **W:** Birdbath **S:** Nestbox
American robin *Turdus migratorius*	SR (some overwinter)	All	Will nest in a variety of locations (a common bird of urban and suburban areas); likes to eat berries; often seen on lawns	**F:** Cornbread, bread, raisins (soaked in prune juice), fruit (e.g., Nanking cherries), mealworms, sunflower seeds (crushed), suet **W:** Birdbath **S:** Nesting shelf **O:** Nesting material, mud
PASSERIFORMES – Catbirds and Thrashers				
Gray catbird *Dumetella carolinensis*	SR	G/P	Dense shrubs and thickets	**F:** Fruit, mealworms **W:** Birdbath
PASSERIFORMES – Starlings				
European starling *Sturnus vulgaris*	SR (some overwinter; introduced)	All (except extreme north)	Treed areas; likes to be around human habitation	**F:** ✪ **W:** Birdbath **S:** Nestbox

Bird Species **Common Name** • *Scientific Name*	**Status** SR-Summer resident PR-Permanent resident • M-Migrant WR-Winter resident	**Natural Region** G-Grassland • P-Parkland B-Boreal Forest • F-Foothills R-Rocky Mountain	**Breeding or Overwintering Habitat, Plantings**	**Attractamts** F -Supplemental Food W-Water S-Shelter/Housing O-Other ✪-Refer to Chapter 14—*Common Alberta Feeder Birds*
PASSERIFORMES – Waxwings				
Bohemian waxwing *Bombycilla garrulus*	WR	Summer: B (north) Winter: G/P	Nests in open boreal forest; likes (among others) the fruits of mountain-ash, saskatoon, choke cherry, pin cherry and dogwood, especially during winter and early spring	**F:** Berries, orange pieces, other fruit (frozen or dried, especially bananas and a mixture or apples and raisins),suet, corn (cracked) **W:** ?
Cedar waxwing *Bombycilla cedrorum*	SR (some overwinter)	All	Nests in open poplar woods, urban areas; likes to eat same as Bohemian	**F:** As for Bohemian **W:** ? **O:** Nesting material (bits of string, etc.)
PASSERIFORMES – Wood-warblers				
Yellow warbler *Dendroica petechia*	SR	All	Shrubby areas (e.g., wild rose thickets) near water	**F:** Sugar-water solution
Yellow-rumped warbler *Dendroica coronata*	SR	B/F/R	Coniferous or mixed woods	**F:** Sugar-water solution?
Common yellowthroat *Geothlypis trichas*	SR	All	Brushy areas near wetlands	
PASSERIFORMES – Sparrows				
Spotted towhee *Pipilo maculatus*	SR	G/P (south)	Thickets in grassland areas	**F:** Sunflower seeds (shelled or chopped), corn (fine cracked), peanuts, millet, mealworms, suet
American tree sparrow *Spizella arborea*	M (some overwinter)	All (during migration) B (nests in northern)	Wooded areas	**F:** ✪
Chipping sparrow *Spizella passerina*	SR	All	Open deciduous and mixed woods, lawns and gardens	**F:** ✪
Clay-coloured sparrow *Spizella pallida*	SR	All	Shrubby areas	**F:** Sunflower seeds (shelled), millet, canary seed, weed seeds, suet
Vesper sparrow *Pooecetes gramineus*	SR	All	Open pastures and meadows	
Savannah sparrow *Passerculus sandwichensis*	SR	All	Damp, low-lying areas with dense vegetation	**F:** Millet, cornbread, suet, sunflower seeds (shelled)
Fox sparrow *Passerella iliaca*	SR	B/F/R	Dense woodland thickets	**F:** Sunflower seeds (shelled), millet, peanuts (chopped), corn (cracked), suet
Lincoln's sparrow *Melospiza lincolnii*	SR	P/B/F/R	Wet meadows, wooded thickets	**F:** Sunflower seeds (shelled), millet, suet
Song sparrow *Melospiza melodia*	SR	All	Shrubby areas (especially with willows), around wetlands	**F:** Sunflower seeds (shelled), millet, canola, peanuts (chopped), nygur seed, suet
White-throated sparrow *Zonotrichia albicollis*	SR	P/B/F/R	Nests at edges of aspen woods; during migration — everywhere	**F:** ✪
Harris's sparrow *Zonotrichia querula*	M (occasionally overwinters)	All (during migration; usually overwinters in south)	Wooded or shrubby areas, hedgerows	**F:** Sunflower seeds (shelled or shopped), millet
White-crowned sparrow *Zonotrichia leucophrys*	SR	G (extreme southeast)/ P (west)/ B/F/R	Shrubby woodlands	**F:** ✪
Dark-eyed junco *Junco hyemalis*	SR (some overwinter)	P/B/F/R	Nests in wooded areas; likes to eat weed seeds	**F:** ✪
PASSERIFORMES – Grosbeaks and Buntings				
Rose-breasted grosbeak *Pheucticus ludovicianus*	SR	P/B/F	Nests in mixed woods; widespread during migration	**F:** ✪
PASSERIFORMES – Blackbirds and Allies				
Red-winged blackbird *Agelaius phoeniceus*	SR	All	Wetlands, lakes, ponds	**F:** ✪
PASSERIFORMES – Blackbirds and Allies continued				
Brewer's blackbird *Euphagus cyanocephalus*	SR	G/P/F/ B(south)	Roadsides, pastures, aspen groves	
Common grackle *Quiscalus quiscula*	SR	G/P/B	Parks, golf courses, wet areas, roadsides	**F:** Sunflower seeds, corn (cracked), millet, cereal grains
Brown-headed cowbird *Molothrus ater*	SR	All (except extreme north)	Lays eggs in nests of other birds, often in open areas near cattle	**F:** Sunflower seeds, corn (cracked)
Baltimore oriole *Icterus galbula*	SR	G/P/ B (south)/ F (south)/ R (south)	Poplar woods	**F:** ✪ **O:** Nesting material (pieces of string, etc.)
PASSERIFORMES – Finches and Grosbeaks				
Gray-crowned rosy-finch *Leucosticte tephrocotis*	PR (Rocky Mountain) WR (elsewhere)	G/P/F (all above, winter only) R	Nests in alpine areas; can be found in open areas during the winter	**F:** ✪
Pine grosbeak *Pinicola enucleator*	PR (Rocky Mountain) WR (elsewhere)	G/P/B/F (all above, winter only) R	Coniferous and mixedwood forests; likes to eat lilac seeds	**F:** ✪ **W:** Birdbath
Purple finch *Carpodacus purpureus*	SR	P/B/F/R	Open mixed and coniferous woodlands; nests in coniferous trees; feeds in deciduous trees	**F:** ✪
House finch *Carpodacus mexicanus*	PR (some overwinter)	G/P (range is expanding)	Mixed woods; agricultural areas; often at feeders in urban areas close to human habitation	**F:** ✪ **S:** Nestbox
Red crossbill *Loxia curvirostra*	PR	P/B/F/R (irruptive)	Coniferous groves and forests (prefers pine forests)	**F:** Sunflower seeds, nygur
White-winged crossbill *Loxia leucoptera*	PR	P/B/F/R (irruptive)	Spruce forests and mixed woods	**F:** Sunflower seeds, nygur
Common redpoll *Carduelis flammea* **Hoary redpoll** *Carduelis hornemanni*	WR	All (irruptive)	All habitats; like to eat birch, alder, lilac, seeds	**F:** ✪
Pine siskin *Carduelis pinus*	PR	All (irruptive)	Nests in coniferous and poplar woods; eats spruce, birch, alder seeds	**F:** ✪
American goldfinch *Carduelis tristis*	SR	G/P/ B (south)/ F/R	Open deciduous areas, urban and suburban gardens; likes to feed in weedy fields, as well as in gardens that have thistle, larch, alder, birch, cosmos, zinnia, sunflower, hollyhock, delphinium, black-eyed Susan, cornflower, coreopsis and yellow batchelor button (likes the seeds)	**F:** ✪ **W:** Birdbath **O:** Nesting material (dog hair, etc.)
Evening grosbeak *Coccothraustes vespertinus*	WR (some now breed in the province)	All (irruptive)	Nests in forests; in winter—everywhere; likes to eat poplar, ash, maple seeds	**F:** ✪ **W:** Birdbath
PASSERIFORMES – Weaver Finches				
House sparrow *Passer domesticus*	PR (introduced)	All	All	**F:** ✪ **W:** Birdbath **S:** Nestbox

APPENDIX 4

Some Alberta Mammals

This table provides information on some of the more common mammals that might appear in a yard or garden in Alberta.

LEGEND

MAMMAL SPECIES
The mammals are listed in taxonomic order, and the scientific and common names follow Jones et al. (1997). The order to which the species belongs is in full capitals and bold-face type; the common name of the family is in bold-face type following the order. The common name and scientific name of the species are below the order and family names.

STATUS
The status given for each species applies to Alberta as a whole; regional variations will occur.

NATURAL REGION
This section indicates in which natural region(s) the mammal species may be observed.

Grassland **P**arkland **B**oreal Forest
Foothills **R**ocky Mountain

See Chapter 3 for more information on the province's natural regions. The Canadian Shield natural region, in the province's northeast, has not been included here.

Mammal Species Common Name • *Scientific Name*	Status	Natural Region G-Grassland P-Parkland B-Boreal Forest F-Foothills R-Rocky Mountain	Habitat	Plantings	Supplemental Food	Structural Attractants	Notes
INSECTIVORA – Shrews							
Masked shrew *Sorex cinereus*	Resident	G(north)/P/B/F/R	Grasslands, meadows, uplands and deadfall in coniferous, deciduous and mixedwood forests	Requires vegetative cover (thick grass, treed areas)	Grains, sunflower seeds, nuts, fruit, mealworms		Shrews are primarily insect eaters, but they also eat other animals and seeds
Pygmy shrew *Sorex hoyi*	Resident	As for masked shrew	As for masked shrew	As for masked shrew	As for masked shrew		As for masked shrew
Dusky shrew *Sorex monticolus*	Resident	All (including eastern G)	As for masked shrew	As for masked shrew	As for masked shrew		As for masked shrew
CHIROPTERA – Bats							
Little brown bat *Myotis lucifugus*	Migratory	G (north)/P/B/F/R	Widely distributed throughout the province, especially where there are wetlands			Bat house	Outside lights, left on at night, attract moths and other night-flying insects, which in turn attract bats
Big brown bat *Eptesicus fuscus*	Hibernate near their summer range	All (except NE corner of province)	As for little brown bat			Bat house	As for little brown bat
LAGOMORPHA – Pikas, Rabbits and Hares							
Snowshoe hare *Lepus americanus*	Quite common resident; population is subject to cycles; active throughout the year	G (except central south)/P/B/F/R	Forests and woodlands, shrub thickets, hedgerows	Beets (for leaves), Swiss chard, parsley, carrots (for tops), yarrow, sunflowers (for seeds), apples	Beet leaves, Swiss chard, parsley, carrot tops, yarrow, sunflower seeds, apples	Rock pile, brush pile, rabbit/hare house	Needs sufficient cover; will browse the terminal buds and girdle the stems of young deciduous trees; eats garden vegetables
White-tailed jackrabbit *Lepus townsendii*	Locally common resident, even in towns and cities; active throughout the year	G/P/B (south)	Open grasslands and open meadows	Eats grass, will feed in open lawn areas	Sunflower seeds		
RODENTIA – Squirrels							
Least chipmunk *Eutamias minimus*	Quite common resident; hibernates	G (except central south)/P/B/F/R	A variety of habitats in brushy and open, wooded areas		Seeds, nuts, berries, raisins, bread	Rock pile, brush pile, nestbox, upturned pot	
Woodchuck (Groundhog) *Marmota monax*	Widely distributed but fairly uncommon resident; hibernates	P/B	Meadows, fields, pastures near wooded areas; river valleys, rock piles, agricultural and residential areas		Oats, corn	Rock pile, brush pile, old building	Will eat crops and garden vegetables
Franklin's ground squirrel *Spermophilus franklinii*	Resident; hibernates	P/B (southeast)	Dense grassy areas, hedges, brush borders, edges of spruce forests		Oats, wheat, sunflower seeds, bur oak acorns, crab apples	Rock pile, brush pile	
Richardson's ground squirrel *Spermophilus richardsonii*	Resident; hibernates	B/P/B(south)	Well-grazed pastures, meadows, roadsides, yards, cemeteries, golf courses (wherever grass is mowed)		As for Franklin's ground squirrel	As for Franklin's ground squirrel	
Thirteen-lined ground squirrel *Spermophilus tridecemlineatus*	Resident; hibernates	G/P/B (southeast)	Brushy edges, areas with tall grass		As for Franklin's ground squirrel	As for Franklin's ground squirrel	
Eastern gray squirrel *Sciurus carolinensis*	Introduced resident; locally common (Calgary, Okotoks)	Calgary, Okotoks	Deciduous forests; urban residential and park areas	Hardwoods	Sunflower seeds, nuts (especially peanuts), fruit, dried bread	Nestbox, snag with natural cavities	Aggressive; predator of nestlings and wild bird nests; will displace other animals
Red squirrel *Tamiasciurus hudsonicus*	Common resident	G (Cypress Hills)/P/B/F/R	Mixedwood forests; fairly common in urban areas where there are conifers	Prefers to eat coniferous cones, especially spruce; where there are no conifers, will eat the samaras of Manitoba maple	Sunflower seeds, nuts, fruit	Nestbox, snag with natural cavities	Will go into torpor during extremely cold periods in the winter; predator of nestlings; aggressive at feeding stations
Northern flying squirrel *Glaucomys sabrinus*	Resident; active year-round	P(north)/B/F/R	Coniferous and mixedwood forests	Berry- and nut-producing shrubs and trees	Sunflower seeds, nuts, fruit	Nestbox, snag with natural cavities	Active at night, especially at dusk and dawn

Mammal Species Common Name • *Scientific Name*	Status	Natural Region G-Grassland P-Parkland B-Boreal Forest F-Foothills R-Rocky Mountain	Habitat	Plantings	Supplemental Food	Structural Attractants	Notes
RODENTIA – Pocket gophers							
Northern pocket gopher *Thomomys talpoides*	Common resident; active year-round	G/P/B(southeast)	Meadows, pastures, gardens, ditches, lawns	Grass, garden vegetables and alfalfa			Although seldom seen, its dirt mounds are familiar
RODENTIA – Beaver							
American beaver *Castor canadensis*	Common resident; remains active all winter beneath the ice and in lodges	All	Lakes, marshes, slow-moving streams and rivers	Will girdle and/or cut down deciduous trees			Is found only where there are suitable water conditions
RODENTIA – Mice, Voles and Muskrat							
Deer mouse *Peromyscus maniculatus*	Very common resident; active year-round	All	Almost all habitats; may be common in urban areas		Sunflower seeds, food scraps	Occupies houses, old buildings; found sometimes in refuse; often attracted to yards with bird feeders, especially in winter	Essential prey for many species, particularly in winter; may carry hantavirus
House mouse *Mus musculus*	Introduced; very common	All (except extreme north and northwest)	Wherever there is human habitation; sometimes found in grasslands or on farmland	Wetland vegetation			Considered a pest species
Southern red-backed vole *Clethrionomys gapperi*	Resident; active year-round	G (except central and east)/P/B/F/R	Woodlands	Grains, herbaceous vegetation	Grain, sunflower seeds, nuts, fruit		
Meadow vole *Microtus pennsylvanicus*	Resident; active year-round	All	Fields, meadows, woodlands, grasslands	As for southern red-backed vole	As for southern red-backed vole		
Common muskrat *Ondatra zibethicus*	Common resident	All	Sloughs, lakes, ponds, marshes and streams	Wetland vegetation			
RODENTIA – Jumping Mice							
Meadow jumping mouse *Zapus hudsonius*	Quite common resident in suitable habitat; hibernates; nocturnal	P/B/F	Moist meadows				Likes to be near water; lives in northern half of province
Western jumping mouse *Zapus princeps*	As for meadow jumping mouse	G/P/B (south)/F/R	Moist meadows				Likes to be near water; lives in southern half of province
RODENTIA – Porcupines							
Common porcupine *Erethizon dorsatum*	Common resident; active year-round	All	Mixed forests, riparian areas, aspen parkland	Eats tree bark	Salt		May kill trees or ornamental plantings
CARNIVORA – Canids							
Coyote *Canis latrans*	Common resident, although population numbers vary	All	Wide range of habitats, from farmland and grassland to open woodlands	Mainly carnivorous but may eat insects, berries and vegetation		May den in protected bushy areas or cut-banks	Typically preys on smaller animals; in large urban centres, coyotes are usually found only along river valleys
Red fox *Vulpes vulpes*	Resident, increasing in numbers; may enter urban areas	All	Wide range of habitats, from farmland and grassland to boreal forest	Meat, carrion; also invertebrates, fruit, berries		May den in cut-banks, culverts or protected, bushy areas	Predator of ground-nesting birds and small mammals
CARNIVORA – Raccoons							
Common raccoon *Procyon lotor*	Unstable population; active year-round	G (southeastern part of province, but range is expanding)	Open, wooded areas associated with river and creek valleys, or ponds	Corn, berry-producing trees and shrubs	Nuts, berries, fresh corn, pet food, sunflower seeds, grains, eggs, honey	Nestbox	Appears to be spreading west and northward in Alberta
CARNIVORA – Mustelids							
Ermine *Mustela erminea*	Fairly common resident; active year-round	G (except southeast)/P/B/F/R	Wooded areas		Suet	Rock pile, brush pile, old building	
Long-tailed weasel *Mustela frenata*	As for ermine	G/P/B (south)/F/R	Grasslands, forests		Suet	As for ermine	
Least weasel *Mustela nivalis*	As for ermine	All	Variety of habitats		Suet	As for ermine	
American mink *Mustela vison*	As for ermine	All	Stream banks, lakeshores and forest edges; may visit yards in urban areas near suitable habitat		Suet	As for ermine	
American badger *Taxidea taxus*	Fairly common resident; hibernates	G/P/B (southeast)	Open habitats				
CARNIVORA – Skunks							
Striped skunk *Mephitis mephitis*	Common resident; hibernates	All	Forest edges, urban areas, farms	Will forage in lawns, fields and woods for insect larvae	Suet, sunflower seeds, nuts, fruit, table scraps	Building, wood pile	
ARTIODACTYLA – Cervids							
Mule deer *Odocoileus hemionus*	Common resident throughout most of Alberta	All	River valleys, coulees, mixedwood forests, brushy prairie, sageflats, sandhills	Will browse apple, poplar and birch, as well as alder, saskatoon and other species of shrubs	Sunflower seeds, canola, oats, alfalfa pellets, seeds, hay, apples, corn, salt licks/salt blocks		
White-tailed deer *Odocoileus virginianus*	Common resident in the south and in central areas	All (except extreme northeast)	Deciduous forests with open glades, farm shelterbelts, riparian forests, meadows, farmland	Will browse apple, poplar and birch, as well as alder and several other species of shrubs	Sunflower seeds, canola, oats, alfalfa pellets, hay, apples, piles of decaying leaves, corn, salt licks/salt blocks		
Moose *Alces alces*	Common resident in wooded areas	G (north, west and Cypress Hills)/P/B/F/R	Mixedwood forests, lakesides, bogs, streams	Will browse shrubs, young trees and aquatic vegetation			Will visit backyard water gardens!

APPENDIX 5
RESOURCE FILE

NATURESCAPE ALBERTA
Box 785, Red Deer, AB T4N 5H2
PHONE/FAX: (403) 347-8200
WEBSITE: www.naturescape.ab.ca

NATURESCAPE B.C.
Box 9354, Stn. Provincial Government,
Victoria, BC V8W 9M1
PHONE: 1-800-387-9853
WEBSITE: www.env.gov.bc/hctf/nature.htm

NATURESCAPE WEBSITES
There are hundreds of websites that deal with the many topics related to NatureScaping. Simply use a search engine to find sites related to your topic of interest. We have listed several sites here, and both the NatureScape Alberta and Naturescape B.C. websites list links to other sites. This Resource File will be maintained on the NatureScape Alberta website.

NATURESCAPING-RELATED COURSES
We will post up-to-date information on courses or workshops on the NatureScape Alberta website. The Ellis Bird Farm usually offers one or two summer workshops on topics related to NatureScaping (see Demonstration Wildlife Gardens, below). Contact your local nature centre, horticultural society, natural history organization, garden centre or wildlife store for information on courses and programs.

BOTANICAL GARDENS
Devonian Botanic Garden
University of Alberta
Edmonton, AB T6G 2E1
PHONE: (780) 987-3054; FAX: (780) 987-4141
E-MAIL: idymock@gpu.srv.ualberta.ca
WEBSITE: www.discoveredmonton.com/devonian

DEMONSTRATION WILDLIFE GARDENS
Devonian Botanic Garden
University of Alberta
Edmonton, AB T6G 2E1
PHONE: (780) 987-3054; FAX: (780) 987-4141
E-MAIL: idymock@gpu.srv.ualberta.ca
WEBSITE: www.discoveredmonton.com/devonian

Ellis Bird Farm Ltd.
Box 5090, Lacombe, AB T4L 1W7
PHONE/FAX: (403) 346-2211
WEBSITE: www.ellisbirdfarm.ab.ca

HORTICULTURAL SOCIETIES AND NURSERY TRADES ASSOCIATIONS

Alberta Horticultural Association (AHA) and Affiliates
c/o Marilyn McArthur, RR 3,
Red Deer, AB T4N 5E3
PHONE/FAX: (403) 346-4902
For a list of Alberta Horticultural Societies, contact AHA.

Landscape Alberta Nursery Trades Association
2nd Fl., 10215-176 St.,
Edmonton, AB T5S 1M1
PHONE: (780) 489-1991; FAX: (780) 444-2152
E-MAIL: lanta@planet.eon.net
WEBSITE: www.canadiannursery.com

ORGANIC GARDENING/HERITAGE SEED PRESERVATION

The Garden Institute
1406, 5325 Calgary Trail,
Edmonton, AB T6H 4J8
PHONE: (780) 461-9958; FAX: (780) 469-6314
E-MAIL: slrempel@freenet.edmonton.ab.ca
WEBSITE: www.mkids.com/Garden/

Seeds of Diversity
Box 36, Station Q, Toronto, ON M4T 2L7
PHONE: (905) 623-0353
E-MAIL: mail@seeds.ca
WEBSITE: www.seeds.ca

NATURESCAPED SCHOOL GROUNDS

Edmonton Area
Devonian Botanic Garden
University of Alberta, Edmonton, AB T6G 2E1
PHONE: (780) 987-3054; FAX: (780) 987-4141
E-MAIL: idymock@gpu.srv.ualberta.ca
WEBSITE: www.discoveredmonton.com/devonian

Calgary Area
Schoolyard Naturalization Coordinator,
Calgary Zoo
Box 3036, Station B, Calgary, AB T2M 4R8
PHONE: (403) 232-9335; FAX: (403) 261-9091

Red Deer Area
Outdoor Classroom Coordinator, Joseph Welsh Elementary School
4401-37 Ave., Red Deer, AB T4N 2T5
PHONE: (403) 346-6377; FAX: (403) 346-5187

British Columbia
Greening Schoolgrounds
1836 McNicoll Ave., Vancouver, BC V6J 1A4
PHONE: (604) 264-1026; FAX: (604) 264-1087
E-MAIL: lgeorge@telus.net
WEBSITE: www.greengrounds.org

National
The Evergreen Foundation
Suite 5A, 355 Adelaide St. West,
Toronto, ON M5V 1S2
PHONE: (416) 596-1495; FAX: (416) 596-1443
WEBSITE: www.evergreen.ca

NATIVE PLANT AND SEED SOURCES

For an up-dated, yearly list, contact the Alberta Native Plant Council (see information below). For a list of Alberta native plant and seed sources on the internet, check with the Alberta Native Plant Council (see below) or the Evergreen Foundation (see above under NATURESCAPED SCHOOL GROUNDS).

Alberta Native Plant Council
Box 52099, Edmonton, AB T6G 2T5
PHONE: (780) 427-5209; FAX: (780) 427-5980
E-MAIL: ksanders@sandnarrows.com
WEBSITE: www.anpc.ab.ca

Alberta Nurseries & Seeds Ltd.
Box 20, Bowden, AB T0M 0K0
PHONE: (403) 224-3545; FAX: (403) 224-2455
E-MAIL: dectod@telusplanet.net
WEBSITE: www.marketland.net

ALCLA Native Plant Restoration Inc.
3208 Bearspaw Dr. NW,
Calgary, AB T2L 1T2
PHONE: (403) 282-6516; FAX: (403) 282-7090
E-MAIL: fedkenhp@cadvision.com

Aquatic Enterprises
1404 Meadow Brook Dr., Airdrie, AB T4A 2B3
PHONE: (403) 948-3412; FAX: (403) 948-3378
WEBSITE: www.aquaticent.ab.ca

Bearberry Creek Greenhouses, Nursery and Watergardens
RR 2, Sundre, AB T0M 1X0
PHONE: (403) 638-4231; FAX: (403) 638-4793

Bedrock Seed Bank
Box 54044, Forest Heights Station,
Edmonton, AB T6A 3Y7
PHONE/FAX: (780) 448-1722
E-MAIL: bedrock@theoffice.net
WEBSITE: www.bedrockseedbank.com

Blooming Prairie
9535-76 Ave., Edmonton, AB T6C 0K1
PHONE: (780) 431-1451; FAX: (780) 433-6440
E-MAIL: blooming@oanet.com

Borealis Botanicals
Box 91, Cochrane, AB T0L 0W0
PHONE: (403) 932-2583; Fax (403) 932-2538
E-MAIL: borealis@cadvision.com
WEBSITE: www.cadvision.com/borealis

Bow Point Nursery
Box 16, Site 3, RR 12, Calgary, AB T3E 6W3
PHONE: (403) 686-4434; FAX: (403) 242-8018
E-MAIL: bowpoint@agt.net

Calgary Zoological Society
Box 3036, Station B, Calgary, AB T2M 4R8
PHONE: (403) 232-9300; FAX: (403) 237-7582
WEBSITE: www.calgaryzoo.ab.ca

Cheyenne Tree Farms
Box 69008, Kensington Post Office,
Edmonton, AB T6V 1G7
PHONE: (780) 456-2464; FAX: (780) 456-4707
E-MAIL: cheyennetf@aol.com

Coaldale Nurseries
Box 1267, Coaldale, AB T1M 1N1
PHONE: (403) 345-4633; FAX: (403) 345-2866

(The) Conservancy
51563, Range Road 212A,
Sherwood Park, AB T8G 1B1
FAX: (780) 922-4355
E-MAIL: gardenshoppe@compuserve.com

Coyote Coulee Seeds
RR 2, Cessford, AB T1R 1E2
PHONE: (403) 566-2485

Devonian Botanic Garden
The Friends of the Garden, University of Alberta, Edmonton, AB T6G 2E1
PHONE: (780) 987-3054; FAX: (780) 987-4141
E-MAIL: idymock@gpu.srv.ualberta.ca
WEBSITE: www.discoveredmonton.com/devonian

Dynamic Seeds Ltd.
Box 813, Fairview, AB T0H 1L0
PHONE: (780) 835-5435; FAX: (780) 835-3064
E-MAIL: dsl@telusplanet.net

Eagle Lake Nurseries Ltd.
Box 2340, Strathmore, AB T1P 1K3
PHONE: (403) 934-3622; FAX: (403) 934-3626
E-MAIL: eglake@telusplanet.net

Eastern Slopes Rangeland Seeds Ltd.
Box 273, Cremona, AB T0M 0R0
PHONE: (403) 637-2473; FAX: (403) 637-2724

Eve's Leaves
9850-154 St., Edmonton, AB T5P 2G6
PHONE: (780) 489-0919; FAX: (780) 483-5886
E-MAIL: eve@inversionmixers.com

Enviroscapes
Box 38, Warner, AB T0K 2L0
PHONE: (403) 733-2160; FAX: (403) 733-2161
E-MAIL: enscapes@telusplanet.net

Foothills Nurseries *(wholesale)*
2626-48 St. SE, Calgary, AB T2B 1M4
PHONE: (403) 203-3338; FAX: (403) 248-6305
E-MAIL: fhnurser@telusplanet.net

Four Seasons Nursery
Box 638, 5122-50 St., Barrhead, AB T0G 0E0
PHONE/FAX: (780) 674-2693

Greenview Nurseries
Box 12, Site 16, RR 7, Calgary, AB T2P 4G7
PHONE: (403) 936-5936; FAX: (403) 936-5981

Grumpy's Greenhouses and Gardens
Box 2488, Pincher Creek, AB T0K 1W0
PHONE: (403) 627-4589; FAX: (403) 627-2909
E-MAIL: grumpys@telusplanet.net

Hanna's Seeds
Box 849, Lacombe, AB T0C 1S0
PHONE: 1-800-661-1529 or (403) 782-6671;
FAX: (403) 782-6503
WEBSITE: www.hannaseeds.com

Hillson Nursery *(wholesale)*
Box 39, Rochester, AB T0G 1Z0
PHONE/FAX: (780) 698-3956

K & C Silviculture
Box 25019, Red Deer, AB T4R 2M2
PHONE: (403) 347-3002; FAX: (403) 347-3899
E-MAIL: kcss@agt.net
WEBSITE: www.silviculture.com

Knutson & Shaw Growers
Box 295, Vulcan, AB T0L 2B0
PHONE: (403) 485-6321; (403) 485-6323
E-MAIL: knshaw@telusplanet.net

Northern Vigor Seeds Ltd. (*wholesale*)
8002 Mission Heights Dr., Grande Prairie, AB T8W 1Y9
PHONE/FAX: (780) 532-1344
E-MAIL: roskac@telusplanet.net

Parkland Nurseries
RR 2, Red Deer, AB T4N 5E2
PHONE: (403) 346-5613; FAX: (403) 346-4443
E-MAIL: parklandgc@cnnet.com

Pickseed
Box 3230, Sherwood Park, AB T8A 2A6
PHONE: 1-800-265-3925 or (780) 464-0350
E-MAIL: pickseed@telusplanet.net
WEBSITE: www.pickseed.com

Prairie Fire Resources
Box 607, Crossfield, AB T0M 0S0
PHONE: (403) 946-4115; FAX: (403) 226-0218
E-MAIL: nativeplants@prairiefire-resources.com
WEBSITE: www.prairiefire-resources.com

Prairie Seeds Inc.
1805-8 St., Nisku, AB T9E 7S8
PHONE: 1-800-222-6443 or (780) 955-7345;
FAX: (780) 955-7718
WEBSITE: www.prairieseeds.com

(The) Professional Gardener Company Ltd. *(wholesale)*
915-23 Ave. SE, Calgary, AB T2G 1P1
PHONE: (403) 263-4200; FAX: (403) 273-0029
E-MAIL: progar@telusplanet.net

Rangeland Seeds Ltd.
Box 928, Vulcan, AB T0L 2B0
PHONE: (403) 485-6448

Seaborn Seeds
Box 298, Rocky Mountain House, AB T0M IT0
PHONE: (403) 729-2267; FAX: (403) 729-3428

Springbank Wild Flowers
PHONE: (403) 288-3661; FAX: (403) 288-6343
WEBSITE: www.springbankwildflowers.com

Sunstar Nurseries
810-167 Ave. NE, RR 6, Site 6, Box 17,
Edmonton, AB T5B 4K3
PHONE: (780) 472-6103; FAX: (780) 472-9218
E-MAIL: sunstar@netcom.ca

Vale's Greenhouses
3rd Ave. and 3rd St. NW, Box 186,
Black Diamond, AB T0L 0H0
PHONE: (403) 933-4814

Wild Rose Consulting Ltd.
15109-77 Ave., Edmonton, AB TSR 3B5
PHONE: (780) 413-9280; FAX: (780) 413-9281
E-MAIL:wildrose.consulting@powersurfr.com

ENVIRONMENTAL/CONSERVATION ORGANIZATIONS (CANADA)

Canadian Environmental Law Association (CELA)
Suite 401, 517 College St.,
Toronto, ON M6G 4AZ
PHONE: (416) 960-2284; FAX: (416) 960-9392
E-MAIL: cela@web.net
WEBSITE: www.web.net.cela

Canadian Nature Federation (CNF)
Suite 606, 1 Nicholas St., Ottawa, ON K1N 7B7
PHONE: 1-800-267-4088 or (613) 562-3447
FAX: (613) 562-3371; E-MAIL: cnf@cnf.ca
WEBSITE: www.cnf.ca

Canadian Wildflower Society
43 Anaconda, Scarborough, ON MIL 4M1
PHONE: (416) 261-6227

Canadian Wildlife Federation (CWF)
2740 Queensview Drive, Ottawa, ON K2B 1A2
PHONE: 1-800-563-WILD or (613) 721-2286;
FAX: (613) 721-2902
E-MAIL: info@cwf-fcf.org
WEBSITE: www.cwf-fcf.org

Earth Day Canada
Suite 250, 144 Front Street West,
Toronto, ON M5J 2L7
PHONE: (416) 599-1991; Fax (416) 599-3100
E-MAIL: earthday@istar.ca
WEBSITE: www.earthday.ca

(The) Evergreen Foundation
Suite 5A, 355 Adelaide St. West,
Toronto, ON M5V 1S2
PHONE: (416) 596-1495; FAX: (416) 596-1443
WEBSITE: www.evergreen.ca

North American Native Plant Society
90 Wolfrey Ave, Toronto, ON M4K 1K8
PHONE/FAX: (416) 466-6428
E-MAIL: jheditor@idirect.ca

Sierra Club of Canada
412, 1 Nicholas St., Ottawa, ON KIN 7B7
PHONE: (613) 214-4611; FAX: (613) 241-2292
E-MAIL: sierra@web.net

World Wildlife Fund Canada (WWF)
Suite 504, 90 Eglinton Ave. E.,
Toronto, ON M4P 2Z7
PHONE: 1-800-267-2632
WEBSITE: www.wwfcanada.org

ENVIRONMENTAL/CONSERVATION ORGANIZATIONS (ALBERTA)

Alberta Conservation Association
14515-122 Ave., Edmonton, AB T5L 2W4
PHONE: 1-877-969-9091 or (780) 415-1334;
FAX: (780) 427-5695
E-MAIL: edmfish@env.gov.ab.ca

Alberta Fish and Game Association
6924-104 St., Edmonton, AB T6H 2L7
PHONE: (780) 437-2342; FAX: (780) 438-6872
E-MAIL: office@afga.org
Web site: www.afga.org

Alberta Lake Management Society
c/o CW-405 Biological Sciences Building,
University of Alberta, Edmonton, AB T6G 2E9
PHONE: (780) 492-1294; FAX: (780) 492-9234
E-MAIL: mark.serediak@ualberta.ca
WEBSITE: www.biology.ualberta.ca/alms

Alberta Native Plant Council
Box 52099, Edmonton, AB T6G 2T5
PHONE: (780) 427-5209; FAX: (780) 427-5980
E-MAIL: ksanders@sandnarrows.com
WEBSITE: www.anpc.ab.ca

Destination Conservation
10511 Saskatchewan Dr.,
Edmonton, AB T6E 4S1
PHONE: (780) 433-8711; FAX: (780) 439-5081
E-MAIL: info@dc.ab.ca
WEBSITE: www.dc.ab.ca

Ducks Unlimited Canada - Alberta
200, 10720-178 St., Edmonton, AB T5S 1J3
PHONE: (780) 489-2002; FAX: (780) 489-1856
E-MAIL: du_edmonton@ducks.ca
WEBSITE: www.ducks.ca

Ellis Bird Farm Ltd.
Box 5090, Lacombe, AB T4L 1W7
PHONE/FAX: (403) 346-2211
WEBSITE: www.ellisbirdfarm.ab.ca

Federation of Alberta Naturalists
Box 1472, Edmonton, AB T5J 2N5
PHONE: (780) 427-8124; FAX: (780) 422-2663
E-MAIL: fan@connect.ab.ca
WEBSITE: www.connect.ab.ca/~fan

Global, Environmental and Outdoor Education Council, Alberta Teachers Association
11010-142 St., Edmonton, AB T5N 2R1
PHONE/FAX: (780) 678-0071
E-MAIL: geoec@agt.net
WEBSITE: www.rockies.ca/eoec

Land Stewardship Centre of Canada
17503-45 Ave. (Imrie House)
Edmonton, AB T6M 2N3
PHONE: (780) 483-1885; FAX: (780) 486-9599
E-MAIL: Lsc@compusmart.ab.ca
WEBSITE: www.Landstewardship.org

SEEDS Foundation
Suite 202, 25 St. Michael St.,
St. Albert, AB T8N 1C7
E-MAIL: seeds@telusplanet.net
WEBSITE: http://greenschools.ca/seeds

REGIONAL ALBERTA NATURAL HISTORY ORGANIZATIONS

Bow Valley Naturalists
Box 1693, Banff, AB T0L 0C0

Buffalo Lake Naturalists
Box 1802, Stettler, AB T0C 2L0

Calgary Field Naturalists' Society
Box 981, Station M, Calgary, AB T2P 2K4

Edmonton Bird Club
Box 1111, Edmonton, AB T5J 2M1

Edmonton Natural History Club
Box 1582, Edmonton, AB T5J 2N9

Ft. McMurray Field Naturalists' Society
152 Cote Bay, Ft. McMurray, AB T9H 4R9

Grasslands Naturalists
Box 2491, Medicine Hat, AB T1A 8G8

Lethbridge Naturalists' Society
Box 1691, Station Main, Lethbridge, AB T1J 4K4

Peace Parkland Naturalists
Box 1451, Grande Prairie, AB T8V 4Z2

Red Deer River Naturalists
Box 785, Red Deer, AB T4N 5H2

Vermilion River Naturalists
6510-53 Ave. Vermilion, AB T9K 1X7

BIRD CONSERVATION

American Birding Association, Inc. (ABA)
Box 6599, Colorado Springs, Colorado USA 80934-6599
PHONE: (719) 578-1614; FAX: (719) 578-1480
WEBSITE: www.americanbirding.org

American Bird Conservancy (ABC)
Suite 400, 1250-24th St. NW, Washington, DC USA 20037
PHONE: (202) 778-9619; FAX: (202) 778-9778
WEBSITE: www.abcbirds.org

Fatal Light Awareness Program (FLAP)
Suite 0116-207, 65 Front Street West,
Toronto, ON M5J 1E6
PHONE: (905) 831-FLAP
WEBSITE: www.flap.org

North American Bluebird Society (NABS)
Box 74, Darlington,
Wisconsin, USA 53530-0074
PHONE: (608) 329-6403; FAX: (608) 329-7057
WEBSITE: www.nabluebirdsociety.org

Purple Martin Conservancy (PMC)
24 Willow Lee Estates,
Mulhurst Bay, AB T0C 2C0
PHONE/FAX: (780) 389-2220
E-MAIL: dmckinon@telusplanet.net

Purple Martin Conservation Association (PMCA)
Edinboro University of Pennsylvania,
Edinboro, Pennsylvania USA 16444
PHONE: (814) 734-4420; FAX: (814) 734-5803
WEBSITE: www.edinboro.edu/~jhill/pmca/pmca.html

BAT CONSERVATION

Bat Conservation International (BCI)
Box 162603, Austin, Texas USA 78716-2603
PHONE: (512) 327-9721; FAX: (512) 327-9724
E-MAIL: members@batcon.org
WEBSITE: www.batcon.org

Bat Conservation Society of Canada (BCSC)
Box 56042, Airways Postal Outlet,
Calgary, AB T2E 8K5
VOICE MAIL: (403) 860-BATS
E-MAIL: BCSC@BatsCanada.org
WEBSITE: www.batscanada.org

NATURE CENTRES

Alberta Birds of Prey Centre
Box 1150, Coaldale, AB T1M 1M9
PHONE: (403) 345-4262; FAX: (403) 345-6668
WEBSITE: www.AlbertaBirds.com

Beaverhill Lake Nature Centre
Box 30, Tofield, AB T0B 2J0
PHONE: (780) 662-3191; FAX: (780) 662-3929

Bud Miller All Seasons Park Centre
c/o City of Lloydminster, 5011-49 Ave.,
Lloydminster, SK S9V 0Y8
PHONE: (780) 875-4497; FAX: (780) 875-4495

Fish Creek Environmental Learning Centre
13931 Woodpath Road SW,
Calgary, AB T2W 5R6
PHONE: (403) 297-7827; FAX: (403) 297-7849
WEBSITE: www.gov.ab.ca/env/parks/prov_parks/fishcreek

Helen Schuler Coulee Centre
910-4 Ave. S, Lethbridge, AB TIJ 0P6
PHONE: (403) 320-3064; FAX: (403) 320-4275
E-MAIL: hscc@city.lethbridge.ab.ca

Inglewood Bird Sanctuary
c/o Calgary Parks and Recreation, Box 2100,
Station M, Calgary, AB T2P 2M5
PHONE: (403) 269-6688; FAX: (403) 221-3775
WEBSITE: www.gov.calgary.ab.ca

John Janzen Nature Centre
Box 2359, Edmonton, AB T5J 2R7
PHONE: (780) 496-2939; FAX: (780) 496-4701
WEBSITE: www.gov.edmonton.ab.ca/parkrec/

Kerry Wood Nature Centre
6300-45 Ave., Red Deer, AB T4N 5H2
PHONE: (403) 346-2010; FAX: (403) 347-2550
E-MAIL: kwnc@telusplanet.net
WEBSITE: www.city.red-deer.ab.ca/kerry/index.html

Muskoseepi Park Pavilion
c/o City of Grande Prairie, Bag 4000
Grande Prairie, AB T8V 6V3
PHONE: (780) 539-0451; FAX: (780) 539-5229
E-MAIL: lgogal@city.grande-prairie.ab.ca

Police Point Intrepretive Centre
Box 2491, Medicine Hat, AB T1A 8G8
PHONE: (403) 529-6225; FAX: (403) 526-6408

Strathcona Wilderness Centre
Strathcona Recreation, Parks and Culture,
2025 Oak St., Sherwood Park, AB T8A 0W9
PHONE: (780) 922-3939; FAX: (780) 922-6415

WILDLIFE REHABILITATION CENTRES

Alberta Birds of Prey Centre
(only for birds of prey but see page 181 [wholesale] under Foothills Nurseries)
Box 1150, Coaldale, AB TIM 1M9
PHONE: (403) 345-4262; FAX: (403) 345-6668
WEBSITE: www.AlbertaBirds.com

Alberta Society for Injured Birds of Prey *(Strathcona Raptor Centre)*
51562 Range Road 222,
Sherwood Park, AB T8C 1H4
PHONE: (780) 922-3024; FAX: (780) 922-2084
E-MAIL: asibp@freenet.edmonton.ab.ca

Calgary Wildlife Rehabilitation Society
Box 152, Suite 234, 5149 Country Hills
Blvd. NW, Calgary, AB T3A 5K8
PHONE: (403) 239-2488; FAX: (403) 241-1961

Cochrane Ecological Institute - Cochrane Wildlife Reserve
Box 484, Cochrane, AB T0L 0W0
PHONE: (403) 932-5632; FAX: (403) 932-6303
E-MAIL: cei@cadvision.com
WEBSITE: www.ceinst.org

Kestrel Wildlife Care Centre
22556 Township Road 511,
Sherwood Park, AB T8C 1H1
PHONE: (780) 464-5445; FAX: (780) 449-3632

Medicine River Wildlife Rehabilitation Centre
Box 115, Spruce View, AB T0M 1V0
PHONE: (403) 346-WILD; FAX: (403) 728-3782
E-MAIL: mrwrc@telusplanet.net
WEBSITE: www.telusplanet.net/public/mrwrc

Rocky View Wildlife Recovery Centre
Box 68, Madden, AB T0M 1L0
PHONE: (403) 946-2361; FAX: (403) 946-5689

Wildlife Rehabilitation Society of Edmonton
Box 66065, Heritage Postal Outlet, Edmonton,
AB T6J 6T4
PHONE: (780) 433-0884; HOTLINE: (780) 914-4118

FEDERAL WILDLIFE AGENCIES

Canadian Wildlife Service (CWS)
Environment Canada
200, 4999-98 Ave, Edmonton, AB T6B 2X3
PHONE: (780) 951-8686; FAX: (780) 495-2615
GENERAL WEBSITE: www.cws-scf.ec.gc.ca/cwshom_e.html
PROGRAMS WEBSITE: www.mb.ec.gc.ca/ENGLISH/LIFE/MIGBIRDS/birders.html

PROVINCIAL WILDLIFE AGENCIES

For information, contact

Alberta Environment Information Centre
9920-108 St., Edmonton, AB T5K 2M4
PHONE: (780) 944-0313 (within Alberta, use RITE LINE: 310-0000); FAX: (780) 427-4407
E-MAIL: env.infocent@gov.ab.ca
WEBSITE: www.gov.ab.ca/env/info/infocentre

Alberta Environment (formerly Alberta Environmental Protection), Natural Resources Service (by Region)
For toll-free access (within Alberta) to these offices, first call the RITE LINE: 310-0000. Regional offices are marked with an asterisk; district offices follow.

Northwest Boreal Region
*Peace River 624-6405; Fairview 835-2737; Fort Vermilion 927-4488; Grande Prairie 538-5265; High Level 926-2238; High Prairie 523-6520; Manning 836-3065; Peace River 624-6439; Red Earth 649-3853; Slave Lake 849-7110; Spirit River 864-4101; Valleyview 524-3605

Northeast Boreal Region
*St. Paul 645-6313; Athabasca 675-2419; Bonnyville 826-3142; Cold Lake 639-3377; Edmonton 427-3574; Fort Chipewyan (8:15-noon; Tues.-Thurs.) 697-3511; Fort McMurray 743-7200; Lac La Biche 623-5247; Smoky Lake 656-3556

Northern East Slopes Region
*Edson 723-8244; Barrhead 674-8236; Evansburg 727-3635; Fox Creek 622-3421; Grande Cache 827-3356; Hinton 865-8264; Stony Plain 963-6131; Swan Hills 333-2229; Whitecourt 778-7112

Bow Region

*Canmore 678-2373; Bow 678-5508; Brooks 362-1232; Calgary 297-6423; Cochrane 932-2388; Coronation 578-3224; Drumheller 823-1670; Elbow (8:15-noon) 949-3749; Ghost 673-3663; Hanna 854-5540; High River 652-8320; Kananaskis (1:00-4:30) 591-6300; Oyen (1:00-4:30) 664-3614; Strathmore 934-3422

Parkland Region

*Rocky Mountain House 845-8230; Camrose 679-1225; Drayton Valley 542-6767; Leduc 361-1250; Lloydminster 871-6495; Nordegg (8:15-noon) 721-3965; Olds 556-4215; Ponoka 783-7093; Provost (1:00-4:30) 753-2433; Red Deer 340-5142; Stettler 742-7510; Sundre 638-3805; Vegreville 632-5410; Vermilion 853-8137; Wetaskiwin 361-1250

Prairie Region

*Lethbridge 381-5281; Blairmore 562-3289; Cardston 653-4331; Claresholm 625-1450; Foremost (1:00-4:30) 867-3826; Lethbridge 381-5266; Medicine Hat 529-3680; Pincher Creek 627-1142; Vulcan 485-6971

PROVINCIAL MUSEUM

Provincial Museum of Alberta

12845-102 Ave., Edmonton, AB T5N 0M6
PHONE: (780) 453-9100 (within Alberta, use RITE LINE); FAX: (780) 454-6629
WEBSITE: www.pma.edmonton.ab.ca

VOLUNTEER OPPORTUNITIES—INSECTS AND WORMS

Butterfly Counts

During the months of June and July, one-day counts of Alberta butterflies are conducted. These counts, which are part of the North American Butterfly Association (NABA) Butterfly Counts, enable naturalists to collect important baseline data on butterfly species distribution in the province. Novices can participate in butterfly counts, as long as they join up with someone who is competent at identifying butterflies. To participate in an established count, contact your local naturalist group or check the NABA website, below.

To start a new count, CONTACT: ***Barb Beck***, 10947-36 Ave. Edmonton, AB T6J OB9
E-MAIL: Barb.Beck@ualberta.ca
WEBSITE: http://owlnut.rr.ualberta.ca/~barb/butterfly.html *OR* http://owlnut.rr.ualberta.ca/~barb/bugs.html

Specific details on count rules can be obtained from the North American Butterfly Association.

CONTACT: ***North American Butterfly Association***, 4 Delaware Road, Morristown, NJ USA 07960
PHONE: (973) 285-0907; FAX: (973) 285-0936
WEBSITE: www.naba.org

Canadian Lady Beetle Survey

Sponsored by the Canadian Nature Federation, the Lady Beetle Survey is part of a program called EPIC (Endangered Plants and Invertebrates in Canada). More than 170 species of lady beetles have been introduced into Canada, and there is concern that these introduced species may be crowding out native species by out-competing them for food and habitat. To help determine the characteristics of lady beetle populations, volunteers are asked to survey lady beetles in their yards or neighbourhoods and submit the information on reporting cards.

CONTACT: ***Canadian Nature Federation*** (see address and website above under Environmental/ Conservation Organizations [Canada])

Coast-to-Coast Moth and Butterfly Survey

Sponsored by the Canadian Wildlife Federation, this survey monitors moth and butterfly numbers and distributions.

CONTACT: ***Canadian Wildlife Federation*** (see address and website above under Environmental/ Conservation Organizations [Canada])

Worm Watch Canada

This program will help scientists understand the value of earthworms as indicators of soil quality. Volunteers receive a Worm Watch kit containing sampling instructions and handbook, taxonomic key and reference lists.

CONTACT: ***Worm Watch***, c/o Agriculture and Agri-Food Canada, Lethbridge Research Station, Box 3000, Lethbridge, AB TIJ 4B1
PHONE: (403) 317-2294; FAX: (403) 317-2187
E-MAIL: wormwatch@em.agr.ca
WEBSITE: www.cciw.ca/ecowatch/wormwatch/intro.html
For information on Worm Watch Workshops, CONTACT: ***The Alberta Science Foundation***.
PHONE: (403) 260-1996; FAX: (403) 260-1165.

VOLUNTEER OPPORTUNITIES—AMPHIBIANS

Alberta Amphibian Monitoring Program

The Alberta Amphibian Monitoring Program (AAMP) was initiated because of a need for information on long-term population trends and current distributions of amphibians in Alberta. There are two parts to this program—volunteer data collection and intensive, site-based monitoring. If you participate in the AAMP, you receive a free monitoring manual containing information on the identification, ecology and natural history of Alberta's amphibians. Included with the manual is a cassette tape of amphibian calls and a copy of *Croaks and Trills*, AAMP's newsletter.

CONTACT: ***Alberta Amphibian Monitoring Program***, Alberta Conservation Association/ Natural Resources Service, Alberta Environment, 7th Floor, O.S. Longman Building, 6909-116 St., Edmonton, AB T6H 4P2.
PHONE: Lisa Takats at (780) 427-1249 or Bruce Treichel at (780) 422-9535 (within Alberta, use RITE LINE)
WEBSITE: www.gov.ab.ca/~env/nrs/wildlife/amphib/

VOLUNTEER OPPORTUNITIES—REPTILES

Alberta Snake Hibernaculum Inventory

If you know the location of a snake hibernaculum, please contact the Alberta Conservation Association.

CONTACT: ***Snake Hibernaculum Inventory*** Alberta Conservation Association/Natural Resources Service, Alberta Environment 7th Floor, O.S. Longman Building, 6909-116 St., Edmonton, AB T6H 4P2.
PHONE: Lisa Takats at (780) 427-1249 or Bruce Treichel at (780) 422-9535 (within Alberta, use RITE LINE)

VOLUNTEER OPPORTUNITIES—SPRING WILDLIFE

International Dawn Chorus Day

This international event celebrates the arrival of spring. Festivities are held on the first Monday of May each year. Started by the U.K. Wildlife Trust, it is gaining popularity around the world.

CONTACT: ***U.K. Wildlife Trust***
WEBSITE: www.wildlifetrust.org.uk/urb/anwt/

May Species Count

The purpose of the May Species Count is to identify birds in spring migration, and to document species diversity and abundance of mammals and flowering plants in the spring. The count is always held the last weekend in May.

CONTACT: ***Federation of Alberta Naturalists***, your local ***naturalist group*** or local ***nature centre*** (all addresses above).

VOLUNTEER OPPORTUNITIES—LAKES

Living by Water Project

The Living By Water Project is a special project of a cross-country partnership of conservation organizations. The group is producing educational materials, including brochures, a list of children's activities, and a guidebook, to help waterfront property owners maximize their enjoyment of their land while maintaining the health and integrity of shoreline and lake/river habitats.

CONTACT: ***Living by Water Project***
Sarah Kipp or Clive Callaway, Box 7, Salmon Arm, BC V1E 4N2
PHONE: (250) 832-7405; FAX: (250) 832-6874
E-MAIL: lbywater@jetstream.net.
Or, ***Federation of Alberta Naturalists*** (see Environmental/Conservation Organizations [Alberta])

VOLUNTEER OPPORTUNITIES—BIRDS

Bird Banding

Beaverhill Bird Observatory
Box 1418, Edmonton, AB T5N 2N5
WEBSITE: www.ualberta.ca/~jduxbury/BBO/bbopage.htm

Lesser Slave Lake Bird Observatory
Box 1076, Slave Lake, AB T0G 2A0
PHONE: (780) 849-6585 (Steve Lane - home)
E-MAIL: LSLBO@telusplanet.net

Calgary Bird Banding Society
3426 Lane Cres. SW, Calgary, AB T3E 5X2
PHONE/FAX: (403) 240-2697 (Doug Collister - home)
E-MAIL: collis@telusplanet.net

Bird Counts

Baillie Bird-a-thon
The oldest sponsored bird count in North America, the Baillie Bird-a-thon is held during the month of May and consists of count volunteers attempting to find as many bird species as possible during a 24-hour period. The volunteers raise money by being sponsored at a flat rate, or on a per-species basis. One can support this program by either participating or by sponsoring participants.

CONTACT: ***Bird Studies Canada***
PHONE: 1-888-448-BIRD
E-MAIL: generalinfo@bsc-eoc.org
WEBSITE: www.bsc-eoc.org/brdathon.html

Birdhouse On-line
This program, sponsored by the Cornell Lab of Ornithology, provides volunteers with the opportunity to record the activities in their nestboxes during the nesting season.

CONTACT: ***BirdHouse Online***
WEBSITE: http://birdsource.cornell.edu/birdhouse/

Breeding Bird Survey
The purpose of the Breeding Bird Survey (BBS) is to measure long-term trends in bird populations across North America. The BBS entails recording all birds seen and heard at 50 stops located at 0.8-km (0.5-mi.) intervals along an assigned route each year. The survey begins one half hour prior to sunrise and is conducted according to a set protocol. One survey per route is done per year, usually during June. To participate in a BBS, you need to have the ability to identify birds by song as well as by sight. If you are less experienced but would like to participate, you can go along with a more experienced birder and act as the recorder.

CONTACT: ***Breeding Bird Survey***
c/o Jack Park, 10236-70 St. Edmonton, AB T6A 2T4
PHONE: (780) 469-8127
E-MAIL: jlpark@oanet.com.
WEBSITE: www.cws.scf.ec.gc.ca/owrc/bbs.htm

Christmas Bird Count
A Christmas Bird Count (CBC) is a survey of birds present in a given area on one calendar day during the Christmas period. Volunteer birdwatchers survey an area that is usually a circle with a 12 km radius centred on a fixed geographic point. CBCs provide both passive and active recreational opportunities for participants. "Feeder watchers" record birds at their backyard bird feeders, whereas "bush beaters" spend the day driving roads and hiking through alleyways, parks and coulees, in all kinds of weather.

CONTACT: ***Federation of Alberta Naturalists*** (see Environmental/Conservation Organizations [Alberta]) or your local ***naturalist organization*** (see Regional Alberta Natural History Organizations).

The Great Backyard Bird Count
This count is a continent-wide survey sponsored by the Cornell Lab of Ornithology that takes place for four days in February. Participants can log their observations on-line.

CONTACT: ***The Great Backyard Bird Count***
WEBSITE: http://birdsource.cornell.edu.

Prairie Nest Record Scheme
The aim of this program is to promote the collection and analysis of nesting-related data. Volunteers report data on any bird nests using a nest record card. Nests visited more than once are the most valuable.

CONTACT: ***Prairie Nest Record Scheme***
Canadian Wildlife Service, Environment Canada, Suite 200, 4999-98 Ave., Edmonton, AB T6B 2X3
PHONE: Brenda Dale, Songbird Biologist, at (780) 951-8686 (collect)
E-MAIL: brenda.dale@ec.gc.ca

Project FeederWatch
Project FeederWatch began in 1987 as a winter survey of the birds that visit backyard feeders in North America. The information collected each year helps ornithologists track changes in the abundance and distribution of bird species that use feeders in the winter.

CONTACT: ***Project FeederWatch***
c/o Bird Studies Canada, Box 160
Port Rowan, ON N0E 1M0
PHONE: (519) 586-3531; FAX: (519) 586-3532
E-MAIL: pfw@nornet.on.ca
WEBSITE: www.bsc-eoc.org/pfw.html

Volunteer Nocturnal Owl Surveys
Using various techniques, volunteers and biologists locate and census owls during the months of March and April.

CONTACT: ***Nocturnal Owl Surveys***
c/o Lisa Takats, Beaverhill Bird Observatory, 7th floor, O.S. Longman Building, 6909-116 St., Edmonton, AB T6H 4P2
PHONE: (780) 422-9536 (within Alberta, use RITE LINE)

Other

Adopt-a-Box Program
Sponsored by the ***North American Bluebird Society***, this program enables individuals to "adopt" a nestbox for bluebirds, swallows or chickadees.

CONTACT: ***North American Bluebird Society*** (see Bird Conservation)

Birdquest
Sponsored by the Canadian Nature Federation (CNF), this is an educational program designed to introduce participants to the fascinating world of Canadian birds. BIRDQUEST kits cost $49.95 each. Note: CNF also has other educational programs related to wildlife conservation.

CONTACT: ***Birdquest***
Canadian Nature Federation, Suite 606, 1 Nicholas St., Ottawa, ON KIN 6Z4
PHONE: 1-800-267-4088
WEBSITE: www.cnf.ca/ed_bquest.html

Checklist Program
The aim of the Alberta checklist program is to document bird abundance and breeding status throughout Alberta and the Northwest Territories. Participants can submit records on a checklist provided by the Federation of Alberta Naturalists or via the internet.

Contact: ***Federation of Alberta Naturalists*** (see Environmental/Conservation Organizations [Alberta]).
WEBSITE: www.connect.ab.ca/~fan or www.ntic.qc.ca/~nellus/cbcp_can.html

Project Pigeon Watch
Project Pigeon Watch is an international survey of pigeon colouration and behaviour. There is a $15.00 (US) fee to participate.

CONTACT: ***Project Pigeon Watch***
Cornell Lab of Ornithology, 159 Sapsucker Woods Rd., Ithaca, New York USA 14850
PHONE: 1-800-843-BIRD or (607) 254-2473

Project Recovery
Individuals, school classes or organizations can "adopt" one of 21 species of birds that are banded by Long Point Bird Observatory (LPBO) in Ontario. Adoption fees are tax-creditable and if the bird is recovered, LPBO will contact the adoptee and provide details of the bird's progress.

CONTACT: ***Project Recovery***
Long Point Bird Observatory
Box 160, Port Rowan, ON N0E 1M0
PHONE: (519) 586-3531; FAX: (519) 586-3532

Warbler Watch
The Cornell Lab of Ornithology operates a website for recording observations of fall and spring migrating warblers. The purpose of this program is to map the migratory routes of all North American warbler species.

CONTACT: ***Warbler Watch***
WEBSITE: http://birdsource.cornell.edu

VOLUNTEER OPPORTUNITIES—PLANTS

May Species Count
Held during the last weekend in May, this count enables volunteers to document species of spring flowering plants.

CONTACT: ***Federation of Alberta Naturalists*** (see Environmental/Conservation Organizations [Alberta]) or your local ***naturalist organization*** (see Regional Alberta Natural History Organizations).

Plantwatch
In this program, participants report the bloom times of one or more indicator plants (seven wild plants plus common purple lilac) to research scientists using the Internet.

CONTACT: ***Devonian Botanic Garden***
Department of Botany, University of Alberta, Edmonton, AB T6G 2E9
PHONE: (780) 987-3054; FAX: (780) 987-4141
E-MAIL: E.Beaubien@ualberta.ca
WEBSITE: www.devonian.ualberta.ca/pwatch/

Alberta Wildflower Survey
The purpose of this survey is to observe and record the first spring flowering dates of 15 plant species.

CONTACT: ***Devonian Botanic Garden***
Department of Botany, University of Alberta, Edmonton, AB T6G 2E9
PHONE: (780) 987-3054; FAX: (780) 987-4141
E-MAIL: E.Beaubien@ualberta.ca
WEBSITE: www.devonian.ualberta.ca/pwatch/

SEED EXCHANGES AND PERENNIAL EXCHANGES

Seedy Saturdays
These community-based, educational and seed exchange events are held across Alberta each spring. For details, contact The Garden Institute (see Organic Gardening/Heritage Seed Preservation). Seed exchanges are also available through the Canadian Wildflower Society (see Environmental/Conservation Organizations [Canada]). Check with your local horticultural society, nursery or naturalist groups for perennial exchanges in your area.

RARE PLANTS AND WILDLIFE

Birds
Sightings of rare or out-of-range birds can be reported to the following:

Northern Alberta: (780) 433-BIRD

Southern Alberta: Rare Bird Hotline, Inglewood Bird Sanctuary, (403) 237-8821

Transcripts of the hotlines can be read at the following websites:

- www.interlog.com/~gallantg/canada/albcal.html
- www.birdware.com/lists/rba/_canada/alberta/calgary/rba.htm
- www.camacdonald.com/birding/caalbertaRareBird.htm

If you find a bird with a metal or coloured leg band, a patagial marker (on the wing) or a neck collar, or if you see a colour-marked shorebird, call 1-800-327-BAND.

Rare Plants and Vertebrates
The Alberta Natural Heritage Information Centre (ANHIC) has "tracking" and "watch" lists of rare plants and mosses, and vertebrate animals (including fish, amphibians, reptiles, mammals and birds). All lists can be downloaded directly from the website.

CONTACT: ***Alberta Natural Heritage Information Centre*** (ANHIC)
Alberta Environment, 2nd Flr., 9820-106 St., Edmonton, AB T5K 2J6
PHONE: (780) 427-6639 (within Alberta, use RITE LINE); FAX: (780) 427-5980
E-MAIL: john.rintoul@gov.ab.ca
WEBSITE: www.gov.ab.ca/env/parks/anhic/anhic.html

APPENDIX 6

Complete the two-page form below to receive a complimentary, one-year subscription to the NatureScape Alberta newsletter.
Mail or fax it to: **NatureScape Alberta, c/o RDRN, Box 785, Red Deer, AB T4N 5H2; Fax (403) 347-8200**. Additional forms are available on-line at **www.naturescape.ab.ca** .

Backyard Watch

My yard is ***NatureScape*** certified: ◯ YES ◯ NO

I intend to have my yard ***NatureScape*** certified: ◯ YES ◯ NO

NAME ______________________ ADDRESS ______________________

CITY/TOWN ______________ PROVINCE ______________ POSTAL CODE ______________

PHONE ( ) ______________ FAX ( ) ______________ E-MAIL ______________

◯ **I don't have any data to provide, but I would like to receive your newsletter.** (Cheque or money order for $5 enclosed)

◯ **I would like your free school membership.** (Provide the school name, address, contact teacher and grade on official school letterhead.)

◯ **Please send me additional "Backyard Watch" forms**

After reading this book

I made the following change(s) to my yard or garden ______________________

I now participate in the following volunteer programs (see Appendix 5) ______________________

ATTACH ADDITIONAL SHEETS IF NECESSARY

Topics I would like to see discussed in the newsletter: ______________________

Completing the information below will help us to more accurately determine the food, shelter and habitat requirements of particular species. A summary of all information received will appear in future issues of the NatureScape Alberta newsletter and will be posted on the website. Please use the reverse side of this form or attach additional sheets of paper to provide detailed information about selected observations. For certain species groups (such as ducks, bats, snakes, etc.) indicate the presence with the check box and, if known, the exact species.

Species Checklist

In my [ ] *location: e.g., garden, yard* in [ ] *day / week / month(s)*, [ ] *year* I recorded the following number of species:

[ ] birds [ ] mammals [ ] amphibians & reptiles [ ] butterflies and [ ] other insects & insect-like animals

Birds

- ◯ Canada goose
- ◯ Duck *(species)* ______
- ◯ American kestrel
- ◯ Merlin
- ◯ Ring-necked pheasant
- ◯ Ruffed grouse
- ◯ Rock dove (pigeon)
- ◯ Mourning dove
- ◯ Great horned owl
- ◯ Hummingbird *(species)* ______
- ◯ Downy woodpecker
- ◯ Hairy woodpecker
- ◯ Northern flicker
- ◯ Blue jay
- ◯ Black-billed magpie
- ◯ American crow
- ◯ Common raven
- ◯ Purple martin
- ◯ Tree swallow
- ◯ Barn swallow
- ◯ Black-capped chickadee
- ◯ Boreal chickadee
- ◯ Red-breasted nuthatch
- ◯ White-breasted nuthatch
- ◯ House wren
- ◯ Mountain bluebird
- ◯ American robin
- ◯ European starling
- ◯ Bohemian waxwing
- ◯ Cedar waxwing
- ◯ Yellow warbler
- ◯ Song sparrow
- ◯ White-throated sparrow
- ◯ White-crowned sparrow
- ◯ Dark-eyed junco
- ◯ Pine grosbeak
- ◯ House finch
- ◯ Common redpoll
- ◯ Pine siskin
- ◯ American goldfinch
- ◯ House sparrow

Mammals

- ◯ Bat *(species)* ______
- ◯ Rabbit or Hare *(species)* ______
- ◯ Ground squirrel *(species)* ______
- ◯ Tree squirrel *(species)* ______
- ◯ Shrew, Mouse or Vole *(species)* ______
- ◯ Porcupine
- ◯ Coyote
- ◯ Red fox
- ◯ Weasel *(species)* ______
- ◯ Striped skunk
- ◯ Deer *(species)* ______

Amphibians & Reptiles

- ◯ Tiger salamander
- ◯ Boreal/Western toad
- ◯ Canadian toad
- ◯ Boreal/Striped chorus frog
- ◯ Wood frog
- ◯ Snake *(species)* ______

Some Insects & Insect-like Animals

If listing species, please use reverse side of form or attach additional sheets.

- ◯ Giant silkworm moth
- ◯ Hawk/Hummingbird moth
- ◯ Tiger moth
- ◯ Underwing moth
- ◯ Honey bee
- ◯ Bumble bee
- ◯ Leaf-cutter bee
- ◯ Yellow jacket
- ◯ Hornet
- ◯ Ant
- ◯ Ground beetle
- ◯ Weevil
- ◯ Ladybird beetle
- ◯ Diving beetle
- ◯ Dragonfly
- ◯ Damselfly
- ◯ Jumping spider
- ◯ Orb-weaving spider
- ◯ Daddy longlegs

Butterflies

- ◯ Skipper *(species)* ______
- ◯ Swallowtail *(species)* ______
- ◯ White *(species)* ______
- ◯ Sulphur *(species)* ______
- ◯ Copper *(species)* ______
- ◯ Elfin or Hairstreak *(species)* ______
- ◯ Blue *(species)* ______
- Tortoise shell
  - ◯ Milbert's tortoise shell
  - ◯ Mourning cloak
  - ◯ Other *(species)* ______
- ◯ Anglewing *(species)* ______
- ◯ Lady *(species)* ______
- ◯ Fritillary *(species)* ______
- ◯ Checkerspot *(species)* ______
- ◯ Crescent *(species)* ______
- ◯ Admiral *(species)* ______
- ◯ Wood nymph *(species)* ______
- ◯ Ringlet *(species)* ______
- ◯ Alpine *(species)* ______
- ◯ Arctic *(species)* ______
- ◯ Monarch

Additional Species

GROUP*	SPECIES NAME

***Species group:** B=Bird, M=Mammal, A=Amphibian, R=Reptile, T=Butterfly, I=Other Insect or Insect-like Animal, O=Other.

Animal Species Details

(Attach additional sheets if necessary)

GROUP*	ANIMAL NAME (common or scientific)	DATE(S)	LIFE STAGE	NOTES AND OTHER OBSERVATIONS

***Group:** B=Bird, M=Mammal, A=Amphibian, R=Reptile, T=Butterfly, I=Other Insect or Insect-like Animal, O=Other.

Examples of Life Stages

- # Species recorded in unusually high numbers
- AB ACTIVE BREEDING site (e.g., nest) (please provide details in notes)
- BA BREEDING ADULT(S) observed in suitable habitat
- CB COURTSHIP BEHAVIOUR (please describe)
- DH Mammal DEN or snake HIBERNACULUM
- E EGGLAYING
- FF First FALL record of species (if applicable)
- FL Last FALL record of species
- FY Adult providing FOOD for YOUNG
- MS METAMORPHIC STAGE (e.g., chrysalis, cocoon, nymph, pupa, caterpillar, tadpole)
- NB NEST-BUILDING or adult carrying nest material
- O OTHER (please provide details in notes)
- SF First SPRING record of species
- SL Last SPRING record of species (if applicable)
- UN USED NEST or eggshells found
- Y Recently born or hatched YOUNG

Plant Species Details

(Attach additional sheets if necessary)

PLANT NAME (common or scientific)	DATE(S)	NOTES AND OTHER OBSERVATIONS (e.g., what animal the plant has attracted)

We invite you to share your observations, stories and photos with us (photos returned if self-addressed stamped envelope is included). We'd also like to hear about special activities and websites of interest.

Yard Certification Application

Please complete this application and mail or fax it to:
NatureScape Alberta, c/o RDRN, Box 785, Red Deer, AB T4H 5H2; Fax: (403) 347-8200.
Feel free to use additional sheets of paper. Additional forms are available on-line at **www.naturescape.ab.ca**.

NAME ______________________ ADDRESS ______________________

CITY/TOWN ______________________ PROVINCE ______________________ POSTAL CODE ______________________

PHONE (   ) ______________________ FAX (   ) ______________________ E-MAIL ______________________

Which best describes your property? ◯ URBAN LOT ◯ ACREAGE ◯ OTHER (describe) ____________	Approximate total size of wildlife habitat area(s) [ ] PLEASE CIRCLE ONE: m² / sq.ft. / hectares / acres
Approximate property size *(optional)* [ ] PLEASE CIRCLE ONE: m² / sq.ft. / hectares / acres	How many years have you been providing wildlife habitat on your property? [ ]

FOOD

Plantings (please list by common or scientific name)

TREES AND SHRUBS	NUMBER	PERENNIALS	NUMBER	ANNUALS, VINES, OTHER	NUMBER

Other Food or Supplement

TYPE OF FOOD OR SUPPLEMENT OFFERED (seeds [give type], suet, sugar water, salt, etc.)	FEEDER TYPE (if relevant)	NUMBER (if relevant)	SEASONAL ONLY (which season)

WATER

Water is provided ◯ YEAR-ROUND ◯ SUMMER ONLY

Water garden (PLEASE CIRCLE "m" or "ft.") ☐ m / ft. WIDE X ☐ m / ft. LONG ◯ with WATERFALL ◯ with STREAM

Naturally occurring water source ◯ SPRING ◯ BOG/MARSH ◯ POND ◯ LAKE ◯ CREEK ◯ RIVER

Other water source ◯ PUDDLING AREA ◯ MUD ◯ BIRDBATH (describe type) ____________________

Other (please describe) ____________________

SHELTER AND HOUSING

Please put **NUMBER OF EACH** in box.

Bird nestbox ☐ Type(s) ____________ Bat house ☐ Squirrel box ☐ Rabbit/Hare box ☐

Amphibian shelter ☐ Bumble bee nest site ☐ Ladybird beetle house ☐ Butterfly hibernation shelter ☐

Bee/Wasp nesting tunnels ☐ Type(s) (i.e., drinking straws, blocks, etc.) ____________ Snake hibernaculum ☐

Brush pile ☐ Rock pile ☐ Rock island ☐ Duck nesting tunnel ☐ Snag ☐ Roosting box ☐

Other (please describe) ____________________

OTHER ATTRACTANTS

Please put **NUMBER OF EACH** in box.

Dust bathing area ☐ Bird perch ☐ Drumming log ☐ Toad light ☐ Spider light ☐

Butterfly basking or perching site ☐ Other (please describe) ____________________

Feathers, string or nesting aids (please describe) ____________________

OTHER INFORMATION

Any other information you would like to share with us.

____

____

MAP

Please provide us with a map of your yard and buildings, or NatureScaped school yard. Indicate where your wildlife habitat areas are, as well as where you've placed supplemental food sources, water, shelter/housing and other attractants. We'd appreciate a map drawn to scale (please let us know on the map what scale you've used). If you would like some ideas on how to draw your map, please see the sample site inventories illustrated in Chapter 2.

INDEX

Page numbers in **purple**, bold-face type indicate photographs and illustrations. Page numbers in **green**, bold-face type refer to specific species descriptions/accounts, or, as in the case of insects and spiders, family and subfamily information.

A

B

C

D

E

F

G

Q

R

S

U

V

W

X

Y

Z